JOURNAL FOR THE STUDY OF THE NEW TESTAMENT
SUPPLEMENT SERIES
213

Sheffield Academic Press
A Continuum imprint

Interpolations in the Pauline Letters

William O. Walker, Jr

Journal for the Study of the New Testament
Supplement Series 213

Published by Shcffield Academic Press Ltd
The Tower Building, 11 York Road, London SE1 7NX
71 Lexington Avenue, New York NY 10017-653

www.SheffieldAcademicPress.com
www.continuumbooks.com

British Library Cataloguing-in-Publication Data

A catalogue record for this book is available from the British Library

Typeset by Sheffield Academic Press
Printed on acid-free paper in Great Britain by MPG Books Ltd, Bodmin, Cornwall

ISBN 1-84127-198-5

CONTENTS

PREFACE

I first became seriously interested in the question of interpolations in the Pauline letters almost three decades ago. One day, as I was reading in 1 Corinthians, I was struck by what appeared to me to be the un-Pauline language, ideology and tone of 11.2-16, the passage dealing with the attire (or hairstyle) of men and women while praying and prophesying. I was aware, of course, that some scholars regarded 1 Cor. 14.34-35 (or perhaps vv. 33b-36) as non-Pauline, and I found myself wondering whether the same might also be true of 11.2-16. Particularly interesting to me was the fact that, if these two passages were removed, the seven letters generally regarded as authentically Pauline would contain not a single statement advocating a subordinate position for women in the life of the church or the family. Indeed, without these passages, a very strong case could be made for Paul's radical egalitarianism regarding the status and role of women. Thus, my initial interest in the interpolation question grew out of a more general concern regarding gender issues in the New Testament.

I prepared a paper entitled '1 Corinthians 11.2-16 and Paul's Views Regarding Women', which I presented at the 1973 annual meeting of the Society of Biblical Literature (the paper was later published, in revised form, in the March, 1975, issue of *JBL* [vol. 94]). In this paper, I argued that the passage was, in fact, a non-Pauline interpolation. Some years later, in 1982, I presented a second paper, entitled 'The "Theology of Woman's Place" and the "Paulinist Tradition"', at the annual meeting of the Society of Biblical Literature (SBL) (this paper appeared in the 1983 issue of *Semeia* [vol. 28]). As I explored the literature regarding interpolations, I came to realize that a number of passages in the Pauline letters had been proposed as possible interpolations. I also became familiar with the work of J.C. O'Neill and Winsome Munro, who argued for extensive interpolations throughout the letters. During the past quarter of a century, my own research on interpolations resulted in the publication of a total of eight articles in five different journals—

five of the articles dealing with specific passages (1 Cor. 11.2-16; 11.3-16; 2.6-16; 12.31b–14.1a; Rom. 1.18–2.29) and three with more general aspects of the issue (Paul's views regarding women, the burden-of-proof question as it relates to possible interpolations, and the use of text-critical evidence in the identification of interpolations). Most recently, my article on 'Interpolations in the Pauline Letters' has been accepted for publication in the first volume (*The Pauline Canon*) of a multi-volume series entitled 'Pauline Studies', to be edited by Stanley E. Porter and Brook W.R. Pearson and published by Brill Academic Publishers.

Although my views have changed somewhat over the years regarding certain aspects of the interpolation question (particularly the burden-of-proof issue), much of the present work is based upon these previously-published items. Thus, I welcome this opportunity to express my appreciation for permission to use the indicated materials:

To the Executive Secretary of the Catholic Biblical Association of America: materials from 'Text-Critical Evidence for Interpolations in the Letters of Paul', *CBQ* 50 (1988), pp. 622-31 (parts of Chapters 1, 2, 4, and 7); and 'Is First Corinthians 13 a Non-Pauline Interpolation?', *CBQ* 60 (1998), pp. 484-99 (Chapter 7);

To the Editor of *New Testament Studies*: materials from 'The Burden of Proof in Identifying Interpolations in the Pauline Letters', *NTS* 33 (1987), pp. 610-18 (parts of Chapter 1 and 3); and 'Romans 1.18–2.29: A Non-Pauline Interpolation?', *NTS* 45 (1999), pp. 533-52 (Chapter 8).

To the Editorial Director of the Society of Biblical Literature: materials from '1 Corinthians 11:2-16 and Paul's Views Regarding Women', *JBL* 94 (1975), pp. 94-110 (part of Chapter 5); and

To the Managing Director of Sheffield Academic Press: materials from 'The Vocabulary of 1 Corinthians 11.3-16: Pauline or Non-Pauline?', *JSNT* 35 (1989), pp. 75-88 (part of Chapter 5); and '1 Corinthians 2.6-16: A Non-Pauline Interpolation?', *JSNT* 47 (1992), pp. 75-94 (Chapter 6).

I had hoped—indeed, expected—to complete this book more than a decade ago, but an unanticipated eleven-year term as Dean of the Division of Humanities and Arts at Trinity University intervened. Upon completion of this term, I was granted a year-long administrative leave, for which I am deeply grateful to the former Vice President for Academic Affairs, Edward C. Roy, Jr, and the former President, Ronald K. Calgaard. Without this leave, the project would have been further delayed. I must express my sincere appreciation also for the skilled and conscientious work of members of the staff of the Elizabeth Huth Coates Library at Trinity University, who provided invaluable assistance in locating and securing needed bibliographic materials. Finally, I would be remiss not to acknowledge the encouragement I have received over the years from members of the New Testament guild who urged me to proceed as quickly as possible with this project. These include most notably M. Eugene Boring, Joseph B. Tyson, Robin Scroggs, J.C. O'Neill and (until her untimely death) Winsome Munro. I am particularly grateful to Professors O'Neill and Munro, whose imaginative, conscientious and creative work on the Pauline corpus has served as both an inspiration and a stimulus to my own efforts.

William O. Walker, Jr
San Antonio, TX
August 2001

ACKNOWLEDGMENTS

To the teachers who introduced me to the study of the New Testament: Robert H. Bullock (Austin College); Eugene W. McLaurin (The Austin Presbyterian Theological Seminary); Ernest Best (The Austin Presbyterian Theological Seminary; later at the University of St Andrews and then at the University of Glasgow); Kenneth W. Clark (Duke University); James L. Price (Duke University); and Hugh Anderson (Duke University; later at the University of Edinburgh).

ABBREVIATIONS

AB	Anchor Bible
ABD	David Noel Freedman (ed.), *The Anchor Bible Dictionary* New York: Doubleday, 1992)
ABRL	Anchor Bible Reference Library
ANTC	Abingdon New Testament Commentaries
ANTT	Arbeiten zur neutestamentlichen Textforschung
APCTS	Annual Publications of the College Theology Society
ASR	Aids for the Study of Religion
ATRSup	Anglican Theological Review Supplements
BAGD	Walter Bauer, William F. Arndt, F. William Gingrich and Frederick W. Danker, *A Greek–English Lexicon of the New Testament and Other Early Christian Literature* (Chicago: University of Chicago Press, 2nd edn, 1958)
BDF	F. Blass, A. Debrunner and Robert W. Funk, *A Greek Grammar of the New Testament and Other Early Christian Literature* (Cambridge: Cambridge University Press, 1961)
BETL	Bibliotheca ephemeridum theologicarum lovaniensum
BEvT	Beiträge zur evangelischen Theologie
Bib	*Biblica*
BJS	Brown Judaic Studies
BMI	The Bible and Its Modern Interpreters
BN	*Biblische Notizen*
BTB	*Biblical Theology Bulletin*
BZNW	Beihefte zur *ZNW*
CBQ	*Catholic Biblical Quarterly*
CBQMS	*Catholic Biblical Quarterly*, Monograph Series
CC	*The Christian Century*
CHSHMCP	The Center for Hermeneutical Studies in Hellenistic and Modern Culture: Protocol
CJA	Christianity and Judaism in Antiquity
ConNT	Coniectanea neotestamentica
EBib	Etudes bibliques
EJR	R.J. Zwi Werblowsky and Geoffrey Widoger (eds.), *The Encyclopedia of the Jewish Religion* (New York: Holt, Rinehart & Winston, 1966)
EncJud	*Encyclopaedia Judaica*

ETL	*Ephemerides theologicae lovanienses*
ExpTim	*Expository Times*
FEUNTK	Forschungen zur Entstehung des Urchristentums des Neuen Testaments und der Kirche
FF	Foundations and Facets
FFasc	Forum Fascicles
FFBS	Facet Books, Biblical Series
FFNT	Foundations and Facets: New Testament
GBS	Guides to Biblical Scholarship
GNS	Good News Studies
HCBD	Paul J. Achtemeier *et al.* (eds.), *The HarperCollins Bible Dictionary* (San Francisco: HarperSanFrancisco, 1996)
HDR	Harvard Dissertations in Religion
Her	Hermeneia
HNTC	Harper's NT Commentaries
HTR	*Harvard Theological Review*
IB	*Interpreter's Bible*
IBT	Interpreting Biblical Texts
ICC	The International Critical Commentary
IDB	George Arthur Buttrick (eds.), *The Interpreter's Dictionary of the Bible* (4 vols.; Nashville: Abingdon Press, 1962)
IDBSup	*IDB*, Supplementary Volume
Int	*Interpretation*
IBT	Interpreting Biblical Texts
ITL	International Theological Library
JAAR	*Journal of the American Academy of Religion*
JAARSup	*Journal of the American Academy of Religion*, Supplement Series
JBL	*Journal of Biblical Literature*
JBR	*Journal of Bible and Religion*
JE	*Jewish Encyclopedia* (ed. I. Singer; 12 vols.; New York/London: Funk and Wagnalls, rev. edn, 1925)
JEH	*Journal of Ecclesiastical History*
JewEnc	*The Jewish Encyclopedia*
JHC	*Journal of Higher Criticism*
JP	*Journal of Philology*
JQR	*Jewish Quarterly Review*
JSNT	*Journal for the Study of the New Testament*
JSNTSup	*Journal for the Study of the New Testament*, Supplement Series
JTS	*Journal of Theological Studies*
KEK	Kritisch-exegetischer Kommentar über das Neue Testament (Meyer-Kommentar)
LCL	Loeb Classical Library
LEC	Library of Early Christianity

MBCBSup	Mnemosyne: Bibliotheca Classica Batava. Supplementum
NCB	New Century Bible
NCE	A Norton Critical Edition
NICNT	New International Commentary on the New Testament
NovT	*Novum Testamentum*
NovTSup	*Novum Testamentum*, Supplements
NS	*Neutestamentliche Studien*
NTM	New Testament Message
NTOA	Novum Testamentum et orbis antiquus
NTS	*New Testament Studies*
PC	Proclamation Commentaries
RB	*Revue biblique*
RHPR	*Revue d'histoire et de philosophie religieuses*
RHR	*Revue de l'histoire des religions*
RL	*Religion in Life*
RSPT	*Revue des sciences philosophiques et théologiques*
SBLDS	SBL Dissertation Series
SBibSt	Sources for Biblical Study
SCJ	Studies in Christianity and Judaism
SD	Studies and Documents
SE	*Studia Evangelica I, II, III* (= TU 73 [1959], 88 [1964], etc.)
SEÅSup	Svensk exegetisk årsbok Supplements
Sem	*Semitica*
SHAW	Sitzungsberichte der Heidelberger Akademie der Wissenschaften. Philosophisch-Historische Klasse
SHCT	Studies in the History of Christian Thought
SNT	Studien zum Neuen Testament
SNTE	Studies in New Testament Exegesis
SNTSMS	Society for New Testament Studies Monograph Series
SP	Sacra Pagina
SPHS	Scholars Press Homage Series
SR	*Studies in Religion/Sciences religieuses*
StC	*Studia Catholica*
TBü	Theologische Bücherei
TDNT	Gerhard Kittel and Gerhard Friedrich (eds.), *Theological Dictionary of the New Testament* (trans. Geoffrey W. Bromiley; 10 vols.; Grand Rapids: Eerdmans, 1964–)
TEH	Theologische Existenz Heute
TLZ	*Theologische Literaturzeitung*
TPAPA	*Transactions and Proceedings of the American Philological Association*
TRE	*Theologische Realenzyklopädie*
TSK	*Theologische Studien und Kritiken*
TU	Texte und Untersuchungen

UJEnc	Isaac Landmann (ed.), *The Universal Jewish Encyclopedia: An Authoritative and Popular Presentation of Jews and Judaism since the Earliest Times* (10 vols.; New York: Universal Jewish Encyclopedia, 1939–43)
WTJ	*Westminster Theological Journal*
ZNW	*Zeitschrift für die neutestamentliche Wissenschaft*
ZTK	*Zeitschrift für Theologie und Kirche*

INTRODUCTION

Victor Paul Furnish noted some years ago that 'hypotheses about textual glosses and the presence of even longer interpolated units [in the Pauline letters] have long been a part of textual and literary criticism'.[1] Indeed, a few scholars have argued for extensive glosses and interpolations throughout the Pauline corpus. First advanced in nineteenth-century Germany and the Netherlands,[2] this latter view was revived in France in the 1920s and 1930s by P.-L. Couchoud[3] and Alfred Firmin Loisy[4] and, in the United States in the 1940s, by Robert Martyr Hawkins.[5] In the 1970s J.C. O'Neill maintained that both Galatians and Romans contain numerous glosses and interpolations, some inadvertently included by copyists but many deliberately added,[6] and, a decade later, Winsome Munro argued for an extensive stratum of 'Pastoral' interpolations in the Pauline corpus as a whole (and in

1. Victor Paul Furnish, 'Pauline Studies', in Eldon Jay Epp and George W. MacRae (eds.), *The New Testament and Its Modern Interpreters* (BMI, 3; Philadelphia: Fortress Press; Atlanta: Scholars Press, 1989), pp. 321-50 (324).

2. For a summary and critical evaluation, see Carl Clemen, *Die Einheitlichkeit der paulinischen Briefe an der Hand der bisher mit bezug auf die aufgestellten Interpolations- und Compilationshypothesen* (Göttingen: Vandenhoeck & Ruprecht, 1894).

3. P.-L. Couchoud, 'Reconstitution et classement des Lettres de Saint Paul', *RHPR* 87 (1923), pp. 8-31; 'La première édition de Saint Paul', *RHR* 94 (1926), pp. 242-63.

4. Alfred Firmin Loisy, *Remarques sur la littérature épistolaire du Nouveau Testament* (Paris: Nourry, 1935), *passim*; and *The Origins of the New Testament* (trans. J.P. Jacks; New Hyde Park, NY: University Books, 1962 [French original 1936]), *passim*.

5. Robert Martyr Hawkins, *The Recovery of the Historical Paul* (Nashville: Vanderbilt University Press, 1943), pp. 14-20, 291-92, *et passim*; see also his 'Romans: A Reinterpretation', *JBL* 60 (1941), pp. 129-40.

6. J.C. O'Neill, *The Recovery of Paul's Letter to the Galatians* (London: SPCK, 1972), pp. 1-15, 73-87, *et passim*; and *Paul's Letter to the Romans* (Baltimore: Penguin Books, 1975), pp. 11-22, 264-74, *et passim*.

1 Peter).[7] Most recently, Darrell J. Doughty has asserted that the Pauline letters 'can only be understood as complex redactional compositions, that may include appropriations of early Pauline material, but most certainly include an abundance of later material as well'; thus, in his view, the burden of proof rests with the claim that *any* of the material in the letters is authentically Pauline.[8]

Not surprisingly, such 'radical' proposals have gained little scholarly acceptance. Georg Strecker, for example, acknowledges that glosses and interpolations are 'to be expected' in the Pauline letters but insists that 'nineteenth century Netherlands conjectural criticism went beyond responsible limits'.[9] Similarly, Furnish accuses O'Neill of a 'wholesale resort to hypotheses', asserting that the latter's work intermixes 'highly subjective judgments about content and tone' with 'often-questionable generalizations about the apostle's style and vocabulary', resulting in 'a Paul created in the interpreter's own image'.[10] More peremptorily, Joseph A. Fitzmyer declares that 'short shrift...has to be given to the proposals of O'Neill' regarding interpolations and glosses in Romans.[11]

Nevertheless, the question of later additions to the Pauline letters remains open. Indeed, as Furnish notes, 'several older hypotheses have attracted new supporters' in recent years, 'and some further passages have been added to the list of suspect texts'.[12] Thus, quite apart from the far-reaching proposals of O'Neill and Munro, the roster of proposed interpolations has become rather lengthy. In Romans alone, it

7. Winsome Munro, *Authority in Paul and Peter: The Identification of a Pastoral Stratum in the Pauline Corpus and 1 Peter* (SNTSMS, 45; Cambridge: Cambridge University Press, 1983); cf. also Dennis Ronald MacDonald, *The Legend and the Apostle: The Battle for Paul in Story and Canon* (Philadelphia: Westminster Press, 1983), p. 86: 'The text of the Pauline letters that lies behind all the extant manuscripts bears signs of harmonization with the Pastorals. That is, all extant manuscripts of the corpus contain interpolations from a scribe who knew the Pastorals and who altered the text of Paul's own letters to conform with them'.

8. Darrell J. Doughty, 'Pauline Paradigms and Pauline Authenticity', *JHC* 1 (1994), pp. 95-128 (95).

9. Georg Strecker, *History of New Testament Literature* (trans. Calvin Katter; Harrisburg, PA: Trinity Press International, 1997), p. 40.

10. Furnish, 'Pauline Studies', p. 325.

11. Joseph A. Fitzmyer, *Romans: A New Translation with Introduction and Commentary* (AB, 33; New York: Doubleday, 1993), p. 65.

12. Furnish, 'Pauline Studies', p. 324.

now includes: 1.18–2.29;[13] 1.19–2.1;[14] 1.32;[15] 2.1;[16] 2.16;[17] 3.12-18;[18] 3.24-26;[19] 4.14;[20] 4.17;[21] 4.18-19;[22] 5.1;[23] 5.6-7;[24] 5.12-21;[25] 5.17;[26] 6.13, 19;[27] 6.17;[28] 7.6;[29] 7.25b;[30] 8.1;[31] 8.9-11;[32] 9.5;[33] 10.9;[34] 10.17;[35] 11.6;[36] 12.11;[37] 13.1-7;[38] 13.5;[39] 14.6;[40] 15.4;[41] 16;[42] 16.5;[43] 16.25-27.[44]

13. William O. Walker Jr, 'Romans 1.18–2.29: A Non-Pauline Interpolation?', *NTS* 45 (1999), pp. 533-52.

14. P.N. Harrison, *Paulines and Pastorals* (London: Villiers, 1964), pp. 79-85.

15. Listed without documentation as a proposed 'secondary gloss' by Fitzmyer (*Romans*, p. 65).

16. Rudolf Bultmann, 'Glossen im Römerbrief', *TLZ 72* (1947), pp. 197-202 (200).

17. Bultmann, 'Glossen im Römerbrief', pp. 200-201.

18. J.C. O'Neill, 'Glosses and Interpolations in the Letters of St Paul', in Elizabeth A. Livingstone (ed.), *SE*, 7; *Papers presented to the Fifth International Congress on Biblical Studies held at Oxford, 1973* (TU, 126; Berlin: Akademie Verlag, 1982), pp. 379-86 (383-84).

19. Charles H. Talbert, 'A Non-Pauline Fragment at Romans 3 24-26?', *JBL* 85 (1966), pp. 287-96.

20. See n. 15 above.

21. See n. 15 above.

22. See n. 15 above.

23. See n. 15 above.

24. Leander E. Keck, 'The Post-Pauline Interpretation of Jesus' Death in Rom. 5,6-7', in Carl Andresen and Günter Klein (eds.), *Theologia Crucis—Signum Crucis: Festschrift für Erich Dinkler zum 70. Geburtstag* (Tübingen: J.C.B. Mohr [Paul Siebeck], 1979), pp. 237-48.

25. O'Neill, 'Glosses and Interpolations', pp. 384-85.

26. See n. 15 above.

27. Wayne H. Hagen, 'Two Deutero-Pauline Glosses in Romans 6', *ExpTim* 92 (1981), pp. 364-67.

28. Bultmann, 'Glossen im Römerbrief', p. 202.

29. See n. 15 above.

30. Bultmann, 'Glossen im Römerbrief', pp. 198-99.

31. Bultmann, 'Glossen im Römerbrief', p. 199.

32. François Refoulé, 'Unité de l'Epître aux Romains et histoire du salut', *RSPT* 71 (1987), pp. 219-42.

33. See n. 15 above.

34. See n. 15 above.

35. Bultmann, 'Glossen im Römerbrief', p. 199.

36. See n. 15 above.

37. See n. 15 above.

38. E.g., Ernst Barnikol, 'Römer 13: Der nichtpaulinische Ursprung der absoluten Obrigkeitsbejahrung von Römer 13,1-7', *Studien zum Neuen Testament*

Similarly, in the other letters,[45] serious questions have been raised regarding the authenticity of such passages as: 1 Cor. 1.2;[46] 2.6-16;[47] 4.6c;[48] 4.17;[49] 6.14;[50] 7.29-31;[51] 10.1-22;[52] 11.2-16 (or, more likely,

und zur Patristik. Erich Klostermann zum 90. Geburtstag dargebracht (ed. Der Kommission für spätantike Religionsgeschichte, Deutsche Akademie der Wissenschaften zu Berlin; TU, 77; Berlin: Akademie Verlag, 1961), pp. 65-133; James Kallas, 'Romans xiii.1-7: An Interpolation', *NTS* 11 (1965), pp. 365-74; Walter Schmithals, *Der Römerbrief als historisches Problem* (SNT, 9; Gütersloh: Gerd Mohn, 1975), pp. 185-97; Munro, *Authority in Paul and Peter*, pp. 16-19, 56-57; and Winsome Munro, 'Romans 13.1-7: Apartheid's Last Biblical Refuge', *BTB* 20 (1990), pp. 161-68.

39. Bultmann, 'Glossen im Römerbrief', p. 200.

40. See n. 15 above.

41. Leander E. Keck, 'Romans 15.4: An Interpolation?', in John T. Carroll, Charles H. Cosgrove and E. Elizabeth Johnson (eds.), *Faith and History: Essays in Honor of Paul W. Meyer* (SPHS; Atlanta: Scholars Press, 1990), pp. 125-36.

42. John Knox ('The Epistle to the Romans: Introduction and Exegesis', *IB*, IX, p. 654) regards the interpolation theory as 'the least difficult' of the possibilities 'and therefore the most likely to be true'; see the entire discussion, pp. 365-68.

43. See n. 15 above.

44. Rom. 16.25-27 is widely regarded as an interpolation. For the most comprehensive argumentation, see Ehrhard Kamlah, 'Traditionsgeschichtliche Untersuchungen zur Schlussdoxologie des Römerbriefes' (unpublished doctoral dissertation, University of Tübingen, 1955). For more extensive interpolation hypotheses regarding Romans, see, for example, Schmithals, *Der Römerbrief als historisches Problem*; and Martin Widmann, 'Der Israelit Paulus und sein antijüdischer Redaktor. Eine literarkritische Studie zu Röm. 9–11', in Ernst Ludwig Ehrlich and Bertold Klappert with Ursula Ast (eds.), *'Wie gut sind deine Zelte, Jaakow...' Festschrift zum 60. Geburtstag von Reinhold Mayer* (Gerlingen: Bleicher, 1986), pp. 150-58.

45. On 1 and 2 Corinthians, see, e.g., Schmithals, *Der Römerbrief als historisches Problem*, pp. 202-209; and Wolfgang Schenk, 'Korintherbriefe', *TRE*, IXX, pp. 620-40 (621-22). On 1 Corinthians, see, e.g., Wolfgang Schenk, 'Der 1. Korintherbrief als Briefsammlung', *ZNW* 60 (1969), pp. 219-43; and Jerome Murphy-O'Connor, 'Interpolations in 1 Corinthians', *CBQ* 48 (1986), pp. 81-94.

46. Johannes Weiss, *Der erste Korintherbrief* (KEK, 5; Göttingen: Vandenhoeck & Ruprecht, 9th edn, 1910), pp. 2-4; Günther Zuntz, *The Text of the Epistles: A Disquisition Upon the Corpus Paulinum* (Oxford: Oxford University Press, 1953), pp. 91-92.

47. Martin Widmann, '1 Kor 2 6-16: Ein Einspruch gegen Paulus', *ZNW* 70 (1979), pp. 44-53; and William O. Walker, Jr, '1 Corinthians 2.6-16: A Non-Pauline Interpolation?', *JSNT* 47 (1992), pp. 75-94.

48. Only the words τὸ μὴ ὑπὲρ ἃ γέγραπται; John Strugnell, 'A Plea for

only vv. 3-16);[53] 11.23-26;[54] 12.31b–14.1a;[55] 14.33b-36 (or, more likely, only vv. 34-35);[56] 15.3-11;[57] 15.21-22;[58] 15.31c;[59] 15.44b-48;[60] 15.56;[61] 2 Cor. 6.14–7.1;[62] Gal. 2.7-8;[63] Phil. 1.1c;[64] 2.6-7;[65] 1 Thess.

Conjectural Emendation in the New Testament, with A Coda on 1 Cor 4.6', *CBQ* 36 (1974), pp. 543-58 (555-58).

49. Weiss, *Der erste Korintherbrief*, p. xli.

50. Udo Schnelle, '1 Kor 6.14—Eine nachpaulinische Glosse', *NovT* 25 (1983), pp. 217-19.

51. O'Neill, 'Glosses and Interpolations', pp. 381-83.

52. Lamar Cope, 'First Corinthians 8–10: Continuity or Contradiction?', *ATRSup* 11 (1990), pp. 114-23.

53. William O. Walker, Jr, '1 Corinthians 11.2-16 and Paul's Views regarding Women', *JBL* 94 (1975), pp. 94-110; Lamar Cope, '1 Cor 11.2-16: One Step Further', *JBL* 97 (1978), pp. 435-36; G.W. Trompf, 'On Attitudes toward Women in Paul and Paulinist Literature: 1 Corinthians 11.3-16 and Its Context', *CBQ* 42 (1980), pp. 196-215; William O. Walker, Jr, 'The Vocabulary of 1 Corinthians 11.3-16: Pauline or Non-Pauline?', *JSNT* 35 (1989), pp. 75-88.

54. Jean Magne, 'Les paroles sur la coupe', in Joël Delobel (ed.), *Logia: Les paroles de Jésus—The Sayings of Jesus: Mémorial Joseph Coppens* (BETL, 59; Leuven: Peeters/Leuven University Press, 1982), pp. 485-90; *From Christianity to Gnosis and From Gnosis to Christianity: An Itinerary through the Texts To and From the Tree of Paradise* (trans. A.F.W. Armstrong; BJS, 286; Atlanta: Scholars Press, 1993), p. 33; and 'A Summary History of the Eucharist' (unpublished paper, 1999), p. 3.

55. Eric L. Titus, 'Did Paul Write I Corinthians 13?', *JBR* 27 (1959), pp. 299-302; and William O. Walker, Jr, 'Is First Corinthians 13 a Non-Pauline Interpolation?', *CBQ* 60 (1998), pp. 484-99.

56. E.g. Gerhard Fitzer, *Das Weib schweige in der Gemeinde: Über den unpaulinischen Charakter der mulier-taceat Verse in 1. Korinther 14* (TEH NS, 110; Munich: Chr. Kaiser Verlag, 1963); Murphy-O'Connor, 'Interpolations in 1 Corinthians', pp. 90-92; and Gordon D. Fee, *The First Epistle to the Corinthians* (NICNT; Grand Rapids: Eerdmans, 1987), pp. 699-708.

57. Robert M. Price, 'Apocryphal Apparitions: 1 Corinthians 15.3-11 as a Post-Pauline Interpolation', *JHC* 2 (1995), pp. 69-99.

58. O'Neill, 'Glosses and Interpolations', pp. 384-85.

59. Dennis R. MacDonald, 'A Conjectural Emendation of 1 Cor 15.31-32: Or the Case of the Misplaced Lion Fight', *HTR* 73 (1980), pp. 265-76.

60. Widmann, '1 Kor 2 6-16', pp. 47-48.

61. Friedrich Wilhelm Horn, '1 Korinther 15,56—ein exegetischer Stachel', *ZNW* 82 (1991), pp. 88-105.

62. E.g. Willem K.M. Grossouw, 'Over de echtheid van 2 Cor 6,14–7,1', *StC* 26 (1951), pp. 203-206; Joseph A. Fitzmyer, 'Qumrân and the Interpolated Paragraph in 2 Cor. 6,14–7,1', *CBQ* 23 (1961), pp. 271-80; Joachim Gnilka, '2 Cor 6.14–7.1

2.13-16;[66] 4.1-8; 4.10b-12; 4.18; 5.1-11;[67] 5.12-22; 5.27.[68]

Despite repeated suggestions that particular passages in the Pauline letters are to be regarded as later additions, however, 'there has been no general scholarly agreement on the probability, or even the plausibility, of any of these hypotheses about glosses and interpolations'.[69] Indeed, as Munro notes, 'no particular passage, not even the benediction in Romans 16.25-27, has gained undisputed interpolation status'.[70] In a more general sense, Doughty observes that interpolation theories 'are not generally presupposed by Pauline scholarship'; further, they actually 'encounter fierce resistance in some quarters'.[71] According to

in the Light of the Qumran Texts and the Testaments of the Twelve Patriarchs', in Jerome Murphy-O'Connor (ed.), *Paul and Qumran: Studies in New Testament Exegesis* (SNTE; Chicago: Priory, 1968), pp. 48-68; and Hans Dieter Betz, '2 Cor 6.14–7.1: An Anti-Pauline Fragment?', *JBL* 92 (1973), pp. 88-108.

63. Ernst Barnikol, 'The Non-Pauline Origin of the Parallelism of the Apostles Peter and Paul: Galatians 2.7-8' (trans. Darrell J. Doughty with B. Keith Brewer), *JHC* 5 (1998), pp. 285-300 (German original, published in Ernst Barnikol (ed.), *Forschungen zur Enstehung des Urchristentums des Neuen Testaments und der Kirche* (Kiel: Walter G. Mühlau, 1931).

64. Wolfgang Schenk, *Die Philipperbriefe des Paulus: Kommentar* (Stuttgart: W. Kohlhammer, 1984), pp. 78-82, 334.

65. Ernst Barnikol, *Prolegomena zur neutestamentlichen Dogmengeschichte*. II. *Philipper 2. Der marcionitische Ursprung des Mythos-Satzes Phil. 2,6-7* (FEUNTK, 7; Kiel: Mühlau, 1932).

66. E.g. Karl Gottfried Eckart, 'Der zweite echte Brief des Apostels Paulus an die Thessalonicher', *ZTK* 58 (1961), pp. 30-44; Birger A. Pearson, '1 Thessalonians 2.13-16: A Deutero-Pauline Interpolation', *HTR* 64 (1971), pp. 79-94; and Daryl Schmidt, '1 Thess 2.13-16: Linguistic Evidence for an Interpolation', *JBL* 102 (1983), pp. 269-79.

67. Gerhard Friedrich, '1. Thessalonischer 5,1-11, der apologetische Einschub eines Späteren', *ZTK* 70 (1973), pp. 288-315.

68. On 1 Thessalonians 2.13-16; 4.1-8, 10b-12, 18; 5.12-22, 27, see Eckart, 'Der zweite echte Brief des Apostels Paulus'.

69. Furnish, 'Pauline Studies', p. 325.

70. Winsome Munro, 'A Paradigmatic Shift in Pauline Studies?' (unpublished paper presented at the 1983 Annual Meeting of the Society of Biblical Literature in Dallas, Texas), p. 4.

71. Doughty, 'Pauline Paradigms', pp. 95-96. For the characterization of Titus' interpolation proposal regarding 1 Cor. 13 as 'criticism run amok', see Fee, *The First Epistle to the Corinthians*, p. 626 n. 6 (Fitzmyer's dismissive assertion that 'short shrift' should be given to O'Neill's argument for numerous interpolations and glosses in Romans has already been noted). See also, e.g., Frederik W. Wisse,

Munro, scholars are more inclined to view entire epistles as pseudonymous than to agree that 'short pockets of material' are non-Pauline additions. At least in part, she suggests, this is because it is simply more difficult to establish 'the alien character of relatively small blocks of writing' than of 'complete compositions'.[72] Along somewhat the same lines, Lamar Cope observes that 'by and large we have treated the letters of Paul in terms of units'. Once it has been established that particular letters are either Pauline or non-Pauline, 'they have been treated as wholes', with little attention to the possibility of non-Pauline passages within otherwise authentically Pauline letters or, for that matter, of authentically Pauline passages within otherwise non-Pauline writings. In Cope's view, '*every passage* needs to be subjected to scrutiny with regard to its origin, not just the letters as a whole'; further, 'the very same arguments which justify assigning a letter as a whole to Paul need to be marshaled in support of each passage, and vice versa'.[73]

All of this is surely true, but a major problem, in my own judgment, is the fact that most of the debate regarding glosses and interpolations has focused directly upon individual passages, with little or no systematic attention to some rather important preliminary issues. These include: (1) the *a priori* probability of interpolations in the Pauline letters; (2) whether direct text-critical evidence is an essential prerequisite for the recognition of individual interpolations; (3) the burden-of-proof question as it relates to the identification of interpolations; and (4) what types of data would count as evidence for interpolation in specific instances. What is now needed, if the discussion is to proceed in a fruitful manner, is a careful consideration of these preliminary issues.

Before proceeding further, however, certain terminological distinctions are necessary. First, it is important to distinguish between 'gloss' and 'interpolation'. Furnish speaks of 'glosses and...even longer

'Textual Limits to Redactional Theory in the Pauline Corpus', in James E. Goehring *et al.* (eds.), *Gospel Origins and Christian Beginnings: In Honor of James M. Robinson* (FFasc, 1; Sonoma, CA: Polebridge Press, 1990), pp. 167-78, for the argument that 'redactional theory [including interpolation hypotheses] that steps outside the bounds of textual evidence and minimizes the burden of proof is counter-productive and a hindrance to Pauline studies' (p. 178).

72. Munro, 'A Paradigmatic Shift?', pp. 4-5.

73. Cope, 'First Corinthians 8–10', pp. 117-18.

interpolated units' in such a way as perhaps to suggest that the only difference between the two is length.[74] Indeed, Fitzmyer's designation of such substantial units of text as Rom. 1.19-21, 3.10-18 and 13.1-7 as 'smaller secondary glosses' might imply that the terms 'gloss' and 'interpolation' are to be used interchangeably.[75] Such, however, is not the case. To be sure, both glosses and interpolations are units of foreign material now appearing in the text of a document. Moreover, as Leander E. Keck notes, 'it is not always possible to differentiate precisely what is gloss and what is interpolation'.[76] Nevertheless, there is a significant difference between the two, at least in principle.

A gloss is an explanatory note or comment, generally written in the margin or occasionally between the lines of a manuscript by a reader, scribe, or possibly even the author of the document in which it now appears.[77] Apparently not intended as an addition to the body of the text, a gloss was designed merely to clarify, explain, or comment upon an item in the text. At times, however, a scribe might copy a gloss into the body of the document, mistakenly assuming that it was intended to be part of the text; the gloss might subsequently be reproduced in later transcriptions of the text and thus might now appear in one or more of the surviving manuscripts. As a likely example of such a gloss, Bruce M. Metzger cites the clause in some manuscripts at Rom. 8.1: μὴ κατὰ σάρκα περιπατοῦσιν ἀλλὰ κατὰ πνεῦμα ('walking not according to the flesh but according to the spirit').[78] This, he believes, 'was originally an

74. Furnish, 'Pauline Studies', p. 324.

75. Fitzmyer, *Romans*, p. 65.

76. Leander E. Keck, *Paul and His Letters* (PC; Philadelphia: Fortress Press, 2nd edn, 1988), p. 18.

77. For a distinction among 'glosses' ('brief explanations of difficult words or phrases'), 'scholia' (random 'interpretive remarks' intended 'to instruct the reader'), 'commentaries' ('systematically developed' comments intended 'to elucidate' an entire passage), 'catenae' ('"chains" of comments extracted from older ecclesiastical writers'), and 'onomastica' ('philological aids' purporting 'to give the meaning and etymology of proper names'), see Bruce M. Metzger, *The Text of the New Testament: Its Transmission, Corruption, and Restoration* (Oxford: Oxford University Press, 3rd edn, 1992), pp. 27-28. In this study, however, 'gloss' refers to any type of explanatory note or comment originally written in the margin or between the lines of a manuscript.

78. In fact, Codex A (fifth century), Codex D (sixth century), and some other witnesses have only μὴ κατὰ σάρκα περιπατοῦσιν with ἀλλὰ κατὰ πνεῦμα being added by correctors of A and D and a few other witnesses.

explanatory note (perhaps derived from v. 4) defining "those who are in Christ Jesus" '.[79] Numerous other examples could be cited.

Unlike a gloss, an interpolation is foreign material inserted deliberately and directly into the text of a document. As already noted, however, a gloss might be copied by a scribe into the body of a manuscript, be reproduced in later transcriptions, and thus now appear in some or perhaps even all of the surviving texts. In such cases, the distinction between gloss and interpolation becomes problematic. In the present study, the term 'interpolation' will be applied to any substantial addition to the text,[80] with no attempt to determine whether the passage in question originated as a gloss or as an interpolation *per se*.

A distinction is also to be noted, at least in principle, between 'interpolation' and 'redaction'. This distinction has been illustrated by means of an agricultural metaphor: 'interpolation is like pushing a shovel in the ground, separating two portions of soil, inserting something, and removing the shovel; evidence is left, but the breaks are reasonably clean and contained'. 'Redaction, on the other hand, much more closely resembles a plant which has grown in the ground; in pulling it up, the roots come too, and it is unclear where the redaction ends'.[81] Thus, as James H. Charlesworth points out, 'interpolations are insertions into the text that disrupt the flow of thought or add specific details', 'they can be removed because of their linguistic structure,

79. Metzger, *The Text of the New Testament*, p. 194. As an example of an absurdity resulting from 'heedlessness that passes comprehension', Metzger cites 2 Cor. 8.4: 'after εἰς τοὺς ἁγίους a good many minuscule manuscripts have added the gloss δέξασθαι ἡμᾶς. It appears that a scribe of one of these manuscripts wrote in the margin beside δέξασθαι ἡμᾶς the comment ἐν πολλοῖς τῶν ἀντιγράφων οὕτως εὕρηται ('it is found thus in many of the copies'). Then the scribe of a subsequent manuscript...incorporated this comment on the gloss directly in his text as though it were part of the apostle Paul's instructions to the Corinthians!'

80. By 'substantial addition', I mean material comprising at least two sentences and usually more (that is, not single words, phrases, clauses, or even sentences).

81. Eugene Harrison Lovering, Jr, 'The Collection, Redaction, and Early Circulation of the Corpus Paulinum' (unpublished doctoral dissertation, Southern Methodist University, 1988), p. 105. As his source for this metaphor, Lovering cites James H. Charlesworth, 'Reflections on the SNTS Pseudepigrapha Seminar at Duke on the Testaments of the Twelve Patriarchs', *NTS* 23 (1977), pp. 296-304 (303). Although Charlesworth does here distinguish between 'interpolation' and 'redaction', the metaphor employed by Lovering (and attributed to Charlesworth) does not appear.

which is usually...self-contained' and 'they might contain terms, symbols, or ideas foreign—or even antithetical—to the context'. Redactions, however, 'are passages embedded into the fabric of the document and cannot be excised'; 'early sources are so reworked from a new perspective that they cannot be distinguished from the more recent sections'. As in the case of interpolations and glosses, however, 'it is often impossible to distinguish between an interpolation and a redaction', for 'an apparent interpolation might be a passage in which the redactor has failed to achieve the usual integration, transition or flow or thought', and 'interpolations are often made to documents which are redactional in character'.[82] Nevertheless, a distinction is clear, at least in principle: an interpolation is a discrete addition to the text while redaction is the rewriting of a text in such a way as to incorporate new material.

Finally, it should be noted that the present study will employ the term 'interpolation' in a somewhat restricted sense, referring only to material that was neither composed by Paul nor included by Paul in the letter in which it now appears. Material composed by Paul for some other occasion but secondarily inserted at its present location, either by Paul or by someone else, will not be regarded as an interpolation, nor will material composed by someone other than Paul but secondarily inserted in one of the letters by Paul himself. In short, the present study is concerned only with non-Pauline material that has been added to one of the Pauline letters by someone other than Paul.

The plan of the book is as follows. The first four chapters will address the important preliminary issues noted above: the *a priori* probability of interpolations in the Pauline letters (Chapter 1), whether direct text-critical evidence is an essential prerequisite for the recognition of individual interpolations (Chapter 2), the burden-of-proof question as it relates to the identification of interpolations (Chapter 3), and specific types of data that count as evidence in the identification of interpolations (Chapter 4). Illustrations in Chapter 4 will be taken primarily from 1 Cor. 14.34-35, which many scholars regard as a non-Pauline interpolation. The next four chapters will argue that 1 Cor. 11.3-16 (Chapter 5), 1 Cor. 2.6-16 (Chapter 6), 1 Cor. 12.31b–14.1a (Chapter 7), and Rom. 1.18–2.29 (Chapter 8) are, in fact, non-Pauline interpolations. The last two chapters (Chapters 9 and 10) will summarize the

82. Charlesworth, 'Reflections', p. 303.

arguments advanced by other scholars for viewing five additional passages as interpolations: Rom. 16.25-27; 2 Cor. 6.14–7.1; 1 Thess. 2.13-16; Rom. 13.1-7; 1 Cor. 10.1-22. Finally, in the Epilogue, I shall briefly address the question of interpolations and the canonical authority of Scripture.

Chapter 1

THE *A PRIORI* PROBABILITY OF INTERPOLATIONS IN THE PAULINE LETTERS*

Before attempting to identify specific passages as possible non-Pauline interpolations, it is important to ask whether it is reasonable to assume, simply on *a priori* grounds, that the Pauline letters, as we now have them, are in fact likely to contain such interpolations. In an attempt to answer this question, I will first call attention to the undoubted presence of interpolations in other ancient literature, including early Christian writings. Then, I will consider certain aspects of the literary history of the Pauline corpus that would appear to bear upon the question of interpolations in the letters. Finally, I will note the actual evidence of numerous textual alterations in the surviving manuscripts of the Pauline letters, including short additions to the text.

1. *Interpolations in Other Ancient Literature*

As Eugene Harrison Lovering, Jr, has noted, 'Almost no one will deny that interpolations made their way into the widest diversity of materials in the ancient world'; moreover, 'the ancients were fully aware of this and literary critics occupied themselves with sorting out the secondary elements'.[1] It should also be noted that 'interpolation was not [necessarily] considered forgery' in antiquity.[2]

* Chapters 1, 2, 3 and 4 include material taken from William O. Walker, Jr, 'The Burden of Proof in Identifying Interpolations in the Pauline Letters', *NTS* 33 (1987), pp. 610-18; and 'Text-Critical Evidence for Interpolations in the Letters of Paul', *CBQ* 50 (1988), pp. 622-31. All of these materials are used here with permission from the original publishers.

1. Lovering, 'The Collection', p. 109.

2. Solomon Zeitlin, *Josephus on Jesus with Particular Reference to the Slavonic Josephus and the Hebrew Josippon* (Philadelphia: The Dropsie College for Hebrew and Cognate Learning, 1931), p. 67.

That interpolations were introduced into many of the Classical writings cannot be questioned. Indeed, Robert M. Grant points out that 'among educated people in the Hellenistic age it was common knowledge that the works of the most ancient theological poets were not preserved in precisely the form in which their authors had left them'.[3] For example, ancient literary critics 'believed, presumably not without some grounds for their belief, that Homer had suffered interpolation as well as omission, and that it was possible for critics to recover something like the original text'.[4] Thus, Zenodotus, the first head of the renowned library in Alexandria (third century BCE), 'was a famous textual critic, well known for his ability to ferret out interpolations in the text of Homer'.[5] For the identification of such interpolations, Zenodotus relied upon four principles of criticism: 'Interpolations, he claimed, could be detected (1) if they broke the continuity of the poem, (2) if they lacked poetic art or were unsuitable to the characters of gods and men, (3) if they contained errors about ancient events, (4) if they differed from the usual style of the poet'.[6] Similarly, one of Zenodotus' successors, the grammarian Aristarchus (second century BCE), was 'expert in discovering interpolations in Homer'.[7] In modern times, Karl Maurer has asserted that 'the fact [of interpolations in Homer] is notorious',[8] and George Melville Bolling, among others, has identified numerous interpolations in the texts of both the *Iliad* and the *Odyssey*.[9] It is also relevant to note that an 'expanded text' of Homer's *Odyssey* appears in Book XVIII of the *Kestoi*, an early-third-century work

3. Robert M. Grant, *The Letter and the Spirit* (New York: Macmillan; London: SPCK, 1957), pp. 15-16. For the full discussion, see pp. 15-18 and 19-23.

4. Grant, *The Letter and the Spirit*, p. 17.

5. Robert M. Grant, 'Marcion and the Critical Method', in Peter Richardson and John C. Hurd (eds.), *From Jesus to Paul: Studies in Honour of Francis Wright Beare* (Waterloo, ON: Wilfrid Laurier University Press, 1984), p. 211; cf. Rudolf Pfeiffer, *History of Classical Scholarship from the Beginnings to the End of the Hellenistic Age* (Oxford: Clarendon Press, 1968), pp. 105-22 (108-13).

6. Grant, *The Letter and the Spirit*, p. 16.

7. Robert M. Grant, *Heresy and Criticism: The Search for Authenticity in Early Christian Literature* (Louisville, KY: Westminster/John Knox Press, 1993), p. 16; cf. Pfeiffer, *History of Classical Scholarship*, pp. 210-33 (214-19, 227-32).

8. Karl Maurer, *Interpolation in Thucydides* (MBCBSup, 150; Leiden: E.J. Brill, 1995), p. 181.

9. George Melville Bolling, *The External Evidence for Interpolation in Homer* (Oxford: Clarendon Press, 1925).

written by the Christian author Sextus Julius Africanus.[10] Interpolations have also been detected in the works of other Classical authors including Orpheus, Musaeus, Hippocrates, Aristophanes, Euripedes and Thucydides.[11] Regarding Thucydides, Maurer, though generally conservative in his conclusions regarding particular passages, has recently concluded that 'a somewhat crude insertion of glosses and other notes into the text of Thuc[ydides] is not a nineteenth-century mirage, but a historical fact for which there is abundant evidence'.[12]

Of direct relevance to the question of interpolations in the Pauline letters is the almost certain presence of interpolations in precisely the genre of ancient literature most closely akin to these letters: the letters of philosophers (e.g. Plato, Aristotle, Epicurus and Seneca) and particularly those 'letters of exhortation in which teachers seek to guide and mold the characters of disciples'.[13] As both Stanley K. Stowers and William G. Doty[14] note, many of these letters are pseudonymous;[15] more to the point, however, is the fact that the Epicurean correspondence, for example, 'has been very heavily edited (redacted) by Epicurus's followers who amplified the master's teachings and adapted them to later situations'.[16] This may well provide a precedent for the presence of interpolations in the letters of Paul, which, of course, can also be seen as 'letters of exhortation in which [a teacher] seek[s] to guide and mold the characters of disciples'.

Beyond this, however, there is ample evidence that early Christians themselves introduced interpolations into Jewish writings that they regarded as in some manner deficient, defective, or less 'Christian' than

10. Walter Bauer, *Orthodoxy and Heresy in Earliest Christianity* (trans. Team from Philadelphia Seminar on Christian Origins; ed. Robert A. Kraft and Gerhard Krodel; Philadelphia: Fortress Press, 1971), pp. 160-65.

11. Regarding Orpheus, Musaeus, and Hippocrates, see, e.g., Grant, *Heresy and Criticism*, pp. 21-22, 61-66; regarding Aristophanes and Euripedes, see, e.g., Maurer, *Interpolation in Thucydides*, p. 181.

12. Maurer, *Interpolation in Thucydides*, p. xi; for a review of the evidence, see the entire book.

13. Stanley K. Stowers, 'Greek and Latin Letters', *ABD*, IV, pp. 290-93 (292).

14. Stowers, 'Greek and Latin Letters', p. 292; and William G. Doty, *Letters in Primitive Christianity* (GBS; Philadelphia: Fortress Press, 1973), p. 23.

15. According to Stowers ('Greek and Latin Letters', p. 292), these 'show marked similarities to pseudonymous Christian letters such as the Pastoral Epistles (1 Timothy, 2 Timothy, Titus)'.

16. Stowers, 'Greek and Latin Letters', p. 292.

might be desired. It is widely agreed, for example, that material was added to the Greek text of Flavius Josephus in order to create a non-Christian testimony to the messiahship and resurrection of Jesus[17] (indeed, some scholars attribute this material to Eusebius, the fourth-century Bishop of Caesarea and eminent church historian).[18] Similarly, the late-second-century critic, Celsus, charged that Christians had added interpolations to the *Sibylline Oracles* in order to provide pagan support for the truth of the Christian religion, and this charge is regarded as 'more than justified' by most modern scholars.[19] Indeed, there is now general agreement that early Christians rewrote and expanded not only the *Sibylline Oracles* but also various other ancient Jewish pseudepigraphical texts including the Hellenistic *Synagogal Prayers*, the *Testaments of the Twelve Patriarchs*, the *Martyrdom and Ascension of Isaiah* and *4 Ezra*.[20] In short, it appears that interpolation

17. Josephus, *Ant.* 18.3.3. For judicious reviews of the evidence, see, for example, Louis H. Feldman, 'Josephus', *ABD*, III, pp. 981-98 (990-91); and John P. Meier, *A Marginal Jew: Rethinking the Historical Jesus*. I. *The Roots of the Problem and the Person* (ABRL; New York: Doubleday, 1991), pp. 56-88; for a treatment of the matter by a classicist, see, e.g., Eva Matthews Sanford, 'Propaganda and Censorship in the Transmission of Josephus', *TPAPA* 66 (1935), pp. 127-45.

18. E.g. Solomon Zeitlin (*The Rise and Fall of the Judaean State: A Political, Social and Religious History of the Second Commonwealth*. I. *37* B.C.E.*–66* C.E. [Philadelphia: Jewish Publication Society of America, 2nd edn, 1969], p. 152) simply asserts that 'the well-known Christ passage in Josephus was interpolated in the fourth century by the Church historian Eusebius'; for argumentation, see his 'The Christ Passage in Josephus', *JQR* 18 (1927–28), pp. 237-40; and *Josephus on Jesus*, pp. 61-70, 93-100. Cf., however, e.g., D.S. Wallace-Hadrill, 'Eusebius of Caesarea and the *Testimonium Flavianum* (Josephus, *Antiquities*, XVIII. 63f.)', *JEH* 25 (1974), pp. 353-62 (361): 'It is...exceedingly improbable that Eusebius himself is to be held responsible for the alteration of Josephus's text, as some have held him to be'. In the most recent contribution to the debate, K.A. Olson ('Eusebius and the *Testimonium Flavianum*', *CBQ* 61 [1999], pp. 305-22) concludes: 'Complete certainty is unattainable, but we have very good reasons to suppose that Eusebius wrote the *Testimonium*'.

19. Grant, *Heresy and Criticism*, pp. 24; see also, e.g., John J. Collins, 'Sibylline Oracles', *ABD*, VI, pp. 2-6.

20. See, e.g., James H. Charlesworth, 'Christian and Jewish Self-Definition in Light of the Christian Additions to the Apocryphal Writings', in E.P. Sanders with A.I. Baumgarten and Alan Mendelson (eds.), *Jewish and Christian Self-Definition*. II. *Aspects of Judaism in the Greco-Roman Period* (Philadelphia: Fortress Press, 1981), pp. 27-55. According to Charlesworth (p. 28), the Christian additions to the pseudepigraphical writings 'can be grouped into four types': (1) 'very minor

was a rather widely-practiced Christian way of dealing with Jewish writings.

James H. Charlesworth claims that, although they apparently felt free to rewrite the Jewish pseudepigraphical writings, 'early Christians used and transmitted the Old Testament and Old Testament Apocrypha with little, if any, modification'.[21] If true, this might suggest that interpolation was regarded by Christians as appropriate only in the case of writings that had not been accorded the status of 'Scripture' and thus shed some light upon the question of *when* the Pauline letters would have been subject to interpolation (that is, *before* they came to be regarded as 'Scripture'). As a matter of fact, however, it is clear that by the second century Jewish scholars were engaged in expunging what they, at least, regarded as 'Christian additions' to the Septuagint (LXX).[22] Indeed, Justin Martyr's text of the LXX 'contained some remarkable interpolations' that 'appear to be of Christian origin'; Justin, however, was 'so sure of their genuineness that he accuse[d] the Jews of having removed them from their copies'.[23] Moreover, O'Neill has noted that Rom. 3.13-18 was incorporated into most manuscripts of Psalm 13 in the LXX (Ps. 14 in the Hebrew Bible) and from there into both the Vulgate and the Prayer Book version of the Psalms.[24]

The addition of Christian interpolations was clearly not confined, however, to non-Christian documents. For example, Dionysius, Bishop of Corinth in the middle of the second century, claimed that 'heretics' had both added materials to and deleted materials from his letters.[25] Similarly, Irenaeus (late-second century) 'express[ed] the greatest apprehension that his writings against heretics would be altered',[26] and the late-fourth-century writer Rufinus claimed that many of the Greek

interpolation[s] which may be found in only some of the manuscripts', (2) 'interpolations result[ing] from extensive redactional activity [that] comprise at least a paragraph', (3) 'massive Christian additions either at the beginning or the end [of a document]', and (4) 'massive rewriting'.

21. Charlesworth, 'Christian and Jewish Self-Definition', p. 27.

22. Melvin K.H. Peters, 'Septuagint', *ABD*, V, pp. 1093-104 (1097).

23. Henry Barclay Swete, *An Introduction to the Old Testament in Greek* (rev. Richard Rusden Ottley; Cambridge: Cambridge University Press, 2nd edn, 1914), pp. 423-24; cf. Zeitlin, *Josephus on Jesus*, p. 67.

24. O'Neill, 'Glosses and Interpolations', p. 384.

25. Grant, *Heresy and Criticism*, p. 12.

26. Bauer, *Orthodoxy and Heresy*, p. 166.

patristic writings had been interpolated.[27] Other examples could be cited.

But what about the writings that now comprise the Hebrew Scriptures and the Christian New Testament? Were they also subject to interpolation? Reference has already been made to Christian interpolations in the LXX. It is also well known that Marcion (mid-second century) removed numerous alleged interpolations from the Gospel of Luke and the letters of Paul;[28] indeed, Robert M. Grant has argued that Marcion was familiar both with 'current theories about interpolated religious documents' and with 'the editorial procedures of the great Hellenistic textual critics' who sought to eliminate such interpolations.[29] Quite apart from Marcion's controversial claims, however, both Munro and O'Neill point out that various forms of textual expansion can be detected in many—perhaps even most—of the writings that are now regarded as Jewish and/or Christian Scripture. Munro observes that both the Pentateuch and the New Testament Gospels are now widely viewed as consisting of multiple strata of tradition and redaction,[30] and O'Neill asserts that 'outside the New Testament epistles, we should all agree that every book of the Bible is either a compilation of various pieces, or a basic document to which additions have been made'.[31] Specific examples cited by Munro and O'Neill include the book of Genesis ('probably based on a double tradition, JE, to which has been added another tradition, P'), Jeremiah ('the prophet's oracles with many subsequent additions'), Proverbs ('a collection, but a collection of at least two sorts of material'), the Gospels of Matthew and Luke ('the enlarging of Mark, or a body of material remarkably like it'), the Gospel of John (an expansion 'of the so-called "Gospel of Signs"'), 2 Peter (an expansion of Jude), and 'the longer recension' of the Epistles of Ignatius (an expansion of an earlier version). Indeed, as has already been suggested in the case of the Synoptic Gospels, expansion of existing documents could result in the creation of entirely new works that survived alongside the earlier writings. Thus, for

27. Grant, *Heresy and Criticism*, p. 111.

28. See, e.g., Grant, *Heresy and Criticism*, pp. 33-47; and 'Marcion and the Critical Method', pp. 207-15.

29. Grant, *Heresy and Criticism*, p. 34; cf. also his 'Marcion and the Critical Method'.

30. Munro, 'A Paradigmatic Shift?', pp. 2-3.

31. O'Neill, 'Glosses and Interpolations', pp. 379-80.

example, Ephesians has often been viewed as a redactional expansion of Colossians,[32] and 2 Thessalonians shows such remarkable similarities to 1 Thessalonians not only in structure but also in 'sequence of thought, clauses, turns of phrase and expressions' as to suggest literary dependence.[33]

Numerous other likely examples of textual expansion could be cited. For example, the 'adulterous woman' pericope in most manuscripts of John's Gospel (7.53–8.11) is almost certainly a later interpolation,[34] and the same is probably true regarding the 'longer ending' of Mark (16.9-20)[35] and perhaps also the final chapter of John (ch. 21).[36]

Also of clear relevance at this point are the numerous distinctive readings appearing in the so-called 'Western Text' of the Gospels, Acts, and (to a lesser extent) the Pauline letters. This text 'is usually longer and more expansive in its language than the Alexandrian text (one-eighth longer in Acts)' and contains a number of what most scholars regard as 'substantial additions' (that is, 'interpolations'). At the same time, however, there are also 'some celebrated instances

32. Noting that 'almost one-third of the former book appears in the latter, and approximately one-half of the sentences in the latter book include language from the former', Charles B. Puskas, Jr (*The Letters of Paul: An Introduction* [GNS; Collegeville, MN: Liturgical Press, 1993], p. 115) refers to Colossians and Ephesians as 'literary siblings'. A more accurate metaphor, however, would probably be 'literary parent and child'.

33. Edgar M. Krentz, 'Thessalonians, First and Second Epistles to the', *ABD*, VI, pp. 515-23 (520) (quoting W. Bornemann, *Die Thessalonicherbriefe* [KEK, 10; Göttingen: Vandenhoeck & Ruprecht, 5th and 6th edn, 1894], p. 473).

34. For a summary of the evidence, see, e.g., C.K. Barrett, *The Gospel According to John: An Introduction with Commentary and Notes on the Greek Text* (Philadelphia: Westminster Press, 2nd edn, 1978), pp. 589-91.

35. For a summary of the evidence and the conclusion that the verses represent a later addition, see, e.g., C.S. Mann, *Mark: A New Translation with Introduction and Commentary* (AB, 27; Garden City, NY: Doubleday, 1986), pp. 672-76. For an extensive review of the evidence followed by the cautious conclusion that the verses are likely original, however, see William R. Farmer, *The Last Twelve Verses of Mark* (SNTSMS, 25; Cambridge: Cambridge University Press, 1974). For the conclusion that the question is 'still open and perhaps "insoluble at present"', see Kenneth W. Clark, 'The Theological Relevance of Textual Variation in Current Criticism of the Greek New Testament', *JBL* 85 (1966), pp. 1-16 (9-10).

36. For a summary of the arguments, see, e.g., Raymond E. Brown, *The Gospel According to John (xiii–xxi): Introduction, Translation, and Notes* (AB, 29A; Garden City, NY: Doubleday, 1970), pp. 1077-82.

where the 'Western' text is shorter and lacks certain phrases or clauses which do occur in the otherwise shorter Alexandrian text' (the so-called 'Western Non-Interpolations').[37] A few scholars have argued that these 'non-interpolations' represent the original readings (that is, that the 'non-Western texts' contain interpolations at these points).[38] In any case, the variant readings (whether additions or deletions) make it clear that materials were sometimes added to and/or deleted from the texts of the New Testament writings.[39] Richard I. Pervo has suggested that the type of Christianity reflected in the distinctive readings of the Western Text 'has many affinities to right-wing Deutero-Paulinism of second century C.E. Asia Minor'. Moreover, in his view, these readings demonstrate that one technique used by representatives of this type of Christianity was 'the revision of texts through addition and deletion'; indeed, they 'show that there were people quite willing to attempt such modifications' of early Christian writings.[40]

As a final testimony to the practices of both redactional expansion and editorial excision in the early church, Munro cites Rev. 22.18-19:

> I warn every one who hears the words of the prophecy of this book: if any one adds to them, God will add to him the plagues described in this book, and if any one takes away from the words of the book of this prophecy, God will take away his share in the tree of life and in the holy city, which are described in this book.

Although debate continues regarding specific passages, the basic point made by Munro and O'Neill would appear to be incontrovertible: there is clear evidence that both Jewish and early Christian writings (including those that eventually attained the status of 'Scripture') were subject to various types of editorial expansion. But what about the

37. Eldon Jay Epp, 'Western Text', *ABD*, VI, p. 910; see the entire article, pp. 909-12.

38. For a discussion of the matter that rejects this view, see, e.g., Klyne Snodgrass, ' "Western Non-Interpolations" ', *JBL* 91 (1972), pp. 369-79.

39. Howard Eshbaugh ('Theological Variants in the Western Text of the Pauline Corpus' [unpublished doctoral dissertation, Case Western Reserve University, 1975], p. 202) suggests that what he terms 'theological variants' in the Western text of the Pauline letters 'show the fluidity of the text in the early church'.

40. Richard I. Pervo, 'Social and Religious Aspects of the "Western" Text', in Dennis E. Groh and Robert Jewett (eds.), *The Living Text: Essays in Honor of Ernest W. Saunders* (Lanham, MD: University Press of America, 1985), pp. 229-41 (241, 230, 231, 239).

letters of Paul? Did they experience the same treatment? Noting 'the addition of between three and six post-Pauline letters to an original body of Pauline writings' as evidence 'that Paul was not exempt' from such treatment, Munro asks, 'Why then should the remaining "genuine" letters...be assumed to be immune?'[41] Similarly, O'Neill asserts that 'there seems to be no reason why Paul's letters should be any different'.[42]

To be sure, one might object that the letters of Paul represent a distinctively different literary genre than do these other biblical writings. Thus, they may not have been subject to the same kinds of literary processes. Responding to this objection, O'Neill agrees that the letters are 'a distinct literary form', but he goes on to observe that 'they are odd as letters anyway'. Noting that 'no ancient letters, except letters modelled on Paul's, are so long or so like treatises in parts', O'Neill suggests 'that the oddness of Paul's letters' may be due to the fact that they 'have been treated in exactly the same way as the rest of the sacred books contained in the Old and New Testaments canons'—in short, 'they are odd as letters' precisely because they have 'been glossed and interpolated'.[43]

Is it the case, however, that the Pauline letters are 'odd as letters', as O'Neill asserts? Stanley K. Stowers maintains that 'the Greek Christian tradition of letter writing is a marked modification of but not a departure from the non-Christian tradition'.[44] John L. White goes further, claiming that Christian letters differ significantly from ordinary Greek letters: 'Even a superficial comparison shows that, with few exceptions, Christian letters are considerably longer than ordinary Greek letters'.[45] This would appear to support O'Neill's contention regarding the 'oddness' of the Pauline letters. Doty, however, claims that 'the Pauline letters are briefer' than their Hellenistic counterparts.[46] The reason for

41. Winsome Munro, 'Interpolation in the Epistles: Weighing Probabily', *NTS* 36 (1990), pp. 431-43 (432).

42. O'Neill, 'Glosses and Interpolations', p. 380.

43. O'Neill, 'Glosses and Interpolations', p. 380.

44. Stowers, 'Greek and Latin Letters', p. 292.

45. John L. White, *Light from Ancient Letters* (FFNT; Philadelphia: Fortress Press, 1986), pp. 18-19; cf. also his 'Letter', *HCBD*, p. 601: 'By comparison with [ordinary Greek letters], New Testament letters tend to be longer and somewhat more literary'.

46. Doty, *Letters in Primitive Christianity*, p. 42.

the apparent contradiction is that the Hellenistic letter-writing tradition has been preserved in two quite distinct forms, which White terms respectively 'the documentary tradition' (papyri and ostraca) and 'the literary tradition' (the classical and later writers). White (and apparently O'Neill) are comparing the Pauline letters with the former, while Doty has in mind the latter. Even Doty observes, however, that 'the letter form which developed in the Pauline letters was richer than either the brief private letters or the more developed letter-essays of Hellenism'.[47] Similarly, Stowers states that the New Testament letters 'resemble neither the common papyri from the very lowest levels of culture and education nor the works of those with the highest levels of rhetorical training'; rather, 'they fall somewhere in between'.[48] In short, the Pauline letters differ in significant respects both from the 'ordinary Greek letters' and from 'the more developed letter-essays of Hellenism'. Thus, the basic thrust of O'Neill's point regarding 'the oddness of Paul's letters' would appear to be valid, even though his specific reference to length and treatise-like features applies more to 'the documentary letter tradition' than to 'the literary tradition'. As letters in the Hellenistic world, the letters of Paul are 'odd', and, as O'Neill suggests, this 'oddness' may result from the fact that they, like other ancient writings, have been interpolated.

Thus, there appears to be no reason for assuming that the Pauline letters would have been any less subject to textual expansion than were other documents that now comprise the Hebrew Scriptures and the Christian New Testament. Moreover, as a possible precedent, the presence of interpolations has already been noted in the Hellenistic literary genre most closely resembling these letters: the letters of philosophers and moralists to their disciples. Finally, as will be discussed later, most scholars agree that at least some of the Pauline letters were in fact subject to various forms of editorial activity; thus, for example, 2 Corinthians is widely regarded as a 'composite' letter, composed of parts of at least two originally separate letters.

By way of summary and conclusion: the undoubted presence of interpolations in other ancient literature—Classical, Hellenistic, Jewish and Christian—would lead us to expect, simply on *a priori* grounds, that the Pauline letters, as we now have them, are likely to contain non-

47. Doty, *Letters in Primitive Christianity*, p. 42.

48. Stanley K. Stowers, *Letter Writing in Greco-Roman Antiquity* (LEC, 5; Philadelphia: Westminster Press, 1986), p. 25.

Pauline interpolations. Indeed, two of my colleagues in the Trinity University Department of Classical Studies—one a specialist in Greek literature and the other in Latin literature—have recently informed me that they would be quite surprised if there were no interpolations in the letters of Paul.[49]

2. *Relevant Aspects of the Literary History of the Pauline Corpus*

This *a priori* probability of interpolations in the Pauline letters is strengthened by a consideration of certain aspects of the literary history of the Pauline corpus. Daryl Schmidt suggests that 'the better we understand the...process that formed the Pauline corpus and shaped it into a part of the emerging Christian canon, the clearer it becomes that the final canonical text reflects evidence of both editing and textual revision'. Indeed, it is Schmidt's view that 'the...process that produced a corpus of published letters...went through several stages at which "interpolations" to the original letters were added for their published recension'.[50]

Unfortunately, we know considerably less about the early history of the Pauline corpus that we might wish,[51] and it is obviously beyond the scope of the present study to attempt a comprehensive reconstruction. There are, however, two relatively clear points regarding this history that are directly relevant to the question of interpolations in the Pauline letters.

1. *The individual Pauline letters have come down to us not as separate documents but only as parts of a collection—indeed, a collection that was assembled, preserved and transmitted by the early church under the name of Paul.* The oldest extant manuscript, P^{46}, originally contained 10 letters,[52] and Codices Vaticanus (B), Sinaiticus (א), Alexandrinus (A) and Ephraemi (C) apparently had 14. Thus, as Jerome

49. Professors Joan B. Burton and Colin M. Wells.

50. Daryl Schmidt, 'Identifying Seams in Authentic Pauline Letters: Evidence for Letter Fragments and Interpolations' (unpublished paper prepared for the Paul Seminar of the Westar Institute, Santa Rosa, CA, 1998), p. 2.

51. To my knowledge, the most comprehensive survey is Lovering's doctoral dissertation, 'The Collection'.

52. In the following order: Romans, Hebrews, 1 and 2 Corinthians, Ephesians, Galatians, Philippians, Colossians, 1 and 2 Thessalonians; missing were Philemon and the Pastoral Letters.

Murphy-O'Connor observes, 'despite the very definite individuality of the Pauline letters, not a single one has been transmitted separately'; rather, 'each has come down to us associated with others attributed to the apostle'.[53] Similarly, Leander E. Keck declares that 'we do not have access to Paul's [individual] letters as he wrote [or dictated] them, but only to the letters as they were at some point incorporated into a collection'.[54] It remains unclear just how this collection came into being—whether through a gradual and informal process of the sharing of individual letters among the churches, by the conscious and deliberate work of one or more collectors, or by some combination of the two.[55] In any case, the letters are now available to us only as parts of a collection that was assembled, preserved, and transmitted by the early church.

It is important to note, however, that we have no way of knowing exactly what materials may have been available to a collector of the Pauline letters or, indeed, what the physical condition of these materials may have been. Early Christians who preserved letters from Paul very likely also preserved other writings, some of them perhaps of unknown origin. Prolonged use of such writings—whether Pauline or non-Pauline—would have resulted in physical deterioration and

53. Jerome Murphy-O'Connor, *Paul the Letter-Writer: His World, His Options, His Skills* (GNS, 41; Collegeville, MN: Liturgical, 1995), p. 114.

54. Keck, *Paul and His Letters*, p. 19.

55. See, e.g., Murphy-O'Connor, *Paul the Letter-Writer*, pp. 114-18, for a discussion of 'The Evolutionary Theory' and 'The Big Bang Theory'; for a somewhat similar but more detailed discussion of 'theories of sudden collection' and 'theories of gradual growth', see Lovering, 'The Collection', pp. 283-345. For a more elaborate taxonomy that categorizes the various hypotheses 'according to the distance they posit between the career of the Apostle Paul and the collection of his letters', see Robert M. Price, 'The Evolution of the Pauline Canon' (unpublished paper prepared for Meeting of the Paul Seminar of the Westar Institute, Santa Rosa, CA, 1995), pp. 119-30: (1) 'Pauline Testament' Theories (the letters collected by Paul himself); (2) 'Paper Apostle' Theories (the letters collected immediately following Paul's death to 'replace the irreplaceable Apostle'); (3) 'Snowball' Theories (the gradual exchange of letters among various Pauline centers); and (4) 'Second Coming' Theories (a period of neglect of the Pauline letters, followed by 'the labors of a single individual, the first collector of the Pauline Epistles', who makes Paul 'a literary influence' in the early church). See also, e.g., Harry Y. Gamble, *The New Testament Canon: Its Making and Meaning* (GBS; Philadelphia: Fortress Press, 1985), pp. 36-46; and his 'The Canon of the New Testament', in Epp and MacRae (eds.), *The New Testament and Its Modern Interpreters*, pp. 201-43 (205-208).

perhaps fragmentation of the scrolls or codices. What was available to a collector, therefore, may have consisted of more-or-less miscellaneous assortments of written materials, in various stages of deterioration, fragmentation and perhaps combination, with no clear distinction between Pauline and non-Pauline texts. If the goal of a collector was to include *all* available Pauline writings, as appears at least plausible, the tendency almost inevitably would have been to err on the side of *in*clusion, not *ex*clusion. Thus, non-Pauline materials may well have been introduced into the Pauline corpus quite unintentionally, perhaps on more than one occasion and by more than one hand.

In short, 'the letters of Paul as we have them cannot be simply equated with what Paul himself wrote [or dictated]'; rather, 'what the letters present us with is Paul as he was transmitted by the church'.[56] This, in my judgment, makes it reasonable to assume, simply on *a priori* grounds, that the letters are likely to contain non-Pauline interpolations, whether intentionally or inadvertently added.

2. *This collection of materials assembled, preserved and transmitted by the early Church under the name of Paul represents both 'an* expanded *Paul' and 'an* abbreviated *Paul', but it is also 'an* edited *Paul'.*[57] Indeed, the collection can be termed 'the letters of Paul' only with serious qualifications. It surely omits some authentically Pauline letters,[58] it undoubtedly includes at least one and probably as many as seven writings that are non-Pauline in origin,[59] and—most significantly

56. Keck, *Paul and His Letters*, p. 19.

57. Leander E. Keck and Victor Paul Furnish, *The Pauline Letters* (IBT; Nashville: Abingdon Press, 1984), p. 50.

58. One could assume *a priori* that some letters written by Paul almost certainly would not have survived. In addition, there are apparent references in 1 Cor. 5.9 and 2 Cor. 2.4, 7.8 and 10.10 to letters that are no longer extant, at least in their entirety and as separate documents. Note also the reference in Col. 4.16 to 'the letter from Laodicea'. See, however, Lovering, 'The Collection', p. 15: 'There is no reason to think that all of Paul's letters were preserved, but there is inconclusive basis for presuming that they were not'; 'there is, finally, insufficient evidence to decide the question'.

59. The earliest extant manuscripts—P^{46} (late-second or early-third century), א and B (fourth century), and A and C (fifth century)—originally included not only the seven letters now generally regarded as authentically Pauline (Philemon is missing from P^{46}) but also letters whose Pauline authorship is disputed (2 Thessalonians, Colossians, Ephesians, and the Pastorals [missing from P^{46}]) and one whose non-Pauline origin is virtually certain (Hebrews). For discussion of the disputed

for purposes of the present study—at least some of the letters almost certainly have been subject to various forms of editing. Indeed, as Keck observes, 'what we have are those forms of Paul's letters that were prepared for church use long after Paul himself wrote them'.[60]

There is, of course, considerable debate regarding the exact nature and extent of this editing, as well as just when in the history of the corpus it would have occurred. According to Harry Gamble, 'the tacit assumption of most literary critics' appears to be that individual letters 'were independently edited and only later on incorporated into the corpus in redacted form'.[61] Walter Schmithals and others, however, maintain 'that the Pauline correspondence was collected, edited, and put into general circulation at a particular point in time by a single individual working under the compulsion of a ruling intention'.[62] David Trobisch argues for something of a mediating position: some of the letters were initially collected and edited by Paul himself; then, following Paul's death, one or more expanded editions appeared, to be followed finally by a comprehensive edition incorporating all available previous editions.[63]

Quite apart from the question of timing, however, it is generally agreed that the editing was of two types: 'one kind created some of the letters as we now have them, the other made modifications in what had been created'.[64] For example, it is now widely held that what we know as 2 Corinthians is a 'composite' letter, comprising parts of at least two originally separate Pauline letters,[65] and 'partition' hypotheses have

letters and Hebrews, see, e.g., Raymond F. Collins, *Letters That Paul Did Not Write: The Epistle to the Hebrews and the Pauline Pseudepigrapha* (GNS, 28; Wilmington, DE: Michael Glazier, 1988).

60. Keck, *Paul and His Letters*, p. 18.

61. Harry Y. Gamble, 'The Redaction of the Pauline Letters and the Formation of the Pauline Corpus', *JBL* 94 (1975), pp. 403-18 (403-404).

62. Gamble, 'The Redaction', p. 404; see Walter Schmithals, *Paul and the Gnostics* (trans. John E. Steely; Nashville: Abingdon Press, 1972), pp. 239-74.

63. David Trobisch, *Die Entstehung der Paulusbriefsammlung: Studien zu den Anfängen christlicher Publizistik* (NTOA, 10; Freiburg: Universitätsverlag; Göttingen: Vandenhoeck & Ruprecht, 1989); and *Paul's Letter Collection: Tracing the Origins* (Minneapolis: Fortress Press, 1994).

64. Keck and Furnish, *The Pauline Letters*, p. 50.

65. For a summary of the evidence for the 'two-letter hypothesis', see, e.g., Victor Paul Furnish, *II Corinthians: Translated with Introduction, Notes, and Commentary* (AB, 32A; Garden City, NY: Doubleday, 1984), pp. 30-32, 35-41. As

also been advanced regarding Philippians,[66] 1 Corinthians[67] and Romans.[68] Indeed, Keck asserts that, 'of the seven undoubtedly genuine letters, only in the case of Philemon can we be certain that what we have is virtually identical with what Paul wrote'.[69]

In short, it is now generally acknowledged that the Pauline letters were assembled, preserved and transmitted by the early church only as parts of an edited collection—what today would be termed an edited 'anthology'. Further, most scholars would grant, at least in principle, that the editing of the letters would almost certainly have included some editorial additions. Indeed, Helmut Koester asserts that 'if the letters of Paul are...not preserved as direct copies of the original autographs, but as later editions, it is not surprising that they also contain a number of editorial additions'.[70] Finally, it is my own judgment that Munro is surely correct when she maintains that 'it strains credulity to assume that [these editorial additions] would have been confined to brief connections and minor improvements'.[71]

3. *Textual Additions in the Surviving Manuscripts of the Pauline Letters*

I have noted the undoubted presence of interpolations in other ancient literature—Classical, Hellenistic, Jewish and even Christian. Further, I have called attention to the fact that we possess the Pauline letters only as parts of a collection that was assembled, edited, preserved and transmitted by the early Church under the name of Paul. Both points, in my judgment, strongly suggest that the Pauline letters, as we now have them, are likely to contain non-Pauline interpolations. This probability

Furnish notes (pp. 32-33), however, other scholars have argued for as many as six original letters. For an argument supporting the unity of 2 Corinthians, see most recently J.D.H. Amador, 'Revisiting 2 Corinthians: Rhetoric and the Case for Unity', *NTS* 46 (2000), pp. 92-111.

66. See, e.g., F.W. Beare, *A Commentary on the Epistle to the Philippians* (HNTC; San Francisco: Harper & Row, 1959), pp. 1-5.

67. For discussion, see, e.g., Raymond F. Collins, *First Corinthians* (SP, 7; Collegeville, MN: Liturgical Press, 1999), pp. 10-14.

68. For discussion, see, e.g., Fitzmyer, *Romans*, pp. 55-67.

69. Keck, *Paul and His Letters*, p. 17.

70. Helmut Koester, *Introduction to the New Testament.* II. *History and Literature of Early Christianity* (Berlin: W. de Gruyter, 2nd edn, 2000), p. 54.

71. Munro, *Authority in Paul and Peter*, p. 19.

is significantly strengthened, however, by yet a third consideration: the surviving manuscripts of these letters provide abundant evidence of actual textual alterations including numerous short additions to the text.

As is well known, the extant manuscripts contain countless variant readings[72] (indeed, except in the case of brief fragments, no two of the texts are identical in every detail!). Most of the variants represent simply inadvertent errors on the part of copyists: obvious misspellings, transpositions, omissions, repetitions, and the like. Others, however, appear to be intentional variations, intended to correct, clarify, or even amplify the text;[73] among these, are numerous glosses (marginal or interlinear comments that were later incorporated into the text).

In principle, one of the purposes of critical texts is the elimination of such glosses, and many of them have in fact been omitted in the recent texts.[74] Lloyd Gaston asserts, however, that 'many who argue in principle against the whole concept [of interpolations] nevertheless continue to use a Greek text which is full of short interpolations [or glosses]'. In his view, 'the new Textus Receptus',[75] as he and others now term it, 'fearing to lose even a single Pauline word, has surely erred on the side of inclusion', for 'the longer reading seems always to have been preferred'.[76] As an example, Gaston cites Gal. 3.19a, where virtually all translators and commentators follow the longer reading. Gaston, however, argues for serious consideration of the shorter

72. For a distinction between a 'reading' ('any textual difference or any varying text formulation in a MS found by comparison with the same passage in any other ms') and a 'variant' (a textual difference that is '"significant" or meaningful in the major tasks of New Testament textual criticism' such as 'determining MS relationships, locating MSS within New Testament textual history and transmission, and in establishing the original or earliest possible New Testament text'), see Eldon Jay Epp, 'Textual Criticism: New Testament', *ABD*, VI, pp. 412-35 (413-14).

73. For a discussion of the various types of alterations, see Metzger, *The Text of the New Testament*, pp. 186-206.

74. See, e.g., O'Neill, 'Glosses and Interpolations', p. 379: 'We all accept that Paul's letters have been glossed, for we all use an edition of the New Testament [i.e., "Nestle or one of its derivatives"] in which, in effect, a systematic attempt has been made to eliminate glosses' [i.e., either by suppressing or by moving to the foot of the page 'the numerous glosses...which appeared in the Textus Receptus'].

75. The 3rd edn of the United Bible Societies text/26th edn of the Nestle-Aland text.

76. Lloyd Gaston, Letter to William O. Walker Jr (September 6, 1985).

reading.[77] Although a judgment regarding the accuracy of the 'always' in Gaston's assertion would require a comprehensive examination of the text, a random check of a few passages in the Pauline letters suggests that the longer reading is at least often preferred. Indeed, in 1 Thessalonians alone, Helmut Koester notes five passages in which the 26th edition of Nestle-Aland added in brackets words that were omitted in the previous edition, and Koester concludes regarding all five cases: 'it can be said with great certainty that these words are not part of the original text'.[78] Moreover, in the case of the Gospels, Schmidt asserts that the 'new Textus Receptus' appears to be 'definitely inclined toward the longer Byzantine text' and that 'the most consistent canon applied…seems to be "when in doubt, insert" '.[79]

The relevance of such observations for the question of possible interpolations in the Pauline letters is obvious: a predisposition to follow the longer reading of disputed texts may blind the interpreter to the presence of numerous glosses and/or short interpolations, and this, in turn, may create a presumption against the presence of longer additions to the text. Conversely, acknowledgment of the glosses and/or short interpolations may open the exegete to the possibility of more substantial insertions.

In any case, it is clear that the surviving manuscripts of the Pauline

77. Lloyd Gaston, 'Angels and Gentiles in early Judaism and in Paul', *SR* 11 (1982), pp. 65-75 (74 n. 43); see also Howard Eshbaugh, 'Textual Variants and Theology: A Study of the Galatians Text of Papyrus 46', *JSNT* 3 (1979), pp. 60-72 (62-63). The longer reading is τί οὖν ὁ νόμος; τῶν παραβάσεων χάριν προσετέθη (usually translated as, 'Why then the law? It was added because of transgressions'); a shorter reading, however, is τί οὖν ὁ νόμος τῶν πράξεων; ('Why then the law of deeds?' or perhaps, 'What then is the law of deeds?'), with τῶν παραβάσεων χάριν προσετέθη ('It was added because of transgressions') missing. Gaston notes: (1) that the shorter reading is found in the earliest extant manuscript (P^{46}), (2) that the shorter reading is cited twice by Irenaeus, (3) that the longer reading contradicts the context (3.15, 22), (4) that the source of the longer reading is easily explained from Rom. 5.20, and (5) that the shorter reading is the *lectio difficilior* in that it speaks of a 'law of deeds'.

78. Helmut Koester, 'The Text of 1 Thessalonians', in Dennis E. Groh and Robert Jewett (eds.), *The Living Text: Essays in Honor of Ernest W. Saunders* (Lanham, MD: University Press of America, 1985), pp. 220-32 (227).

79. Daryl Schmidt, 'Response', in G.D. Kilpatrick, *A Textus Receptus Redivivus? Protocol of the Thirty-Second Colloquy, 12 March 1978* (ed. Edward C. Hobbs; CHSHMCP, 32; Berkeley: The Center for Hermeneutical Studies in Hellenistic and Modern Culture, 1978), pp. 24-26 (26).

letters contain numerous short additions to the text. This leads O'Neill to ask, 'If St Paul's letters as we have them almost certainly contain glosses, is it also likely that they contain interpolations?' Perhaps for rhetorical reasons, his own answer is only a *probable* 'Yes'.[80] In light of the other *a priori* considerations discussed above, however, my own response would be, 'Yes, the Pauline letters almost certainly contain not only brief glosses but also more substantial interpolations'.

4. *Conclusion*

The widespread presence of interpolations in other ancient literature—Classical, Hellenistic, Jewish and Christian—is virtually certain. The Pauline letters were assembled, preserved and transmitted by the early Church only as parts of an expanded, abbreviated and edited collection. The surviving manuscripts of these letters bear witness to numerous alterations, including short additions to the text. In my judgment, these considerations lead almost inescapably to the conclusion, simply on *a priori* grounds, that the Pauline letters, as we now have them, are likely to contain non-Pauline interpolations. Indeed, as Munro asserts, 'it strains credulity to assume that interpolation did not take place'.[81]

Assuming, now, that the Pauline letters are likely to contain non-Pauline interpolations, the problem facing the interpreter becomes that of identifying these interpolations. Before attempting such identification, however, three additional preliminary issues must be raised: (1) whether direct text-critical evidence is an essential prerequisite for the recognition of individual interpolations; (2) the burden-of-proof question as it relates to the identification of individual interpolations; and (3) what types of data would count as evidence for interpolation in specific instances.

80. O'Neill, 'Glosses and Interpolations', p. 379.
81. Munro, 'Interpolation in the Epistles', p. 431.

Chapter 2

THE ABSENCE OF DIRECT TEXT-CRITICAL EVIDENCE FOR INTERPOLATION

1. *Introduction*

In the previous chapter, I concluded that it would be reasonable, simply on *a priori* grounds, to anticipate the likely presence of non-Pauline interpolations in the Pauline letters. Before any such interpolations can confidently be identified, however, a potentially serious objection must be confronted: *the surviving manuscripts of the Pauline letters provide very little direct text-critical evidence of interpolation.* Indeed, such evidence can be cited for only two passages.

The first of these passages is Rom. 16.25-27. These verses are missing altogether from a few witnesses, and in the others they appear variously at the end of ch. 14, at the end of ch. 15, at the end of ch. 16, at the end of both chs. 14 and 15, and at the end of both chs. 14 and 16.[1] To be sure, such text-critical evidence, in and of itself, proves neither the non-Pauline origin of the passage[2] nor that it represents a secondary addition to Paul's Roman letter.[3] In conjunction with other types of evidence, however, these data have often been used to support the conclusion that Rom. 16.25-27 is a non-Pauline interpolation.[4]

1. For details, see, e.g., Fitzmyer, *Romans*, p. 48.

2. The passage might have been composed by Paul for some other occasion and secondarily added to the Roman letter.

3. Conceivably, the passage might have been an original part of the letter that was subsequently moved to other locations and occasionally even omitted altogether.

4. See, e.g., Fitzmyer, *Romans*, p. 753: 'It is probably not an authentic Pauline composition, but a doxology that was added to the letter at the time of the formation of the Pauline corpus of letters'. For a discussion of the evidence, see, e.g., Ernst Käsemann, *Commentary on Romans* (trans. Geoffrey W. Bromiley; Grand Rapids: Eerdmans, 1980), pp. 421-28.

The other passage for which direct text-critical evidence of possible interpolation exists is 1 Cor. 14.34-35. These verses appear in all of the extant manuscripts, but in texts of the 'Western' tradition they stand at the end of ch. 14 rather than after v. 33. Arguing on the basis of the text-critical criterion of 'transcriptional probability',[5] Gordon D. Fee concludes that this passage most likely originated as a marginal gloss that was subsequently incorporated into the text at two different places.[6] In Fee's view, this conclusion is confirmed by considerations of 'intrinsic probability'.[7]

Apart from these two passages, every proposed interpolation in the Pauline letters appears in all extant manuscripts of the letters, and indeed at the same location in all of the manuscripts. This raises the crucial question: Is it possible—or, perhaps more to the point, is it likely—that a passage might appear in all of the surviving manuscripts—indeed, appear at the same location in all of the manuscripts—and yet be a non-Pauline interpolation? In other words, does the absence of direct text-critical evidence inevitably deal a fatal blow to interpolation hypotheses? For some scholars, the answer appears to be a clear 'Yes'. Harry Y. Gamble, for example, maintains that 'when textual revisions have taken place they have left their marks in the [manuscript] evidence'.[8] Kurt and Barbara Aland go further, asserting that 'every reading ever occurring in the New Testament textual tradition is stubbornly preserved, even if the result is nonsense'; indeed, in their view, 'major disturbances in the transmission of the New Testament text can always be identified with confidence, even if they occurred during the second century or at its beginning'.[9] Finally,

5. That is, 'that form of the text is more likely the original which best explains the emergence of all the others'.

6. Fee, *The First Epistle to the Corinthians*, pp. 699-700. For the view that the marginal gloss came from Paul himself, see, e.g., E. Earle Ellis, 'The Silenced Wives of Corinth (I Cor. 14:34-5)', in Eldon Jay Epp and Gordon D. Fee (eds.), *New Testament Textual Criticism: Its Significance for Exegesis: Essays in Honour of Bruce M. Metzger* (Oxford: Clarendon Press; New York: Oxford University Press, 1980), pp. 213-20.

7. That is, 'what an author is most likely to have written'. For a summary of the evidence, see, e.g., Fee, *The First Epistle to the Corinthians*, pp. 701-708. For detailed argumentation that 1 Cor. 14.34-35 is a non-Pauline interpolation, see, e.g., Fitzer, *Das Weib schweige in der Gemeinde.*

8. Gamble, 'The Redaction', p. 418.

9. Kurt Aland and Barbara Aland, *The Text of the New Testament: An*

Frederik W. Wisse decries 'redactional theory that steps outside the bounds of textual evidence' as 'counter-productive and a hindrance to Pauline studies'.[10]

As a preliminary response to such views, I suggest that the absence of direct text-critical evidence for interpolation should be seen as precisely what it is: the *absence* of evidence. C.K. Barrett has reminded us that 'the evidence of the [extant manuscripts] can tell us nothing about the state of the Pauline...literature before its publication' (presumably late in the first century).[11] Barrett's reminder can be pushed a bit further, however: the evidence of the manuscripts provides no clear and certain information regarding the state of the Pauline literature prior to the date of the oldest surviving manuscript of the letters[12]—that is, near the end of the second century.[13] Despite the conscientious and skilled efforts of generations of textual critics, we can make only educated guesses regarding the text of the Pauline letters during the first century and more of their existence. As regards possible interpolations, we can be certain only that a particular passage appeared at its present location in the Pauline corpus near the end of the second century. Whether it was included earlier and, if so, how much earlier, simply cannot be decided on the basis of direct text-critical evidence. In the face of otherwise compelling evidence for

Introduction to the Critical Editions and to the Theory and Practice of Modern Textual Criticism (trans. Erroll F. Rhodes; Grand Rapids: Eerdmans; Leiden: E.J. Brill, 2nd edn, 1989), p. 295.

10. Wisse, 'Textual Limits', pp. 168-78 (178). See also, e.g., Ellis, 'The Silenced Wives of Corinth', p. 220; and E. Earle Ellis, 'Traditions in 1 Corinthians', *NTS* 32 (1986), pp. 481-502 (488 and 498 n. 58).

11. C.K. Barrett, *A Commentary on the First Epistle to the Corinthians* (HNTC; New York: Harper & Row, 1968), p. 14.

12. To be sure, citations in second-century Christian writers can sometimes shed light upon the early text of the letters, but this would be of little direct help in identifying possible interpolations.

13. Various dates have been suggested for the oldest extant manuscript, P^{46}, ranging from late-first century to the first half of the third century; for discussion, see., e.g., Philip W. Comfort and David P. Barrett (eds.), *The Complete Text of the Earliest New Testament Manuscripts* (Grand Rapids: Baker Book House, 1999), pp. 18 and 194-97. Although Comfort and Barrett (p. 196) suggest a date 'sometime after 125', most scholars have settled on a date around the end of the second century; see, e.g., Aland and Aland, *The Text of the New Testament*, p. 87, and Metzger, *The Text of the New Testament*, p. 37. Other extant manuscripts date from the fourth century and later.

interpolation, this absence of direct text-critical evidence should not be allowed to decide the issue.[14]

At the same time, however, it must be acknowledged that any interpolation now appearing in all of the extant manuscripts would necessarily have been inserted prior to the date of the oldest surviving manuscript—that is, before the end of the second century.[15] Thus, we must ask whether it is reasonable to assume that interpolations were in fact introduced into the Pauline letters prior to the end of the second century.

2. *Interpolations Prior to the End of the Second Century?*

In a remarkable study of what he terms 'the orthodox corruption of Scripture', Bart D. Ehrman notes that 'Christianity in the second and third centuries was in a remarkable state of flux'; more specifically, he points out that 'this was an age of competing interpretations of Christianity'.[16] Ehrman then demonstrates that 'the scribes of the second and third centuries in fact altered their texts of Scripture at significant points in order to make them more orthodox on the one hand and less susceptible to heretical construal on the other'—in short, 'to make them "say" what they were already thought to "mean"'. They did this 'either by importing their [own view] into a text that otherwise lacked it or by modifying a text that could be taken to support contrary views'. Indeed, it is Ehrman's view that 'the vast majority of all textual variants originated during...the second and third centuries'.[17]

Although Ehrman focuses his attention on the second and third centuries, what he says would appear to be particularly relevant to the early part of the second century and also to the latter years of the first

14. As will be discussed in Chapter 4, there may also be various types of *indirect* text-critical evidence for interpolation.

15. According to Gamble ('The Redaction', p. 418), 'if it has to be suspected on the basis of internal evidence that a given letter has been subjected to editorial revision, such revision must have occurred before that letter entered into the stream of textual transmission'. As will become evident in what follows, I myself would modify the last clause of Gamble's statement to read, 'before that letter entered into the [*surviving*] stream of textual transmission'.

16. Bart D. Ehrman, *The Orthodox Corruption of Scripture: The Effect of Early Christological Controversies on the Text of the New Testament* (Oxford: Oxford University Press, 1993), pp. 3, 24.

17. Ehrman, *The Orthodox Corruption of Scripture*, pp. 25, 26, 29.

century. In fact, Ehrman cites the view of 'a wide-range of eminent textual specialists who are otherwise not known for embracing compatible views' that 'the period of relative creativity was early, that of strict reproduction late'.[18] The Alands agree. Noting that the text of the New Testament writings 'was a "living text" in the Greek literary tradition, unlike the text of the Hebrew Old Testament, which was subject to strict controls because (in the oriental tradition) the consonantal text was holy)', they acknowledge that 'until the beginning of the fourth century the text of the New Testament developed freely'. Significantly, however, they go on to say that 'this was all the more true of the early period, when the text had not yet attained canonical status, *especially in the earliest period when Christians considered themselves filled with the Spirit*'.[19] Similarly, Kenneth W. Clark asserts that '*the earliest stage of transmission* was marked by an attitude of freedom in theological interpretation'.[20] This 'earliest period when the Christians considered themselves filled with the Spirit', which was also 'the earliest stage of transmission', must surely include the time between Paul (mid-first century) and the date of the oldest surviving manuscript of the Pauline letters (late-second century). Thus, if the Alands and Clark are correct, it can only be assumed that alterations of the text were even more numerous and significant before the end of the second century than we know them to have been later. This, in turn, clearly increases the likelihood that interpolations were introduced during this earliest period.

Koester apparently agrees. Speaking of the Gospels in terms that would be equally applicable to the Pauline letters, he makes explicit what is implied in the words of the Alands and Clark. Koester declares that 'the problems for the reconstruction of the textual history of the canonical Gospels in *the first century of transmission* are immense'. Asserting that 'textual critics of the New Testament writings have been surprisingly naïve in this respect', Koester goes on to note that 'textual critics of classical texts know that *the first century of their transmission* is the period in which the most serious corruptions occur'. Koester also

18. Ehrman, *The Orthodox Corruption of Scripture*, p. 44 n. 112, 28. Cf., however, Wisse, 'Textual Limits', p. 176: 'if we judge by the interpolations in New Testament writings for which there is textual evidence then it appears that the numbers increase rather than decrease after the second century'.

19. Aland and Aland, *The Text of the New Testament*, p. 68 (emphasis added).

20. Clark, 'The Theological Relevance', p. 7 (emphasis added).

observes that 'the Gospels [and the same could be said regarding the Pauline letters], from the very beginning, were not archival materials but used texts'; this, in his judgment, 'is the worst thing that could happen to any textual tradition' because 'a text, not protected by canonical status, but used in liturgy, apologetics, polemics, homiletics, and instruction of catechumens is most like to be copied frequently and is thus subject to frequent modifications and alterations'.[21] Thus, according to Koester, 'whatever evidence there is indicates that not only minor, but also substantial revisions of the original texts have occurred [during the first century of their transmission]'.[22] Indeed, Clark even asks whether 'there really was a stable text at the beginning'. Noting that 'the earliest witnesses to the NT text even from the first century already show such variety and freedom that we may well wonder if the text remained stable long enough to hold a priority', he concludes: 'it may be doubted that there is evidence of one original text to be recovered'.[23] Thus, 'editorial revision' of the Pauline texts (including interpolation) very likely began almost as soon as the letters appeared and continued, largely unchecked, until the letters acquired canonical or at least quasi-canonical status.

In short, it would appear that the period between the actual composition of Paul's letters (mid-first century) and the date of the earliest extant manuscript of the these letters (late-second century at best) was precisely the time during which the letters would have been most susceptible to alteration, including interpolation.[24] Indeed, the circumstances of the time provided ample motivation, opportunity and the means for the introduction of such interpolations. All of this, in my

21. Helmut Koester, 'The Text of the Synoptic Gospels in the Second Century', in Petersen (ed.), *Gospel Traditions in the Second Century*, pp. 19-37 (19-20) (emphasis added).

22. Koester, 'The Text of the Synoptic Gospels', p. 37.

23. Clark, 'The Theological Relevance', p. 16.

24. Even Wisse ('Textual Limits', p. 175) agrees that 'the strongest argument in favour of setting the early history of transmission of the text apart from the later periods is the fact that it took some time for the Pauline corpus to gain full canonical status'; thus, 'Christian scribes would have been very reluctant to tamper with the text of a canonical writing but would have felt free to introduce changes before a text was recognized as apostolic and authoritative'. For a discussion of this issue as it relates to the Gospels and more particularly to the Synoptic Problem, see William O. Walker, Jr, 'An Unexamined Presupposition in Studies of the Synoptic Problem', *RL* (1979), pp. 41-52.

judgment, makes it reasonable to assume that interpolations are likely to have been introduced into the Pauline letters prior to the date of the earliest surviving manuscript—some, no doubt, accidental and inadvertent; others, however, almost certainly intentional.

This conclusion, however, leads to further questions: If interpolations were in fact introduced into the Pauline letters prior to the end of the second century, why is there no direct text-critical evidence of such interpolations? What became of the manuscripts that presumably did not contain these interpolations? Why have they not survived?

3. *What Became of the Manuscripts?*

An initial response to these questions is to note that precisely the same questions could also be raised regarding other early manuscripts of the Pauline letters. First, not a single early manuscript of an individual Pauline letter has survived. Even if the individual letters first circulated only as parts of a collection, and this appears unlikely,[25] they must first have existed as separate documents. Nevertheless, no early manuscripts of individual letters have survived. Why not? What became of these manuscripts? Second, no manuscripts have survived of earlier collections of the Pauline letters. That such earlier collections once existed is virtually certain. It is clear, for example, that Clement of Rome, Ignatius, Polycarp and the author of 2 Peter were acquainted with more than one of the letters. Moreover, the early appearance of pseudo-Pauline letters suggests that Paul's writings were known outside the particular communities to which they were addressed. Indeed, Gamble believes that there is evidence for the early existence of two forms of a 10-letter collection (not including the Pastorals or Hebrews).[26] In whatever form these earlier collections may have existed, however, not a single manuscript of any such collection has survived.[27] Why not?

25. For a cogent argument to this effect, see Lucetta Mowry, 'The Early Circulation of Paul's Letters', *JBL* 63 (1944), pp. 73-86.

26. Gamble, 'The Canon of the New Testament', pp. 205-208; and Harry Y. Gamble, 'Canon: New Testament', *ABD*, I, pp. 852-61 (853-54).

27. To be sure, P^{46} now contains only nine letters (in the following order): Romans, Hebrews, 1 and 2 Corinthians, Ephesians, Galatians, Philippians, Colossians and 1 Thessalonians. Most scholars assume that 2 Thessalonians was originally included, but not the Pastorals. Thus, P^{46} apparently attests a ten-letter collection. It does not fit the presumed usual model of such a collection, however,

What became of these manuscripts? Finally, no manuscripts have survived of earlier forms of any of the Pauline letters. As has already been noted, 2 Corinthians is widely regarded as a 'composite' letter, compilation theories have also been proposed for certain others of the letters, and it is widely assumed that the letters were subject to various types of editorial activity prior to their ultimate publication as parts of the Pauline corpus. If manuscripts of earlier forms of these letters ever existed, however, they have not survived. Why not? What became of these manuscripts?

If early manuscripts of individual letters have not survived, if manuscripts of earlier collections of letters have not survived, and if manuscripts not reflecting other types of editorial revision have not survived, why should it be assumed that manuscripts not containing presumed interpolations would have survived?

It is impossible, of course, to know the fate either of the autographs or of any copies of the Pauline letters that were made prior to the latter part of the second century. The manuscripts may simply have deteriorated and disintegrated from constant use (or from neglect), or they may have perished during the Roman persecutions of the period.[28] There is, however, another quite plausible scenario. *All that survived was manuscripts of the final edited collection of the Pauline corpus—manuscripts that are all remarkably similar to each other*. All other versions of the letters disappeared. This inevitably raises the question: Was the disappearance of earlier versions of the letters related in any way to the publication of the final edited collection? Of course, the collection may simply have rendered earlier versions superfluous, with the result that they gradually disappeared. It is surely possible, however, that once the final edited collection appeared, earlier versions of the letters were deliberately suppressed by Christians themselves.

because it omits Philemon and includes Hebrews. Thus, it appears to be something of an anomaly so far as the history of the Pauline corpus is concerned.

28. See, e.g., Metzger, *The Text of the New Testament*, p. 201 n. 1: 'Their early loss is not surprising, for during persecutions the toll taken by imperial edicts aiming to destroy all copies of the sacred books of Christians must have been heavy. Furthermore, simply the ordinary wear and tear of the fragile papyrus, on which at least the shorter Epistles of the New Testament had been written...would account for their early dissolution. It is not difficult to imagine what would happen in the course of time to one much-handled manuscript, passing from reader to reader, perhaps from church to church (see Col. iv.16), and suffering damage from the fingers of eager if devout readers as well as from climatic changes'.

We know that Paul and his letters were the subject of considerable controversy, particularly during the second century.[29] At one extreme were groups of Jewish Christians who rejected Paul because of his views regarding justification and the Jewish Law and, indeed, regarded him as a false apostle. At the opposite extreme, Marcion was convinced that all of the Apostles except Paul had misunderstood Jesus and that Paul was the only true Apostle. Eventually, the precursors of 'Catholic' Christianity accepted both the apostleship and the letters of Paul but only after, in various ways, the more radical features of his thought had been 'domesticated' or 'tamed'.[30]

It is also clear that at least two significantly different versions of the Pauline corpus circulated in the second century: the one accepted by Marcion (no longer extant) and that recognized by his opponents (the only surviving version).[31] Marcion accused his opponents of adding materials to the letters; they accused him of excising these materials. As a matter of historiographical principle, we cannot simply reject the word of Marcion about this and accept the word of his opponents. Indeed, P.-L. Couchoud argued many years ago that it was Marcion who preserved the original text of the Pauline letters and that the now-extant manuscripts include numerous interpolations.[32] Without necessarily going this far, it would appear reasonable to acknowledge that Marcion's opponents may well have made additions to the text of the Pauline letters.[33] All we can know with certainty is that the surviving

29. See, e.g., Wayne A. Meeks (ed.), *The Writings of St. Paul: Annotated Text, Criticism* (NCE; New York: W.W. Norton, 1972), pp. 149-213, and, for a short summary, pp. 149-50.

30. See, e.g., Maurice F. Wiles, *The Divine Apostle: The Interpretation of St. Paul's Epistles in the Early Church* (Cambridge: Cambridge University Press, 1967).

31. According to Harry Y. Gamble (*Books and Readers in the Early Church: A History of Early Christian Texts* [New Haven: Yale University Press, 1995], pp. 59-60), 'There is also evidence, though less direct, of yet a third early edition of the Letters of Paul' consisting of 'letters to seven churches': that is, Corinth (1 and 2 Corinthians treated as a single unit), Rome, Ephesus, Thessalonica (1 and 2 Thessalonians treated as a single unit), Galatia, Philippi, and Colossae (Colossians and Philemon treated as a single unit).

32. Couchoud, 'Reconstitution et classement' and 'La première édition'.

33. See, e.g., Hermann Detering, 'The Dutch Radical Approach to the Pauline Epistles', *JHC* 3 (1996), pp. 163-93 (177): 'There is no excuse in an unprejudiced investigation for excluding from the outset the possibility of the Marcionite edition

text of the Pauline letters is the text promoted—and perhaps produced—by the historical winners in the theological and ecclesiastical struggles of the second and third centuries. Marcion's version simply disappeared, and other versions, if they existed, met the same fate—examples, no doubt, of the well-documented practice of suppression and even destruction of texts that were regarded by some Christians as deficient, deviant, or dangerous.[34] That such suppression and destruction of texts could occur, even as late as the fifth century, is well illustrated by the fate of Tatian's Diatessaron: as Frank W. Beare notes, 'The Syrian episcopate...made a determined and successful effort to end the use of the *Diatessaron*', which 'was so thoroughly suppressed that no copy of it has ever been discovered, apart from a single leaf of vellum containing a fragment of the Greek text of it'.[35]

W.H.C. Frend points out that before the end of the second century, a common 'Rule of Faith' was accepted by 'the great Church', the basic tradition of the Church was the same wherever Christians lived, and the Canon of Scripture 'had still to undergo [only] some minor modifications'. In short, 'The Church in 180 was probably more united than it ever has been before or since'.[36] If this is true, then it is certainly possible that the emerging 'orthodox' leadership of the churches might have 'standardized' the text of the Pauline corpus in the light of its own views and practices,[37] suppressing and even destroying all deviant texts

of the *Paulina* being older and more original than the canonical, even if only for methodological reasons... It would seem that the general opinion still is that only Marcion could have had a *Tendenz*. It seems to remain inconceivable that the Catholic Church, too, which, like the Marcionite Church, constituted itself in the second century, might have had a strong interest in finding its theological interests already represented in the documents of the apostolic time. But the possibility that the Catholic Church of the second century introduced its theological tendency into the Pauline Epistles cannot be a priori precluded.'

34. See, e.g., Morton Smith, *Jesus the Magician* (New York: Harper & Row, 1978), pp. 1-2; Elaine Pagels, *The Gnostic Gospels* (New York: Random House, 1979), pp. xvii-xix; and Arthur Vööbus, 'Syriac Versions', *IDBSup*, pp. 848-54 (851).

35. F.W. Beare, 'Canon of the New Testament', *IDB*, I, pp. 520-32 (532).

36. W.H.C. Frend, *Martyrdom and Persecution in the Early Church: A Study of a Conflict from the Maccabees to Donatus* (Garden City, NY: Doubleday, 1967), p. 223.

37. See, e.g., Bauer, *Orthodoxy and Heresy*, pp. 147-94 (160-67).

and manuscripts. Thus, what Wisse characterizes as 'a remarkably unified text without a hint of major editing'[38] may well point not to a uniform transmission of the text from the very beginning but rather to such a deliberate standardizing of the text at some point(s) in its transmission.[39] This would explain why it is that we have no manuscripts dating from earlier than the latter part of the second century and why all of the surviving manuscripts are so remarkably similar.

What the earlier text of Paul's letters may have been remains, probably forever, shrouded in the mists of obscurity. Suppression and destruction of earlier manuscripts would suggest, however, that these manuscripts may have differed in significant ways from the standardized text that survived (surely, this was the case with Marcion's version!); otherwise, it is difficult to understand why they would have disappeared so completely. We know that the surviving version of the Pauline letters includes passages not found in the Marcionite version; it may also include passages not found in other earlier versions either of the collected letters or of individual letters. Thus, the surviving version may well contain interpolations for which no direct text-critical evidence exists—interpolations that would have been introduced prior to the end of the second century and would now appear in all extant manuscripts of the Pauline letters. In short, it may be that we have no manuscripts lacking presumed interpolations simply because such manuscripts were destroyed by the early church.

To be sure, Wisse has suggested that what has just been proposed constitutes a 'conspiracy theory' regarding the disappearance of manuscripts.[40] If such a theory appears unlikely, another, perhaps less-controversial, scenario is also possible. Robert M. Price suggests that 'scribes comparing longer with shorter versions of the same epistle [that is, versions with and without interpolations] would harmonize the

38. Wisse, 'Textual Limits', p. 174.

39. See, e.g., O'Neill, *Paul's Letter to the Romans*, p. 14: 'Admittedly it is hard to see how various additions made to different manuscripts at different times should have produced such a uniformly attested text. How do a paragraph added in one manuscript and an explanatory note added in another come together in the one recognized text? The answer must be that at various stages in the transmission of the text powerful editors collected together as many manuscripts as possible and made a standard edition which became the one uniformly copied thereafter in that part of the church.'

40. Wisse, 'Textual Limits', p. 177.

two, always following the longer reading'; in other words, 'scribes would on the whole prefer to transcribe the longer text, being unwilling to lose anything precious'. Thus, interpolations (if they existed) would be copied into new manuscripts. Once the longer texts appeared, they almost certainly would be preferred[41] and thus preserved by the early Church. Shorter manuscripts, not containing the added material, would be regarded as incomplete or defective and therefore either destroyed or allowed to fall into disuse and thus disrepair and eventual disintegration.[42] Thus, it would by no means be surprising that interpolations might appear in all of the surviving manuscripts of the Pauline letters. The fact that the surviving manuscripts betray so little evidence of interpolation, or indeed of any type of editing, suggests merely that such editing had virtually come to an end by the close of the second century—that is, once the text of the letters had been standardized.[43]

4. *Conclusion*

I have suggested that the absence of direct text-critical evidence for interpolation must be seen as precisely what it is: the *absence* of evidence, which, in the face of otherwise compelling evidence for interpolation, should not be allowed to decide the issue. Further, I have argued that the Pauline letters would have been most susceptible to textual alteration, including interpolation, precisely during the period

41. Assuming, to be sure, that the longer readings were not judged to be heretical or otherwise unacceptable.

42. Price, 'The Evolution of the Pauline Canon', p. 128; cf., e.g., Mowry, 'The Early Circulation', p. 86 n. 28: the 'textual additions' in various early copies of Paul's letters 'survived', but 'their omissions tended to disappear'.

43. Ingo Broer ('"Der Ganze Zorn Ist Schon Über Sie Gekomen': Bemerkungen zur Interpolationshypothese und zur Interpretation von 1 Thess 2,14-16', in Raymond F. Collins [ed.], *The Thessalonian Correspondence* [BETL, 87; Leuven: Leuven University Press/Peeters, 1990], pp. 142-45) appeals to evidence from *1 Clement*, Ignatius and Polycarp in an attempt to demonstrate that knowledge of a collection of Pauline letters in the late-first and early-second centuries was sufficiently widespread to rule out the notion of numerous interpolations. There is no way to know, however, whether the version(s) of the Pauline letters known by these authors may have differed from the version that survived or, if so, how significant these differences may have been. Thus, evidence that they knew one or more of the Pauline letters by no means proves that these letters were not subject to interpolation either before or after they wrote.

prior to the date of the oldest surviving manuscript. Finally, I have proposed plausible answers to the question of why no manuscripts not containing presumed interpolations have survived. In light of such considerations, it would appear that the presence of a passage in all of the surviving manuscripts should carry little if any weight in determining whether this passage is a non-Pauline interpolation. In short, the absence of direct text-critical evidence for interpolation by no means invalidates the conclusion of Chapter 1 that it is reasonable, simply on *a priori* grounds, to assume the likely presence of non-Pauline interpolations in the Pauline letters.

Chapter 3

The Burden of Proof in the Identification of Interpolations

Crucial to any discussion of possible interpolations in the Pauline letters is the twofold question regarding the burden of proof: Does the burden of proof rest with the argument for or with the argument against interpolation, and just how onerous is this burden? In the most general sense, the burden-of-proof question relates simply to the issue of whether the Pauline letters do or do not contain non-Pauline interpolations (yet to be identified). I have argued in Chapters 1 and 2 that, despite the almost total absence of direct text-critical evidence to this effect, the probable presence of non-Pauline interpolations in the Pauline letters is to be assumed simply on *a priori* grounds. If my argument was successful, it would appear that the burden of proof now rests with any argument that the Pauline letters do *not* contain non-Pauline interpolations. Moreover, the weight of this burden would appear to be rather heavy. Unless compelling evidence to the contrary can be adduced, it is to be assumed that the Pauline letters, as we now have them, are likely to contain non-Pauline interpolations.

As regards individual passages, however, the matter is somewhat more complicated. Here, most scholars would agree that the burden of proof rests with the argument for interpolation. In the absence of cogent arguments to the contrary, it is to be assumed that any passage in a letter judged otherwise authentically Pauline was itself either composed by Paul, included by Paul in the letter, or both. Recently, however, Darrell J. Doughty has challenged this view. Assuming 'that the Pauline writings are redactional compositions' that 'may or may not contain authentic Pauline material', Doughty maintains that the burden of proof rests with the argument *for* authenticity, whether of an entire letter or of any portion thereof.[1] Although I have a certain degree of

1. Doughty, 'Pauline Paradigms and Pauline Authenticity', pp. 95-128 (126).

sympathy for Doughty's position, it is my own judgment that the safer principle is the *via media* enunciated by E.P. Sanders and others: 'the burden of proof falls...on the one who argues a case'—whatever this case may be.[2] Thus, if one argues *for* interpolation, the burden of proof rests with the argument for interpolation; equally, however, if one argues *against* interpolation, the burden of proof rests with the argument against interpolation.[3] In later chapters, I will attempt to demonstrate that certain passages in the Pauline letters are in fact non-Pauline interpolations. Thus, I will accept the burden of proof in the argument. It will be my responsibility, in other words, to make the case that these passages are to be viewed as interpolations.

This, however, is not the end of the matter. One must also ask just how onerous this burden of proof really is. If discussions of possible interpolations focus simply upon individual passages, as has typically been the case, the burden would appear quite heavy indeed. Thus, Winsome Munro complains that 'scholars advancing theories of interpolation' are confronted with 'an insurmountable obstacle which no amount of evidence or argument is allowed to overcome', for theirs is the task 'of proving beyond any doubt that a passage does not owe its presence to the author of the whole'.[4] In each case, they must convincingly demonstrate both that the passage does not 'fit' in its present context and that certain of its features are 'non-Pauline'. Beyond this, many would insist that a plausible 'occasion' (e.g. motivation and opportunity) for the presumed interpolation must be established.[5] Further, as has already been noted, some would require direct

2. E.P. Sanders, *Jesus and Judaism* (Philadelphia: Fortress Press, 1985), p. 13; see also, e.g., Willi Marxsen, *The Beginnings of Christology: A Study of Its Problems* (trans. Paul J. Achtemeier; FFBS, 22; Philadelphia: Fortress Press, 1969), p. 8; M.D. Hooker, 'Christology and Methodology', *NTS* 17 (1971), p. 485; and Ben F. Meyer, *The Aims of Jesus* (London: SCM Press, 1979), p. 83 and p. 277 n. 8.

3. See, e.g., Winsome Munro, 'Criteria for Determining the Authenticity of Pauline Letters: A Modest Proposal' (unpublished paper prepared for Meeting of the Paul Seminar of the Westar Institute, Santa Rose, CA, 1994), p. 4: 'I strongly urge that the Paul Seminar of the Westar Institute decide to level the playing field by insisting that there be as much onus on the assertion of Pauline authorship as its denial'.

4. Munro, 'A Paradigmatic Shift?', p. 7.

5. Regarding partition theories, Lovering ('The Collection', p. 36) insists that 'a scholar must be able to suggest a historically probable occasion and motive for a redactor to have put together the several letters which that scholar thinks originally

text-critical evidence—that is, that the passage be missing from one or more of the surviving manuscripts or versions of the text, or at least that it be variously located in these texts.[6] Finally, in a more general sense, a persuasive case must be made (or at least assumed) that it is not unreasonable, simply on *a priori* grounds, to expect interpolations in the Pauline letters.[7] It is within this context that Munro appeals for 'scholarly openness, both to the concept of later expansion of the text, and to the probability that particular passages or sets of passages are later additions or rewritten versions, even if the evidence falls short of "proof" in an absolute sense'.[8]

It is in the spirit of such 'scholarly openness' that I have addressed the general question of the *a priori* probability of interpolations in the Pauline letters, concluding that the burden of proof now rests with any argument against such interpolations. It is in the same spirit that I now address the burden-of-proof question as it relates to individual passages. As already noted, I acknowledge that the burden of proof here rests with the argument for interpolation. I now submit, however, that this burden is significantly lighter than has generally been assumed.

If, as I have argued, it is reasonable to assume the probable presence of non-Pauline interpolations in the Pauline letters, the relevant question regarding individual passages is no longer simply, 'Is this passage an interpolation?' Rather, it becomes, 'Is this passage one of the interpolations that are likely to be found in the Pauline letters?' To be sure, the difference is a subtle one, but it is important—not least in terms of its psychological impact upon the exegete. As Frederik W. Wisse notes, 'certainty about the reality of redactional changes [including interpolations] in the Pauline letters...will inevitably influence the researcher's attitude towards the text'.[9] In the absence of *a priori* reasons to expect interpolations, it should not be surprising that most exegetes are

existed into the form in which we now know them'. By implication, Lovering insists upon the same regarding interpolation hypotheses.

6. This is the major thrust of Wisse, 'Textual Limits'.

7. See, e.g., Frederik W. Wisse, 'The Nature and Purpose of Redactional Changes in Early Christian Texts: The Canonical Gospels', in Petersen (ed.), *Gospel Traditions in the Second Century*, pp. 39-53 (41): 'Before we can argue for a specific interpolation we must first establish the probability that early Christian texts were extensively redacted'.

8. Munro, 'Interpolation in the Epistles', p. 432.

9. Wisse, 'Textual Limits', p. 173.

dubious regarding arguments that particular passages are in fact interpolations. Given the assumption of the probable presence of interpolations, however, one would expect a greater degree of openness to interpolation hypotheses regarding particular passages.

While acknowledging what I have termed 'its psychological impact upon the exegete', however, Wisse insists that 'certainty about the reality of redactional changes in the Pauline letters has no obvious bearing on the burden of proof in individual cases'.[10] If Wisse is thinking strictly of *statistical* probability, I must, of course, agree. There are, however, other forms of probability (or perhaps 'plausibility' is here the preferable word), and it is some of these other forms that I now wish to explore.

Quite apart from any *a priori* probability of interpolations, of course, there always exists at least the theoretical possibility that a particular passage in the Pauline letters might be an interpolation. Once the *a priori* probability of interpolations is granted, however, the authenticity of every passage in the Pauline letters is thereby called into question: if there are indeed likely to be interpolations in the letters, then this or that particular passage may indeed be such an interpolation.

In short, it can no longer simply be assumed that *any* passage was an original part of the letter in which it now appears, or indeed that it is authentically Pauline. It may be, or it may not be. The problem becomes that of determining which of the materials are original and Pauline and which are not. Everything is 'up for grabs'. Thus, Doughty appears to be correct when he observes, 'Once one grants the probability of secondary interpolations, the roller coaster is already plunging down the first drop, and the ride will be furious'.[11] Indeed, it is because of considerations such as these that Doughty assigns the burden of proof to the argument *for* authenticity.[12] Without going so far as Doughty, I believe that the mere probability of interpolations in the letters significantly lightens the burden of proof for arguments that particular passages are in fact interpolations—not statistically, to be sure, but in terms of logical plausibility.

The burden of proof becomes lighter still once one or more passages are confidently identified as actual interpolations. If a letter contains one non-Pauline interpolation, it may well contains others. Thus, for

10. Wisse, 'Textual Limits', p. 173.
11. Doughty, 'Pauline Paradigms and Pauline Authenticity', p. 102.
12. Doughty, 'Pauline Paradigms and Pauline Authenticity'.

example, if Rom. 16.25-27 is in fact a non-Pauline interpolation, as most scholars apparently have concluded, then it is by no means inappropriate to look for other interpolations in the Roman letter. Similarly, if 1 Cor. 14.34-35 is an interpolation, as many believe, then 1 Corinthians may well contain additional interpolations. Further, if one letter contains non-Pauline interpolations, other letters may contain them as well—particularly in light of the fact that the letters have been preserved not as separate documents but only as parts of an edited collection.

Indeed, if a series of interpolations could confidently be identified either in the Pauline corpus as a whole or in specific letters, it might even be possible to strengthen the argument for additional interpolations by appealing to the widely-recognized but somewhat controversial legal principle of 'pattern of behavior'. This principle holds that 'evidence of the habit of a person or of the routine practice of an organization, whether corroborated or not and regardless of the presence of eyewitnesses, is relevant to prove that the conduct of the person or organization on a particular occasion was in conformity with the habit or routine practice'.[13] In other words, evidence of a particular *pattern* of behavior on the part of an individual or a group is relevant in determining whether the individual or group is likely to have committed a *specific* act of the type exhibited in the pattern. Thus, evidence that early Christians exhibit a pattern of introducing interpolations into the Pauline letters would be relevant in ascertaining both whether they are likely also to have introduced additional interpolations (yet to be identified) and whether they are likely, in fact, thus to have inserted a particular passage suspected on other grounds of being an interpolation.

To be sure, any argument based upon such 'pattern-of-behavior' evidence would necessarily appeal to logical plausibility, not statistical probability, and could serve only a corroborative function in support of other types of evidence for interpolation. Nevertheless, the force of such an argument should not be minimized. Indeed, one might even reason as follows (again, in terms not of statistical probability but

13. *Federal Rules of Evidence: 1998–99 Edition including Amendments Effective December 1, 1998* (St Paul, MN: West Group, 1998), p. 35. See also p. 36: 'Agreement is general that habit evidence is highly persuasive as proof of conduct on a particular occasion'; 'surely any sensible man in investigating whether X did a particular act would be greatly helped in his inquiry by evidence as to whether he was in the habit of doing it'.

rather of logical plausibility): the more interpolations there are, the more interpolations there are likely to be; and the more interpolations there are likely to be, the more likely it is that this or that particular passage is in fact an interpolation.

In conclusion, it is my judgment that while the burden of proof still rests with any claim that a particular passage in the Pauline letters is a non-Pauline interpolation, the weight of this burden is considerably lighter than has generally been assumed. In the first instance, it is significantly reduced by the mere *a priori* probability of interpolations in the Pauline letters. It is then further reduced by the confident identification of one or more actual interpolations in the letters. Finally, the confident identification of a series of actual interpolations would, in my view, constitute appropriate grounds for the *prima facie* presumption both that additional interpolations are likely to be found and that particular passages suspected on other grounds of being interpolations may well in fact be interpolations.

Chapter 4

EVIDENCE FOR INTERPOLATION

Some years ago, Victor Paul Furnish lamented the fact 'that so far no firm and convincing techniques or criteria [had] been developed to aid in the identification of glosses and interpolations' in the Pauline letters. As evidence, he cited what he viewed as 'the wholesale resort to hypotheses', the 'highly subjective judgments about content and tone', and the 'often-questionable generalizations about the apostle's style and vocabulary' that characterized the work of J.C. O'Neill. Indeed, in Furnish's judgment, what O'Neill had produced was 'a Paul created in the interpreter's [that is, O'Neill's] own image'.[1]

Furnish is surely correct that, insofar as is possible, attempts to identify interpolations in the Pauline letters should avoid both 'subjective judgments about content and tone' and 'questionable generalizations about the apostle's style and vocabulary'. Further, they should by no means produce 'a Paul created in the interpreter's own image'. It should be noted, however, that 'subjective judgments' and 'generalizations' are to some extent inevitable when one attempts to distinguish between possible earlier and later materials in the same document. Thus, with regard to the work of Thucydides, Karl Maurer observes:

> It is obvious that in the matter of interpolation as in everything else an editor must trust in part to his [*sic*] mere intuition; for the [manuscripts] themselves, made not by machines but persons, embody centuries of concrete historical reality; and for reasons invisible to us, any particular case may defy a general pattern.[2]

Thus, in the case of particular passages in the Pauline letters, subjective judgments (including what Maurer terms 'mere intuition') will inevitably result in differing conclusions regarding the actual presence or absence of interpolation.

1. Furnish, 'Pauline Studies', p. 325.
2. Maurer, *Interpolations in Thucydides*, p. 187.

Maurer also asserts, however, that 'there are patterns' that can aid in the recognition of interpolations,[3] thereby suggesting that it is possible, at least in principle, to identify these patterns. More explicitly, Winsome Munro insists that it is 'possible to apply criteria to direct attention to the kind of elements in the text that can point to interpolation'. Indeed, in her view, agreement regarding criteria for the identification of interpolations 'is essential, not only to establish what is not original to a given writer, but also to confirm that the rest can be assumed to be "genuine"'. Otherwise, 'every part of every epistle should be suspect, for there is no way to determine which passages may properly be called into question, or judged to be secondary additions'.[4]

Characteristically, criteria for identifying interpolations have been invoked, if at all, on a more-or-less *ad hoc* basis. In the 1940s, Robert Martyr Hawkins offered some helpful suggestions regarding criteria, but his comments were far too sketchy and programmatic to be persuasive to most readers.[5] In his treatment of Galatians and Romans, O'Neill mentions and makes use of a variety of criteria, but he provides no comprehensive and systematic discussion of these criteria.[6] In a separate article, however, appealing to the practice of scholars of the Hebrew Bible, O'Neill lists 'contradictions' and 'changes in style' as the relevant criteria for the identification of interpolations.[7] In addition, Eugene Harrison Lovering, Jr, discusses a number of criteria employed by advocates of 'partition' theories, and most of these apply rather well, *mutatis mutandis*, to the identification of interpolations.[8]

To my knowledge, however, Munro is the first to attempt a systematic and more-or-less comprehensive treatment of the question of criteria for the identification of interpolations.[9] She identifies nine types of criteria for such identification. The first five, which she labels 'initial

3. Maurer, *Interpolations in Thucydides*, p. 187.

4. Munro, 'Interpolation in the Epistles', p. 433.

5. Hawkins, *The Recovery of the Historical Paul*; see also his 'Romans: A Reinterpretation'.

6. O'Neill, *The Recovery of Paul's Letter to the Galatians*; and *Paul's Letter to the Romans*.

7. O'Neill, 'Glosses and Interpolations', p. 380.

8. Lovering, 'The Collection', pp. 66-81.

9. Munro, *Authority in Paul and Peter*, pp. 21-25; 'Interpolation in the Epistles', pp. 431-443; and 'Criteria for Determining the Authenticity', pp. 78-80 and esp. 79-80.

indicators', are direct textual, ideological, stylistic/linguistic, and contextual criteria, plus the criterion of literary dependence. The last four, which she calls 'confirming factors', are literary/historical coherence, omission in external attestation, contextual plausibility and historical plausibility; these four, however, 'generally only carry weight if there are other good reasons [that is, initial indicators] to think a passage may be interpolated'.[10]

For the most part, I am in agreement with Munro regarding how interpolations are to be identified. I prefer, however, to speak of 'types of evidence for interpolation' rather than 'criteria for the identification of interpolations'. In part, this is because 'criteria' might imply a greater degree of certainty than is actually warranted (that is, *if* a passage satisfies certain specified criteria, then it *is* a non-Pauline interpolation). Perhaps more importantly, 'criteria' tends to focus one's attention on the more theoretical aspects of the debate regarding interpolation, not on the actual *evidence* that must be examined in determining whether a particular passage is in fact an interpolation. Beyond this, I have chosen not to include 'literary dependence', both because I regard such dependence as virtually impossible to establish[11] and because any putative evidence of literary dependence might also serve as evidence of common authorship.[12] In addition, I will not treat 'omission in external attestation' as a separate category but rather subsume it under the rubric of text-critical evidence. Finally, I will organize what Munro terms 'literary/historical coherence', 'contextual plausibility' and 'historical plausibility' somewhat differently under the categories of 'comparative', 'situational', 'motivational' and 'locational evidence'. Thus, I propose to discuss eight types of evidence that might indicate the presence of an interpolation. Following Munro's distinction, I categorize these as 'initial indicators' of possible interpolation (text-critical,

10. Munro, 'Interpolation in the Epistles', p. 440.

11. Note, for example, the difficulty in establishing the direction of literary dependence in studies of the Synoptic Problem. Using the same evidence, some scholars argue for Matthew's dependence upon Mark while others insist upon the exact opposite.

12. If literary dependence upon a document that is clearly post-Pauline could be established, this, of course, would indicate non-Pauline (post-Pauline) authorship of the passage in question. This, however, is difficult to establish, and there is always the risk of circular argumentation.

contextual, linguistic, ideational and comparative evidence) and 'confirming factors' (situational, motivational and locational evidence).

It is essential to keep in mind, as Munro points out, that no one type of evidence for interpolation 'can stand by itself'. Different kinds of 'analyses can correct and complement each other'. In the final analysis, 'the judgment as to whether any passage is interpolated depends on a variety of factors and depends on no one infallible criterion'; rather, it is a matter of taking into account the cumulative effect of converging lines of evidence'.[13] The strongest possible argument for interpolation, of course, would appeal to all eight types of evidence; in most cases, however, this is not possible.

In the discussion that follows, I will illustrate each of the various types of evidence for interpolation by reference to 1 Cor. 14.34-35. I have chosen this passage because, of all the proposed interpolations in the Pauline letters, it alone appears to exhibit one form or another of all eight types.[14] From time to time, however, I will also refer to other passages for illustrative purposes.

1. *Text-Critical Evidence for Interpolation*

Text-critical evidence for interpolation would be data in early witnesses to the text—manuscripts, versions, lectionaries and/or ecclesiastical writers—suggesting that a passage may at one time not have been a part of the Pauline letter in which it now appears. At least three possible types of such evidence are to be noted: (1) the absence of a passage from one or more of the ancient witnesses; (2) the appearance of a passage at different locations in various of the witnesses; and (3) the failure of an early Christian writer to cite a passage when demonstrable familiarity with the letter in which the passage now appears and congruence of subject matter would lead one to expect such a citation.[15]

13. Munro, *Authority in Paul and Peter*, pp. 21, 23, 24-25.

14. For a full discussion of the evidence that this passage is a non-Pauline interpolation, see Fitzer, *Das Weib schweige in der Gemeinde*; for a summary, see, e.g., Fee, *The First Epistle to the Corinthians*, pp. 699-708.

15. Yet another indication of possible interpolation might be the presence—immediately preceding, near the beginning, near the end, and/or immediately following what appears to be a more-or-less self-contained passage—of one or more apparently insignificant textual variants that could be interpreted as attempts to

a. *The Absence of a Passage from One or More of the Ancient Witnesses*
The first and most obvious type of text-critical evidence for interpolation would be the absence of a passage from one or more of the ancient manuscripts, versions and/or lectionaries. It is important to note, however, that the evidence of the various witnesses is by no means of equal value. Thus, as Bruce M. Metzger points out, 'witnesses are to be weighed rather than counted'. In other words, 'those witnesses that are found to be generally trustworthy in clear-cut cases deserve to be accorded predominant weight in cases when the textual problems are ambiguous and their resolution is uncertain'. To this end, attention must be paid to 'the date and character of the witnesses' (or, even more importantly, 'the date and character of the type of text that [a witness] embodies'), 'the geographical distribution of the witnesses', and 'the genealogical relationship of texts and families of witnesses'.[16] Thus, a passage that appears in most of the witnesses may nevertheless be judged a later addition to the text if, in terms of 'quality', the witnesses omitting the passage 'outweigh' those including it. Such is the case, for example, with Jn 7.53–8.11, which is found in the vast majority of the manuscripts and some of the early versions but is omitted by virtually all of the 'best' manuscripts.[17] Thus, on the basis of the text-critical evidence alone, it is now generally agreed that this passage represents a later addition to the text of the Fourth Gospel.

Of all the proposed interpolations in the Pauline letters, however, only the doxology of Rom. 16.25-27 is missing from any of the witnesses. To be sure, the doxology appears in all of the 'best' manuscripts,[18] but there is significant evidence for an early version of Romans without it. The verses apparently were not in the texts used by Marcion (second century), Priscillian (fourth century), or Jerome

improve an otherwise rough transition between the passage in question and its immediate context. Although this obviously involves text-critical matters, it will be treated below as a form of *contextual* evidence for interpolation.

16. Bruce M. Metzger, *A Textual Commentary on the Greek New Testament: A Companion Volume to the United Bible Societies' Greek New Testament (Third Edition)* (New York: United Bible Societies, 1971), pp. xxv-xxvi; see also his *The Text of the New Testament*, p. 209.

17. For a summary of the evidence, see, e.g., Barrett, *The Gospel According to St. John*, pp. 589-91.

18. As will be noted below, however, it is variously located in these manuscripts.

(fourth/fifth centuries), and Harry Gamble, Jr, has argued that 'this patristic testimony is buttressed by...the complete omission of the doxology' in the original Old Latin text.[19] If Gamble is correct, text-critical evidence for an early text without Rom. 16.25-27 is stronger than has generally been assumed. Moreover, it is appropriate at this point to invoke the text-critical principle of 'transcriptional probability'—what a scribe is most likely to have done. On the face of it, it appears more likely that a copyist would have added Rom. 16.25-27 to a text not containing it than that one would have deleted it from a text in which it originally appeared. In this particular case, however, special problems regarding the earliest form of the Roman letter significantly complicate the issue.[20] In any case, the absence of Rom. 16.25-27 from some of the witnesses—even though they do not include any of the 'best' manuscripts—lends some support to the view that this passage is a later addition to the text of Paul's Roman letter.[21]

Philip B. Payne has attempted to show that there is some evidence for an early text lacking 1 Cor. 14.34-35.[22] His argument is fourfold: (1) ancient witnesses to the text consistently separate vv. 34-35 from v. 33 by intervals or paragraph markings; (2) Codex Vaticanus (fourth century) has a 'bar-umlaut' siglum between vv. 33 and 34 similar to sigla that elsewhere in Vaticanus appear to indicate awareness of a textual variant; (3) the Latin Codex Fuldensis (sixth century) contains a marginal gloss, apparently intended to replace vv. 34-40, that lacks vv. 34-35; and (4) the minuscule Manuscript 88* (twelfth century), which has vv. 34-35 after v. 40 rather than after v. 33, appears to have been copied from a manuscript that did not contain vv. 34-35 at all.

19. Harry Y. Gamble, Jr, *The Textual History of the Letter to the Romans: A Study in Textual and Literary Criticism* (SD, 42; Grand Rapids: Eerdmans, 1977), pp. 25- 26; see the entire discussion on pp. 24-29.

20. For a discussion of 'the fourteen-chapter form', 'the fifteen-chapter form', and 'the sixteen-chapter form' of Romans, see, e.g., Gamble, *The Textual History*, pp. 15-35.

21. The conclusion that the passage is in fact an interpolation, however, depends more heavily upon the second type of text-critical evidence to be discussed, together with considerations of vocabulary, style and ideational content.

22. Philip B. Payne, 'Fuldensis, Sigla for Variants in Vaticanus, and 1 Cor. 14.34-5', *NTS* 41 (1995), pp. 240-62; *idem*, 'MS. 88 as Evidence for a Text without 1 Cor. 14.34-5', *NTS* 44 (1998), pp. 152-58; and, most recently, Philip B. Payne and Paul Canart, 'The Originality of Text-Critical Symbols in Codex Vaticanus', *NovT* 42 (2000), pp. 105-13.

Curt Niccum, however, has vigorously disputed Payne's conclusions regarding Codex Vaticanus and Codex Fuldensis, insisting that in the case of Vaticanus Payne has 'confused two separate markings' and that the marginal gloss in Fuldensis was intended as a replacement only for vv. 36-40.[23] My own judgment is that Payne's arguments, while interesting and suggestive, are not sufficient to establish the probability of an early text lacking 1 Cor. 14.34-35. Thus, I conclude, at least provisionally, that the first type of text-critical evidence for interpolation—the absence of a passage from one or more of the early witnesses—can be found in the Pauline letters only for Rom. 16.25-27. Moreover, the evidence for interpolation is not conclusive even here.

b. *The Appearance of a Passage at Different Locations in Various of the Witnesses*

A second possible type of text-critical evidence for interpolation would be the appearance of a passage at different locations in various of the ancient manuscripts, versions and/or lectionaries. Again, however, it is important to take into account the 'quality' of the witnesses in assessing the weight of such evidence. In the case of Rom. 16.25-27, the evidence for some type of displacement is impressive. This passage is missing completely from some witnesses. Beyond this, it is variously located after ch. 15 in the oldest surviving manuscript,[24] after ch. 16 in most of the 'best' witnesses,[25] after ch. 14 in a number of witnesses, after both ch. 14 and ch. 16 in a few witnesses including one manuscript from the fifth century (A), and after both ch. 14 and ch. 15 in one fourteenth-century manuscript. Such evidence indicates great uncertainty in the early Church regarding the appropriate location of the passage and at least suggests that it may be a later addition to the text of Paul's Roman letter. Moreover, the case for interpolation is strengthened by the fact, noted above, that the passage does not appear at all in some of the witnesses.

In the case of 1 Cor. 14.34-35 the evidence is more ambiguous. Although these verses appear after v. 33 in the vast majority of the surviving witnesses, they follow v. 40 in a few. According to Gordon

23. Curt Niccum, 'The Voice of the Manuscripts on the Silence of Women: The External Evidence for 1 Cor. 14.34-5', *NTS* 43 (1997), pp. 242-55.

24. P^{46} (late-second or early-third century).

25. Including א (fourth century), B (fourth century), C (fifth century), and D (sixth century).

D. Fee, however, these few instances constitute 'the entire Western Tradition'.[26] If Fee is correct, this supports the view that the early Church was uncertain regarding the proper location of these verses, and this, in turn, strengthens the possibility that the passage may constitute a later addition to the text. Niccum, however, disputes Fee's claim, insisting that, 'far from being the reading of the entire Western tradition, the transposition is the product of a local text'.[27] My own judgment is that the mere fact of the varied location of a passage raises some question regarding its original inclusion in the text; obviously, however, the testimony of 'the entire Western Tradition' would carry significantly more weight than that of 'a local text'.

At this point, Fee also appeals to the principle of 'transcriptional probability'. He proposes that the appearance of 1 Cor. 14.34-35 both after v. 33 and after v. 40 suggests three possible scenarios: (1) the words originally stood after v. 33 and were subsequently moved to a later position; (2) they originally stood after v. 40 and were subsequently moved to an earlier position; or (3) they were not an original part of the text, 'but were a very early marginal gloss that was subsequently placed in the text at two different places'. In Fee's judgment, the third option is clearly preferable because it 'best fits Bengel's first principle', which states: 'That form of the text is more likely the original which best explains the emergence of all the others'. Thus, Fee judges it likely that 1 Cor. 14.34-35 represents a later addition to the text of Paul's Corinthian letter.[28] Robert Hull, Jr, however, argues that Fee has misappropriated Bengel's first principle, which applies only to 'attested textual variation, not conjectural emendation'.[29] My own view is that, while Bengel's principle as stated applies only to 'attested textual variation', it may well be appropriate to expand it in such a manner as also to include 'conjectural emendation' if there are sound arguments for the proposed emendation. Surely, Fee's third scenario—the original absence of 1 Cor. 14.34-35—is one possible explanation for the varied location of the passage in the surviving manuscripts, and as such it should be given serious consideration. In short, the

26. Fee, *The First Epistle to the Corinthians*, p. 699 n. 1.

27. Niccum, 'The Voice of the Manuscripts', p. 252.

28. Fee, *The First Epistle to the Corinthians*, p. 699.

29. In a paper presented to the New Testament Textual Criticism Section of the 1990 Annual Meeting of the Society of Biblical Literature, New Orleans, LA, cited by Niccum ('The Voice of the Manuscripts', p. 243).

appearance of 1 Cor. 14.34-35 at different locations in various of the witnesses does indeed constitute evidence, inconclusive though it be, that the passage may be an interpolation.

c. *Inexplicable Failure of an Early Christian Writer to Cite a Passage*
A third type of text-critical evidence for interpolation—indirect, to be sure, and based upon an argument from silence—might be the failure of an early Christian writer to cite a passage when demonstrable familiarity with the letter in which the passage now appears and congruence of subject matter would lead one to expect such a citation. Here, the inference might be that the passage was not included in the text known by this writer. Thus, for example, Payne notes that 1 Cor. 14.34-35 is cited by none of the Apostolic Fathers and, indeed, by no early ecclesiastical writer prior to Tertullian (160–240 CE). Particularly significant, in Payne's view, is the fact that Clement of Alexandria (died c. 215 CE) cites 1 Cor. 14.6, 9, 10, 11, 13, 20, and 'discusses the behaviour of women in church' and yet, contrary to 1 Cor. 14.34-35, 'calls both men and women without distinction to silence in church'. This, according to Payne, 'may imply that 1 Cor. 14.34-35 was not in [Clement's] text of 1 Corinthians'.[30] In response, however, Niccum notes that 'Clement was also familiar with 1 Tim 2, yet Clement never cites vv. 11-12' (another passage mandating the silence of women). Thus, 'following Payne's line of reasoning, one could argue that Clement's New Testament text also lacked these verses!' Further, according to Niccum, Clement discusses not 'women's behaviour *in* church, but the Christian couple's proper demeanor while going *to* church and the impressions given to outsiders'. Thus, according to Niccum, Clement's failure to cite 1 Cor. 14.34-35 is irrelevant to the interpolation hypothesis. Indeed, it is his judgment that 'one cannot determine the text of a Church Father' in the manner proposed by Payne.[31]

It is not my purpose here to resolve the debate between Payne and Niccum regarding 1 Cor. 14.34-35. Rather, I have sought only to illustrate how this third type of text-critical evidence for interpolation might be used and to indicate some of the problems raised by such use.

30. Payne, 'Fuldensis', pp. 247-48; see also his 'MS. 88 as Evidence', pp. 155-56.

31. Niccum, 'The Voice of the Manuscripts', p. 244 n. 11.

Niccum has suggested that a failure to pay close attention to details may obscure significant differences in subject matter between a proposed interpolation in the Pauline letters and the statement of an early Christian writer. To this, I would add that any argument for interpolation based upon this third type of text-critical evidence is, by its very nature, an argument from silence with all of the weaknesses inherent to such arguments. There might be any number of reasons why an early Christian writer would not cite a passage that, in our judgment today, would clearly be relevant and even important for the subject matter at hand. Furthermore, it is often difficult to determine whether an early Christian writer is citing a specific passage in one of the Pauline letters or simply expressing common sentiments or drawing upon a shared body of tradition, belief, or practice. For example, *1 Clem.* 49.2-50.2 is a paean to love somewhat similar to that found in 1 Corinthians 13. Thus, it might be assumed that the author of *1 Clement* was familiar with 1 Corinthians 13. I will argue in Chapter 7, however, that this is not the case. Indeed, because the author of *1 Clement* clearly knew 1 Corinthians, I regard the differences between the two passages as evidence that 1 Corinthians 13 may well have been missing from this author's text of 1 Corinthians and thus may be a non-Pauline interpolation. Such arguments, however, are far from conclusive.

In short, this third type of text-critical evidence for interpolation must be used with great caution. Nevertheless, in conjunction with other types of evidence, it may serve a corroborative function and thereby strengthen the case for interpolation. Further, it might even provide an initial clue that would lead to a search for other, more cogent evidence.

d. *Conclusion regarding Text-Critical Evidence for Interpolation*

At most, text-critical evidence—of any of the three types noted—can suggest only that a passage may at one time not have been a part of the letter in which it now appears, at least not in its present location. Such evidence cannot show that the passage is non-Pauline in origin, for it may have been composed by Paul for some other purpose but secondarily inserted at its present location in one of the letters. Moreover, such evidence cannot show conclusively that the passage was inserted by someone other than Paul.[32] Thus, text-critical evidence alone forms an

32. In the case of 1 Cor. 14.34-35, for example, Ellis ('The Silenced Wives of

inadequate basis for concluding that a passage is a non-Pauline interpolation as defined for purposes of the present study. For this, support is needed from other types of evidence.

2. *Contextual Evidence for Interpolation*

Contextual evidence for interpolation would be data suggesting that a passage may not 'fit' in its present location in one of the Pauline letters and thus may represent a secondary addition to the text. There are within the Pauline corpus a number of passages that exhibit little or no apparent conceptual, stylistic and/or 'tonal'[33] relation to their immediate contexts. Indeed, they appear to 'interrupt' these contexts and, in some cases, even to contradict them conceptually. When such passages are removed, there often results a smooth conceptual, stylistic and/ or 'tonal' connection between what immediately precedes and what immediately follows;[34] indeed, as James H. Charlesworth notes, 'when the passage is removed, the flow of thought is often clarified or improved'.[35] In addition, the passages themselves can often stand alone as independent, self-contained units. Finally, such contextual 'interruptions' are sometimes accompanied by one or both of the following phenomena: (1) the repetition—near the end of the passage in question or in the verse immediately following—of a significant word or phrase from the verse immediately preceding the passage; and (2) the presence—immediately preceding, near the beginning, near the end and/or immediately following—of one or more apparently insignificant textual

Corinth', pp. 213-20) suggests that the passage was originally a marginal gloss inserted either by Paul himself or at his direction and later copied into the text; see also, e.g., Stephen C. Barton, 'Paul's Sense of Place: An Anthropological Approach to Community Formation in Corinth', *NTS* 32 (1986), pp. 225-46 (229-30).

33. 'Tonal' refers to the emotional or atmospheric quality of the discourse (e.g. 'a happy tone of voice', 'a sad tone of voice', or 'an angry tone of voice', 'the tone of the debate was hostile', 'the tone of the statement was threatening', or 'the tone of the question was friendly').

34. In some cases, of course, an interpolator or a later copyist, seeking to smooth out an otherwise rough transition between the passage in question and its immediate context, may have made slight modifications in the material immediately preceding and/or following the passage; in such cases, the removal of the passage in question might result in a less smooth transition from the material preceding to that immediately following the passage.

35. Charlesworth, 'Christian and Jewish Self-Definition', p. 30.

variants. Both phenomena could be interpreted as attempts to improve an otherwise rough transition between the passage in question and its immediate context.

a. *Conceptual, Stylistic and/or 'Tonal' Interruption of the Context*
Regarding 1 Cor. 14.34-35, Fee observes that 'one can make much better sense of the structure of Paul's argument without these intruding sentences', which have little, if anything, to do with the subject matter of the surrounding material. Indeed, 'these two verses simply lack any genuine correspondence with either the overall argument of chs. 12-14 or the immediate argument of vv. 26-40'. Chapter 12 is a general discussion of 'spiritual gifts', culminating in the exhortation to 'desire the higher gifts' (v. 31a).[36] Chapter 14 constitutes Paul's 'balanced guidelines for tongues with interpretation and prophecy with discernment'. The preliminary conclusion appears at v. 33: 'For God is not a God of confusion but of peace as in all the churches of the saints'. This is followed by a kind of 'rhetorical aside' (vv. 36-38): 'an *ad hominen* argument against those in the community who in the name of being *pneumatikos* ('spiritual') are leading [the Corinthian] church in another direction'. Finally, vv. 39-40 represent 'a concluding wrap-up of the whole matter'. Verses 34-35, however, represent a complete, self-contained unit of material that is in no way dependent upon its present context. Indeed, 'even if one were to conclude that vv. 34-35 are authentic, they would appear to be best understood as something of an afterthought to the present argument'.[37] In short, 1 Cor. 14.34-35 is a self-contained unit that interrupts the context in which it appears, and its removal leaves a complete and coherent discussion of spiritual gifts in chs. 12 and 14. Such evidence suggests that the passage may represent a secondary addition to the text.

In the case of 1 Cor. 14.34-35, the contextual evidence for interpolation is primarily conceptual in nature: the subject matter of the passage interrupts that of its context. In other cases, the evidence is also stylistic and/or 'tonal'. For example, as will be discussed in Chapters 7 and

36. I will argue in Chapter 7 that 1 Cor. 12.31b–14.1 is a non-Pauline interpolation. If it is not an interpolation, it must be seen as something of a digression in which Paul sets forth 'a still more excellent way' of dealing with the diversity of spiritual gifts within the Christian community (discussed in ch. 12) before indicating his own preference (ch. 14).

37. Fee, *The First Epistle to the Corinthians*, pp. 701-702.

8, 1 Cor. 12.31b–14.1a interrupts its context both conceptually and stylistically and Rom. 1.18–2.29 reflects a significant difference in 'tone' from the material immediately preceding.

b. *Repetition of Significant Word or Phrase*

An additional phenomenon suggesting that a self-contained passage that appears to 'interrupt' its context may be an interpolation is the repetition—near the end of the passage in question or in the verse immediately following—of a significant word or phrase from the verse immediately preceding the passage. This might represent an attempt, either by the interpolator or by a later scribe, to improve an otherwise rough transition between the passage and its immediate context. In 1 Cor. 12.31a, for example, Paul encourages his readers to 'be zealous for the greater gifts' (τὰ χαρίσματα τὰ μείζονα).[38] This is repeated in 14.1b-c with the substitution of 'the spiritual gifts' (τὰ πνευματικά) for 'the greater gifts' (τὰ χαρίσματα τὰ μείζονα) and the addition of 'and especially that you may prophesy' (μᾶλλον δὲ ἵνα προφητεύητε). With the elimination of 12.31b–14.1a as a non-Pauline interpolation, it would become necessary also to remove either 12.31a or 14.1b. Thus, either 12.31a or (more likely) 14.1b may have been added to provide a smoother transition between 12.31b–14.1a and its immediate context. This may constitute evidence that 12.31b–14.1a is in fact an interpolation.

c. *Apparently Insignificant Textual Variants*

Yet another phenomenon suggesting that a self-contained passage that appears to 'interrupt' its context may be an interpolation is the presence—immediately preceding, near the beginning, near the end and/or immediately following the passage—of one or more apparently insignificant textual variants. Like the repetition of a significant word or phrase, this might reflect an attempt to improve an otherwise rough transition between the passage in question and its immediate context. For example, as will be discussed in Chapter 5, textual variants in 1 Cor. 11.17 suggest that various editors and/or copyists may have attempted in different ways to improve what otherwise would have been a rather rough transition from v. 16—and, indeed, from the entire preceding passage, vv. 3-16. Somewhat differently, a textual variant in

38. Or κρεί(ττ)ονα.

1 Cor. 12.31a may represent a later assimilation to the wording of 13.13 following the addition of 12.31b–14.1a to the text. Again, this might be viewed as an attempt to link an interpolation more closely with its immediate context.

d. *Conclusion regarding Contextual Evidence for Interpolation*
As in the case of text-critical evidence, contextual evidence alone cannot show that a passage is non-Pauline in origin or that it was included at its present location by someone other than Paul. At most, such evidence can indicate only that the passage may represent a secondary addition to the text. Thus, neither text-critical nor contextual evidence—either alone or in combination—constitutes a sufficient basis for concluding that a passage is a non-Pauline interpolation as defined for purposes of the present study. For this, support is needed from other types of evidence.

3. *Linguistic Evidence for Interpolation*

Linguistic evidence for interpolation would be the presence of what appear to be non-Pauline vocabulary (choice of words and phrases and/or specific meanings attached thereunto) and/or stylistic features (genre, grammar and syntax, various types of rhetorical and artistic devices, and the like). The use of such linguistic evidence is, however, always problematic. The peculiar subject matter of a passage or even the vocabulary of the intended readers (or 'opponents') may dictate a distinctive terminology; moreover, peculiarities of language may indicate simply the author's use of traditional material. Thus, as G.W. Trompf notes, 'By itself an appeal to linguistic idiosyncracy in this or that passage attributed to Paul does not yield positive conclusions'.[39] Nevertheless, with specific reference to 1 Cor. 11.3-16, Trompf offers the following suggestion: 'if the language of 11.3-16 could be reckoned characteristically Pauline, the case for excursus as against interpolation could be strongly upheld'; if, on the other hand, the language should turn out to be distinctively non-Pauline, the evidence could be 'slightly tipped in favor of deutero-Pauline authorship'.[40]

39. Trompf, 'On Attitudes toward Women', p. 202; cf. Munro, *Authority in Paul and Peter*, pp. 22-23.

40. Trompf, 'On Attitudes toward Women', pp. 202-203.

Such a conclusion may be somewhat premature, however, because of the ambiguity of the term 'characteristically Pauline' and the implication that linguistic features in a suspected interpolation will necessarily be either 'characteristically Pauline' or 'distinctively non-Pauline'. As a matter of fact, at least in principle, 'characteristically Pauline' features might be of two different types: (1) *distinctively Pauline* (present in the authentic Pauline materials but not in other early Christian literature); or (2) *Pauline, but not distinctively so* (present both in the authentic Pauline letters and in other early Christian literature). By the same token, 'distinctively non-Pauline' features might be of two different types: (1) *non-Pauline, but not identifiably post-Pauline* (present neither in the authentic Pauline letters nor in the extant post-Pauline Christian literature); and (2) *distinctively post-Pauline* (present in early post-Pauline Christian literature[41] including the pseudo-Pauline writings[42] but not in the authentic Pauline letters).

The identification of these four types of linguistic features suggests the following principles to be applied in the use of linguistic features as possible evidence for interpolation in the letters of Paul: (1) the presence of *distinctively Pauline* linguistic features strengthens the case for Pauline authorship;[43] (2) the presence of linguistic features that are *Pauline, but not distinctively so* provides somewhat weaker support for Pauline authorship; (3) the presence of linguistic features that are *non-Pauline, but not identifiably post-Pauline*, strengthens the case against Pauline authorship; and (4) the presence of *distinctively post-Pauline linguistic features* strengthens the case not only against Pauline authorship but also against Paul's use of material written by

41. Inasmuch as Paul's letters represent the earliest extant Christian literature, 'early post-Pauline Christian writings' includes everything else in the New Testament as well as, e.g., the Apostolic Fathers.

42. I am here assuming that the Pastoral Letters (1 Timothy, 2 Timothy, and Titus), Ephesians, Colossians, and probably 2 Thessalonians are pseudo-Pauline; see, e.g., Collins, *Letters That Paul Did Not Write*.

43. This is not conclusive, however, because it is to be expected that the author of an interpolation might well imitate some 'characteristically' and perhaps even 'distinctively' Pauline linguistic features (unless, of course, the passage was inserted into the letter by someone other than its author, in which case the author may not have been familiar with any of the Pauline letters). Thus, in the face of otherwise compelling arguments against Pauline authorship, the presence of such features should not be allowed to decide the matter.

someone else; this is particularly true when the features can be identified as *characteristically pseudo-Pauline*.[44]

In particular cases, of course, the weight of the linguistic evidence for or against interpolation depends upon a number of considerations. These include the relative frequency of the various types of linguistic features, the extent to which these features might have been dictated by the specific subject matter of the passage, the 'literary' and/or 'rhetorical expectations' of the intended readers,[45] and possibly even the linguistic features employed by supposed 'opponents'.[46]

a. *The Vocabulary of 1 Corinthians 14.34-35*

At several points, the vocabulary of 1 Cor. 14.34-35 appears not to be characteristically Pauline: (1) the verb σιγάω ('to keep silent') appears elsewhere in the undisputed Pauline letters only at Rom. 16.25 (part of a passage regarded by most scholars as a non-Pauline interpolation) and 1 Cor. 14.28, 30 (the passage immediately preceding 14.34-35); otherwise, the verb is found in the New Testament only in Luke and Acts.[47] (2) The verb ἐπιτρέπω ('to permit'), is found elsewhere in the undisputed letters only at 1 Cor. 16.7, where it is in the active voice (not passive as in 14.34) and refers not to a regulation regarding human conduct (as in 14.34) but simply to the Lord 'permitting' Paul to visit the Corinthians.[48] Otherwise, the verb is found in the New Testament only in the Gospels[49] and in the pseudo-Pauline 1 Tim. 2.12. In the Gospels, as in 1 Cor. 16.7, it is always in the active voice and refers to

44. This fourth principle, however, must be used with caution. It is clear, for example, that the Gospels and Acts (here assumed to be post-Pauline in their canonical form) contain traditional (perhaps pre-Pauline) materials. Thus, certain of the linguistic features now appearing in the Gospels and Acts may actually be pre-Pauline features. The same may be true of other post-Pauline (including pseudo-Pauline) writings: they may contain earlier materials and thus exhibit linguistic features that are pre-Pauline rather than post-Pauline. In short, the distinction between pre-Pauline and post-Pauline linguistic features is fraught with difficulty.

45. For example, the vocabulary and literary style of a passage might vary depending upon the intellectual and educational level of the intended readers.

46. An author might adopt the vocabulary and style of the 'opponents' in order to 'meet them on their own turf'.

47. Lk. 9.36; 18.39; 20.26; Acts 12.17; 15.12, 13.

48. For the same idea and the same verb as in 1 Cor. 14.34, however, see the pseudo-Pauline 1 Tim. 2.12.

49. Mt. 8.21//Lk. 9.59, 61; Mt. 19.8//Mk 10.4; Mk 5.13//Lk. 8.32; Jn 19.38.

someone 'permitting' (or not 'permitting') someone (or something) else to do something. Only in 1 Cor. 14.34 is it in the passive voice, and only in 1 Cor. 14.34 and 1 Tim. 2.12 does it refer to the activity of women.[50] (3) The verb ὑποτάσσω ('to be subject') appears frequently in the authentically Pauline letters, but in all except three cases it refers to submission either to God (1 Cor. 15.28), to Christ (1 Cor. 15.27, 28; Phil. 3.21), to God's law (Rom. 8.7), to God's righteousness (Rom. 10.3), or to 'futility' (Rom. 8.20). Apart from 1 Cor. 14.34, the verb refers to submission to humans at only three places, the first of which is regarded by some as part of a non-Pauline interpolation: Rom. 13.1, 5 (governing authorities); 1 Cor. 14.32 (prophets); 1 Cor. 16.16 (Christian leaders).[51] In the pseudo-Pauline Colossians, Ephesians and Titus, however, it almost always has in mind submission to other human beings.[52] (4) The verb ἐπερωτάω ('to ask') appears elsewhere in the undisputed letters only at Rom. 10.20, in a quotation from Isa. 65.1. Otherwise, the verb is found in the New Testament only in the Gospels.[53] (5) The adjective αἰσχρός ('shameful') is found elsewhere in the undisputed letters only at 1 Cor. 11.16, which is part of another suspected non-Pauline interpolation. Otherwise, the adjective is found in the New Testament only in the pseudo-Pauline Eph. 5.12 and Tit. 1.11. (6) The phrase 'just as even the law says' (καθὼς καὶ ὁ λόγος λέγει), as it stands in v. 34, appears also not to be characteristically Pauline. As Raymond F. Collins notes, 'Paul generally expresses a somewhat negative view of the law' (cf. 1 Cor. 15.56), and 'when he wants to develop a scriptural argument he cites the pertinent passage of Scripture (cf. 9.9; 14.21), rather than making a merely general reference under the rubric of "the law" '.[54] In short, much of the vocabulary

50. In 1 Cor. 14.34, they are not permitted to speak in church; in 1 Tim. 2.12, they are not permitted to teach or have authority over men.

51. In the Pseudo-Pauline writings, however, the verb almost always refers to submission to humans: husbands (Eph. 5.24; Col. 3.18; Tit. 2.5; cf. 1 Pet. 3.1, 5), masters (Tit. 2.9; cf. 1 Pet. 2.18), and governing authorities (Tit. 3.1; cf. 1 Pet. 2.13). The only exception is Eph. 1.22, where it speaks of submission to Christ.

52. Christians to one another (Eph. 5.21), women to men (Col. 3.18; Eph. 5.24; Tit. 2.5; cf. 1 Pet. 3.1, 5), slaves to masters (Tit. 2.9; cf. 1 Pet. 2.18), and subjects to rulers (Tit. 3.1; cf. 1 Pet. 2.13; Rom. 13.1, 5). The only exception is Eph. 5.24, which speaks of the church being in submission to Christ.

53. Mt. 16.1; Mt. 22.46//Mk 12.34//Lk. 20.40; Mk 9.32; 11.29; Lk. 2.46; 6.9.

54. Collins, *First Corinthians*, p. 515 (note, however, that Collins regards 1 Cor. 14.34-35 as Pauline). To be sure, 1 Cor. 9.8 reads, ἢ καὶ ὁ λόγος λέγει ('does not

of 1 Cor. 14.34-35 appears to be not only non-Pauline but also distinctively post-Pauline.

It is true that certain linguistic features appear to link 1 Cor. 14.34-35 with its immediate context. These include the verbs σιγάω ('to keep silent', cf. 14.28, 30), λαλέω ('to speak', 21 times in ch. 14), and ὑποτάσσω ('to be subject', cf. 14.32). Fee suggests, however, that these verbs 'are used in such completely different ways [in 14.34-35] as to make them suspect'. As an example, he observes that 'there is not a single absolute use of the verb "to speak" in its other 21 occurrences in this chapter, yet it is twice so used here'.[55] Thus, the vocabulary of 1 Cor. 14.34-35 appears to suggest non-Pauline authorship.

b. *Literary Style or Form*

Initially, it might appear difficult to argue that the literary style or form of 1 Cor. 14.34-35 is non-Pauline. Elsewhere, however, both G.W. Trompf and I have suggested the presence in certain New Testament writings of a specific literary form or genre that appears to have been developed for the express purpose of 'keeping women in their place'. Characteristically, this form consists of three elements: (1) a general statement, assertion or command regarding the proper status, role, attire and/or demeanor of women; (2) a reason or justification (theological, historical, rational or pragmatic) for the statement, assertion or command; and (3) a 'mitigation', 'softening of the blow' or 'saving phrase' to make the statement, assertion or command less offensive to women. Examples of this form are to be found at 1 Cor. 11.3-16; 14.34-35; Col. 3.18-19; Eph. 5.22-33; 1 Tim. 2.8-15; Tit. 2.4-5; 1 Pet. 3.1-7.[56] Significant for the purposes of the present study is the fact that all of these examples except two appear in pseudo-Pauline or non-Pauline writings. The two exceptions are 1 Cor. 11.3-16 and 14.34-35. In Chapter 5, I will argue that 1 Cor. 11.3-16 is a non-Pauline interpolation. In short,

even the law say…?'), but Paul then cites the appropriate scriptural passage.

55. Fee, *The First Epistle to the Corinthians*, p. 702.

56. For my initial suggestion of this form, see Walker, '1 Corinthians 11:2-16', p. 102 n. 35. Subsequently, Trompf ('On Attitudes toward Women', pp. 205-206, 210-11), without reference to any specific literary form *per se*, and with somewhat different terminology than that suggested by me, identified essentially the same three formal elements. My own full statement of the proposal appears in William O. Walker, Jr, 'The "Theology of Woman's Place" and the "Paulinist" Tradition', *Semeia* 28 (1983), pp. 101-12.

this particular literary form appears to be characteristic not of the authentically Pauline letters but rather of the post-Pauline and particularly pseudo-Pauline writings. Thus, its appearance at 1 Cor. 14.34-35 may indicate that these verses are a non-Pauline interpolation.

Examples of apparently non-Pauline literary style or form in other proposed interpolations will be noted in the following chapters.

c. *Conclusion regarding Linguistic Evidence for Interpolation*

Unlike text-critical and contextual evidence, linguistic evidence may indeed point to non-Pauline authorship of a passage. When the vocabulary and/or literary style or form of a passage differ significantly from those appearing elsewhere in the authentically Pauline writings, this may be an indication that the passage was composed by someone other than Paul. It does not necessarily mean, of course, that someone other than Paul inserted the passage at its present location in one of the Pauline letters: Paul may well have used material written by someone else for his own purposes. As already noted, however, the appearance of distinctively *post-Pauline* and particularly *pseudo-Pauline* linguistic features may well indicate that the passage was composed after the lifetime of Paul and thus that its presence in one of the Pauline letters is to be attributed to someone other than Paul.

As Munro warns, however, extreme caution is necessary in the use of linguistic evidence for the identification of possible interpolations. First, there is the very real danger of circular argumentation: 'to determine which stylistic characteristics [including vocabulary] do or do not pertain to a certain writer, a prior judgment is required as to what he [*sic*] has written'. Second, the same author may exhibit different linguistic features, depending upon the intended audience, subject matter, situation, purpose or even which section of a letter is under consideration. Third, the vocabulary of the intended readers (or even of the 'opponents') may dictate a distinctive terminology. Fourth, an author's linguistic usage may change with the passing of time. Finally, peculiarities of language may indicate simply the author's use of materials composed by someone else. Nevertheless, as Munro concludes, 'stylistic unity tends to confirm authenticity [or common authorship], while stylistic diversity strengthens the possibility that more than one hand has been at work in the text'.[57]

57. Munro, *Authority in Paul and Peter*, p. 22.

4. *Ideational Evidence for Interpolation*

Ideational evidence for interpolation would be data suggesting that significant features of the substantive content of a passage are not characteristically Pauline or, in some cases, perhaps that they are even anti-Pauline. In the discussion of linguistic evidence for interpolation, a distinction was made among features that are (1) distinctively Pauline, (2) Pauline, but not distinctively so, (3) non-Pauline, but not identifiably post-Pauline, and (4) distinctively post-Pauline. The same distinction is appropriate when dealing with ideational evidence for interpolation: features of the first type constitute significant evidence for Pauline authorship; those of the second type, somewhat weaker evidence for Pauline authorship; those of the third type, evidence against Pauline authorship; and those of the fourth type, stronger evidence against Pauline authorship as well as evidence that the passage in question was added to the Pauline letter after the time of Paul and thus by someone other than Paul. Evidence for interpolation is further strengthened if the features appear to be characteristic of the pseudo-Pauline writings. Finally, if it can be shown that the ideas expressed in a passage are not only different from but also antithetical to Pauline thought as seen elsewhere in the authentic letters, the most reasonable assumption is that the passage was neither composed by Paul nor included by him in the letter. Thus, it is likely to be a non-Pauline interpolation as defined for purposes of the present study.

It has already been noted that the ideational content of 1 Cor. 14.34-35 has no apparent relation to that of its context. More to the point, it is often noted that these verses stand in obvious contradiction to 11.3-16, 'where it is assumed without reproof that women pray and prophesy in the assembly'.[58] Thus, it would appear that the author of 11.3-16 cannot also have been the author of 14.34-35.[59] In Chapter 5, however, I will argue that 11.3-16 is a non-Pauline interpolation. Thus, at most, the apparent contradiction indicates only that Paul could not have been the author of both passages. If 11.3-16 is in fact non-Pauline, then, at least in principle, 14.34-35 might have been written by Paul.

58. Fee, *The First Epistle to the Corinthians*, p. 702.

59. For a contrary argument, however, see, e.g., Trompf, 'On Attitudes toward Women', pp. 209-10, 214-15. Trompf suggests that the two passages, both of which he regards as interpolations, may well have come from 'the same hand'.

It would appear, however, that the ideas expressed in 1 Cor. 14.34-35 are indeed non-Pauline and even anti-Pauline—more so even than those in 11.3-16. Even the immediate context in ch. 14 apparently assumes that women are included among those who speak in church (note the 'all' in vv. 5, 18, 23, 24, 31, and the 'each one' of v. 26). More importantly, 1 Cor. 14.34-35 contradicts Paul's avowed egalitarianism as articulated in Gal. 3.27-28 (that is, in Christ 'there is neither Jew nor Greek, there is neither slave nor free, there is neither male nor female; for you are all one in Christ Jesus'); his surprisingly even-handed discussion of sex, marriage and divorce in 1 Corinthians 7;[60] and the very positive and non-discriminatory manner in which he speaks of women with whom he has been associated in the work of the church.[61] Indeed, it stretches the imagination to think that this Paul might also have written (or approved) the sentiments expressed in 1 Cor. 14.34-35! Thus, the ideational evidence suggests that 1 Cor. 14.34-35 is likely non-Pauline in the double sense of non-Pauline authorship and non-Pauline insertion in Paul's letter to the Corinthians.

Here, then, for the first time, is a type of evidence that may point to interpolations that are non-Pauline in the double sense of non-Pauline composition and non-Pauline inclusion in one of the Pauline letters. As in the case of linguistic evidence, however, extreme caution is required in the use of ideational evidence for interpolation. First, the same author may (and Paul certainly sometimes does) express different ideas, depending upon the intended audience, subject matter, situation, purpose, or even which section of a letter is under consideration; moreover, an author's ideas, like his/her vocabulary and literary style, may change with the passing of time. Second, significant conceptual differences may simply be an indication that the author is incorporating alien material into his/her own work.

5. *Comparative Evidence for Interpolation*

Comparative evidence for interpolation would be data suggesting that significant features of a passage—linguistic, ideational and/or situational—are more closely akin to those of known non-Pauline (and

60. See, e.g., Robin Scroggs, 'Paul and the Eschatological Woman', *JAAR* 40 (1972), pp. 283-303 (294-97).

61. E.g. 1 Cor. 16.19; Rom. 16.1-2, 3-5, 6, 7, 12, 13, 15; Phil. 4.2-3; Phlm. 1.

particularly post-Pauline and pseudo-Pauline) writings than to those of the authentically Pauline letters. Munro refers to this phenomenon as 'literary or historical coherence'. As she states it, 'The case for dissociation [from Paul] is considerably strengthened if it can be argued that an alleged interpolation coheres with material belonging to another milieu'.[62] Thus, comparative evidence for interpolation can often be seen as the 'flip-side' of linguistic, ideational and/or situational evidence: the latter 'dissociate' a passage from Paul, while the former 'associates' it with someone other than Paul. When a passage can thus be both 'dissociated' from Paul and 'associated' with a non-Pauline and particularly a post-Pauline author, this may serve as compelling evidence that the passage was neither composed by Paul nor inserted by him at its present location in one of the Pauline letters.

I have already suggested that the literary form or genre of 1 Cor. 14.34-35 appears to be characteristically post-Pauline and even pseudo-Pauline. In addition, certain other linguistic, ideational and situational features of the passage that appear to be non-Pauline are found in pseudo-Pauline writings. In particular, this passage bears a close resemblance to the pseudo-Pauline 1 Tim. 2.11-12. Both employ the verb ἐπιτρέπειν to enjoin silence on the part of women; both require that women be 'submissive' (using the same linguistic root: ὑποτάσσειν in 1 Cor. 14.34 and ὑποταγή in 1 Tim. 2.11), presumably to men, an idea that is also present elsewhere in the pseudo-Pauline writings;[63] and both suggest that men should be the teachers of women, not *vice versa*. In addition, the use of the adjective αἰσχρός in 1 Cor. 14.35 is similar to that in 1 Cor. 11.16, which is also regarded by some as a non-Pauline interpolation, and the adjective appears elsewhere in the New Testament only at the pseudo-Pauline Eph. 5.12 and Tit. 1.11. Moreover, although it is not elsewhere suggested in the authentically Pauline writings (except perhaps in 1 Cor. 11.3-16, which may be an interpolation) that the role and status of women were regarded as a problem during Paul's lifetime, there is ample evidence of this in the pseudo-Pauline writings, which contain strong restrictions regarding the status and role of women.[64] Such evidence suggests that 1 Cor. 14.34-35 may

62. Munro, *Authority in Paul and Peter*, p. 24.

63. Col. 3.18; Eph. 5.24; Tit. 2.5; cf. also 1 Pet. 3.1, 5 (all using the verb ὑποτάσσειν).

64. Col. 3.18; Eph. 5.22-33; 1 Tim. 2.9-15; Tit. 2.3-5; cf. also 1 Pet. 3.1-6.

have been written (and added to Paul's Corinthian letter) sometime after the death of the apostle and, indeed, that it may have originated in the same circles that produced some of the pseudo-Pauline literature.

6. *Situational Evidence for Interpolation*

Situational evidence for interpolation would be data suggesting that a passage reflects a situation, occasion or set of circumstances different from that reflected in the remainder of the letter in which the passage appears, and perhaps even from that known or believed to have prevailed during Paul's lifetime.

The situational evidence for regarding 1 Cor. 14.34-35 as a non-Pauline interpolation is largely inferential. Apart from this passage and perhaps 1 Cor. 11.3-16 (which is regarded by some as a non-Pauline interpolation), there is nothing whatsoever in the undisputed letters to suggest that the activity of women in the church was regarded as a problem by Paul or during Paul's lifetime. Clearly, however, such activity came to be regarded as problematic in the post-Pauline Church. This suggests that 1 Cor. 14.34-35 may not have been composed until after the time of Paul.

Great caution must be exercised, however, in the use of this type of evidence. Reconstruction of the situation presupposed by a text is generally highly speculative. Moreover, a situation reflected in a particular passage may in fact have prevailed during Paul's own lifetime despite the absence of other evidence to this effect; thus, arguments for interpolation based upon situational evidence are almost always arguments from silence. For these reasons, unless one can be certain that the situation presupposed by a passage existed only after the time of Paul, situational evidence for interpolation can serve only a corroborative function in the case of passages suspected on other grounds of being interpolations. To the extent that such evidence does in fact point to interpolation, however, it suggests both non-Pauline authorship and non-Pauline insertion of a passage at its present location in one of the Pauline letters.

7. *Motivational Evidence for Interpolation*

Motivational evidence for interpolation would be data suggesting plausible reasons why a particular passage might have been added to one of the Pauline letters. For the most part, such evidence would involve considerations of the ideational content of the proposed interpolation. The question would be, 'Why would someone wish to add this material to one of Paul's letters?' In other words, 'Why would someone wish to attribute this material to Paul?' Conceivably, however, the primary consideration might be linguistic in nature. In the case of 1 Cor. 12.31b–14.1a, for example, an interpolator might simply wish to give Paul credit for the magnificent encomium on love; in this case, both ideational and linguistic factors might be involved.

The motivational evidence for regarding 1 Cor. 14.34-35 as a non-Pauline interpolation is closely related to the situational evidence. After the time of Paul, the status and role of women in the Church apparently came to be regarded as something of a problem. Thus, it may have appeared desirable to have the Apostle say something to address the problem. Hence, the addition of a passage such as 1 Cor. 14.34-35 to one of the authentically Pauline letters.

Motivational evidence for interpolation, however, is inevitably highly speculative in nature. Moreover, plausible reasons for the addition of a passage to a Pauline letter might also constitute evidence that the passage was included by Paul himself. Thus, like situational and comparative evidence, motivational evidence is of value only in the case of passages already suspected on other grounds of being non-Pauline interpolations.

8. *Locational Evidence for Interpolation*

Locational evidence for interpolation would be data suggesting plausible reasons why a passage might have been inserted specifically at its present location, not somewhere else, in one of the Pauline letters. Such evidence might involve items of either an ideational or a linguistic nature. In the former case, it would be the content of the passage that led to its insertion at its present location; in the latter, some feature(s) of vocabulary and/or literary style or form.

If 1 Cor. 14.34-35 is in fact a later addition to Paul's Corinthian letter, why was it inserted precisely at its present location and not elsewhere?[65] In a general sense, of course, vv. 34-35, like all of ch. 14 and indeed both chs. 12 and 14, have to do with public worship. There are,

65. As already noted, some manuscripts place vv. 34-35 at the end of ch. 14, not after v. 33. This, however, does not significantly affect the locational evidence for interpolation.

however, more specific linguistic and ideational features that appear to link these verses to their immediate context: (1) ch. 14 as a whole deals with 'speaking' in church, a theme that also characterizes vv. 34-35; (2) v. 28 speaks of 'keeping silent in church', a notion that is picked up in v. 34; (3) v. 32 speaks of 'being subject', an idea that reappears at v. 34 (using the same verb, ὑποτάσσεσθαι); (4) v. 33 includes the phrase 'in all of the churches', and this reappears almost verbatim in v. 34 ('in the churches'). In short, it may simply have been the common themes of 'speech', 'silence' and 'submission', together with the setting of public worship 'in the churches', that led to the insertion of 14.34-35 precisely at its present location in 1 Corinthians. More specifically, however, the verses may have been added at this point because, as Dennis Ronald MacDonald suggests, 'some scribe…feared that others might interpret the egalitarian treatment of spiritual gifts in 1 Corinthians to mean that Paul included women in the prophetic office'. According to MacDonald, 'the scribe knew better, for he had read (pseudo-)Paul's comment in 1 Timothy that women must remain silent; therefore, he added vv. 33b-36[66] in order to clarify what he understood to have been Paul's position on the matter'.[67]

One might argue, of course, that the commonalities between 1 Cor. 14.34-35 and its context point to Pauline authorship of the verses in question. As Fee notes, however, what appear to be common themes are treated so differently in vv. 34-35 as to make suspect any such argument.[68] For example, ch. 14 as a whole is concerned with the speech of *prophets and speakers in 'tongues'*, while vv. 34-35 addresses the speech of *women*. Similarly, in v. 28 it is *speakers in 'tongues'* who are to keep silent *unless an interpreter is available*, while in v. 34 it is *all women* who are to keep silent. Further, in v. 32 it is *'the spirits of prophets'* that are subject *to a particular class of people* (prophets), while in v. 34 it is *women* who are to be subject *to men*. In short, the exclusive focus on women in vv. 34-35 distinguishes these verses from the remainder of ch. 14.

Like motivational evidence for interpolation, locational evidence is inevitably highly speculative in nature and is of value only in the case of passages already suspected on other grounds of being non-Pauline

66. Murphy-O'Connor ('Interpolations in 1 Corinthians', p. 90) argues convincingly that the interpolation does not include vv. 33b and 36.

67. MacDonald, 'A Conjectural Emendation', p. 267.

68. Fee, *The First Epistle to the Corinthians*, p. 702.

interpolations. Indeed, such evidence might constitute grounds for attributing the presence of a passage to Paul himself.

9. *Conclusion*

In principle, any or all of the following conclusions might be drawn on the basis of text-critical, contextual, linguistic, ideational, comparative, situational, motivational and/or locational evidence: (1) a particular passage at one time may not have appeared at its present location in one of the Pauline letters; (2) it appears not to 'fit' at this location; (3) significant features of its vocabulary and/or literary style or form appear to be non-Pauline; (4) certain of its ideas appear to be non-Pauline or even anti-Pauline; (5) it is more closely akin to non-Pauline and particularly post-Pauline and/or pseudo-Pauline materials than to the authentically Pauline writings; (6) it appears to reflect a situation not otherwise known to have prevailed during the lifetime of Paul; (7) there are plausible reasons why it might have been added to one of the Pauline letters; and (8) there are plausible reasons why it might have been inserted specifically at its present location in one of the letters. Seldom, if ever, however, is it possible to draw all of these conclusions regarding a particular passage. Generally, what is required is a careful assessment of various lines of evidence, resulting in a conclusion that can be affirmed with a greater or lesser degree of confidence, depending upon the evidence.

Another important consideration, however, must not be overlooked. It has already been noted that a passage might appear in all of the surviving witnesses to the text—and indeed at the same location in all of the witnesses—and nevertheless be a non-Pauline interpolation. Analogous observations can be made regarding contextual, linguistic, ideational, situational, comparative, motivational and locational evidence. A passage might appear to 'fit' perfectly within its context and nevertheless be a non-Pauline interpolation. In such case, the interpolator would simply have composed or adapted the passage in such a way as to make it 'fit'. Similarly, an interpolator might deliberately imitate Paul's vocabulary and/or literary style, thereby producing an interpolation with linguistic features remarkably similar to those of Paul himself. Further, a passage might express ideas that are in agreement, or at least not in conflict, with those of Paul himself and nevertheless be a non-Pauline interpolation. Additionally, a passage might both reflect a situation known to have existed during Paul's lifetime and appear more closely akin to the authentically Pauline letters than to non-Pauline (including pseudo-Pauline) writings and nevertheless be a non-Pauline interpolation. Finally, there might be no apparent reasons for the secondary insertion of a passage into one of the Pauline letters, either at its present location or elsewhere, and the passage might nevertheless be a non-Pauline interpolation. Thus, as has already been noted in the case of text-critical evidence, the absence of evidence for interpolation—whether contextual, linguistic, ideational, situational, comparative, motivational or locational—must always be seen as precisely what it is: the *absence* of evidence. In the face of otherwise compelling evidence for interpolation, the absence of one or more particular types of evidence should not be allowed to decide the issue. Indeed, it must be acknowledged that the Pauline letters may well contain non-Pauline interpolations that, because of such absence of evidence, will never be identified.

In short, the attempt to identify non-Pauline interpolations in the Pauline letters must be satisfied with probabilities not certainties. The most that can be said with confidence is that the letters are likely to contain interpolations and that certain individual passages probably are in fact such interpolations.

As regards 1 Cor. 14.34-35, the following can be said: the text-critical evidence suggests that it may represent a secondary addition to the text of Paul's letter to the Corinthians. The linguistic and ideational evidence suggest non-Pauline authorship of the passage, and indeed the latter suggests that it was someone other than Paul who inserted the verses in the Pauline letter. The situational and comparative evidence suggest composition of the passage after the time of Paul and both non-Pauline authorship and non-Pauline insertion. The motivational and locational evidence provide plausible reasons why someone other than Paul might both have composed the passage and inserted it at precisely its present location in Paul's Corinthian letter. Thus, the cumulative weight of the evidence appears to support the view that 1 Cor. 14.34-35 is a non-Pauline interpolation.

In the case of other proposed interpolations, the evidence is less clearcut. As has already been noted, there is direct text-critical evidence for interpolation only in the cases of Rom. 16.25-27 and perhaps 1 Cor. 14.34-35. In the case of Rom. 16.25-27, there appears to be little if any contextual evidence for interpolation; nevertheless—

primarily on the basis of text-critical, linguistic, ideational and comparative evidence—it is regarded as an interpolation by most scholars. Here as elsewhere, any case for interpolation must be based upon the convergence of different lines of evidence and conclusions must be qualified in light of the consistency and strength of the evidence. It is my own judgment, however, that a careful analysis of the evidence can at times lead to the reasonably confident conclusion that a passage is a non-Pauline interpolation.

In this chapter, I have presented evidence for viewing 1 Cor. 14.34-35 as a non-Pauline interpolation. In Chapters 5, 6, 7 and 8, I will argue that the following passages are also interpolations: 1 Cor. 11.3-16; 2.6-16; 12.31b–14.1a; Rom. 1.18–2.29. Finally, in Chapters 9 and 10, I will summarize the evidence for placing five additional passages in the same category: Rom. 16.25-27; 2 Cor. 6.14–7.1; 1 Thess. 2.13-16; Rom. 13.1-7; 1 Cor. 10.1-22. Altogether, arguments will have been presented for viewing ten passages as non-Pauline interpolations. It is my own judgment that there are surely more—perhaps many more.

Chapter 5

1 CORINTHIANS 11.3-16*

1. *Introduction*

It is widely acknowledged that 1 Cor. 11.2-16—or, more likely, only vv. 3-16[1]—presents serious problems for the exegete. Wayne A. Meeks, for example, refers to it as 'one of the most obscure passages in the Pauline letters',[2] and Gordon D. Fee observes that it

> is full of notorious exegetical difficulties, including (1) the 'logic' of the argument as a whole, which in turn is related to (2) our uncertainty about the meaning of some absolutely crucial terms and (3) our uncertainty about prevailing customs, both in the culture(s) in general and in the church(es) in particular (including the whole complex question of early Christian worship).[3]

Along somewhat different lines, Robin Scroggs suggests that 'in its present form this is hardly one of Paul's happier compositions'. In his view, 'the logic is obscure at best and contradictory at worst'. Moreover, 'the word choice is peculiar; the tone, peevish'.[4]

In light of such difficulties, it is not surprising that Pauline authorship of the passage has from time to time been questioned. More than 60 years ago, for example, Alfred F. Loisy suggested that vv. 3-16 (but

* Much of this chapter represents a revised version of my articles '1 Corinthians 11:2-16', and 'The Vocabulary of 1 Corinthians 11.3-16'. It is included here with permission from the original publishers.

1. In the past, most of the discussion has focused on 1 Cor. 11.2-16. As will become clear, however, it is now my own judgment that the proposed interpolation most likely does not include v. 2.

2. Meeks, *The Writings of St. Paul*, p. 38.

3. Fee, *The First Epistle to the Corinthians*, p. 492.

4. Scroggs, 'Paul and the Eschatological Woman', p. 297. Suggesting that 'all these difficulties point to some hidden agenda, hidden probably to the Apostle himself as well as to his readers', Scroggs proposes that this 'hidden agenda' might be Paul's fear of homosexuality (n. 38).

not v. 2) were of non-Pauline origin.[5] More recently, Winsome Munro concluded that vv. 2-16 represent one among a rather large number of 'Pastoral' interpolations in the Pauline corpus.[6] Quite independently of the work of Loisy and Munro, I argued in 1975 that 1 Cor. 11.2-16 is a non-Pauline interpolation.[7]

Reactions to my proposal were mixed. Jerome Murphy-O'Connor acknowledged the difficulties posed by the passage but nevertheless asserted that my arguments for interpolation were 'highly questionable on both factual and methodological grounds' and that my hypothesis must be rejected.[8] In a later article, he attempted to clarify the situation in Corinth and Paul's response to it in such a way as to demonstrate the internal coherence of the passage in question and thus to refute my claim that it is non-Pauline.[9] Others who rejected my arguments included John P. Meier,[10] Anthony C. Thiselton,[11] William F. Orr and

5. Loisy, *Remarques sur la littérature épistolaire*, pp. 60-62.

6. Winsome Munro, 'Two Strata in 1 Cor. 10 and 11' (unpublished paper presented at the 1971 Annual Meeting of the Society of Biblical Literature, Atlanta, GA); 'Authority and Subjection in Early Christian "Paideia" with Particular Reference to the Pauline Corpus and 1 Peter' (unpublished doctoral dissertation, Columbia University, 1974); 'Patriarchy and Charismatic Community in "Paul"', in Judith Plaskow and Joan Arnold Romero (eds.), *Women and Religion* (ASR, 1; Missoula, MT: American Academy of Religion/Scholars Press, rev. edn, 1974), pp. 189-98 (191-92); 'Post-Pauline Material in 1 Cor. 10, 11, and 14 with Confirmation from 2 Cor 6.14–7.1' (unpublished paper, 1977); and *Authority in Paul and Peter*, especially pp. 69-75.

7. Walker, '1 Corinthians 11:2-16 and Paul's Views regarding Women'; see also 'The "Theology of Woman's Place"'; and 'The Vocabulary of 1 Corinthians 11.3-16'.

8. Jerome Murphy-O'Connor, 'The Non-Pauline Character of 1 Corinthians 11:2-16?', *JBL* 95 (1976), pp. 615-21.

9. Jerome Murphy-O'Connor, 'Sex and Logic in 1 Corinthians 11:2-16', *CBQ* 42 (1980), pp. 482-500; see also his 'Interpolations in 1 Corinthians', pp. 87-90. According to Murphy-O'Connor, Paul is not concerned in 1 Cor. 11.2-16 with the presence or absence of a head covering (e.g. a veil or shawl); rather, the problem is that of men with elaborately arranged long hair and women with disordered hair. The former was associated with homosexuality and the latter more generally with a lack of feminity.

10. John P. Meier, 'On the Veiling of Hermeneutics (1 Cor. 11:2-16)', *CBQ* 40 (1978), pp. 212-26 (218 n. 12).

11. Anthony C. Thiselton, 'Realized Eschatology at Corinth', *NTS* 24 (1978), pp. 510-26 (520-21).

James Arthur Walther,[12] as well as Elisabeth Schüssler Fiorenza.[13] Indeed, Fee characterizes my proposal as 'a counsel of despair'.[14] On the other hand, shortly after the appearance of my own work, Lamar Cope published an article in which he supported the case for interpolation, suggesting, however, that the addition includes only vv. 3-16 and not v. 2[15]—a suggestion that I have now accepted. In my judgment, however, the most significant and impressive arguments for the non-Pauline character of the passage have come from G.W. Trompf.[16]

In this chapter, it is my intention to reformulate the arguments that 1 Cor. 11.3-16 is a non-Pauline interpolation, taking into account the contributions of Munro, Cope and Trompf as well as my own further reflections regarding the matter. As a way of emphasizing their importance in the identification of interpolations, I will pay particular attention to the linguistic features of the passage. In addition, of course, I will address considerations of a text-critical, contextual, ideational, comparative, situational, motivational and locational nature.

Before proceeding to such matters, however, it is important to consider the nature of the Corinthian correspondence itself. As was indicated in Chapter 1, it is widely accepted that the Pauline writings must have undergone some revision at the hands of one or more editors. Evidence of such editorial activity has often been noted particularly in

12. William F. Orr and James Arthur Walther, *I Corinthians: A New Translation: Introduction with a Study of the Life of Paul, Notes, and Commentary* (AB, 32; Garden City, NY: Doubleday, 1976), pp. 259, 261, 262.

13. Elisabeth Schüssler Fiorenza, 'The Study of Women in Early Christianity: Some Methodological Considerations', in Thomas J. Ryan (ed.), *Critical History and Biblical Faith: New Testament Perspectives* (APCTS; Villanova: College Theology Society/Horizons, 1979), pp. 30-58 (36-37, 47, p. 54 n. 17, p. 58 n. 43); cf. also her *In Memory of Her: A Feminist Theological Reconstruction of Christian Origins* (New York: Crossroad, 1983), pp. 227-30. Schüssler Fiorenza treats my hypothesis as an example of the type of 'revisionist apologetics' that seeks to formulate a 'canon within the canon' by declaring 'one string of the tradition as unauthentic and therefore not normative'. In response, I note that I did not enter at all into the question of the Canon, nor did I deal in any way whatsoever with the question of what is or is not normative. For my own views regarding the matter, see the Epilogue of this book.

14. Fee, *The First Epistle to the Corinthians*, p. 492 n. 3.

15. Cope, '1 Cor. 11.2-16', pp. 435-46.

16. Trompf, 'On Attitudes toward Women', pp. 196-215. Richard A. Horsley (*1 Corinthians* [ANTC; Nashville: Abingdon Press, 1998], pp. 152-57) summarizes the arguments for interpolation but apparently reserves judgment on the matter.

the Corinthian correspondence. Thus, most scholars regard 2 Corinthians as a 'composite' letter, composed of parts of at least two originally separate communications,[17] and the same has sometimes been argued regarding 1 Corinthians.[18] For example, Walter Schmithals argued some years ago that the material now contained in 1 Corinthians derives from two separate letters.[19] Following modification of his

17. For a summary of the evidence, see, e.g., Furnish, *II Corinthians*, pp. 30-32, 35-41. Indeed, Günther Bornkamm (*Die Vorgeschichte des sogenannten Zweiten Korintherbriefes* [SHAW, 2; Heidelberg: Winter, 1961]; reprinted with Addendum in his *Gesammelte Aufsätze*. IV. *Geschichte und Glaube* [BevT, 53; Munich: Chr. Kaiser Verlag, 1971], pp. 162-94; cf. his 'The History of the Origin of the So-Called Second Letter to the Corinthians', *NTS* 8 [1961–62], pp. 258-64; and *Paul* [trans. D.M.G. Stalker; New York: Harper & Row, 1971], pp. 244-46) maintained that 2 Corinthians comprises parts of five different letters, written at different times to deal with different situations, and that its various parts were perhaps not combined until near the end of the first century. Bornkamm identified the letters, arranged chronologically, as: Letter A (2.14–7.4); Letter B (10.1–13.14); Letter C (1.1–2.13; 7.5-16); Letter D (8.1-24); and Letter E (9.1-15). On the grounds of its non-Pauline vocabulary and theological contents, as well as the fact that it breaks the context, he regarded 6.14–7.1 as a non-Pauline interpolation. As to why chs. 10–13, which form the second part chronologically, would have been placed last by the editor, Bornkamm suggested that because heresy was regarded in the early Church as one of the perils of the last days, warnings against it were characteristically located at the end of writings. Otherwise, in his view, Letter C contains the basic material, into which Letter A was inserted and to which Letters D and E were added. Bornkamm's reconstruction, with some modifications, has been accepted by a number of scholars. For an argument supporting the unity of 2 Corinthians, however, see most recently Amador, 'Revisiting 2 Corinthians'.

18. For a summary and critique of various proposals, see, e.g., Robert Jewett, 'The Redaction of I Corinthians and the Trajectory of the Pauline School', *JAARSup* 44 (1978), pp. 389-44 (396-402).

19. Walter Schmithals, *Gnosticism in Corinth: An Investigation of the Letters to the Corinthians* (trans. John E. Steely; Nashville: Abingdon Press, 1971), pp. 87-101. Unlike Bornkamm, Schmithals regarded 2 Cor. 6.14–7.1 as authentically Pauline (p. 94 esp. n. 21) and included it in the earlier of the two letters. Thus, in his view, Letter A consisted of 2 Cor. 6.14–7.1; 1 Cor. 6.12-20; 9.24–10.22; 11.2-34; 15; 16.13-24; while Letter B included 1 Cor. 1.1–6.11; 7.1–9.23; 10.23–11.1; 12.1–14.40; 16.1-12. To complete his analysis of the Corinthian correspondence, Schmithals divided 2 Corinthians into four letters: Letter C (2.14–6.13; 7.2-4); Letter D (10.1–13.13); Letter E (9.1-15); and Letter F (1.1–2.13; 7.5–8.24). Like Bornkamm, Schmithals suggested that the collection may have been made near the end of the first century (pp. 88-89). Jewett ('The Redaction of I Corinthians')

reconstruction by Wolfgang Schenk,[20] Schmithals divided the materials into five letters.[21] More modestly, Jean Héring, argued that 1 Corinthians comprises material from two separate letters.[22]

Even scholars who regard 1 Corinthians as a unity, however, have often detected the presence of one or more interpolations. Thus, Murphy-O'Connor observes that 'anyone familiar with recent literature on 1 Corinthians will have noticed an increasing tendency to discern interpolations in this letter, some only a single verse, but others almost a complete chapter'. Murphy-O'Connor continues: 'The number of proposals is sufficient to constitute a definite trend'. Proposed interpolations discussed by Murphy-O'Connor include: 1 Cor. 2.6-16; 4.6c; 6.14; 11.3-16; 14.34-35; 15.31-32; 15.44b-48 (he does not, however, include 1 Cor. 12.31b–14.1a!).[23]

In my own judgment, the appearance of so many proposals regarding interpolations in 1 Corinthians, together with arguments for the 'composite' nature of the letter, justifies—indeed requires—a careful examination of any passage exhibiting features that are typically characteristic of interpolations. Thus, I now proceed to such an examination of 1 Cor. 11.3-16.

divides 1 Corinthians into four original letters: Letter A (11.2-34); Letter B ([2 Cor. 6.14–7.1]; 6.12-20; 9.24–10.22; 15.1-58; 16.13-24); Letter C (1.1–6.11; 7.1–8.13; 9.19-23; 10.23–11.1; 12.1-31a; 14.1c-40; 12.31b–13.13; 16.1-12); and Letter D (9.1-18). In his view, Letter C was the 'frame letter', into which, at various points, a redactor inserted portions of Letters B, C and D. Jewett also identifies six non-Pauline interpolations: 1.2b; 4.17c; 7.17b; 11.16; 14.1a-b; 14.33b-36.

20. Schenk, 'Der 1. Korintherbrief als Briefsammlung'. Schenk divided 1 Corinthians into four original letters: Letter A (1 Cor. 1.1-9; [2 Cor. 6.14–7.1]; 6.1-11; 11.2-34; 15; 16.13-24); Letter B (9.1-18; 9.24–10.22; 6.12-20; 5.1-13); Letter C (7.1–8.13; 9.19-23; 10.23–11.1; 12.1-31a; 14.1c-40; 12.31b–13.13; 16.1-12); and Letter D (1.10–4.21).

21. Walter Schmithals, 'Die Korintherbriefe als Briefsammlung', *ZNW* 64 (1973), pp. 263-88. The five are: Letter A (11.2-34); Letter B (6.1-11; [2 Cor. 6.14–7.1]; 6.12-20; 9.24–10.22; 15.1-58; 16.13-24); Letter C (5.1-13; 7.1–8.13; 9.19-22; 10.23–11.1; 12.1-31a; 14.1c-40; 12.31b–13.13; 16.1-12); Letter D (4.1-21); and Letter F (9.1-18; [2 Cor. 6.3-13; 7.2-4]).

22. Jean Héring, *The First Epistle of Saint Paul to the Corinthians* (trans. A.W. Heathcote and P.J. Allcock; London: Epworth Press, 1962), pp. xiii-xiv. Letter A consists of 1.1–8.13; 10.23–11.1; 16.1-4, 10-14, while Letter B includes 9.1–10.22; 11.2–15.58; 16.5-9, 15-24. Chapter 13 is 'a special addition'.

23. Murphy-O'Connor, 'Interpolations in 1 Corinthians' (quotations from p. 81).

2. *Text-Critical Evidence for Interpolation*

There is no direct text-critical evidence suggesting that 1 Cor. 11.3-16 might be an interpolation. The passage appears in all of the extant manuscripts—and indeed at the same location in all of the manuscripts. As was noted in Chapter 2, however, the absence of direct text-critical evidence for interpolation should be seen as precisely what it is: the *absence* of evidence. In the face of otherwise compelling arguments for interpolation, this absence of evidence should not be allowed to decide the issue.

3. *Contextual Evidence for Interpolation*

While there is no direct text-critical evidence suggesting that 1 Cor. 11.3-16 might be an interpolation, there is significant contextual evidence. Trompf has provided a detailed analysis of this evidence, in which he demonstrates 'that the whole passage sits ill at ease in the context of 1 Cor. 10:1–11:34'—indeed, 'that Paul's discussions in 1 Corinthians 10–11 proceed much more smoothly if we omit 11.3-16 from the text'.[24] These conclusions are supported by a number of considerations relating to what Trompf terms both the 'narrower' and the 'broader' context of the passage.

a. *The Extent of the Proposed Interpolation*

Before exploring these contextual considerations, however, a decision must be made regarding the exact extent of the proposed interpolation. In my 1975 article, I acknowledged the possibility that the interpolation might begin only at v. 3 but nevertheless argued for the inclusion of v. 2. At least three considerations would appear to support this view. First, most of the material in v. 2 could easily have been derived from v. 1 and vv. 17-34—that is, from the passages immediately preceding and immediately following the proposed interpolation. The words ἐπαινῶ δὲ ὑμᾶς ὅτι ('I commend you because') may derive from οὐκ ἐπαινῶ ὅτι ('I do not commend [you] because') in v. 17; μου μέμνησθε ('you remember me') is perhaps reminiscent of μιμηταί μου γίνεσθε

24. Trompf, 'On Attitudes toward Women', pp. 197-98; see the entire discussion, pp. 197-202. In what follows, I am greatly indebted to Trompf, although I depart from his analysis at certain points.

('be imitators of me') in v. 1; and καθῶς παρέδωκα ὑμῖν τὰς παραδόσεις κατέχετε ('you maintain the traditions even as I have delivered them to you') may have been suggested by ἐγὼ γὰρ παρέλαβον ἀπὸ κυρίου ὃ καὶ παρέδωκα ὑμῖν ('for I received from the Lord what I also delivered to you') in v. 23 (cf. also 15.1-3a). Second, the inclusion of v. 2 in the interpolation makes possible a smooth transition from v. 1 to v. 17. Without vv. 2-16, the τοῦτο of v. 17 (usually translated as 'the following') would almost certainly refer not forward to what follows in 11.17-34 but back to the command in 11.1 (or perhaps all of 10.31–11.1). Thus, v. 17 would be translated somewhat as follows: 'But in commanding this [that is, to become imitators of Paul's rather "situational" approach to matters of eating and drinking], I am not commending the fact that when you come together it is not for the better but for the worse'; in other words, 'situationalism' has its limits, where the peace and purity of the church are involved! Third, the transition from 11.1 to 11.2 is problematic, suggesting that the latter may not originally have followed the former. Verse 1 commands the readers to become 'imitators' (μιμηταί) of Paul just as he is of Christ. Verse 2, however, commends the readers for 'remembering' (μέμνησθε) the writer in all things and maintaining the 'traditions' (παραδόσεις) just as he has delivered them. Neither the preceding verse (11.1) nor indeed the preceding passage (10.1–11.1), however, makes any mention of 'traditions'. Thus, unless v. 2 is a part of the proposed interpolation, it would appear to mark the beginning of a new section of the letter (a section, indeed, that might be expected to deal with the 'traditions'). The most natural place to see the beginning of a new section, however, is 12.1, with its περὶ δὲ τῶν πνευματικῶν (cf. περὶ δὲ ὧν ἐγράψατε in 7.1, περὶ δὲ τῶν εἰδωλοθύτων in 8.1, and περὶ δὲ τῆς λογείας τῆς εἰς τοὺς ἁγίους in 16.1).

In his response to my article, however, Cope argued against the inclusion of v. 2 in the proposed interpolation.[25] For the following reasons, I have become convinced that he is correct. First, with the removal of vv. 3-16, vv. 2 and 17 form one logically clear and syntactically complete sentence: 'I commend you because you remember me in everything and maintain the traditions even as I have delivered them to you; but in the following instructions I do not commend you, because when you come together it is not for the better but for the

25. Cope, '1 Cor. 11.2-16', pp. 435-36.

worse'.[26] As Cope notes, 'the adversative conjunction δέ [v. 17] is now appropriate', because 'Paul commends the Corinthians for proper maintenance of the words of the supper tradition (παρέδωκα in vv. 2 and 23) but objects to their practices connected with that tradition'.[27] Second, the substantive and 'tonal' connection between v. 2 and vv. 3-16 is at least as problematic as that between v. 1 and v. 2. As has already been noted, v. 2 commends the readers for 'remembering' (μέμνησθε) the writer in all things and maintaining the 'traditions' (παραδόσεις) he has delivered (παρέδωκα). With such an introduction, one would expect the verses immediately following not only to reflect and even amplify this positive expression of commendation but also to deal with the 'traditions'. Verses 3-16, however, contain nothing at all by way of commendation; rather, the writer appears to be somewhat less than happy regarding the attire and/or hairstyle of men and women in Christian worship. Moreover, vv. 3-16 make no mention of 'traditions'. Third, vv. 17-34 do in fact pick up the references in v. 2 both to 'commendation' and to the 'traditions' (παραδόσεις) the writer has delivered (παρέδωκα). The former is turned into its opposite ('I do not commend') in v. 17 (see also v. 22) and is followed by a denunciation of the Eucharistic practices of the readers, while the latter is amplified in v. 23 ('For I received [παρέλαβον] from the Lord what I also delivered [παρέδωκα] to you') with reference to the Eucharistic tradition. In short, while the link between v. 1 and v. 2 is problematic, that between v. 2 and vv. 17-34 is both clear and logical.

For these reasons, it is now my own judgment that the proposed interpolation includes only vv. 3-16 and not v. 2.

b. *The Narrower Context of 1 Corinthians 11.3-16*

Much of the evidence for interpolation relating to the 'narrower' context of 1 Cor. 11.3-16 has already been cited, but three points call for reiteration. First, with the removal of vv. 3-16, vv. 2 and 17 form one logically clear and syntactically complete sentence. Second, there is no apparent substantive or 'tonal' connection between v. 2 and vv. 3-16. Third, there is a clear substantive connection between v. 2 and vv. 17-34. Two additional points, however, must be noted. Fourth, apart from

26. Four different readings are attested for v. 17. As Fee (*The First Epistle to the Corinthians*, pp. 534-35 n. 15) observes, however, 'eventually these all come out at the same place' so far as the sense of the verse is concerned.

27. Cope, '1 Cor. 11.2-16', pp. 435-36.

the obvious fact that both passages have to do with public worship, there is no apparent substantive connection, and indeed little 'tonal' connection, between vv. 3-16 and vv. 17-34. The former verses deal with the attire and/or hairstyle of men and women in worship, while the latter address certain abuses of the Eucharistic practices of the readers. Moreover, as Fee notes, 'the style of argumentation [in vv. 2-16]...is much less impassioned than that in vv. 17-34 (indeed the differences are as night and day)'.[28] Fifth, although vv. 3-16 clearly deal with public worship, Paul explicitly states in v. 18 that *the first point* (πρῶτον) to be made regarding the assembled community has to do with factions within the community. This would make little sense if he had just discussed the attire and/or hairstyle of men and women in Christian worship.

In short, 1 Cor. 11.3-16 neither logically follows 11.2 nor logically precedes 11.17-34. Moreover, without vv. 3-16, v. 2 leads clearly into vv. 17-34, both syntactically and logically. Finally, 11.3-16 constitutes a complete, self-contained unit that can stand on its own, independent of its present context. Thus, the passage may well be an interpolation.

c. *The Broader Context of 1 Corinthians 11.3-16*

According to Trompf's detailed analysis, 1 Cor. 10.1–11.2 and 11.17-34 'hold together as a continuous argument concerned with eating and drinking'.[29] I agree, although I would also include chs. 8 and 9 in the analysis. Chapter 8 discusses whether it is permissible for Christians to eat food offered to idols. This discussion leads, in ch. 9, to the related issue of Christian liberty. Then, beginning at 10.1, Paul draws a series of links between eating and drinking and various forms of unacceptable behavior: (1) Hebrews who ate and drank the 'spiritual food' and 'spiritual drink' in the wilderness but then fell into idolatry and immorality (10.1-13); (2) Christians who 'partake of the table of demons' and 'drink the cup of demons' and thus become guilty of idolatry

28. Fee, *The First Epistle to the Corinthians*, p. 491; cf. n. 2: 'it lacks almost all of the evidences of rhetoric and emotion that pervade the rest of the letter'. Fee also notes (p. 530) that, while in 1 Cor. 11.3-16 Paul 'can appeal to shame, propriety, and custom (as well as theological presuppositions and church practice)', in vv. 17-34 'there is only attack and imperative'.

29. Trompf, 'On Attitudes toward Women', p. 198; see the entire discussion, pp. 198-201. Although my own analysis of 1 Cor. 10.1–11.2 and 11.17-34 is heavily indebted to that of Trompf, it proceeds somewhat differently at certain points.

(10.14-22);[30] and (3) Christians who irresponsibly exercise their liberty by eating food offered to idols and thereby compromise the conscience of their fellow Christians (10.23-30). The third section of ch. 10 leads to the following summary (10.31–11.1):

> So, whether you eat or drink, or whatever you do, do all to the glory of God. Give no offense to Jews or to Greeks or to the church of God, just as I try to please all people in everything I do, not seeking my own advantage, but that of many, that they may be saved. Be imitators of me, as I am of Christ.

The connection between eating and drinking and unacceptable behavior continues in 11.2, 17-34. In v. 2, Paul 'commends' (ἐπαινῶ) the readers because they 'remember' (μέμνησθε) him in everything and maintain the (Eucharistic) 'traditions' (παραδόσεις) even as he delivered (παρέδωκα) them, but in vv. 17-34 he does not 'commend' (οὐκ ἐπαινῶ) them for their misbehavior in the actual administration of the Eucharist. Reinforcing the connection between ch. 10 and 11.17-34 is the fact that 10.14-22 already contains clear allusions to the Eucharist.

The proposed interpolation (1 Cor. 11.3-16), however, has nothing whatsoever to do with eating and drinking or, indeed, with such unacceptable behavior as idolatry, immorality and abuse of Christian liberty. Rather, it constitutes a complete, self-contained unit whose subject matter—the proper attire and/or hairstyle for men and women in Christian worship—appears to be totally unrelated to that of the material both immediately preceding and immediately following. If 1 Corinthians is divided into two letters, as Héring proposes, 11.3-16 interrupts an otherwise connected discussion of 'the bread' and 'the cup of the Lord' (10.14-22 and 11.17-34).[31] Even if 1 Corinthians is regarded as a unit, however, 11.3-16 nevertheless interrupts an otherwise connected discussion of the relation between eating and drinking and various forms of unacceptable behavior (10.1–11.1 and 11.17-34). Thus, the passage appears not to 'fit' at its present location in Paul's Corinthian letter. Indeed, if it belongs anywhere in 1 Corinthians, the most appropriate place would appear to be somewhere in the proximity of ch. 12 or ch. 14, which deal with 'speaking' in public worship.[32]

30. Cope ('First Corinthians 8–10') argues, however, that 1 Cor. 10.1-22 may well be a non-Pauline interpolation.

31. Héring, *The First Epistle*, pp. xiii-xiv.

32. It should be noted, however, that both Schmithals ('Die Korintherbriefe als Briefsammlung') and Jewett ('The Redaction of I Corinthians') regard 11.2-34 as a

The difference in 'tone' between 1 Cor. 11.3-16 and the passage immediately following (vv. 17-34) has already been noted. Fee also points out, however, that 11.3-16 'lacks almost all of the evidences of rhetoric and emotion that pervade the rest of the letter'.[33] Trompf amplifies the point, noting that 'the argumentation of 11.3-16 does not carry the conviction which abounds in the rest of 1 Corinthians'. 'The arguments in defence of head-covering are much less assured and their grounds more diffuse' than elsewhere in the letter. The request that the readers judge for themselves (v. 13) and the appeals to nature (vv. 14 and 15) and custom (v. 16) 'show up as flimsy supports when set beside [Paul's] usual reliance on Christ's commands, the scripture, the kerygma or the Spirit'.[34] All of this, in my judgment, suggests that 1 Cor. 11.3-16 may well be a secondary addition to the text of Paul's Corinthian letter.

d. *Repetition of a Significant Word*

Yet another piece of contextual evidence that 1 Cor. 11.3-16 may be an interpolation must be noted. As was pointed out in Chapter 4, the repetition—near the end of a proposed interpolation or in the verse immediately following—of a significant word or phrase from the verse immediately preceding the passage often indicates the work of 'an editor who is making an insert'.[35] In the case of 1 Cor. 11.3-16, the verb ἐπαινῶ appears both in v. 2 (the verse immediately preceding the proposed interpolation) and in v. 17 (the verse immediately following). This repetition may indicate that the interpolator (or perhaps a later editor) is attempting to pick up again the train of thought that was interrupted by the insertion of the proposed interpolation.

e. *Apparently Insignificant Textual Variants*

A final piece of contextual evidence that 1 Cor. 11.3-16 may have been added secondarily to Paul's Corinthian letter is textual evidence for

separate letter dealing with two aspects of public worship: the attire and/or hairstyle of men and women and the proper observance of the Eucharist.

33. Fee, *The First Epistle to the Corinthians*, p. 491 n. 2.

34. Trompf, 'On Attitudes toward Women', p. 204.

35. Meeks, *The Writings of St. Paul*, p. 41. Meeks makes reference here specifically to 1 Cor. 12.31b–13.13, which separates 12.31a and 14.1, but his remarks are equally applicable to 11.3-16; cf. also 2 Cor. 6.11-13 and 7.24, which are separated by 6.14–7.1, which is widely regarded as an interpolation.

four different readings in the verse immediately following the passage (v. 17): (1) παραγγέλλων οὐκ ἐπαινῶ,[36] (2) παραγγέλλω οὐκ ἐπαινῶν,[37] (3) παραγγέλλων οὐκ ἐπαινῶν,[38] and (4) παραγγέλλω οὐκ ἐπαινῶ.[39] Here, as Fee notes, 'the text shows considerable confusion... as to which is the main verb and which the participle'.[40] It was noted in Chapter 4 that the appearance—immediately preceding, near the beginning, near the end and/or immediately following what appears to be a more-or-less self-contained passage—of one or more apparently insignificant textual variants might indicate that editors or copyists have attempted in different ways to improve what they regarded as a rather rough transition between the passage in question and its immediate context. Just so, the textual variants in 1 Cor. 11.17 appear to reflect different attempts to smooth the transition from v. 16 (and indeed from the entire passage, vv. 3-16) to v. 17; thus, they may suggest that 1 Cor. 11.3-16 is a secondary addition to the Corinthian letter.

f. *Conclusion regarding Contextual Evidence*

There is, in my judgment, considerable contextual evidence suggesting that 1 Cor. 11.3-16 represents a secondary addition to Paul's Corinthian letter. Such evidence, of course, by no means indicates that the passage was composed by someone other than Paul, or even that it was added to the letter by someone other than Paul; for this, other types of evidence would be required.

4. *Linguistic Evidence for Interpolation*

As was noted in Chapter 4, linguistic features can be classified according to the following four types: (1) *distinctively Pauline*; (2) *Pauline, but not distinctively so*; (3) *non-Pauline, but not identifiably post-Pauline*; and (4) *distinctively post-Pauline*. Features of the first type strengthen the case for Pauline authorship, while those of the second type provide somewhat weaker support. Features of the third type strengthen the case against Pauline authorship, and those of the fourth

36. This reading follows ℵ, F, G, Ψ, and the majority of the mmanuscripts.
37. Found in A, C, and the Latin and Syriac versions.
38. Found in B.
39. Found in D* and a minuscule.
40. Fee, *The First Epistle to the Corinthians*, p. 534 n. 15.

type strengthen the case both against Pauline authorship and against Paul's use of material written by someone else (this is particularly true when the features can be identified as characteristically pseudo-Pauline). In what follows, I will discuss the relevant linguistic features of 1 Cor. 11.3-16 in terms of the four types.

It should be noted, however, that it is often difficult to maintain a distinction between *linguistic* and *ideational* features in a passage. In the case of 1 Cor. 11.3-16, for example, the use of both κεφαλή ('head') and φύσις ('nature') involves both. Thus, the assignment of certain features to one or the other of the categories is, to some extent, necessarily arbitrary.

a. *Linguistic Features that Are Distinctively Pauline*

Very few, if any, of the significant linguistic features of 1 Cor. 11.3-16 can be regarded as distinctively Pauline—that is, characteristic of the authentic Pauline letters but not of other early Christian literature. Possible exceptions are καταισχύνειν ('to dishonor') in vv. 4 and 5, ἀτιμία ('disgrace') in v. 14, and perhaps συνήθεια ('practice' or 'custom') in v. 16. Καταισχύνειν appears eight times elsewhere in the authentic letters of Paul[41] and otherwise only four times in early Christian literature (nowhere in the Pseudo-Pauline writings).[42] 'Ατιμία appears five times elsewhere in the authentic letters of Paul[43] and otherwise only twice in early Christian literature (including once in the pseudo-Pauline writings);[44] it is perhaps significant, too, that ἀτιμία and δόξα ('glory') appear as opposites in 2 Cor. 6.8, just as they do in 1 Cor. 11.14-15. Συνήθεια probably appears at one other place in the authentic letters of Paul,[45] and otherwise it is found four times in early Christian literature (nowhere in the pseudo-Pauline writings and only once in the New Testament).[46] It is doubtful whether any of these words should really be

41. 1 Cor. 1.27 (×2); 11.22; 2 Cor. 7.14; 9.4; Rom. 5.5; 9.33; 10.11.

42. Lk. 13.17; 1 Pet. 2.6; 3.16; *Herm. Man.* 15.5.2.

43. 1 Cor. 15.43; 2 Cor. 6.8; 11.21; Rom. 1.26; 9.21.

44. 2 Tim. 2.20; *Diogn.* 5.14. Trompf ('On Attitudes toward Women', p. 204 n. 23) suggests, however, that the usage of both καταισχύνειν and ἀτιμία in 1 Cor. 11.3-16 is 'distinctly narrow in application' as compared with the usages elsewhere in the Pauline letters.

45. It is the better attested reading for 1 Cor. 8.7; many manuscripts, however have συνείδησις ('consciousness' or 'conscience').

46. Jn 18.39; Ignatius, *Eph.* 5.1; *Herm. Man.* 5.2.6; *Diogn.* 2.1.

regarded as distinctively Pauline, but, even if they are, they are insufficiently numerous or striking to provide much positive support for Pauline authorship of 1 Cor. 11.3-16.

b. *Linguistic Features that Are Pauline, But Not Distinctively So*

Many of the linguistic features of 1 Cor. 11.3-16 should be regarded as characteristically but not distinctively Pauline—that is, typical both of the authentic Pauline letters and of other early Christian writings. All other things being equal, the presence of such features may lend some support to the case for Pauline authorship. Included here are such words as θέλειν ('to wish'), εἰδέναι ('to know'), πᾶς ('every'), ἀνήρ ('man'), εἶναι ('to be'), Χριστός ('Christ'), γυνή ('woman'), Θεός ('God'), προσεύχεσθαι ('to pray'), προφητεύειν ('to prophesy'), ἔχειν ('to have'), ὀφείλειν ('to owe'), εἰκών ('image'), δόξα ('glory'), ὑπάρχειν ('to be'), ἄγγελος ('angel'), κρίνειν ('to judge'), διδάσκειν ('to teach'), διδόναι ('to give'), and various pronouns, conjunctions, prepositions, articles, and the like. All of this language is common in early Christian literature and thus in no way distinctively Pauline.

Particular attention should be called to the phrase ἐν κυρίῳ ('in the Lord') in v. 11. This phrase occurs 33 times elsewhere in the authentic letters of Paul,[47] but it also appears 13 times in the pseudo-Pauline writings[48] and once in Revelation.[49] Thus, it cannot be regarded as a distinctively Pauline phrase; within the New Testament, however, it is limited almost exclusively to the Pauline and pseudo-Pauline writings.[50] This suggests that if 1 Cor. 11.3-16 is in fact an interpolation, its linguistic affinities are to be found, at least in part, in the pseudo-Pauline Colossians and Ephesians.

c. *Linguistic Features that Are Non-Pauline, But Not Identifiably Post-Pauline*

Some of the linguistic features of 1 Cor. 11.3-16 appear to be non-Pauline but not identifiably post-Pauline—that is, they appear neither

47. 1 Thess. 3.8; 4.1; 5.12; Gal. 5.10; 1 Cor. 1.31; 4.17; 7.22, 39; 9.1, 2; 15.58; 16.19; 2 Cor. 2.12; 10.17; Rom. 14.14; 16.2, 8, 11, 12 (×2), 13, 22; Phil. 1.14; 2.19, 24, 29; 3.1; 4.1, 2, 4, 10; Phlm. 16, 20.

48. 2 Thess. 3.4, 12; Col. 3.18, 20; 4.7, 17; Eph. 2.21; 4.1, 17; 5.8; 6.1, 10, 21.

49. Rev. 14.13.

50. This may be an indication that pseudo-Pauline writers made use of otherwise distinctively Pauline vocabulary.

elsewhere in the authentic Pauline letters nor in other extant early Christian writings. Such is the case, for example, with the phrase 'praying or prophesying' (προσευχόμενος ἢ προφητεύων; προσευχο-μένη ἢ προφητεύουσα) in vv. 4 and 5, which appears nowhere else in the Pauline corpus or, indeed, in the entire New Testament.[51] The same is true of the adjective ἀκατακάλυπτος in vv. 5 and 13, the cognate verb κατακαλύπτεσθαι in vv. 6 and 7,[52] the verb κομᾶν ('to have long hair') in vv. 14-15, and the cognate noun κόμη ('hair') in v. 15, all of which occur nowhere else in early Christian literature and whose use here appears to be dictated by the distinctive subject matter of the passage.[53] Similarly, ξυρᾶν ('to shave') in vv. 5 and 6 and κείρειν ('to shear') in v. 6 appear nowhere else in the Pauline corpus (including the pseudo-Pauline writings) and elsewhere only rarely in early Christian literature,[54] and περιβόλαιον (v. 15) occurs elsewhere in early Christian literature only once in Hebrews (Heb. 1.12, which is a quotation from Ps. 101.27 LXX) and once in the second-century *Epistle of Aristeas* (158); once again, however, the use of these terms in 1 Cor. 11.3-16 apparently stems from the subject matter of the passage. Finally, φιλόνεικος ('contentious') in v. 16 appears elsewhere in early Christian literature only at *1 Clem.* 45.1, where, however, it is used in a positive, not a negative, sense.[55]

A further example of a linguistic feature in 1 Cor. 11.3-16 that appears to be neither Pauline nor identifiably post-Pauline is the juxta-position of εἰκών ('image') and δόξα ('glory') in the phrase εἰκὼν καὶ δόξα Θεοῦ ('image and glory of God') in v. 7. Although each of the two terms is fairly common, both in the Pauline letters[56] and elsewhere

51. See Trompf, 'On Attitudes toward Women', pp. 203-204 (p. 204 n. 22).

52. The meaning of κατακαλύπτεσθαι and of ἀκατακάλυπτος, like that of κατὰ κεφαλῆς ἔχων (v. 4) is a matter of dispute. For discussion, see, e.g., Murphy-O'Connor, 'Sex and Logic in 1 Corinthians 11:2-16', pp. 483-91; and Fee, *The First Epistle to the Corinthians*, pp. 496-97.

53. For a discussion of some of the questions raised by these terms including how they are to be translated, see, e.g., Dennis Ronald MacDonald, *There is No Male and Female: The Fate of a Dominical Saying in Paul and Gnosticism* (HDR, 20; Philadelphia: Fortress Press, 1987), pp. 73-80, and the literature cited there.

54. Ξυρᾶν at Acts 21.24 and κείρειν at Acts 8.32; 18.18; *1 Clem.* 16.2; *Barn.* 5.2 (all except Acts 18.18 are in quotations from Isa. 53.7).

55. But cf. φιλονεικία in Lk. 22.24 and *Mart. Pol.* 18.1.

56. Apart from 1 Cor. 11.3-11, εἰκών appears six times in the authentic letters of Paul (1 Cor. 15.49 [×2], 2 Cor. 3.18; 4.4; Rom. 1.23; 8.29), and δόξα is found 54

in early Christian literature,[57] nowhere except in 1 Cor. 11.7 are they juxtaposed as apparent synonyms (εἰκὼν καὶ δόξα Θεοῦ).[58]

A final example of a linguistic feature in 1 Cor. 11.3-16 that appears to be neither characteristically Pauline nor identifiably post-Pauline is the reference to 'nature' (φύσις) in v. 14. To be sure, Paul uses the word nine times outside this passage,[59] and it appears occasionally in other early Christian writings,[60] but never in the 'hypostasized' or even 'personified' sense found here, which is reminiscent of contemporary Stoic and some rabbinic Jewish notions.[61] Thus, the usage appears to

times (1 Thess. 2.6, 12, 20; Gal. 1.5; 1 Cor. 2.7, 8; 10.31; 15.40, 41 [×4], 43; 2 Cor. 1.20; 3.7 [×2], 8, 9 [×2], 10, 11 [×2], 18 [×3]; 4.4, 6, 15, 17; 6.8; 8.19, 23; Rom. 1.23; 2.7, 10; 3.7, 23; 4.20; 5.2; 6.4; 8.18, 21; 9.4, 23 [×2]; 11.36; 15.7; 16.27; Phil. 1.11; 2.11; 3.19, 21; 4.19, 20).

57. Εἰκών appears twice in the pseudo-Pauline Colossians (1.15; 3.10) and 14 times elsewhere in the New Testament (Mt. 22.20; Mk 12.16; Lk. 20.24; Heb. 10.1; Rev. 13.14, 15 [×3]; 14.9, 11; 15.2; 16.2; 19.20; 20.4), and δόξα appears 20 times in the pseudo-Pauline writings (2 Thess. 1.9; 2.14; Col. 1.11, 27 [×2]; 3.4; Eph. 1.6, 12, 14, 17, 18; 3.13, 16, 21; 1 Tim. 1.11, 17; 3.16; 2 Tim. 2.10; 4.18; Tit. 2.13) and some 91 times elsewhere in the New Testament.

58. The two words do, however, occasionally appear in the same context in the authentic Pauline letters (2 Cor. 3.18; 4.4; Rom. 1.23). See Murphy-O'Connor, 'Sex and Logic in 1 Corinthians 11:2-16', p. 495, for the argument that Paul juxtaposed δόξα and εἰκών in 1 Cor. 11.7 'in order to signal unambiguously that he was no longer speaking of *anēr*, as he actually is (v. 4), but of *anēr* as he was intended to be by God' (that is, 'the addition of *doxa theou* directed attention to the state of humanity before the Fall').

59. Gal. 2.15; 4.8; Rom. 1.26 (where the cognate adjective φυσικός also appears, as it does in v. 27); 2.14, 27; 11.21, 24 (×3). See Chapter 8, however, for the argument that Rom. 1.26 and 2.14 are parts of a non-Pauline interpolation (Rom. 1.18–2.29).

60. Eph. 2.3; Jas 3.7 (×2); 2 Pet. 1.4; Ignatius, *Eph.* 1.1; Ignatius, *Trall.* 1.1; *Barn.* 10.7; *Diogn.* 9.6.

61. Rom. 1.26-27 and 2.14 are not really parallels, for they do not represent a 'hypostasizing' or 'personification' of 'nature' as a 'quasi-divine' reality or power such as is found in Stoicism and in 1 Cor. 11.14. In Romans, the adjective φυσικός, the prepositional phrase παρὰ φύσιν and the noun φύσις as an adverbial dative should properly be translated, respectively, simply as 'natural', 'unnatural' and 'naturally'. A similar interpretation should be applied to the references to φύσις in Gal. 2.15; 4.8; Rom. 2.27; 11.21, 24. Barrett (*A Commentary on the First Epistle to the Corinthians*, p. 256), among others, maintains that φύσις in 1 Cor. 11.14 refers to 'the natural world as God made it, rather than (in the Stoic manner) [to] Nature as a quasi-divine hypostasis'. This interpretation is far from evident in the passage

be characteristic neither of the Pauline nor of the early post-Pauline Christian writings.

Admittedly the appearance of these apparently non-Pauline but not identifiably Post-Pauline linguistic features cannot be decisive for determining the authorship of 1 Cor. 11.3-16, but, all other things being equal, their very number lends some support to the case for non-Pauline composition.

d. *Linguistic Features that Are Distinctively Post-Pauline*

A number of the linguistic features of 1 Cor. 11.3-16 appear to be distinctively post-Pauline—that is, characteristic of the early post-Pauline Christian writings but not of the authentic letters of Paul. Indeed, what is most striking about these features is that, at least for the most part, they appear to be not only post-Pauline but also distinctively *pseudo*-Pauline. The first such feature is the opening clause in v. 3: θέλω δὲ ὑμᾶς εἰδέναι ('And I wish you to know'). Although each word in the clause, taken individually, is characteristic (but not distinctive) of the authentic Pauline letters,[62] the clause as a whole is not. Paul regularly uses a negative clause to express essentially the same idea: οὐ θέλω (or θέλομεν)...ὑμᾶς ἀγνοεῖν ('I [or 'we'] do not wish you to be ignorant'), followed in every case except one by ἀδελφοί ('brothers');[63] indeed, this negative formulation occurs twice in 1 Corinthians itself (shortly before 1 Cor. 11.3-16 at 10.1 and shortly after at 12.1) and once in 2 Corinthians (1.8). In the one instance where Paul expresses the idea with a positive formulation (Phil. 1.12), he employs words that are distinctively different from those found in 1 Cor. 11.3 (γινώσκειν δὲ

itself, however, and apparently derives from Barrett's assumption that the author of 1 Cor. 11.3-16 must be the same as the author of Romans. For a highly illuminating treatment of the topic, see Helmut Koester, 'φύσις, φυσικός, φυσικῶς', *TDNT*, IX, pp. 251-77 (271-75 [on Paul]).

62. Θέλειν ccours some 53 times outside this passage in the authentic Pauline letters (1 Thess. 2.18; 4.13; Gal. 1.7; 3.2; 4.9, 17, 20, 21; 5.17; 6.12, 13; 1 Cor. 4.19, 21; 7.7, 32, 36, 39; 10.1, 20, 27; 12.1, 18; 14.5, 19, 35; 15.38; 16.7; 2 Cor. 1.8; 5.4; 8.10, 11; 11.12, 32; 12.6, 20 [×2]; Rom. 1.13; 7.15, 16, 18, 19 [×2], 20, 21; 9.16, 18 [×2], 22; 11.25; 13.3; 16.19; Phil. 2.13; Phlm. 14). The infinitive form, εἰδέναι, is found four times in the authentic Pauline letters (1 Thess. 4.4; 5.12; 1 Cor. 2.2; 8.2); it also appears four times, however, in the pseudo-Pauline writings (Col. 2.1; 4.6; Eph. 1.18; Tit. 1.16); otherwise, it appears only twice in the entire New Testament (Lk. 20.7; 22.34). Δέ and ὑμᾶς are, of course, frequent.

63. 1 Thess. 4.13; 1 Cor. 10.1; 12.1; 2 Cor. 1.8; Rom. 1.13; 11.15.

ὑμᾶς βούλομαι, 'and I wish you to know') and, as in all but one of the negative formulations, concludes the clause with ἀδελφοί ('brothers'). The words of 1 Cor. 11.3, however, appear almost *verbatim* in the pseudo-Pauline Col. 2.1 (θέλω γὰρ ὑμᾶς εἰδέναι), their only other occurrence in the entire New Testament. Thus, the opening clause of 1 Cor. 11.3-16 appears to be both non-Pauline and, indeed, pseudo-Pauline in character.

A second linguistic feature of 1 Cor. 11.3-16 that is atypical of the authentic Pauline letters and at least similar to pseudo-Pauline usage is the word κεφαλή ('head'), which appears nine times in the passage.[64] At least the three references in v. 3 are metaphorical, not literal, in their meaning, and the same may well be true of the second reference both in v. 4 and in v. 5 and the reference in v. 10; thus, at least three and perhaps as many as six of the nine references to κεφαλή in 1 Cor. 11.3-16 are metaphorical.[65] Elsewhere in the authentic Pauline letters, however, the word occurs only twice, and, in both instances, it carries its literal meaning: 'head' of the human body.[66] Κεφαλή is more frequent, however, in the pseudo-Pauline writings, where it appears six times,[67] always with a metaphorical rather than a literal meaning: Christ is the κεφαλή of his body, the church (Col. 1.18; Eph. 5.23); the κεφαλή from which the body grows (Col. 2.19; Eph. 4.15-16); the κεφαλή over all things for the church, which is his body (Eph. 1.22); and the κεφαλή of all rule and authority (Col. 2.10). Most significantly, Eph. 5.23, like 1 Cor. 11.3, speaks of man (ἀνήρ) as the κεφαλή of woman (γυνή). It is true that Paul perhaps hints at a metaphorical use

64. Three times in v. 3, twice each in vv. 4 and 5, and once each in vv. 7 and 10. On κεφαλή, see Heinrich Schlier, 'κεφαλή, ἀνακεφαλαιόομαι', *TDNT*, III, pp. 673-82.

65. Scroggs ('Paul and the Eschatological Woman', pp. 297-302 [298-99 n. 41] and others have argued that the meaning of κεφαλή here is 'source', not 'head' in the sense of 'leader' or 'ruler', and that the point being made has to do with the order of creation rather than with importance, authority, or preeminence; cf., e.g., Stephen Bedale, 'The Meaning of κεφαλή in the Pauline Epistles', *JTS* 5 (1954), pp. 211-15. Although I am not persuaded at this point (indeed, there may even be a *double entendre*), the fact remains that, however κεφαλή is to be in interpreted in v. 3, the reference is metaphorical, not literal.

66. Rom. 12.20 is a quotation of Prov. 25.21-22, and 1 Cor. 12.21 is a part of Paul's analogy between the human body and the church as the 'body of Christ' (1 Cor. 12.12-27).

67. Col. 1.18; 2.10, 19; Eph. 1.22; 4.15; 5.23.

of κεφαλή in 1 Cor. 12.12-27, where he speaks of the church as 'the body of Christ' (cf. 1 Cor. 6.15a; 10.16b-17; Rom. 12.4-5), and in 2 Cor. 11.2, where he refers to Christ as the 'husband' (ἀνήρ) of the Church (cf. Rom. 7.1-6, esp. v. 4), but it is only in the pseudo-Pauline writings that the metaphor of Christ as the 'head' (κεφαλή) is actually employed. Thus, the metaphorical use of κεφαλή in 1 Cor. 11.3-16 appears to be not only non-Pauline but also pseudo-Pauline.

A third linguistic feature of 1 Cor. 11.3-16 that is non-Pauline but 'reminiscent of deutero-Pauline terminology' consists of 'words chosen to stress shameful actions or encourage propriety'.[68] As already noted, such is not the case with καταισχύνειν ('to dishonor') in vv. 4 and 5, ἀτιμία ('disgrace') in v. 14, and ὀφελεῖν ('to owe'). Αἰσχρός ('disgraceful', v. 6), however, occurs nowhere else in the authentic Pauline letters and is found elsewhere in the New Testament only in the pseudo-Pauline writings (twice)[69] and once in a passage regarded by many as another non-Pauline interpolation dealing with women (1 Cor. 14.35). Similarly, πρέπον ('proper', v. 13) appears nowhere else in the authentic letters of Paul,[70] but the cognate verb, πρέπειν, occurs three times with the same meaning in the pseudo-Pauline writings[71] and only twice more in the entire New Testament.[72] Thus, it appears that the words αἰσχρός and πρέπον represent linguistic features that are non-Pauline and, indeed, pseudo-Pauline.

A fourth example of a pseudo-Pauline linguistic feature in 1 Cor. 11.3-16 is perhaps to be found in the use of the verb κτίζειν for 'create' (v. 9). Elsewhere in the authentic Pauline letters, the verb appears only at Rom. 1.25 in participial form as a circumlocution for 'God';[73] it is found seven times in the pseudo-Pauline writings,[74] however, and in six of the seven, as in 1 Cor. 11.9, it refers to the act of creating rather than to the creator.[75]

68. Trompf, 'On Attitudes toward Women', p. 204.

69. Eph. 5.12; Tit. 1.11.

70. Elsewhere in the New Testament, it appears only at Mt. 3.15.

71. Eph. 5.3; 1 Tim. 2.10; Tit. 2.1.

72. Heb. 2.10; 7.26.

73. For the argument that 1.18–2.29 is a non-Pauline interpolation, however, see Chapter 8. The cognate noun, κτίσις, appears nine times in the authentic Pauline letters (Gal. 6.15; 2 Cor. 5.17; Rom. 1.20, 25; 8.19, 20, 21, 22, 39) but only twice in the pseudo-Pauline writings (Col. 1.15, 23).

74. Col. 1.16; 3.10; Eph. 2.10, 15; 3.9; 4.24; 1 Tim. 4.3.

75. The one exception is Col. 3.10.

A fifth example of an apparently non-Pauline and perhaps post-Pauline linguistic feature in 1 Cor. 11.3-16 is the clause, εἰ δέ τις δοκεῖ... in v. 16. To be sure, a similar clause appears at five other places in the authentic Pauline letters, three of them in 1 Corinthians.[76] Although the meaning of the clause is clear in each of the other instances ('If anyone supposes [himself/herself/ to be...'), the translation of the verb δοκεῖ in 1 Cor. 11.16 is problematic. Here it cannot carry its usual meaning of 'suppose', 'think' or even 'seem'; thus, suggestions include 'is disposed', 'wants' and 'intends to be'. Moreover, in every case except 1 Cor. 11.16, the clause is followed either by an imperative[77] or by an indicative that relates clearly and logically to the prior condition.[78] In 11.16, however, the logical relation of ἡμεῖς τοιαύτην συνήθειαν οὐκ ἔχομεν οὐδὲ αἱ ἐκκλησίαι τοῦ Θεου ('we do not have such a custom nor [do] the churches of God') to εἰ δέ τις δοκεῖ φιλόνεικος is anything but clear. Thus, the clause, εἰ δέ τις δοκεῖ... in 11.16 appears to be distinctively different from the similar clause elsewhere in the authentic Pauline letters. Further, Robert Jewett suggests that it may represent 'a garbled adaptation of [the] rather similar clause in 1 Cor. 14.37': εἴ τις δοκεῖ προφήτης εἶναι ἢ πνευματικός ('if anyone supposes himself/herself to be a prophet').[79] Indeed, it should be noted that similar clauses also appear at 1 Cor. 3.18 and 8.12. Thus, the clause in v. 16 may derive from someone (presumably later than Paul) who was familiar with 1 Cor. 3.18, 8.12 and/or 14.37.

A sixth example of an apparently non-Pauline and perhaps pseudo-Pauline linguistic feature in 1 Cor. 11.3-16 is the phrase αἱ ἐκκλησίαι τοῦ Θεοῦ ('the churches of God') in v. 16. This phrase appears also at

76. 1 Cor. 3.18; 8.2; 14.37; Gal. 6.3; Phil. 3.4. The only other occurrence of the clause in the New Testament is at Jas 1.26.

77. 1 Cor. 3.18b: 'If anyone among you supposes [himself/herself] to be wise in this age, let him/her become foolish, in order that he/she may become wise'; 1 Cor. 14.37: 'If anyone supposes [himself/herself] to be a prophet or a "spiritual", let him/her acknowledge that the things I write to you are a command of the Lord'.

78. 1 Cor. 8.2: 'If anyone supposes [himself/herself] to know anything, he/she does not yet know as it is necessary to know'; Gal. 6.3: 'For if anyone supposes [himself/herself] to be something, being nothing, he/she deceives himself/herself'; Phil. 3.4b: 'If anyone else supposes [himself/herself] to have confidence in [the] flesh, I [have] more'.

79. Jewett, 'The Redaction of I Corinthians', p. 427. Without accepting the view that 1 Cor. 11.3-16 as a whole is a non-Pauline interpolation, Jewett does argue (pp. 427-29) that v. 16 is such an interpolation.

1 Thess. 2.14 and 2 Thess. 1.4, but nowhere else in the New Testament; only at 2 Thess. 1.4, however, does the phrase occur absolutely, as in 1 Cor. 11.16, and 2 Thessalonians should probably be regarded as pseudo-Pauline. In 1 Thess. 2.14, the full phrase is τῶν ἐκκλησιῶν τοῦ Θεοῦ τῶν οὐσῶν ἐν τῇ Ἰουδαίᾳ ἐν Χριστῷ Ἰησοῦ ('the churches of God that are in Judea in Christ Jesus'). Furthermore, as Trompf notes, 1 Corinthians is elsewhere 'noted for the consistent use of the phrase "church of God" in the singular, and of all places just before and after the controversial passage'.[80] 'Apart from plural references to the churches of Galatia and Asia in 16.1, 19, the *appeal to authority* with the plural ἐκκλησίαι of 11.16b links with the comparable appeal in 14.34 (a better substantiated interpolation) to "the churches of the saints", and thus the usage is more likely to be deutero-Pauline than not.'[81] Thus, αἱ ἐκκλησίαι τοῦ Θεοῦ, used absolutely, may well represent a distinctively non-Pauline and, indeed, pseudo-Pauline linguistic feature.[82]

Finally, although the exact meaning of the phrase is problematic, the use of ἐξουσίαν ἔχειν ('to have authority') in v. 10 also appears to be non-Pauline and perhaps even pseudo-Pauline in character. Paul normally uses ἐξουσία in a non-personalized way to mean 'authority' in the sense of 'power', 'right' or 'freedom',[83] and the phrase ἐξουσίαν ἔχειν apparently has a quite different meaning elsewhere in 1 Corinthians.[84] In 1 Cor. 15.24, however, ἐξουσία is juxtaposed with ἀρχή and δύναμις, and in Rom. 13.1-2 (in the plural) it is juxtaposed with ἄρχοντες in such a way as to suggest a personified reference to 'rulers'

80. 1 Cor. 10.32; 11.22; cf. also 1.2; 15.9.

81. Trompf, 'On Attitudes toward Women', p. 203 n. 18.

82. Trompf ('On Attitudes toward Women', p. 203) calls attention to 'that curious, dissociating, self-consciously authoritarian *hēmeis* in v. 16, with the accompanying appeal to customs prevailing among the "churches of God"' as an example of a non-Pauline linguistic feature; acknowledging (p. 203 n. 18) that 'there are other places where, in being defensive, Paul associates himself with others', Trompf nevertheless asserts that 'Paul's habit is to appeal to his own labors, not to make the kind of pontifical pronouncements based on ecclesiastical authority we find in 11:16'.

83. See 1 Cor. 7.37; 8.9; 9.4, 5, 6, 12, 18; 2 Cor. 10.8; 13.10; Rom. 9.21.

84. 1 Cor. 7.37; 9.4; cf. Rom. 9.11; see Trompf, 'On Attitudes toward Women', p. 204 (204 n. 24).

or 'governing authorities'.[85] Then, in the pseudo-Pauline Colossians and Ephesians, ἐξουσία is consistently used in a personalized manner to speak of (supernatural and evil) powers and rulers.[86] Which, if any, of these meanings is intended for ἐξουσία in 1 Cor. 11.10 is far from certain; indeed, the entire phrase, ἐξουσίαν ἔχειν ἐπὶ τῆς κεφαλῆς ('to have authority over' or 'upon the head'), is filled with difficulties.[87] Nevertheless, the association of ἐξουσίαν ἔχειν ἐπὶ τῆς κεφαλῆς with διὰ τοὺς ἀγγέλους ('because of the angels'), itself highly problematic,[88] at least raises the possibility of a meaning for ἐξουσία similar to that found in Colossians and Ephesians: if the angels are to be regarded as evil powers, then the meaning may be that women must have a ruler (and a sign of this ruler on their heads) in order not to come under the domination of the angels. If so, then the use of ἐξουσία in 1 Cor. 11.10 is yet another indication that the entire passage may have more affinities with the pseudo-Pauline than with the authentically Pauline writings.

e. *Conclusion*

This examination of significant linguistic features in 1 Cor. 11.3-16 suggests: (1) that very few, if any, of these features are 'distinctively Pauline'; (2) that many are 'Pauline but not distinctively so'; (3) that some are 'non-Pauline but not identifiably post-Pauline; and (4) that a significant number are 'distinctively post-Pauline' and indeed pseudo-Pauline. Thus I conclude that the evidence provided by the linguistic features of 1 Cor. 11.3-16 significantly strengthens the case both against Pauline authorship of the passage and against Paul's inclusion of the passage in the Corinthian letter. Indeed, all other things being equal, this evidence would, in my judgment, 'tip the scales' toward viewing the passage as a non-Pauline interpolation.

85. Cf. also Tit. 3.1. For the view that Rom. 13.1-7 is a non-Pauline interpolation, see, e.g., Barnikol, 'Römer 13'; and Kallas, 'Romans xiii.1-7'.

86. Col. 1.13, 16; 2.10, 15; Eph. 1.21; 2.2; 3.10; 6.12.

87. For a discussion of the problems, with references to the relevant literature, see MacDonald, *There Is No Male and Female*, pp. 76-79.

88. See MacDonald, *There Is No Male and Female*, pp. 76-79, and the literature there cited.

5. *Ideational Evidence for Interpolation*

The ideational evidence for regarding 1 Cor. 11.3-16 as a non-Pauline interpolation is quite strong. The first and most obvious consideration is what the passage says regarding the relation between men and women. Despite attempts 'to rescue the curious passage in 1 Corinthians 11 from ill-odor',[89] its subordination of woman to man is difficult to deny. If, however, the Pastorals, Ephesians and Colossians are regarded as pseudo-Pauline, and 1 Cor. 14.34-35 as a non-Pauline gloss, there is no other passage in the entire Pauline corpus which might even possibly be interpreted as advocating any form of male priority and female subordination. Surely, this fact, coupled with Paul's clear statement of equality in Gal. 3.28, his very positive references to female co-workers,[90] and the other indications of his 'egalitarian' attitude toward women,[91] carries some weight in determining the authenticity of the verses under consideration. To carry the point a bit further, however, 1 Cor. 11.3-16 is remarkably similar in subject matter, vocabulary and 'tone' to 1 Cor. 14.34-35, which is widely regarded as a non-Pauline interpolation, as well as to Col. 3.18, Eph. 5.22-33, 1 Tim. 2.9-15 and Tit. 2.3-5, all of which are likely pseudo-Pauline. In particular, the closest parallel to the notion that man is the κεφαλή of woman, Christ the κεφαλή of man, and God the κεφαλή of Christ is to be found in the pseudo-Pauline Eph. 5.21-24 (especially v. 22).[92] In short, the attitude toward women expressed in 1 Cor. 11.3-16 appears

89. Trompf, 'On Attitudes toward Women', p. 196. See, e.g., Else Kähler, *Die Frau in den paulinischen Briefen unter besonderer Berücksichtigung des Begriffes der Unterordnung* (Zürich: Gotthelf, 1960), pp. 45-46; M.D. Hooker, 'Authority on her Head: An Examination of I Cor. xi.10', *NTS* 10 (1964), pp. 410-16; and Scroggs, 'Paul and the Eschatological Woman'.

90. 1 Cor. 16.19; Phil. 4.2-3; Rom. 16.1-16; cf. also, e.g., Acts 16.14-15; 17.34; 18.18, 26.

91. See, e.g., Trompf, 'On Attitudes toward Women', pp. 210-12, for a summary of the evidence.

92. Trompf ('On Attitudes toward Women', p. 205) also suggests that the 'subordinationism' of Christ to God in 1 Cor. 11.3 is 'stated there with noticeably less subtlety than in other Pauline passages (3.23; 8.6; 15.27-28; Rom. 1.3-4; 8.3; Gal. 1.4; 4.4; Phil. 2.11; Col. 1.15, 19; cf. 1 Tim. 2.5; 6.13-16; 2 Tim. 1.9-10)'. Apparently, the pseudo-Pauline concept is related to certain gnostic or proto-gnostic speculation; see, e.g., Schlier, 'κεφαλή, ἀνακεφαλαιόομαι', pp. 680-81 (676-78).

to be not only non-Pauline (and even anti-Pauline) but also characteristic of the pseudo-Pauline writings.[93]

Closely related to this first ideational feature, as Trompf notes, are the allusions to Genesis in 1 Cor. 11.7-9, 12a, which 'bear a closer resemblance to the more disturbing (dare I say sexist?) argumentation of the deutero-Pauline 1 Tim. 2.13-15 than generally admitted'.[94] According to Trompf, both passages presuppose a setting of worship, both begin with a statement regarding what is appropriate in worship, both are concerned with the attire and role of women, and both appeal to the order of creation to support what they say. Thus, again, 1 Cor. 11.3-16 appears to have greater affinities with the pseudo-Pauline than with the authentically Pauline writings.

A third ideational reason for regarding 1 Cor. 11.3-16 as a non-Pauline interpolation is that in his undoubtedly authentic writings Paul nowhere indicates any concern for such 'incidental' matters as whether men and women should pray and prophesy with their heads covered or uncovered or whether their hair should be long or short or confined or loose. It is impossible to say with certainty just what the actual practices in ancient times were regarding head-coverings and hairstyles,[95] but many scholars believe that the author of the passage in question

93. The following parallel to the apparent 'mitigation' of the subordinationism in vv. 11-12, which occurs twice in the *Gen. Rab.* (8.9 and 22.2), is suggestive: 'In the past Adam was created from dust and Eve was created from Adam; but henceforth it shall be *in our image, after our likeness* [Gen 1:26]: neither man without woman nor woman without man, and neither without the Shekinah' (my emphasis). Although the *Genesis Rabbah* dates from the late-fifth or early-sixth century, it is likely that much of its material originated earlier, and the particular quotation in question is specifically ascribed, respectively, to Rabbi Simlai (c. 250 CE) and Rabbi Akiba (c. 135 CE). If these ascriptions are correct then the parallel to 1 Cor. 11.11-12 existed in an oral form in the early-second century, and it is possible that these verses are based upon earlier rabbinic teaching. Of course, it is also possible that the rabbinic parallel is based upon the New Testament passage. See Madeleine Boucher, 'Some Unexplored Parallels to 1 Cor 11,11-12 and Gal 3,28: The New Testament on the Role of Women', *CBQ* 31 (1969), pp. 50-58.

94. Trompf, 'On Attitudes toward Women', p. 205.

95. See John Coolidge Hurd, Jr, *The Origin of I Corinthians* (New York: Seabury; London: SPCK, 1965), p. 184, especially n. 2. William M. Ramsay (*The Cities of St. Paul: Their Influence on His Life and Thought* [London: Hodder & Stoughton, 1907], pp. 201-205) cites Dio Chrysostom to the effect that the oriental custom of veiling women was practiced in Tarsus and suggests that this accounts for Paul's teachings on the subject.

(assumed by them to be Paul) is arguing for the introduction (or, more likely, the preservation) of an oriental and, specifically, Jewish custom against the Greek custom.[96] Except in matters of sexual purity, Paul appears to have had little concern for such differences between Jews and Greeks; indeed, he expressly disavows such concern in his well-known claim that he has 'become all things to all people' (1 Cor. 9.19-23; cf. 10.32-33), which sounds very much like 'when in Rome, do as the Romans do'.[97] Even in the potentially explosive matter of eating meat that had been offered to idols, Paul refused to set forth any 'legalistic' requirements (1 Cor. 8–10; cf. Rom. 14). Finally, when Paul does give directions or advice regarding specific matters of conduct (again, except in matters of sexual purity), he characteristically supports such directions or advice not by general theological arguments but rather by pragmatic considerations, such as the nearness of the parousia and the need for complete freedom to serve God (1 Cor. 7.26-35), the effects of one's conduct on other Christians (1 Cor. 8; 10.23-29), the edification of the church (1 Cor. 14), or the effect on outsiders (1 Cor. 14.23-25). Indeed, although he regards 1 Cor. 11.3-16 as authentically Pauline, Fee acknowledges that 'there is nothing quite like this in [Paul's] extant letters, where he argues for maintaining a custom, let alone predicating a large part of the argument on shame, propriety, and custom'.[98] Trompf goes even further:

> The onus of proof is now on those who wish to argue that St. Paul, the apostle to the Gentiles, who has just given careful but (by Jewish standards) conspicuously liberal conditions for dining with pagans (10.25-9; cf. Acts 15.20a; 21.25), now wants to impose a very culture-bound regulation which has its basis in the kerygma or fundamental teachings of the earliest church.[99]

96. See Schmithals, *Gnosticism in Corinth*, p. 238; cf. Gerhard Deutsch and Kaufmann Kohler, 'Bareheadedness', *JE*, II, pp. 530-33; Anonymous, 'Head, Covering of', *UJEnc*, V, pp. 262-63; Anonymous, 'Covering of the Head', *EJR*, p. 101; and Meir Ydit, 'Head, Covering of the', *EncJud*, VIII, pp. 2-6.

97. Obviously Paul would have set certain limits to such a policy, but it seems highly unlikely that these limits would have included the matter of head-covering or hairstyle.

98. Fee, *The First Epistle to the Corinthians*, p. 530.

99. Trompf, 'On Attitudes toward Women', p. 202. As regards 'the kerygma or fundamental teachings of the earliest church', see καθὼς παρέδωκα ὑμῖν τὰς παραδόσεις κατέχετε in v. 2 (which, however, I no longer regard as a part of the interpolation).

A fourth ideational reason for regarding 1 Cor. 11.3-16 as a non-Pauline interpolation is its notion of 'man' (ἀνήρ) as the 'glory' (δόξα) of God (v. 7).[100] To be sure, Paul quite often uses the word δόξα, and in a variety of ways, but he never speaks of humans, *in their present existence*, as the 'glory' of God. Indeed, Paul insists quite explicitly and pointedly that, because of sin, humans have lost the 'glory' of God which they had in the beginning (Rom. 3.23).[101] As Scroggs expresses it, 'Man does not possess this δόξα any more than he retains the image [of God]'.[102] One might argue, of course, that although Rom. 3.23 refers to man's *actual* status *subsequent* to the Fall, what 1 Cor. 11.7 has in mind is the status of man *prior* to the Fall and/or his *intended* status.[103] Such an argument, however, has no basis in the text itself and would appear to depend upon certain theological and/or literary presuppositions rather than an exegesis of the passage in question. Scroggs is surely correct in his observation that 1 Cor. 11.7 refers to the *actual* status of 'man *in his present existence* as the image and glory of God'.[104] Elsewhere in the authentic Pauline letters, however, 'glory' is essentially an eschatological concept, applied not to the present status of humankind but only to the new creation that is still to be consummated in the future (see, e.g., Rom. 5.2; 8.18).[105] To be sure, Murphy-O'Connor argues that 'in Christ humanity once again exists as God intended from the beginning, for Christ is the model of authentic humanity (2 Cor. 4.4-6)'. Thus, he can appeal to 2 Thess. 1.14 and 2 Cor. 3.18 as evidence that the theme of 'glory' in 1 Cor. 11.7 is 'fully at home in the authentic letters' of Paul.[106] In response, three points are to be noted: (1) 2 Thessalonians is probably a pseudo-Pauline writing; thus, it should not be used to establish Paul's thought. (2) In any case, there is no reference in 2 Thess. 2.14 to humans *being* the 'glory' of God; rather, the verse speaks of *obtaining* 'the glory of our Lord Jesus

100. On δόξα, see Gerhard Kittel and Gerhard von Rad, 'δοκέω, δόξα, δοξάζω, συνδοξάζω, ἔνδοξος, ἐνδοξάζω, παράδοξος', *TDNT*, II, pp. 233-53.

101. See Robin Scroggs, *The Last Adam: A Study in Pauline Anthropology* (Philadelphia: Fortress Press, 1966), pp. 73-74.

102. Scroggs, *The Last Adam*, p. 70 n. 30.

103. See, e.g., Murphy-O'Connor, 'Sex and Logic in 1 Corinthians 11:2-16', pp. 495-96.

104. Scroggs, *The Last Adam*, p. 70 n. 30 (emphasis added).

105. Scroggs, *The Last Adam*, especially pp. 64-65.

106. Murphy-O'Connor, 'The Non-Pauline Character of 1 Corinthians 11:2-16?', pp. 619-20.

Christ' as the *goal* of the Christian calling and thus appears to look toward the future, not the present. (3) Similarly, 2 Cor. 3.18 does not characterize humans, in their present condition, as *being* the 'glory' of God; rather, it refers to 'the glory of the Lord' as something that humans may *behold*[107] and toward which they may progressively move through a process of transformation (μεταμορφούμεθα ἀπὸ δόξης εἰς δόξαν). In short, according to Scroggs, 1 Cor. 11.7 represents 'an exception to Paul's usual practice, for which δόξα is an eschatological term', for 'Paul has "lapsed" here into non-eschatological thinking'.[108] My own suggestion, however, is that it is precisely this 'lapse' into non-eschatological thinking that betrays the passage as non-Pauline.

A fifth ideational reason for regarding 1 Cor. 11.3-16 as a non-Pauline interpolation is that the idea of being taught by nature in v. 14 (ἡ φύσις αὐτὴ διδάσκει ὑμᾶς) occurs nowhere in the undoubtedly authentic Pauline writings, although it is common in Greek philosophy generally, and in Stoicism in particular.[109] Many scholars have argued otherwise, asserting that Paul, like contemporary rabbinic Judaism, did hold to a notion of a universal moral law or a 'law of nature' and citing Rom. 1.26-27 and 2.14 as parallels to the passage in question (cf. also Rom. 2.27; 11.21, 24; Gal. 2.15; 4.8).[110] I will argue in Chapter 8 that Rom. 1.18–2.29 is a non-Pauline interpolation. Even if the passage is authentically Pauline, however, its references to 'nature' are not really parallels to 1 Cor. 11.14. They do not represent a 'hypostasizing' of 'nature' as a 'quasi-divine' reality or power such as is found in Stoicism and in 1 Cor. 11.14. The adjective φυσικός, the prepositional phrase παρὰ φύσιν, and the noun φύσις as an adverbial dative should

107. Or possibly 'reflect'. For a detailed analysis of the language of 2 Cor. 3.18, see, e.g., Rudolf Bultmann, *The Second Letter to the Corinthians* (trans. Roy A. Harrisville; Minneapolis: Augsburg, 1985), pp. 90-96.

108. Scroggs, *The Last Adam*, p. 70 n. 30.

109. See Morton Scott Enslin, *The Ethics of Paul* (Apex edn; New York: Abingdon, 1957), pp. 19-23, 91, 200.

110. See, e.g., Alan Richardson, *An Introduction to the Theology of the New Testament* (New York: Harper and Brothers, 1958), p. 49; Robert M. Grant, 'Hellenistic Elements in 1 Corinthians', in Allen Wikgren (ed.), *Early Christian Origins: Studies in Honor of Harold R. Willoughby* (Chicago: Quadrangle, 1961), pp. 60-66 (62); and Barrett, *A Commentary on the First Epistle*, p. 256. For a highly illuminating treatment of the topic, see Koester, 'φύσις, φυσικός, φυσικῶς', especially pp. 271-75 (on Paul).

properly be translated, respectively, simply as 'natural', 'unnatural' and 'naturally'.

A sixth ideational reason for regarding 1 Cor. 11.3-16 as a non-Pauline interpolation is the improbability that Paul would have stated that 'for a man to wear long hair is degrading to him' (v. 14b), particularly if the tradition in Acts 18.18 is accurate, which reports that 'at Cenchreae he cut his hair, for he had a vow'.[111] Even if that tradition is not accurate, and Paul himself did not let his own hair grow long, it is nevertheless unlikely that a Jew would have adopted such an attitude toward long hair on a man, because, as Robert C. Dentan points out, 'long hair on men was greatly admired' in the Old Testament,[112] and it appears that Palestinian Judaism, at least, preserved the custom of long hair for men in New Testament times.[113] The statement in 1 Cor. 11.14 sounds much more Greek or Roman than Jewish,[114] and such concern about the length of hair and other related matters would seem to be more characteristic of the post-Pauline than of the Pauline period.[115]

111. I am indebted to my colleague, Francisco O. Garcia-Treto, for calling this to my attention. Cf. also Acts 21.23-24. On the vow, which would undoubtedly have been a Nazarite vow, see, e.g., J. Coert Rylaarsdam, 'Nazarite', *IDB*, III, pp. 526-27, and the bibliography cited there.

112. Robert C. Dentan, 'Hair', *IDB*, II, p. 512.

113. See John L. McKenzie, *Dictionary of the Bible* (Milwaukee: Bruce, 1965), p. 333.

114. See Tertullian, *De corona* 4; Dio Chrysostom, *Or.* 33. 48. McKenzie (*Dictionary of the Bible*, p. 333) says that the author (whom he regards as Paul) 'in speaking to the Corinthians accepts the Roman rather than the Palestinian style'. Barrett (*A Commentary on the First Epistle*, pp. 256-57) observes that Hellenistic portraiture showed men with short hair and women with long hair and cites an interesting parallel to 1 Cor. 11.14-15 in Epictetus, *Diss.* 1.16, 9-14: 'Let us leave the main works (ἔργα) of nature (φύσις), and behold her minor works (πάρεργα). Is there anything less useful than the hair on the chin? What then? Has not nature used this also in the most fitting way possible? Has she not by means of it distinguished the male and the female? Has not the nature of each one of us immediately cried out from afar, I am a man; on this understanding approach me, speak to me, seek nothing else; here are the signs? Again, in regard to women, as she has mingled something gentler in the voice so she has taken away the hair (of the chin)... For this reason we ought to keep the signs that God has given, we ought not to throw them away, nor to confound, so far as we can, the distinctions of the sexes'. Lucian (*Dialogi meretricii* 5.3) similarly shows that it was considered 'unnatural' for a woman to shave (as did the most manly, ἀνδρώδεις, of athletes).

115. Cf. 1 Tim. 2.9; 1 Pet. 3.3.

In short, 1 Cor. 11.3-16 contains a number of ideas that appear to be non-Pauline and, indeed, even anti-Pauline.

6. *Comparative Evidence for Interpolation*

In the preceding sections of this chapter, it has been noted that a number of the linguistic and ideational features of 1 Cor. 11.3-16 appear to be more closely akin to those of the pseudo-Pauline writings than to those of the authentic Pauline letters. As regards linguistic features, a number of words and phrases in the passage were characterized as 'non-Pauline', 'distinctively post-Pauline', and even 'pseudo-Pauline'. As regards ideas, the attitude toward women in 1 Cor. 11.3-16 is both significantly different from that exhibited elsewhere in the authentic Pauline letters[116] and remarkably similar to that found in the pseudo-Pauline and other post-Pauline writings. The same appears to be true regarding a number of other ideas expressed in the passage. This suggests that 1 Cor. 11.3-16 was both composed and inserted into the Corinthian letter by someone other than—indeed, later than—Paul.

7. *Situational Evidence for Interpolation*

Apart from 1 Cor. 14.34-35, which is widely regarded as a non-Pauline interpolation, and 1 Cor. 11.3-16, there is nothing at all in the authentic Pauline letters to suggest that Paul regarded either the role of women in Christian worship or the relation between women and men as problematic. Quite to the contrary, Gal. 3.28, 1 Corinthians 7 and Paul's incidental references to women with whom he shared the work and leadership of the Christian churches make it clear that Paul was radically egalitarian regarding such matters. The pseudo-Pauline writings and 1 Peter, however, indicate quite unmistakably that such matters had become problematic in the post-Pauline Church. This suggests that 1 Cor. 11.3-16 was likely composed after Paul's lifetime.

8. *Motivational Evidence for Interpolation*

The likely motivation both for the composition of 1 Cor. 11.3-16 and for its insertion into Paul's Corinthian letter has already been indicated:

116. With the possible exception of 1 Cor. 14.34-35, which is widely regarded as a non-Pauline interpolation.

the status and role of women, as well as their relation to men, had become problematic in the post-Pauline church, and it now appeared desirable to have 'Paul' himself address the issue. Thus, the matter was addressed both in the pseudo-Pauline writings[117] and by means of interpolations in the authentically Pauline letters.[118]

9. *Locational Evidence for Interpolation*

As to why 1 Cor. 11.3-16 would have been inserted precisely at its present location in the Corinthian letter, since it so obviously breaks the context, one can only guess.[119] Trompf suggests that the choice of location can best be understood by assuming a link between 11.3-16 and 14.33b-35(6). The latter passage, intended to silence women in worship and thus 'to prevent uncontrolled spiritism and disorder in the assembly', quite appropriately was interjected 'at the climax of Paul's treatment of glossalalia and spiritism in church worship'. The former, perhaps intended 'to lead up to the heavy-handed statements against speaking', was inserted 'into the previous section on eating and drinking', which 'at least concerned public worship'. Indeed, in Trompf's view, 'it is difficult to imagine another place where the intrusion [of 11.3-16] could have been made (by a simple use of *de*, cf. 11.3) without altering the text of the original'.[120]

It is quite possible, however, that the passage was composed for some other occasion and only secondarily inserted into Paul's letter. Indeed, the editor who inserted the passage may even have thought that Paul himself was its author, in which case the problem would simply have been that of determining exactly where to locate it among the other materials that now make up the letter.[121] The parts of the present

117. Col. 3.18-19; Eph. 5.22-33; 1 Tim. 2.8-15; Tit. 2.3-5; cf. also 1 Pet. 3.1-7.

118. 1 Cor. 11.3-16; 14.34-35.

119. Betz, in speaking of 2 Cor. 6.14–7.1 as an interpolation, can only refer to 'reasons unknown to us' ('2 Cor 6:14–7:1', p. 108).

120. Trompf, 'On Attitudes toward Women', pp. 214-15.

121. The problem of the relationship between this and other interpolations in the authentic Pauline materials, on the one hand, and the pseudo-Pauline writings, on the other hand, needs much further study. As has been noted, there are definite similarities between 1 Cor. 11.3-16 and both Colossians and Ephesians, on the one hand, and 1 Timothy, on the other hand. This suggests the possibility that the interpolation comes from the same source (or sources) as the pseudo-Pauline writings.

letter may either have originally been parts of different letters or, if parts of the same letter, have somehow been accidentally disarranged. The editor, then, may either simply have left the materials in the order in which he/she found them, attempting only to provide or improve the transitions, or, less likely, have rearranged them in what appeared to be the best order. It is possible, of course, that 11.3-16 was inserted into what was otherwise a reasonably orderly and well-arranged letter, but the likelihood of other interpolations in the Corinthian correspondence argues against this possibility.[122]

If it was an editor who decided where to locate the passage, it may be that the admonition to 'give no offense to Jews or to Greeks or to the church of God' (10.32) provided the opening for a discussion of attire and/or hairstyles in worship. It is also possible that the basic principle was one of verbal parallels. For example, the references to 'the church of God' (ἡ ἐκκλησία τοῦ Θεοῦ) both in 10.32 and in 11.22 (see also 'church' in 11.18) may have suggested the insertion of 11.3-16, with its concluding reference to 'the churches of God' (αἱ ἐκκλησίαι τοῦ Θεοῦ), between the two. Other verbal parallels between 11.3-16 and its immediate context include θέλω ('I wish') in v. 3 (cf. 10.1, 20, 27; 12.1, 18); κεφαλή ('head') in vv. 3, 4, 5, 7, and 10 (cf. 12.21); καταισχύνειν ('to dishonor') in vv. 4 and 5 (cf. 11.22); δόξα ('glory') in vv. 7 (×2) and 15 (cf. 10.31); and ἐν ὑμῖν αὐτοῖς κρίνατε ('judge for yourselves') in v. 13 (cf. κρίνατε ὑμεῖς ὅι φημι in 10.15). To be sure, such verbal parallels might be cited as arguments for Pauline authorship of 1 Cor. 11.3-16, but, as already noted, the significant linguistic differences between this passage and the authentically Pauline materials make this unlikely.

10. *Epilogue*

I have argued that 1 Cor. 11.3-16 is a non-Pauline interpolation. There is also reason to believe that the passage may actually consist of three originally separate and distinct pericopae, each dealing with a somewhat different though related topic.

The *first* such pericope would vv. 3, 8-9 and 11-12. It will be referred

Of course, the interpolation may have been added to Paul's Corinthian letter by someone other than its author.

122. On the work of the editor, see Bornkamm, *Die Vorgeschichte des sogenannten Zweiten Korintherbriefes*, *passim*; this is summarized in his *Paul*, pp. 244-46; see also Schmithals, *Gnosticism in Corinth*, pp. 87-101.

to as 'Pericope A'. These verses, when separated out and combined, form a self-contained unit, which, translated rather literally, reads as follows:

> And I want you to know that the head of every man is Christ, [the] head of woman [is] man, and [the] head of Christ [is] God. For man is not from woman, but woman from man. For also man was not created for the sake of the woman, but woman for the sake of the man. But neither [is] woman without man nor man without woman in [the] Lord; for even as the woman [was] from the man, so also the man [is] through the woman; and all things [are] from God.

The removal of these verses leaves a *second* smoothly-connected and self-contained pericope in vv. 4-7, 10, 13, 16,[123] free of many of the difficulties that the passage presents in its combined form. This second pericope, which will be referred to as 'Pericope B', reads as follows:

> Every man praying or prophesying having [something] down from [the] head[124] dishonors the head, but every woman praying or prophesying with [the] head uncovered dishonors her head; for it is one and the same as having been shaved. For if a woman does not cover herself, let her be shorn; but if [it is] shameful for a woman to be or shorn or shaved, let her be covered. For a man, on the one hand, ought not to be covered [on] the head, being [the] image and glory of God; but the woman, on the other hand, is [the] glory of man. For this reason, a woman ought to have authority upon [or 'over'] [her] head, because of the angels.[125] Judge

123. I will suggest below that vv. 14-15 form the third self-contained pericope in the passage.

124. The meaning of κατὰ κεφαλῆς ἔχων (v. 4) is by no means clear. It's opposite is ἀκατακαλύπτῳ τῇ κεφαλῇ (v. 5; cf. ἀκατακάλυπτον in v. 13 and the repeated use of κατακαλύπτεσθαι in vv. 6 and 7), which almost certainly should be translated as 'with the head uncovered'. Thus, the most obvious meaning of κατὰ κεφαλῆς ἔχων would appear to be, 'having [a covering] down on [the] head' (cf. κατακαλύπτεσθαι τὴν κεγαλήν in v. 7). For discussion, see, e.g., Fee, *The First Epistle to the Corinthians*, pp. 506-508. Murphy-O'Connor ('Sex and Logic in 1 Corinthians 11:2-16', pp. 483-85) argues that the reference is to long hair 'hanging from the head' (cf. v. 14).

125. 'Because of the angels' (διὰ τοὺς ἀγγέλους) has never been satisfactorily explained, although many suggestions have been offered; see Joseph A. Fitzmyer, 'A Feature of Qumrân Angelology and the Angels of I Cor. xi.10', *NTS* 4 (1957–58), pp. 48-58; reprinted with a 'Postscript' in Murphy-O'Connor (ed.), *Paul and Qumran*, pp. 31-47; and in Joseph A. Fitzmyer, *Essays on the Semitic Background of the New Testament* (London: Geoffrey Chapman, 1971; paperback edn, Missoula, MT: Scholars Press, 1974), pp. 187-204, with relevant bibliographical data. Perhaps

among yourselves: is it proper for a woman to pray to God uncovered? And if anyone is inclined to be contentious, we have no such custom,[126] nor [do] the churches of God.

Not only does each of the two pericopae form a smoothly-connected and self-contained unit when thus separated, but it also becomes apparent both that there are very significant differences between the two and that there are plausible reasons for their having been eventually combined, even though the combination actually tends to distort the real meaning of each separate pericope. It has often been noted, for example, that κεφαλή (head), appears to be used in a metaphorical sense in v. 3 (Pericope A) but in a literal sense in vv. 4, 5, 7 and 10 (Pericope B).[127] If the entire passage is left in its combined state, this presents serious problems of interpretation. If, however, the passage is divided as I propose, these problems immediately disappear. There is also a marked difference in literary style between the two pericopae. Scroggs comments on 'the economic use of words' in vv. 11-12;[128] the Greek here has no verbs and is poetic and even cryptic in style. The same is true, although to a somewhat lesser degree, of vv. 3 and 8-9. Taken as a unit, the style of Pericope A stands in notable contrast to the more expansive prose style of Pericope B and, for that matter, of vv.

the phrase διὰ τοὺς ἀγγέλους, which appears somewhat redundant after διὰ τοῦτο at the beginning of v. 10, was originally a part of pericope A and thus was somehow parallel to the διὰ τὴν γυναῖκα and διὰ τὸν ἄνδρα of v. 9. This would mean, however, that something has been lost from the text at some point in its transmission.

126. This is often translated as 'no other practice', but the Greek is ἡμεῖς τοιαύτην συνήθειαν οὐκ ἔχομεν, that is, 'no such practice' as a woman praying to God with her head uncovered (v. 13).

127. See, e.g., Meier, 'On the Veiling of Hermeneutics', p. 218: 'in *Verse 4* and following, Paul confuses his argument—as is his wont—by shifting the meaning of the key word "head"' (Meier's emphasis). See also Scroggs, 'Paul and the Eschatological Woman', p. 299 n. 42: 'The problem, whether the object of the dishonoring in 4*b* and 5*b* is the literal or the metaphorical meaning of κεφαλή, is notorious, and there can hardly be certainty in the matter. The literal meaning makes a little more sense in and of itself, but then that makes vs. 3 meaningless. According to Barrett, J. Weiss considered vs. 3 to be a later gloss, and it is true that removing that verse would solve the problems in 4f., cf. Barrett p. 250. On the assumption that vs. 3 *was* original, however, it seems better to take κεφαλή in the passages to be the same metaphorical use as the word has in vs. 3.' I am proposing, of course to remove not only v. 3 but also vv. 8-9, 11-12, which clearly eliminates the problem.

128. Scroggs, 'Paul and the Eschatological Woman', p. 300 n. 49.

14-15 as well. Finally, Pericope A is a general statement regarding the relation between man and woman in the church, similar in tone and vocabulary to Col. 3.18-19 and Eph. 5.22-33, while Pericope B deals with a specific question, that of head-covering and/or hairstyle in worship, and is in this respect much more closely akin to 1 Tim. 2.9–515 (cf. also 1 Pet. 3.1-7).[129]

The *third* pericope (vv. 14-15), which will be referred to as 'Pericope C', is perhaps not initially as easily distinguishable as are the first two, but there are four strong reasons for separating it from Pericope B. In the first place, it forms a complete and intelligible unit by itself, reading as follows:

> Does not nature itself teach you that, on the one hand, if a man has long hair it is a disgrace to him, but, on the other hand, if a woman has long hair, it is [her] glory; because her hair has been given to her instead of a covering.

In the second place, the material immediately preceding vv. 14 and 15 (Pericope B) is complete and intelligible without Pericope C—much more intelligible, in fact, than with it included, because, in the third place, the two pericopae really deal with different topics. Pericope B is concerned with the question of a head-covering in worship, while Pericope C deals with the proper length of hair for men and women and actually suggests that women do not need any artificial head-covering, since they have their long hair as a natural covering.[130] Finally, in the

129. A consideration of all of the New Testament epistolary passages dealing in detail with the status and role of women and their relationship to men suggests that there was a specific literary form, developed perhaps for the purpose of 'keeping women in their place'. The form characteristically consists of three parts: (1) an assertion or command; (2) the reason (either theological or historical) for the assertion or command; and (3) a 'mitigation' or 'softening of the blow'. The pattern is clearly exhibited in 1 Tim. 2.9-15. For discussion, see Walker, 'The "Theology of Woman's Place"'.

130. Scroggs ('Paul and the Eschatological Woman', p. 298 n. 40) senses something of the problem: 'Paul is actually self-contradictory in the "argument from nature". In 5*b* uncovered hair is equated with a shorn head, while in v. 15 he claims that the long hair was given to woman ἀντὶ περιβολαίου, which has to mean "in place of", "as", or "for" a hair covering. That is, Paul here says the woman's hair is the equivalent of a head-covering. If that is so, why should she need an "artificial" covering in place of the one given her by God? It is in any case the very opposite of a shorn head.' Scroggs, however, is unable to offer a satisfactory solution to the problem.

fourth place, there are significant differences in vocabulary between the two pericopae. Pericope B consistently uses αἰσχρός (v. 6) and the cognate verb καταισχύνειν (vv. 4, 5) to express the idea of 'dishonor' or 'disgrace', while Pericope C uses ἀτιμία (v. 14) for the same idea. Also, Pericope B speaks of man as the 'glory' (δόξα) of God and woman as the 'glory' (δόξα) of man (v. 7), while Pericope C uses δόξα with reference to woman's long hair.[131]

In short, it may well be that 1 Cor. 11.3-16 consists of three originally separate and distinct pericopae, each dealing with a somewhat different topic, yet having in common the fact that all three are concerned with some aspect of the relationship between men and women. Pericopae A and B also have in common the use of the word 'head' (κεφαλή), though used differently in the two, as well as the general idea of the subordination of woman to man. Pericopae B and C also have in

131. J.B. Hurley ('Did Paul Require Veils or the Silence of Women? A Consideration of I Cor 11:2-16 and I Cor 14:33b-36', *WTJ* 35 [1973], pp. 190-220 [193-204]) argues, primarily on the basis of Jewish and Hellenistic custom and LXX vocabulary, that throughout 1 Cor. 11.2-16 the author (whom he regards as Paul) is dealing with essentially the same problem: that of the proper hairstyle and length rather than that of a head covering such as a veil or shawl. The terms κατὰ κεφαλῆς ἔχων (v. 4), κατακαλύπτεται, and κατακαλυπτέσθω (v. 6), and κατακαλύπτεσθαι τὴν κεφαλήν (v. 7) refer to the appropriate custom for women which has the braids of hair pinned or folded on the top or at the back of the head, while ἀκατακάλυπτος (vv. 5, 13) refers to the custom followed by courtesans and prostitutes of allowing the hair to hang loose. Thus, according to Hurley, Paul does not advocate the wearing of a veil or shawl, since the long hair is an adequate head covering (v. 15), but he does insist that women wear their hair up to distinguish them from prostitutes and to indicate their husbands' authority over them (vv. 3-13) and that there be a distinction in hair length between women and men (vv. 14-15).

Hurley's argument is very ingenious, based as it is in part upon the fact that in the LXX the καλύπτω word-group sometimes translates a form of פרע, which would refer to long hair in both the Old Testament and the rabbinic writings (cf. Lev. 13.45; Num. 5.18; cf. *b. Ta'an.* 17b). In reply, however, it must be noted that, while there is often good reason to translate פרע as 'let loose', this does not necessarily mean that the LXX translators so understood it with their use of the καλύπτω word-group, which would not normally have this meaning. Furthermore, even if what I have called pericope B and pericope C do both deal with the question of hair rather than that of an artificial head covering, account must still be taken of the differences in vocabulary between the two pericopae, as well as of the fact that pericope B (according to Hurley) deals with hairstyle, while pericope C deals with hair length.

common their concern for the head or hair, the idea of 'dishonor' or 'shame', and the word 'glory' or 'pride' (δόξα). Thus, it is not difficult to understand how and why the three pericopae might have been combined to form 1 Cor. 11.3-16 as it now stands. Whether they were first combined by the editor who inserted the entire passage in its present place in 1 Corinthians, or whether he found them already combined, cannot at this point be determined. Neither is it certain whether they were first combined to provide material for dealing with some particular problem or question in the church or simply because it was believed that all were written by Paul and thus should be combined and incorporated into the corpus of his correspondence.

Chapter 6

1 CORINTHIANS 2.6-16*

1. *Introduction*

Commentators have often noted that 1 Cor. 2.6-16 'stands out from its context both in style and in content'.[1] Thus, it is not surprising that the authenticity of the passage has been questioned. In a 1979 article, Martin Widmann argues that: (1) numerous linguistic peculiarities seriously call into question Pauline authorship; (2) the passage contradicts what Paul says elsewhere; (3) the consistent use of 'we' and other features distinguishes 2.6-16 form-critically from its immediate context; and (4) the presence of the passage in 1 Corinthians can plausibly be explained as an attempt by Corinthian 'pneumatics' to correct what they saw as Paul's distortion of their position.[2]

Jerome Murphy-O'Connor, however, has examined Widmann's arguments and found them inconclusive.[3] Acknowledging that the exegesis of 1 Cor. 2.6-16 is perhaps more complicated than that of any other suspected interpolation in 1 Corinthians, Murphy-O'Connor concludes that 'Widmann's proposal is a *possible* explanation of the particularities of 2.6-16' but is 'less *probable* than the alternative hypothesis that Paul has taken over the ideas and terms of his opponents'[4]—a view advocated, in fact, by most commentators.[5]

In contrast to both Widmann and Murphy-O'Connor, E. Earle Ellis

* This chapter is a revised version of my article '1 Corinthians 2.6-16: A Non-Pauline Interpolation', and is included here by permission from the original publisher.

1. Hans Conzelmann, *1 Corinthians: A Commentary on the First Epistle to the Corinthians* (trans. James W. Leitch; Her; Philadelphia: Fortress Press, 1975), p. 57.
2. Widmann, '1 Kor 2 6-16'.
3. Murphy-O'Connor, 'Interpolations in 1 Corinthians', pp. 81-84.
4. Murphy-O'Connor, 'Interpolations in 1 Corinthians', p. 83 (his emphasis).
5. See, e.g., Fee, *The First Epistle to the Corinthians*, p. 100.

suggests that the passage, 'which has the literary form of a midrash or exposition of Scripture, probably was created within a (Pauline) group of pneumatics prior to its use' in 1 Corinthians. He cites as evidence of non-Pauline origin: '(1) the shift from the singular...to the plural with the "we", i.e. the pneumatics as the subject...(2) the unity of the section independent of its context, and (3) the considerable number of phrases not found elsewhere in the Pauline literature'.[6] On the basis of such evidence, Ellis concludes that 'on balance, 1 Cor. 2.6-16 is probably a pre-formed piece that Paul has employed and adapted to its present context'.[7]

Three possible explanations of 1 Cor. 2.6-16 thus emerge.[8] (1) it was

6. E. Earle Ellis, '"Spiritual" Gifts in the Pauline Community', *NTS* 20 (1974), pp. 128-44 (130). Non-Pauline phrases include: 'rulers of this age', 'before the ages', 'the spirit of the cosmos', and 'the spirit that is from God'. For a fuller exposition, see Ellis, 'Traditions in 1 Corinthians', especially p. 490.

7. Ellis, 'Traditions in 1 Corinthians', p. 490. Apparently, his principal reason for viewing this passage (and others) as 'tradition' rather than 'interpolation' is the absence of any direct text-critical evidence for interpolation; see his 'The Silenced Wives of Corinth', p. 220; and 'Traditions in 1 Corinthians', pp. 488, 498 n. 58; cf. also, e.g., Wisse, 'Textual Limits to Redactional Theory'.

8. Not included in this study are treatments such as those of Gerd Theissen (*Psychological Aspects of Pauline Theology* [trans. John P. Calvin; Philadelphia: Fortress Press, 1987], pp. 343-93) and Thomas W. Gillespie ('Interpreting the Kerygma: Early Christian Prophecy According to 1 Corinthians 2:6-16', in James E. Goehring *et al.* (eds.), *Gospel Origins and Christian Beginnings: In Honor of James M. Robinson* [FFasc, 1; Sonomo, CA: Polebridge, 1990], pp. 151-66), both of which seek to understand 1 Cor. 2.6-16 within the overall context of Pauline thought. On the basis of a 'psychological' analysis, Theiseen argues that the passage is 'the classic text' for Paul's understanding of 'a pneumatic knowledge that surpasses natural human possibilities but that is expressed in clear language rather than being communicated in glossalalic sounds' (p. 343). Gillespie maintains that 'the unlabeled subject matter' of 1 Cor. 2.6-16 is 'early Christian prophecy' and that 'the function of such prophecy was the interpretation of the apostolic kerygma'; cf. also Gerhard Dautzenberg, 'Botschaft und Bedeutung der urchristlichen Prophetie nach dem ersten Korintherbrief (2.6-16, 12-14)', in J. Panagopoulos (ed.), *Prophetic Vocation in the New Testament and Today* (NovTSup, 45; Leiden: E.J. Brill, 1977), pp. 131-61. My own judgment is that the arguments of Theissen and Gillespie, even if substantially correct, provide little positive support for Pauline authorship of 1 Cor. 2.6-16. Gillespie begs the question by simply assuming Pauline authorship, while Theissen (p. 349 n. 7) rejects both Widmann's interpolation hypothesis and 'assumption of a pre-Pauline source that Paul is said to have commented on critically' by suggesting that 'in formal respects 1 Cor. 2.6-16 is the literary deposit of a

composed by Paul, using ideas and terminology taken from his opponents, (2) it was composed by someone other than Paul but was included in the Corinthian letter by Paul, or (3) it was both written and added to the Corinthian letter by someone other than Paul (not necessarily the same person, however).

My own judgment is that Widmann is correct in viewing 1 Cor. 2.6-16 as a non-Pauline interpolation. I believe, however, that his hypothesis can be strengthened both by detaching it from his reconstruction of the history of the Corinthian correspondence and by adducing additional arguments for non-Pauline authorship. Moreover, I believe that some, at least, of Murphy-O'Connor's critique of Widmann's hypothesis can be rebutted. In what follows, therefore, I will argue that the passage is in fact a non-Pauline interpolation.[9] In the process I will also take into account the opposing arguments of Murphy-O'Connor and others.

2. *Historical Considerations*

Two matters call for preliminary consideration. The first relates to the history of the Corinthian correspondence and the question of how, if it is in fact an interpolation, 1 Cor. 2.6-16 came to be added to what we now know as 1 Corinthians.[10] The question is particularly pressing because, after finding Widmann's form-critical, linguistic and ideational arguments for non-Pauline authorship of the passage inconclusive, Murphy-O'Connor asserts that in the final analysis the interpolation hypothesis stands or falls with 'Widmann's explanation of how the interpolation came to be part of 1 Corinthians'. 'If [this explanation] should prove to be unsatisfactory', Murphy-O'Connor claims, Widmann's 'hypothesis must be declared unacceptable'.[11]

form that was once oral'. I believe, however, that some other (later) author could have inserted 1 Cor. 2.6-16 in such a way as to accomplish exactly what Theissen and Gillespie attribute to Paul. Cf., in this regard, Munro's comments regarding rhetorical criticism of the Gospels in 'Interpolation in the Epistles', pp. 436-37.

9. By 'non-Pauline interpolation', I mean that the passage was neither composed nor placed in the Corinthian letter by Paul.

10. This question involves aspects of what, in Chapter 4, I have termed 'situational', 'motivational' and 'locational' evidence. My own treatment of these types of evidence regarding 1 Cor. 2.6-16, however, will appear later in this chapter.

11. Murphy-O'Connor, 'Interpolations in 1 Corinthians', p. 83.

Widmann's reconstruction of the Corinthian correspondence is based in part upon reconstructions proposed by Wolfgang Schenk and Walter Schmithals.[12] Finding traces of seven different letters in 1 and 2 Corinthians, Widmann suggests that in 'Letter B2'[13] Paul defines true wisdom in such a manner as to indicate that the wisdom of certain 'pneumatics' (πνευματικοί) in Corinth is inauthentic. These pneumatics, according to Widmann, then add 2.6-16 to Paul's correspondence as a corrective.[14] Murphy-O'Connor's rejoinder is that 'no convincing arguments have ever been put forward that would justify the dismemberment of 1 Corinthians' and that 'Widmann's explanation of *how* the interpolation took place is [therefore] utterly implausible'. In addition, Murphy-O'Connor finds it highly unlikely that such an interpolation would have been 'retained when, in [Widmann's] hypothesis, the various letters were collected into what we now know as 1–2 Corinthians'.[15]

I do not agree that Widmann's explanation of how 1 Cor. 2.6-16 came to be a part of 1 Corinthians is *utterly* implausible. Widmann is by no means the only scholar to have questioned the integrity of 1 Corinthians,[16] and once the question is raised, a number of reconstructions become conceivable, including that proposed by Widmann. Thus, 1 Cor. 2.6-16 *may* have become a part of the Corinthian letter in precisely the manner suggested by Widmann (and, if so, the passage clearly is a non-Pauline interpolation). As already indicated, however, Widmann's is only one among a number of proposed reconstructions, and the very multiplicity, inevitably speculative nature and mutual incompatibility of all such reconstructions makes impossible, at least at present, the confident affirmation of any. Thus, none of these reconstructions, including Widmann's, can serve as the primary basis for an interpolation hypothesis. In short, if Widmann's case for viewing 1 Cor. 2.6-16 as an interpolation must stand or fall with his explanation of how the passage came to be a part of 1 Corinthians, it is clear that the verdict must be *non liquet*. At best, what was labeled in Chapter 4

12. Schenk, 'Der 1. Korintherbrief als Briefsammlung'; Schmithals, 'Die Korintherbriefe als Briefsammlung'; Schmithals, *Gnosticism in Corinth*, pp. 87-101.

13. 1 Cor. 1.1–2.5; 3.1–4.21; 2 Cor. 10–13.

14. Widmann, '1 Kor 2 6-16', pp. 50-52.

15. Murphy-O'Connor, 'Interpolations in 1 Corinthians', p. 84.

16. For a brief survey followed, however, by arguments supporting the unity of the letter, see Helmut Merklein, 'Die Einheitlichkeit des ersten Korintherbriefes', *ZNW* 75 (1984), pp. 153-83 (153-56).

as 'situational', 'motivational' and 'locational' evidence can serve as 'confirming factors', which 'generally only carry weight if there are other good reasons [that is, initial indicators] to think a passage may be interpolated'.[17] In short, convincing evidence that the passage is a non-Pauline interpolation must come from other quarters. Thus, I agree with Murphy-O'Connor that Widmann's proposed explanation (or any other) of *how* the interpolation came about lends little if any positive support to the latter's interpolation hypothesis.

I do not agree, however, that Widmann's interpolation hypothesis stands or falls with his explanation of how 1 Cor. 2.6-16 became a part of the Corinthian correspondence. Indeed, I regard this explanation as largely irrelevant to the question at hand. As will become evident in what follows, I believe, *pace* Murphy-O'Connor, that there are cogent contextual, linguistic, ideational and other arguments for viewing the passage as a non-Pauline interpolation.

3. *Text-Critical Evidence for Interpolation*

A second preliminary matter has to do with text-critical considerations. On the face of it, text-critical evidence would appear to constitute the most cogent basis for any interpolation hypothesis.[18] As was noted in Chapter 4, text-critical evidence for interpolation might be of at least three types: (1) the absence of a passage from one or more of the ancient witnesses; (2) the appearance of a passage at different locations in various of the witnesses; and (3) the inexplicable failure of an early Christian writer to cite a passage. So far as I can ascertain, however, such text-critical evidence for interpolation does not exist in the case of 1 Cor. 2.6-16. The passage appears at the same location in all of the earliest witnesses to the text, and I am aware of no inexplicable failure of an early Christian writer to cite it.[19] There are, to be sure, some textual variants shortly before the beginning of the passage, but it would be

17. Munro, 'Interpolation in the Epistles', p. 440.

18. Indeed, some would maintain that such evidence constitutes the *only* cogent basis for interpolation hypotheses.

19. 1 Cor. 2.9 appears to be reflected in *1 Clem.* 23.8; *2 Clem.* 11.7; 13.5; and *Mart. Pol.* 2.3. Note, however, that 1 Cor. 2.9 is apparently a paraphrase of Isa. 64.4 (cf. 52.15; Sir. 1.10). 1 Cor. 2.10 may be reflected in Ignatius, *Phld.* 7.1, but this is far from certain.

difficult to find here any positive support for a theory of interpolation.[20]

As was noted in Chapter 2, however, the absence of text-critical evidence for interpolation must be seen as precisely what it is: the *absence* of evidence. The earliest extant manuscripts of Paul's letters date from the late second century, and it is clear that they represent *edited* versions of the letters. We have little evidence regarding the texts prior to this time. It is precisely during this earlier period, however, that interpolations would most likely have been introduced. Thus, if there are compelling other reasons for regarding 1 Cor. 2.6-16 as an interpolation, the absence of text-critical evidence should not be allowed to decide the issue.

4. *Contextual Evidence for Interpolation*

The most obvious indication that 1 Cor. 2.6-16 may be an interpolation is the abrupt shift at v. 6 from singular ('I') to plural ('we'), from aorist to present tense,[21] and from autobiographical reminiscence to what might be seen as timeless propositions. Furthermore, the passage forms a complete, self-contained unit, which Hans Conzelmann refers to as 'a commonplace of "wisdom"'.[22] Thus, as Widmann notes, 1 Cor. 2.6-16 is to be regarded on form-critical grounds as representing a quite different literary genre from that of its immediate context (2.1-5; 3.1-4).[23] The immediately preceding and following verses represent 'the living forms of an epistolary discourse with the Corinthian community'. On the contrary, 2.6-16 consists of 'the a-historical assertions of the "we" about their pneumatic status'. Indeed, Widmann suggests that 'the self-affirmations of the pneumatics [in 2.6-16] belong to the same type of pneumatic eulogy with which 1 John debates'.[24] In short, the smoothly connected autobiographical summary of 2.1-5, 3.1-4, is interrupted by 2.6-16 with its panegyric to Wisdom and its possessors.

20. For discussions, see, e.g., Metzger, *A Textual Commentary on the Greek New Testament*, p. 546; Conzelmann, *1 Corinthians*, pp. 54-55; and Fee, *The First Epistle to the Corinthians*, p. 88 n. 2.

21. This is noted by Ellis ('Traditions in 1 Corinthians', p. 490) but not by Widmann.

22. Conzelmann, *1 Corinthians*, p. 57.

23. Note, e.g., Ellis' reference ('"Spiritual" Gifts in the Pauline Community', p. 130 n. 5) to 'the unity of the section independent of its context'.

24. Widmann, '1 Kor 2 6-16', p. 50 (translation here and elsewhere mine).

Murphy-O'Connor acknowledges in principle the validity of Widmann's observation but insists that 'in itself it proves nothing'. Focusing only on 'the switch from the singular to the plural and back again', Murphy-O'Connor maintains that the same phenomenon is manifest in 1.18-25 and that in both cases there is 'a very natural explanation' for 'the switch'; Paul 'uses the singular when it is a question of his personal experience (2.1-5) and judgment (3.1-4)' and the plural when he wishes 'to associate himself with Apollos, who had been set over against him by those who thought of themselves as a spiritual elite (πνευματικοί)'. In support of this view, Murphy-O'Connor cites the use of the plural (referring to Paul and Apollos) in 3.5-9.[25] I note, however, that 'the switch from the singular to the plural and back again' is really not at all parallel at the three points mentioned by Murphy-O'Connor. In the cases of 1.18-31[26] and 3.5-9, there is an obvious reason for the change, and, at least in 3.5-9, the identity of the 'we' is clear. Paul begins the account of his first visit to Corinth at 1.14, using the first person singular. The account continues through 1.17, where it is interrupted by a discussion of Christ as the wisdom and power of God (1.18-31); here, the first person plural appears (1.23), apparently to distinguish Paul and his fellow Christian preachers from 'Jews and Greeks'. At 2.1 Paul resumes the account of his visit and, accordingly, returns to the first person singular. If 2.6-16 is an interpolation, the autobiographical account continues in the first person singular at 3.1, shifting momentarily to the plural at 3.9 because here Paul speaks of both himself and Apollos, but returning to the singular at 3.10 in order to distinguish Paul from Apollos and other leaders.[27] In 2.6-16, however, the 'we' is completely anonymous,[28] and there is no apparent reason for the change to the plural (Paul quite naturally could have continued in v. 6 with 'among the mature *I* impart wisdom...'). Thus, I do not regard Murphy O'Connor's argument regarding the shift from singular to plural as valid. Moreover, as already indicated, Murphy-O'Connor ignores the corresponding shift from aorist to present tense.

25. Murphy-O'Connor, 'Interpolations in 1 Corinthians', p. 82; cf. M. Carrez, 'Les "nous" en 2 Corinthiens', *NTS* 26 (1980), pp. 474-86.

26. *Pace* Murphy-O'Connor (and others), I see the complete unit as 1.18-31, not 1.18-25 (note ἡμῖν in v. 30).

27. Note the return to the plural in 4.1, where, again, it is clear that the referents are Paul and Apollos.

28. See, e.g., Conzelmann, *1 Corinthians*, p. 59.

There are, however, other considerations of a contextual nature suggesting that 1 Cor. 2.6-16 may be an interpolation. In principle, the most obvious such indication might be a clear interruption of the subject matter of the text.[29] 'Wisdom', however, is a major theme in 1 Corinthians from 1.17 at least up to 3.23,[30] including 2.6-16. Nevertheless, the latter passage does, in significant ways, interrupt the train of thought of its immediate context. Specific linguistic and ideational differences between 2.6-16 and the surrounding material—and they are both numerous and significant—will be treated below. At this point, however, it should be noted that the removal of 2.6-16 leaves a smoothly connected passage (2.1-5; 3.1-4) dealing with Paul's initial visit to the Corinthians and emphasizing both his own 'weakness' (2.1-5) and the 'fleshly' nature of his hearers (3.1-4). The passage is interrupted, however, by 'an exposition of the exalted status and role of the Christian pneumatic as one who is privy to divine mysteries, a theme that does not appear to have its genesis in the critique of the Corinthian practices'.[31]

Yet another contextual consideration is suggested by Murphy-O'Connor's view that in 1 Cor. 2.6-16 'Paul deliberately takes over the terminology and ideas of his adversaries'.[32] I find this view highly problematic. As Conzelmann has noted, the passage, taken on its own terms, is not really polemical in nature: the 'we' in 2.6-16 are the pneumatics as opposed to 'the powers of this world' and the non-pneumatics, and 'the character of *direct* polemic against the Corinthians attaches to the "we" only through its being placed between 2.1-5 and 3.1ff'.[33] Most translators and commentators, assuming 'an emphatic antithesis'[34] between 2.6-16 and what precedes, render the δέ of v. 6 as 'but' or 'yet' and the λαλοῦμεν as 'we do speak'. Often, however, δέ means 'and' or functions simply 'as a transitional particle pure and

29. See, e.g., 1 Cor. 14.34-35, which many regard as an interpolation.

30. See, e.g., Conzelmann, *1 Corinthians*, p. 57.

31. Ellis, 'Traditions in 1 Corinthians', p. 490. Note again, however, that Ellis regards 1 Cor. 2.6-16 not as an interpolation but rather as an example of Paul's use of 'traditional' materials.

32. Murphy-O'Connor, 'Interpolations in 1 Corinthians', p. 82.

33. Conzelmann, *1 Corinthians*, p. 59 (his emphasis). To be sure, Conzelmann indicates his own belief that the passage is Pauline by adding: 'Paul is obviously here presenting his own wisdom, to which he then adds polemical highlights'.

34. Conzelmann, *1 Corinthians*, p. 60.

simple, without any contrast intended';[35] moreover, λαλοῦμεν would normally be rendered simply as 'we speak' or 'we are speaking'. Thus, apart from its context, the beginning of 2.6 would be translated in a much more neutral manner: 'And we speak wisdom among those who are perfect...'[36] If Paul intended the passage to be polemical, one might expect the polemic to be much less subtle and more explicit and direct.

To carry the point a step further, it is far from clear to me why Paul would at this point choose to adopt in polemical fashion the terminology and ideas of 'opponents'. Indeed, he has yet to intimate that there are any 'opponents' as such. In 1.10-11 he indicates that the source of the difficulty in Corinth is 'dissensions' or 'quarreling *among you*' (not between Paul and his opponents), and he returns to the same idea at 3.3 ('jealousy and strife *among you*'). Only at 1.17 does he first suggest that 'wisdom' might be a part of the problem, and even here there is no mention of 'opponents'.[37] Paul's rejection of 'wisdom' may well be simply the negative aspect of his insistence upon the gospel of the crucified Christ. Nowhere in 1.10–2.5 and 3.1–4.21, with the *possible* exception of 4.8-13,[38] does Paul even hint that there are people in Corinth claiming a superior 'wisdom' that sets them apart from other Christians. Indeed, I suspect that 1 Corinthians has too often been read in light of 2 Corinthians and/or that interpretation of other parts of 1 Corinthians has been unduly influenced by 1 Cor. 2.6-16![39]

35. BAGD, p. 171; note that δέ often 'cannot be translated at all'. Cf., however, e.g., Fee, *The First Epistle to the Corinthians*, p. 101 n. 12: 'Gk. δέ, clearly adversative here and thus rightly translated "however" (cf. "yet" in RSV, GNB, NAB)'.

36. Indeed, it is far from clear to me that 2.6-16, even *in* its present context, is polemical in nature. If anything, it is apologetic in tone: far from attacking the 'wisdom' claimed by others, it rather can be seen as insisting that 'we [too] speak wisdom'. Removed from their present context, however, the verses appear neither polemical nor apologetic.

37. Translation of the phrase ἐν σοφίᾳ λόγου is problematic, but it may mean nothing more than 'eloquent wisdom' (RSV) or 'cleverness in speaking' (BAGD, p. 759), in which case the reference may be simply to Paul's lack of effectiveness as a speaker (cf. 2.1, where λόγος and σοφία appear to be used virtually synonymously).

38. Here, the contrast appears to be simply between the 'apostles' and the Christians in Corinth, not between Paul and his 'opponents'.

39. See William Baird, '"One against the Other": Intra-Church Conflict in 1 Corinthians', in Robert T. Fortna and Beverly R. Gaventa (eds.), *The Conversation*

Another contextual consideration is suggested by Emanuel Hirsch's observation that the repetition of a *catchword* or *phrase* sometimes indicates the insertion of redactional material, with the interpolation either beginning shortly after the first occurrence of the *Schlagwort* and running through the second or including the first occurrence and ending shortly before the second.[40] Just such a phenomenon may occur in the repetitive κἀγὼ ἐλθὼν πρὸς ὑμᾶς, ἀδελφοί (2.1)...κἀγώ, ἀδελπφοί (3.1), occurring shortly before and immediately after 2.6-16. If 2.6-16 is an interpolation, the repetition of κἀγώ and ἀδελφοί may represent the interpolator's way of returning to Paul's autobiographical summary, now interrupted after 2.5 with the insertion of 2.6-16.[41] Observing the apparent logical contrast between 2.6-16 and 3.1-4, the RSV translates the καί in κἀγώ as 'but' and a number of other versions simply leave it untranslated. The NRSV and some other versions, however, correctly render the καί as 'and'. The removal of 2.6-16, of course, would eliminate the contrast between 2.6-16 and 3.1-4 and thus call for the correct translation of καί as 'and'.

Finally, however, it is just possible that 3.1 in its entirety represents a scribe's attempt (or even that of the actual interpolator) to link the interpolation (2.6-16) both to what precedes (2.1-5) and to what follows (3.2-4). The reference to πνευματικοί in v. 1 would relate back to the interpolation (2.6-16), while the remainder of v. 1 would point both back to 2.1-5 and forward to 3.2-4. Moreover, apart from the problem of the καί in 3.1, the removal of both 2.6-16 and 3.1 would

Continues: Studies in Paul and John in Honor of J. Louis Martyn (Nashville: Abingdon Press, 1990), pp. 116-36; Baird argues that 'the search for opponents in 1 Corinthians may be misguided'—indeed, that '[t]he situation reflected in the letter seems to be more complicated, involving not simply Paul against Corinthians, but Corinthians one against the other' (p. 116); see also on p. 119: 'Investigation of the problems of 1 Corinthians should be restricted to the text of 1 Corinthians'.

40. Emanuel Hirsch, 'Stilkritik und Literaranalyse im vierten Evangelium', *ZNW* 43 (1950–51), pp. 129-43; cf. Robert Tomson Fortna, *The Gospel of Signs: A Reconstruction of the Narrative Source Underlying the Fourth Gospel* (SNTSMS, 11; Cambridge: Cambridge University Press, 1970), p. 21; and Munro, *Authority in Paul and Peter*, p. 23. For possible examples in the Fourth Gospel (suggested by Fortna), see Jn 2.3 and 2.5; 4.47 and 4.49; 11.33 and 11.38; and 20.14 and 20.16.

41. This final consideration is, to be sure, rather tenuous. In 1 Corinthians alone, Paul elsewhere addresses his readers as 'brothers' at 1.10, 11, 26; 4.6; 7.24, 29; 10.1; 11.33; 12.1; 14.6, 20, 26, 39; 15.1, 31, 50, 58; and 16.15.

perhaps leave an even smoother, more coherent connection between 2.1-5 and 3.2-4 than would be the case if only 2.6-16 were removed.

In short, appeal can be made to at least four, and possibly as many as six, contextual considerations to support the view that 1 Cor. 2.6-16 is an interpolation:

1. The shift from singular to plural number.
2. The shift from aorist to present tense.
3. The interruption of the autobiographical material with a timeless panegyric to Wisdom.
4. The lack of evidence for the view that 2.6-16 represents Paul's polemical use of the terminology and ideas of his opponents.
5. The possibility that the repetition in 3.1 of the κἀγώ and ἀδελφοί in 2.1 suggests the presence of intrusive material and an attempt in 3.1 to pick up again the threads of 2.1-5.
6. The possibility that 3.1 in its entirety may represent a secondary link between 2.1-5 and 3.2-4.

Thus, on what he terms 'form-critical' grounds and what I have called 'contextual considerations', I agree with Widmann that 1 Cor. 2.6-16 appears to be an interpolation.[42]

5. *Linguistic Evidence for Interpolation*

Further support for regarding 1 Cor. 2.6-16 as an interpolation is based on linguistic peculiarities of the passage. Most of these have been set forth by Ellis and Widmann. Ellis notes the following phrases not found elsewhere in Paul's letters: οἱ ἄρχοντες τοῦ αἰῶνος τοῦτου (vv. 6, 8), πρὸ τῶν αἰώνων (v. 7), ὁ κύριος τῆς δόξης (v. 8), τὸ πνεῦμα τοῦ ἀνθρώπου (v. 11), τὸ πνεῦμα τοῦ κόσμου (v. 12), τὸ πνεῦμα τὸ ἐκ τοῦ Θεοῦ (v. 12), ψυχικὸς ἄνθρωπος (v. 14),[43] and νοῦς Χριστοῦ (v. 16).[44] To these can be added οἱ τέλειοι (v. 6) and τὰ βάθη τοῦ Θεοῦ (v. 10).

42. It is true, of course, that there is some verbal, ideational, and perhaps even structural overlap between 2.6-16 and its context. Such overlap may well say more about why the interpolation appears at this particular point in 1 Corinthians (that is, some congruence in subject matter and terminology) and/or reasons for the content of the interpolation than about any original relation between the passages.

43. Cf. 'old human' in Rom. 6.6; Eph. 4.22; Col. 3.9.

44. Ellis, '"Spiritual" Gifts in the Pauline Community', p. 130 n. 5; and 'Traditions in 1 Corinthians', p. 499 n. 69. Except for 'the Lord of glory' (v. 8), which occurs also in Jas 2.1, none of these phrases is found elsewhere in the New Testament.

Ellis also notes one word not found elsewhere in Paul's letters—διδακτός (v. 13)[45]—another is the adverb πνευματικῶς (v. 14).[46]

Widmann notes a number of 'linguistic, terminological peculiarities in the passage, which', in his judgment, 'allow one to suspect non-Pauline authorship'.[47] These include:

1. Use of 'solemn mystery-language' to characterize Christian proclamation[48] rather than Paul's usual kerygmatic, eschatological terminology.
2. Portrayal of Jesus' crucifixion not in kerygmatic terms but rather as a crime perpetrated by οἱ ἄρχοντες τοῦ αἰῶνος τούτου (v. 8).
3. Reference to political or demonic authorities as οἱ ἄρχοντες τοῦ αἰῶνος τούτου (v. 8).
4. Use of ὁ κύριος τῆς δόξης as a title for Christ (v. 8).
5. Presence of an Apocryphal citation (v. 9).[49]
6. 'Completely unique development of the word-group πνεῦμα, πνευματικός', in which πνεῦμα serves not, as for Paul, 'as a designation for the *heilsgeschichtlich* presence of Christ in the community' but rather 'as organ of knowledge and...as divine self-consciousness' (vv. 10-15).
7. Non-Pauline use of 'the dualistic anthropological conceptual pair Psychic-Pneumatic, originating from Gnostic speech', to differentiate humankind into two classes of people (vv. 14-15).[50]
8. 'Further development of the pneumatic-language' along non-Pauline lines with 'the proud, self-confident statement: ἡμεῖς

45. Διδακτός occurs also in Jn 6.45.

46. A few MSS have πνευματικῶς also in v. 13, but Conzelmann regards this as an assimilation to v. 14' (*1 Corinthians*, p. 67 n. 112). Otherwise, πνευματικῶς occurs only at Rev. 11.8 in the New Testament.

47. Widmann, '1 Kor 2 6-16', pp. 46-48.

48. For fuller treatment of this feature, see, e.g., Conzelmann, *1 Corinthians*, pp. 57-62.

49. It is not completely clear that v. 9 is an Apocryphal citation. See, e.g., Conzelmann, *1 Corinthians*, pp. 63-64. In any case, Widmann also regards 1 Cor. 15.44b-48 as an interpolation ('1 Kor 2 6-16', pp. 47-48).

50. Widmann finds the same phenomenon in 1 Cor. 15.44b-48 but, as noted above (see n. 49 above), argues that these verses are also an interpolation, probably originating from the same hand as 2.6-16.

> δὲ νοῦν Χριστοῦ ἔχομεν' (v. 16), in which 'mind of Christ' is used as a synonym for 'Spirit'.[51]

Murphy-O'Connor acknowledges that the evidence cited by Widmann 'is compatible with' the interpolation hypothesis. Insisting, however, that 'evidence which fits' must be distinguished from 'evidence which proves',[52] he maintains that it is precisely these linguistic data 'which have given rise to the current hypothesis that Paul deliberately takes over the terminology and ideas of his adversaries'. Thus, in his judgment, Widmann's 'list of unique features does not constitute a valid argument'. Murphy-O'Connor also asserts, *pace* Widmann, that it is possible, primarily from Paul's own terminology in the passage, 'to propose a plausible reconstruction of the position that Paul is arguing against in 2.6-16'.[53]

Contrary to Murphy-O'Connor, I believe, on the basis of three considerations, that the linguistic data weigh heavily against Pauline authorship of 1 Cor. 2.6-16. First, without providing a detailed analysis of specific linguistic features cited by Widmann, Murphy-O'Connor simply asserts that the evidence is compatible with both hypotheses regarding the origin of the passage. It is by no means clear just what degree of significance he attaches to each of the various items. My own judgment is that the linguistic data are *more nearly* compatible with the interpolation hypothesis than with the opposing view (for example, the presence within the scope of only 11 verses—a total of barely over 200 words—of two words and at least nine phrases not found elsewhere in the authentic Pauline letters surely cannot be disregarded). Indeed, it is precisely such linguistic data that Ellis cites as one of his principal arguments for non-Pauline (pre-Pauline) authorship of the passage.[54]

Second, Murphy-O'Connor considers the linguistic data in isolation from contextual and ideational considerations. As will be noted below, arguments for interpolation are inevitably *cumulative* in nature. No single argument can be taken as conclusive. When viewed in the light

51. Cf. Rom. 11.34a, 'For who has known the mind of the Lord?', where the implied answer is clearly a resounding 'No one!'

52. See Humphrey Palmer, *The Logic of Gospel Criticism: An Account of the Methods and Arguments Used by Textual, Documentary, Source, and Form Critics of the New Testament* (London: Macmillan; New York: St Martin's, 1968), p. 152.

53. Murphy-O'Connor, 'Interpolations in 1 Corinthians', pp. 82-83; cf. also his *1 Corinthians* (NTM, 10; Wilmington, DE: Michael Glazier, 1979), p. 19.

54. See pp. 138-39 above.

of these other considerations, the linguistic data become even more important.

Third, quite apart from Widmann's 'list of unique features', Ellis has cited a number of other linguistic data that, in my judgment, call into serious question the Pauline authorship of 1 Cor. 2.6-16 (I have added several more).[55] Murphy-O'Connor does not deal with most of these data at all.

Finally, it must be noted that much of the terminology (as well as much of the ideational content) in 2.6-16 is remarkably similar to what is found later in Gnosticism.[56]

In short, I believe that the linguistic data, particularly when viewed in the light of other considerations, constitute a strong argument against Pauline authorship of 1 Cor. 2.6-16.

6. *Ideational Evidence for Interpolation*

Thus far the evidence appears to indicate a non-Pauline *origin* of 1 Cor. 2.6-16 but not necessarily that the passage was included in the Corinthian letter by someone other than Paul (note Ellis' view that it is a *pre*-Pauline piece used by Paul). Even scholars who maintain Pauline authorship, however, have noted significant differences between the thought world of 1 Cor. 2.6-16 and that reflected elsewhere in the authentic Pauline letters (including 1 Corinthians). Indeed, certain features of the passage appear to contradict what Paul says elsewhere, particularly in 1 Cor. 1.17–2.5. Thus, Schmithals notes that 'there suddenly appears [in 1 Cor. 2.6–3.1] a doctrine of wisdom which—formally, at any rate—is genuinely Gnostic and *against* which in the preceding section Paul emphatically set himself'. Indeed, 'what is found in 2.6–3.1 could be the precise exposition of a Gnostic'.[57] Similarly, Hans Conzelmann speaks of 'a contradiction of his previous statements when Paul now announces after all a positive, undialectical possibility of cultivating a wisdom of the "perfect"'. Along the same

55. See pp. 138-39 above.

56. See, e.g., Conzelmann, *1 Corinthians*, pp. 57-69.

57. Schmithals, *Gnosticism in Corinth*, p. 151 (his emphasis). Schmithals sees the unit as 2.6–3.1 rather than 2.6-16. While I might be inclined to agree on ideational grounds, form-critical considerations (that is, return to singular pronoun and aorist tense) raise difficulties. It may be, however, that 3.1 represents a later scribe's attempt to provide a smoother transition between 2.6-16 and 3.1-4.

lines, Conzelmann notes that 1 Cor. 2.6-16, unlike other Pauline materials, 'is dominated by a pneumatic enthusiasm, a distinction between two classes of believer', for 'the pneumatics here do not comprise all Christians, but only a superior class'; moreover, 'the offense of the cross appears to be thrust aside in favor of the direct knowledge of spirit by spirit'. Further, Conzelmann observes that 'the esoterism put forward in this section' is 'the only instance of its kind in Paul'. Not only does the content of 2.6-16 appear to be non-Pauline and perhaps even anti-Pauline; according to Conzelmann, this content 'is in substance not [even] Christian'.[58]

Supporting his interpolation hypothesis, Widmann cites eight significant ideational differences between 1 Cor. 2.6-16 and its immediate context—differences reflecting such antithetical world-views as to seriously undermine any claim that Paul was responsible for the presence of the passage in 1 Corinthians:

1. Christian speech is viewed as the mysterious hidden divine Wisdom or 'the deep things of God' *rather than* as the openly proclaimed word of the cross.
2. Crucifixion is seen as an act committed in ignorance by 'archons of this aeon' *rather than* as the 'ground of salvation established by God in Christ'.
3. A positive evaluation of wisdom is made *rather than* rejecting wisdom and, paradoxically, identifying the preaching of the cross as wisdom.
4. A maturity of pneumatics is exalted *rather than* such 'maturity' being depicted as arrogance and the inferior position and earthly weakness of both preachers and members of the community being emphasized.
5. A distinction between psychics and pneumatics is made, both with predetermined destinies, *rather than* between Jews and Greeks, both with equal need of and access to salvation in Christ.
6. An elaborate understanding is shown of the Spirit as the means of access to 'the depths of God' and supernatural wisdom *rather than* more primitively as the 'strange miraculous power' and eschatological gift work in the 'difficult, weak,

58. Conzelmann, *1 Corinthians*, pp. 57-59.

all-too-human task of mission' and the 'daily practice of faith'.

7. Preaching is understood as 'esoteric mystery-speech' *rather than* as the community's intelligible human 'missionary and catechetical work'.
8. An attitude of 'superiority over all criticism' is displayed *rather than* the realization of being weak, fearful, earthly beings, far from self-honor, far from the goal, and 'therefore ready to submit to every criticism'.[59]

Murphy-O'Connor rejects Widmann's 'second line of argument' (the ideational) as 'specious, because of the eight points [Widmann] mentions only one is not a variant of those listed in his first argument' (the linguistic). In addition, Murphy O'Connor claims that Paul at certain points, 'with tongue in cheek, is merely appropriating the formulae of his adversaries' (e.g. 'the idea that the πνευματικός...is immune from criticism') and that 'there is no real contradiction between the cross as related to men in 2.8 and the cross as related to the will of God in 1.18-25'. He concludes, therefore, that 'Widmann's second line of argument...fails to strengthen his position'.[60]

It is true, of course, that the linguistic and ideational data of 1 Cor. 2.6-16 overlap to a considerable extent (ideas can only be expressed in words!). Nevertheless, I believe that Murphy-O'Connor has failed to do justice to the full range of the ideational data cited by Widmann. First, as already noted, he does not provide a detailed analysis of the linguistic data, simply asserting that they are compatible both with the interpolation hypothesis and with the view that Paul has adopted the terminology and ideas of his opponents. Thus, because he essentially equates Widmann's ideational data with his linguistic data, his rejection of the former carries no more weight than does his rejection of the latter.

In addition, Murphy-O'Connor fails to explain why, throughout an entire passage of 11 verses, Paul would employ both terminology and ideas that appear to be *contradictory* to his views as expressed elsewhere (particularly immediately preceding and following the passage). The only argument cited by Murphy-O'Connor supporting Paul's use

59. Widmann, '1 Kor 2 6-16', pp. 48-50. To some extent, these substantive differences overlap with the linguistic differences already discussed.

60. Murphy-O'Connor, 'Interpolations in 1 Corinthians', p. 83.

of ideas and terms taken from opponents[61] is 'the presence of the same phenomenon in the discussion concerning meat offered to idols (chs. 8–10)'.[62] The latter passage (1 Cor. 8–10), however, is not really analogous in this respect. 1 Corinthians 2.2-16, *in its entirety*, appears to contradict Paul's views as expressed immediately preceding and following in the same letter. In chs. 8–10, on the other hand, we find a dialectic in which Paul apparently quotes from his opponents and then comments upon or amplifies the quotations in such a way as to correct the opponents and thus make clear his own views regarding the matters at hand. To be sure, there are difficulties of interpretation in chs. 8–10, not to mention questions regarding the integrity of the section,[63] but neither the chapters as a whole nor individual units with the chapters can, in my judgment, be regarded as reflecting sustained use of language or ideology of Paul's opponents with which he himself disagrees.

A final point regarding ideational considerations in 1 Cor. 2.6-16 is suggested by Conzelmann, who notes that the passage contains 'traces of a certain theological schema, the "revelation schema": the "mystery" had been decreed by God from eternal ages, but remained hidden, and *now* is revealed'. According to Conzelmann, this schema, 'in its established form', first is found in the deutero-Pauline epistles 'and their neighborhood'.[64] Arguing that the schema 'is not gnostically conceived' and that it 'evolved within the internal life of the Pauline school', Conzelmann then suggests that 'Paul himself is here [in 1 Cor. 2.6-16] developing the beginnings of the schema which was then further developed by his disciples'.[65] My own judgment is that Conzelmann's earlier point should be pursued to its logical conclusion: with

61. An alternative suggestion is that 'Paul, in his eagerness to refute the ideas of his opponents, allows himself to be carried away into linking up with these ideas for the sake of argument, and in so doing is himself drawn a certain distance within their orbit' (Conzelmann, *1 Corinthians*, p. 57 [paraphrasing Rudolf Bultmann]).

62. Murphy-O'Connor, 'Interpolations in 1 Corinthians', p. 82; cf. his 'Freedom or the Ghetto (1 Cor. VIII,1-13; X,23–XI,1)', *RB* 85 (1978), pp. 543-74.

63. See, most recently, Cope, 'First Corinthians 8–10'. Cope argues that 1 Cor. 10.1-22 is a non-Pauline interpolation designed to bring Paul into line with the view of later Christians.

64. See Col. 1.26-27; Eph. 3.5, 9-10; 2 Tim. 1.9-10; Tit. 1.2-3; 1 Pet. 1.20; and Rom. 16.25-27 (almost certainly an interpolation; see, e.g., Käsemann, *Commentary on Romans*, pp. 421-28).

65. Conzelmann, *1 Corinthians*, pp. 57-58.

only two possible exceptions, the schema appears only in the pseudo-Pauline, never in the Pauline, writings. The two possible exceptions are Rom. 16.25-27 (widely regarded as an interpolation)[66] and 1 Cor. 2.6-16 (the passage under present consideration). I regard this as a strong indication of non-Pauline, and indeed post-Pauline, authorship of the latter.

In short, it is my judgment that the ideational content of 1 Cor. 2.6-16 is so significantly different from—and indeed contradictory to—Paul's views as expressed elsewhere in the authentic letters (and particularly in 1 Corinthians) as to make Pauline authorship or Pauline responsibility for the presence of the passage in 1 Corinthians highly unlikely.

7. *Comparative Evidence for Interpolation*

As has already been noted, certain features of the thought-world of 1 Cor. 2.6-16 appear to be more closely akin to that of the post-Pauline and particularly pseudo-Pauline writings than that of Paul's authentic letters. These include: (1) the contrast between 'a secret and hidden wisdom of God' and 'a wisdom of this age [and] of the rulers of this age'; (2) the implied distinction between 'the mature' or 'the perfect' (οἱ τέλειοι) and ordinary Christians; and (3) the presence of what Conzelmann calls 'the revelation schema': 'the "mystery" had been decreed by God from eternal ages, but remained hidden, and *now* is revealed'.[67] The first two items, as has already been suggested, are typical of later Gnostic thought but not of the authentically Pauline writings. With only two possible exceptions, the third appears only in the pseudo-Pauline, never in the Pauline, writings. The two possible exceptions, as already noted, are Rom. 16.25-27 (widely regarded as an interpolation) and 1 Cor. 2.6-16 (the passage under present consideration). In short, much of the ideational content of 1 Cor. 2.6-16 appears not only to be non-Pauline and even anti-Pauline but also post-Pauline. This, in my judgment, lends significant support to the view that the passage is a non-Pauline interpolation in the double sense of non-Pauline authorship and non-Pauline inclusion in the Corinthian letter.

66. Somewhat similar ideas appear in Mt. 13.10-17//Mk 4.10-12; Lk. 8.9-10; Mt. 13.34-35; Mt. 10.26-27//Mk 4.21-22//Lk. 8.16-17; 12.2-3. At least in their present form, however, all of these passages must be regarded as post-Pauline.

67. Conzelmann, *1 Corinthians*, pp. 57-58.

8. *Situational, Motivational and Locational Evidence for Interpolation*

Widmann's explanation of why 1 Cor. 2.6-16 now appears in the Corinthian letter, and indeed why it appears at its present location, has been noted above. I have also suggested that this explanation, because of its inevitably and obviously speculative nature, offers little if any support for Widmann's interpolation hypothesis regarding the passage. As regards the situation and the motivation underlying the possible interpolation, however, I have no better explanation to offer than that proposed by Widmann. My own guess is that the verses would most likely have been added after Paul's death, when the prevalence and popularity of Gnostic-like notions of 'wisdom' made it desirable (at least to someone) to bring Paul into the fold of the 'pneumatikoi'. In the absence of evidence, however, such a guess provides no support for regarding the passage as a non-Pauline interpolation.

Assuming for the moment that 1 Cor. 2.6-16 is in fact a non-Pauline interpolation, it is possible to speculate regarding why the passage might have been added at precisely its present location in the Corinthian letter. First, the primary subject matter of 2.6-16 is 'wisdom', and this is also a major topic in the larger context from 1.17 all the way to the end of ch. 3. Second, 2.6-16 can, as has already been suggested, be viewed as an attempt to correct or at least qualify Paul's apparent deprecation of wisdom in 1.17–2.5. Third, 3.1-4 does in fact make a distinction between 'spiritual people' (πνευματικοί), on the one hand, and, on the other hand, 'fleshly people' (σάρκινοι, σαρκικοί), 'babes in Christ' (νήπιοι ἐν Χριστῷ), or those who 'walk in a human way' (κατὰ ἄνθρωπον περιπατεῖτε).[68] It should be noted, however, that the characteristic feature of those who are not 'pneumatikoi' in 2.6-16 is their non-possession of the Spirit, while in 3.1-4 it is their propensity to jealousy and strife. Thus, despite the apparent similarity, there is a significant difference between 2.6-16 and 3.1-4. Nevertheless, the points of contact between this passage and its immediate context might explain why, if it is an interpolation, it was inserted precisely at its present location.

68. In v. 4, Paul actually refers to the latter simply as ἄνθρωποι. One wonders what the alternative to ἄνθρωποι might be!

9. *Conclusion*

Murphy-O'Connor is surely correct in his view that 'evidence which fits' is not necessarily the same as 'evidence which proves'.[69] 'Proof', however, is rarely if ever possible in matters of literary judgment. In the case of interpolation theories, various types of arguments can be advanced, each of which involves certain problems, such as the danger of circular reasoning. Thus, no argument 'can stand by itself'. Different kinds of criteria must be used to 'correct and complement each other'. 'It is a matter of taking into account the cumulative effect of converging lines of evidence'.[70] The crucial question must always be: in which direction does the *cumulative preponderance* of the evidence point?

It appears to me that Murphy-O'Connor proceeds in atomistic fashion in his critique of Widmann. First, after examining only one of its features, he rejects Widmann's form-critical argument; second, without subjecting them to a detailed analysis, he asserts that Widmann's linguistic data are less than conclusive; third, he dismisses Widmann's summary of ideational contradictions between 2.6-16 and the remainder of 1 Corinthians on the grounds that it represents essentially a repetition of the linguistic date; finally, he rejects Widmann's reconstruction of the history of the Corinthian correspondence. As he finds each separate line of Widmann's argument inconclusive, he drops it from further consideration. Thus, it is my judgment that Murphy-O'Connor fails to take into account the *cumulative* impact of the various lines of evidence supporting the interpolation hypothesis.

My own conclusion, on the other hand, is that the interpolation hypothesis explains the origin of 1 Cor. 2.6-16 more adequately than does the view that Paul has adopted the terminology and ideas of his opponents or that he has, for whatever reason, employed a pre-formed piece of traditional material. This conclusion is based upon the *cumulative* weight of the form-critical, linguistic, ideational, contextual and other data.

69. Murphy-O'Connor, 'Interpolations in 1 Corinthians', p. 82.
70. Munro, *Authority in Paul and Peter*, pp. 21-25.

Chapter 7

1 CORINTHIANS 13*

Commentators have often noted that the relation of 1 Corinthians 13[1] to its immediate context is problematic. The observations of Wayne A. Meeks are typical: 1 Corinthians 13 'interrupts the train of thought; 14.1b would follow logically after 12.31a, while 14.1a repeats 12.31a almost verbatim... Moreover, ch. 13 is a self-contained unit, composed in the style of an encomium on a virtue so familiar in Greek literature'.[2] Many years ago, Johannes Weiss argued that the chapter originally stood somewhere other than in its present position, perhaps after ch. 8.[3] Jean Héring and others have agreed.[4] Without committing himself regarding its original placement, Hans Conzelmann suggested that 'the passage must be expounded in the first instance on its own.[5] At one point, Anton Fridrichsen even argued that ch. 13 was a Christian-Stoic diatribe added to 1 Corinthians by a later hand,[6] though he later rejected this view.[7]

* Much of this chapter represents a slightly revised version of my article, 'Is First Corinthians 13 a Non-Pauline Interpolation', but it also contains material from my 'Text-Critical Evidence for Interpolation'. All of these materials are included here with permission of the original publishers.

1. Actually 12.31b–14.1a. Except when clarity requires greater specificity, however, I will refer to the passage simply as 1 Corinthians 13.

2. Meeks, *The Writings of St. Paul*, p. 41 n. 6; cf., e.g., Orr and Walther, *I Corinthians*, p. 290 (summarizing the views of Johannes Weiss); and Héring, *The First Epistle of Saint Paul*, pp. 133-34.

3. Weiss, *Der erste Korintherbrief*, esp. pp. 309-12.

4. Héring, *The First Epistle of Saint Paul*, p. 134; cf., e.g., Jack T. Sanders, 'First Corinthians 13: Its Interpretation Since the First World War', *Int* 20 (1966), pp. 159-87 (181).

5. Conzelmann, *1 Corinthians*, p. 218.

6. Eduard Lehmann and Anton Fridrichsen, 'I Kor. 13: Eine christlich-stoische Diatribe', *TSK* 94 (1922), pp. 55-95.

7. Anton Fridrichsen, Prescript to E. Hoffmann, 'Zu 1 Cor. 13 und Col. 3,14',

In 1959, Eric L. Titus suggested—apparently independently of Fridrichsen's initial position—that 1 Corinthians 13 might be a non-Pauline interpolation.[8] Perhaps in part because Titus' article is brief (less than four pages) and because it appeared in one of the less well-known journals, it has not, in my judgment, received the scholarly attention it deserves. Indeed, Jerome Murphy-O'Connor, in his discussion of possible interpolations in 1 Corinthians, fails even to mention 1 Corinthians 13.[9] To be sure, Titus' suggestion has occasionally been noted, but it has almost always been rejected, and Gordon D. Fee goes so far as to label it 'criticism run amok'.[10] So far as I am aware, however, no one has submitted Titus' work to a detailed critical examination or undertaken an independent study of the possibility that 1 Corinthians 13 is non-Pauline. It is my intention, therefore, to argue that 1 Corinthians 13 is in fact a non-Pauline interpolation—that is, that it was both composed by someone other than Paul and inserted at its present location in the Corinthian letter by someone other than Paul.

1. *Preliminary Considerations*

Before adducing specific arguments against the authenticity of 1 Corinthians 13, it is important to note certain preliminary considerations mentioned by Titus: (1) 'Pauline authorship [of 1 Corinthians 13] would not be disproved by a demonstration that the passage is out of context at its present location'; (2) 'to deny the hymn on love to Paul is not to deny that he gave love an important place in his thought' or, differently stated, 'an argument against the authenticity of the passage must be made on other grounds than a denial of the importance of love in Paul's thought'; (3) because 'the genuineness of I Corinthians 13 has had almost universal support from critical scholarship', any assertions to the contrary must be made only with caution; and (4) the argument against Pauline authorship, 'if it has any weight at all, must be in its cumulative effect, and not in a single point in isolation'.[11]

Regarding Titus' first, second and fourth points, I can only register

in Anton Fridrichsen (ed.), *Otto Lagercrantz Mnemosynon* (ConNT, 3; Leipzig: Lorentz, 1939), p. 28.

8. Titus, 'Did Paul Write I Corinthians 13?', pp. 299-302.
9. Murphy-O'Connor, 'Interpolations in 1 Corinthians'.
10. Fee, *The First Epistle to the Corinthians*, p. 626 n. 6.
11. Titus, 'Did Paul Write I Corinthians 13?', p. 299.

my own strong agreement. As regards the first, it is surely possible that an authentically Pauline passage might—accidentally or deliberately—have become misplaced, either from elsewhere in 1 Corinthians or from another letter. Regarding the second, I note only Paul's emphasis on love in such passages as Gal. 5.14, 1 Cor. 8.1 and Rom. 13.8-10. With reference to the fourth, I have agreed in Chapter 3 that the burden of proof rests with any argument for interpolation. As regards the third, however, my basic agreement must be somewhat qualified by attention to certain aspects of the nature and history of the Pauline corpus. Titus shares the assumption of most modern scholars that the Pauline corpus represents an *edited* collection including both pseudonymous and composite writings. He further suggests that 'interpolation would serve as an ideal instrument' in the process of adapting the Pauline letters to the changing needs of the early church and that 'the process of "correcting" the tradition, even words of Jesus, which we see at work in the second-century Fathers, may well run back to the earliest times'.[12]

Since Titus' article appeared in 1959, much has been written regarding possible interpolations in the Pauline letters, and, as noted in my Introduction, a number of passages have been so identified. In my judgment, this work has confirmed Titus' view regarding the probability of interpolations in the Pauline corpus. Indeed, I argued in Chapters 2 and 3 that it is to be assumed, simply on *a priori* grounds, that the Pauline letters, as we now have them, are likely to contain non-Pauline interpolations. Thus, the question to be raised regarding any particular passage is simply whether this passage is one of the interpolations that almost certainly exist within the Pauline corpus.

2. *1 Corinthians 13: An Independent, Self-Contained Unit*

Many scholars have observed that 1 Corinthians 13 is an independent self-contained unit, in no way dependent upon chs. 12 and/or 14 either for its unity or for its coherence and meaning. Titus notes, for example, that the chapter 'stands out' in the mind of the average Christian 'in the same way as does the 23rd Psalm or the Matthean version of the Lord's Prayer' and that it 'thrusts itself out from the Corinthian letter as if to

12. Titus, 'Did Paul Write I Corinthians 13?', p. 299; cf. e.g., John Knox, *Chapters in a Life of Paul* (ed. Douglas R.A. Hare; Macon, GA: Mercer University Press, rev. edn, 1987), pp. 5-7; and Keck and Furnish, *The Pauline Letters*, pp. 50-51.

invite special attention'.[13] Even scholars who regard the chapter as integrally related to chs. 12 and/or 14 sometimes speak of it as a 'digression',[14] and some recognize the possibility that 'it had independent existence before having been adapted and inserted here'.[15] Indeed, noting that 1 Cor. 13.13 'seems to constitute a summary of the treatment of three distinct themes'—faith, hope and love—in which it is concluded that, of the three, love is the greatest, Titus suggests that ch. 13 was originally 'the concluding member' of an 'original triad' in which faith, hope and love all received significant treatment.[16]

In short, quite apart from any question of Pauline origin, there are sound reasons for regarding 1 Corinthians 13 as an independent self-contained unit.

3. *1 Corinthians 13: Not Appropriately Located between Chapters 12 and 14*

Various scholars have argued that 1 Corinthians 13 did not originally occupy its present place between chs. 12 and 14 of 1 Corinthians.[17]

13. Titus, 'Did Paul Write I Corinthians 13?', p. 299; cf. e.g., Meeks, *The Writings of St. Paul*, p. 41; and Conzelmann, *1 Corinthians*, p. 218. See also, however, e.g., Fee, *The First Epistle to the Corinthians*, pp. 626-27 n. 9.

14. See, e.g., Fee, *The First Epistle to the Corinthians*, p. 626: 'Both the imperative in 12:31a and the resumptive nature of the imperatives in 14:1 indicate that this is something of a digression in Paul's argument. But as with all such "digressions", it is fully relevant to the context, and without it the succeeding argument would lose much of its force.'

15. Fee, *The First Epistle to the Corinthians*, p. 626. Fee also insists, however, that, if so, the passage 'has been...thoroughly adapted to the context'.

16. Titus, 'Did Paul Write I Corinthians 13?', p. 301. Titus observes: 'There is little in chapter 13 to call for a singling out of faith and hope in this summary manner. Faith is dealt with briefly, though not so as to suggest its enduring quality. Hope is mentioned in verse 7, where it is said that loves hopes all things, but the subject there is love and not hope. But the ending would be perfectly normal if faith and hope had already received consideration, and the writer had arrived at the conclusion that, of the three units of the triad, love was the greatest.'

17. E.g. Héring, *The First Epistle of Saint Paul*, p. 134; and Sanders, 'First Corinthians 13', p. 181. Cf., however, e.g., Nils Johansson ('I Cor. XIII and I Cor. XIV', *NTS* 10 [1964], pp. 383-92), who thinks that 'I Cor. XIV can help to explain why I Cor. XIII was written and why it was placed where it is' (p. 384); and Fee (*The First Epistle to the Corinthians*, p. 626), who holds that 'in its present form [1 Cor. 13] is not only fully Pauline, but also has been so thoroughly adapted to the

This argument is based upon considerations of form and style, content and transitions between ch. 13 and the surrounding material. Closely related to the question of original location, of course, is the possibility that ch. 13 is a Pauline 'digression' or 'excursus'.

a. *Form and Style*

The form and style of 1 Corinthians 13 are significantly different from those of chs. 12 and 14. Whether ch. 13 be regarded as a poem, a hymn, a prose-poem, or something else, it is clear that it represents a literary genre far removed from that of chs. 12 and 14.[18] In terms of specific details of style, ch. 13, unlike chs. 12 and 14, contains not a single imperative verb.[19] Moreover, all of the verbs with people as their subject are in the first person, not the second or third person as in chs. 12 and 14; indeed, except for γινώσκομεν and προφητεύομεν in v. 9 and βλέπομεν in v. 12, all of these verbs are first-person singular, not plural. In short, it is my own judgment that the form and style of 1 Corinthians 13 are such as to raise serious questions regarding the chapter's original placement between chs. 12 and 14.

b. *Content*

Of greater significance, however, are considerations of content. Héring points out that 1 Corinthians 13 'obviously interrupts the discussion on spiritual gifts' found in chs. 12 and 14.[20] As Sanders summarizes the matter, ch. 12 constitutes a discussion of the various charismata, leading to a listing of 'what [Paul] considers to be the valid charismata in descending order of importance' (12.28-30) and the admonition, 'Earnestly desire the greater charismata' (12.31a). Without the intervention of ch. 13, ch. 14, presupposing that the highest gift (apostleship) 'is limited to only a few specially chosen persons', then urges that the

context that such questions [as whether "it had independent existence before having been adapted and inserted here"] seem ultimately irrelevant'.

18. J.F.M. Smit ('The Genre of 1 Corinthians 13 in the Light of Classical Rhetoric', *NovT* 33 [1991], pp. 193-216) discusses the question of genre in detail.

19. It is grammatically possible that ζηλοῦτε in 12.31a and/or 14.1a is indicative rather than imperative; in the context, however, this is highly unlikely (particularly in 14.1a). For a discussion of the issues involved, see J.F.M. Smit, 'Two Puzzles: 1 Corinthians 12.31 and 13.3: A Rhetorical Solution', *NTS* 39 (1993), pp. 246-64 (248-50).

20. Héring, *The First Epistle of Saint Paul*, p. 134.

Corinthians 'desire the highest available [gift]—that is, prophecy'—and explains 'why prophecy is more to be desired than the other charismata, particularly glossalalia'.[21]

While the subject matter of chs. 12 and 14 is 'spiritual gifts' and their role in public worship, ch. 13 says nothing at all about public worship or, indeed, about the community as such; rather, ch. 13 is an encomium on love, and, with its predominance of first-person singular verbs, it focuses on the individual, not the community.

In addition, as a '*critique of pneumatika*',[22] 1 Corinthians 13 does more than merely divert attention away from the principal points of chs. 12 and 14; it appears to declare these points essentially irrelevant. If anything, ch. 13 might be appropriate *after* ch. 14 but certainly not *before* it.[23] At the end of a discussion of the relative value of the various spiritual gifts, it would be a way of saying that all such discussion would become unnecessary and even irrelevant if love prevailed. Coming before ch. 14, however, it turns the latter chapter into an anti-climactic relapse into the controversy that has just been declared irrelevant.[24]

According to Titus, additional items suggesting that 1 Corinthians 13 does not belong between chs. 12 and 14 include: (1) the absence of any clear relation between faith, almsgiving and martyrdom (13.2-3) as well as the subject matter of chs. 12 and 14; (2) the failure to relate

21. Sanders, 'First Corinthians 13', p. 182. Cf. the similar summary in Titus, 'Did Paul Write I Corinthians 13?', p. 300: 'Chapter 14 is a treatise on the superiority of prophecy on the ground that it edifies. If chapter 13 is omitted, the treatment of gifts in chapters 12 and 14 becomes a unity in terms of a hierarchy of values within the list itself'. See, however, Fee (*The First Epistle to the Corinthians*, p. 623), who rejects the idea of reading 1 Cor. 12.28 'as *ranking* the various ministries and gifts, so that Paul might place tongues as the last and least of the gifts'. If Fee is correct, however, it then becomes difficult to interpret Paul's admonition to 'be zealous for the greater gifts' (12.31a).

22. Conzelmann, *1 Corinthians*, p. 233.

23. See, e.g., Sanders, 'First Corinthians 13', pp. 183-87 (my emphasis).

24. Smit ('Two Puzzles', p. 250) goes somewhat further, suggesting that 'in its presentation of charismata and love and in the behavior it demands of the Corinthians 1 Cor. 12:31 is diametrically opposed to 1 Cor. 13:1-13'. For Smit, however, this does not mean that 1 Corinthians 13 is a non-Pauline interpolation; rather, he sees 12.31 as an example of irony: 'At the beginning of a demonstrative passage, in which he devalues the worth of the charismata, Paul ridicules in an ironic manner the Corinthians' pursuit of these gifts as their highest goal' (p. 253).

love as patience, kindness, humility, courtesy, and so on, to the issues under consideration in chs. 12 and 14; (3) a similar failure to relate 'Love bears all things, believes all things, hopes all things, endures all things' (v. 7) to 'the charismatic problem of Christian worship'; and (4) the apparent contradiction between the stress on the importance of gifts (even in ch. 14) and the minimizing of such gifts in ch. 13—a minimizing that is accomplished 'not only by contrasting them with love but also by stressing their ephemeral character'.[25]

Some scholars have argued that the themes and even some of the language of 1 Corinthians 13 are in fact related to themes and language of other parts of the letter, including chs. 12 and 14. Indeed, according to this view, ch. 13 echoes in various ways a number of the issues dealt with elsewhere in 1 Corinthians.[26] Space does not permit a consideration of such possible links in any detail. Suffice it to say that one would expect there to be *some* thematic connections between ch. 13 and its present context, both immediate and larger, even if it is a non-Pauline interpolation; otherwise, it would be difficult to explain why the passage was inserted in the Corinthian letter and indeed in this particular section of the letter. In short, I regard the presence of certain general thematic similarities between 1 Corinthians 13 and its context as, in the final analysis, essentially irrelevant so far as any argument either for or against interpolation is concerned.

c. *Transitions*

The transitions or links between 1 Corinthians 13 and chs. 12 and 14 are 'ragged'.[27] Indeed, as Meeks puts it, the way in which '14.1a repeats 12.31a almost verbatim' could be 'the device of an editor who is making an insert',[28] or, in the words of Titus, the transitions 'have the earmarks of interpolation'.[29] If 12.31b–14.1a were removed, 14.1b would follow smoothly after 12.31a and the entire sentence would read

25. Titus, 'Did Paul Write I Corinthians 13?', pp. 301-302.

26. E.g., Fee, *The First Epistle to the Corinthians*, esp. pp. 626-27. Certainly, this is true of 'tongues' and 'prophecy' (see chs. 12 and 14) and it may also be true of 'knowledge' (see 'wisdom' in chs. 1–3) and possibly of 'boastful' (φυσιοῦται in v. 4; see, e.g., φυσιοῦσθε in 4.6).

27. Conzelmann, *1 Corinthians*, p. 217.

28. Meeks, *The Writings of St. Paul*, p. 41 n. 6.

29. Titus, 'Did Paul Write I Corinthians 13?', p. 300.

either 'but be zealous for the greater gifts[30] and especially that you may prophesy' or 'but be zealous for the spiritual gifts, and especially that you may prophesy'.[31] The words 'but be zealous for' (12.31a) are repeated in 14.1a, which may represent an editorial addition for the purpose of relinking ch. 14 to ch. 12 (with ch. 13 now intervening).[32]

It is perhaps also significant that a few manuscripts read κρείττονα or κρείσσονα ('better') rather than μείζονα ('greater') in 12.31a.[33] Although the latter reading has much stronger textual attestation, it may in fact represent an early editor's assimilation of 12.31a to 13.13, where 'love' is spoken of as the 'greatest' (literally, 'greater' [μείζων]) of the triad, 'faith, hope, love'. Thus, 12.31a, with its command to be zealous for the 'greater' gifts would now point to 13.13, which speaks of 'love' as the 'greatest' (literally, 'greater'). Such a reading, however, simply reinforces the point that ch. 13 interrupts the logical flow of chs. 12 and 14. Without ch. 13, the 'greatest' (or 'best') gift is clearly 'prophecy', not 'love'.

d. *A Digression or Excursus?*

Some commentators have suggested that 1 Corinthians 13 represents 'something of a digression in Paul's argument'.[34] William F. Orr and James Arthur Walther, for example, suggest that the chapter 'was composed by Paul independent of the rest of our I Corinthians', that he then 'inserted it in this discussion at the point where it occurred to him but before he was finished with his discussion of spiritual gifts', and that, 'since the letter was occasional and this occurs in the body of a major section, it was not edited by Paul; and it escaped the editorial hand of the collector of Paul's correpondence'.[35] According to Titus, however, 'It is to be doubted that I Corinthians 13 is typical of the Pauline

30. Another possible reading is 'but be zealous for the better gifts...'

31. Titus ('Did Paul Write I Corinthians 13?', p. 300) remarks that, on the one hand, 'it might be argued that the inclusion of "the higher gifts" in 12.31a prepares the way for "a still more excellent way" of 12.31b and so would be transitional', but, on the other hand, 'it may have been this reference to "higher gifts" that attracted the interpolation at this point, the modifier "higher" calling forth the phrase "still more excellent" of 12.31b. This would be supported by the awkward character of the transition.'

32. Titus, 'Did Paul Write I Corinthians 13?', p. 300.

33. Among the manuscripts is Codex Bezae (D) of the sixth century.

34. Fee, *The First Epistle to the Corinthians*, p. 626.

35. Orr and Walther, *I Corinthians*, p. 290.

parenthesis or digression'. Citing Rom. 5.13 as a typical example of Pauline digression, Titus notes that here 'an abrupt change of thought takes place', and 'Paul is soon lost in his explanatory remark and never returns to complete his sentence'. In 1 Corinthians 13, however, 'there is no tendency to become lost in [the] digression'; rather, Paul 'returns to his main argument even to the repetition of the exact phrase used at the end of chapter 12'.[36]

It is my own judgment that 1 Corinthians 13 is not to be characterized as a digression or excursus. It is rather an interruption that both breaks the logical flow of chs. 12 and 14 and, in a literary style quite foreign to these chapters, declares essentially irrelevant the issues there being discussed.

Such a conclusion does not, of course, necessarily mean that Paul was not the author of 1 Corinthians 13. It might mean simply that he composed the passage for some other purpose or context and that it was subsequently inserted (either by him or by someone else) between chs. 12 and 14 of 1 Corinthians.

4. *1 Corinthians 13: Not Composed by Paul*

Arguments against Pauline authorship of 1 Corinthians involve considerations of form and style, vocabulary, and content. It should be noted, too, that some of the arguments already proposed against an original location of the passage between chs. 12 and 14 are also, in my judgment, arguments against Pauline authorship of the passage.

a. *Form and Style*

In describing the form and style of 1 Corinthians 13, C. Spicq speaks of

> the literary beauty of this chapter, its rhythm, the musical effect of the words resulting from their euphony, the choice of images, the balance and parallelism of the statements, the play of the antitheses, of the chiasm, of the hyperboles, of the anaphora, and the overall lyrical tone.[37]

Meeks refers to 1 Corinthians 13 as a 'prose-poem',[38] and some regard

36. Titus, 'Did Paul Write I Corinthians 13?', p. 300.

37. C. Spicq, *Agapè dans le Nouveau Testament: Analyse de Textes* (Ebib; 3 vols.; Paris: J. Gabalda, 1958–59), II, p. 50 (translation mine); see also Smit, 'The Genre of 1 Corinthians 13', pp. 199-205.

38. Meeks, *The Writings of St. Paul*, p. 41 n. 6.

it as a 'hymn'.[39] Fee and others, however, have questioned whether the passage should really be characterized as 'poetic',[40] and some, noting its rhetorical features, have suggested that it should be viewed as a type of paraenetic exhortation.[41] Nevertheless, Fee also speaks of 'the exalted nature of its prose', acknowledges that it 'soars', and refers to it as 'one of Paul's finest moments'.[42] In light of such considerations, Titus concludes that 'the form of [1 Corinthians 13] is unique in Paul's letters'. To be sure, there are other passages in the authentically Pauline letters that 'indicate poetic sensitivity, rhythm and balance, but nowhere do we find anything approaching the sustained poetic quality of chapter 13'.[43] My own judgment is that Titus is correct: there is nothing else in the undoubted Pauline letters that is even remotely comparable to 1 Corinthians 13 in terms of form and style. Thus, I regard the form and style of the passage as arguments against Pauline authorship.

In and of itself, this conclusion does not necessarily mean that Paul could not here have used (and perhaps adapted) a *topos* on love composed by someone else, as some believe him to have done, for example, with the 'Christ Hymn' in Philippians 2. Given my earlier arguments against the *substantive* appropriateness of 1 Corinthians 13 between chs. 12 and 14, however, I regard this as highly unlikely.

b. *Vocabulary*

J. Smit has called attention to a number of 'conspicuous words and metaphors' in 1 Corinthians 13 that may, in my judgment, indicate non-Pauline authorship.[44] The following words and phrases occur nowhere else in the authentic Pauline writings: δείκνυμι ('show') in 12.31b;[45] ὁδὸν...δείκνυμι ('show...a way') in 12.31b;[46] χαλκὸς ἠχῶν ἢ κύμβαλον

39. E.g. Héring, *The First Epistle of Saint Paul*, p. 134.

40. Fee, *The First Epistle to the Corinthians*, pp. 625-26.

41. E.g. Sanders, 'First Corinthians 13', p. 157; cf. e.g., Fee, *The First Epistle to the Corinthians*, p. 626 n. 3 and p. 627 n. 10.

42. Fee, *The First Epistle to the Corinthians*, pp. 625-26.

43. Titus, 'Did Paul Write I Corinthians 13?', p. 301. According to Titus: 'The famous passage, Philippians 2:5-11, cannot be used to disprove this assertion for, as is widely known, it was in all probability the common property of the Christian community and not a Pauline creation'.

44. Smit, 'The Genre of 1 Corinthians 13', pp. 199-201.

45. Elsewhere, only at 1 Tim. 6.15 in the writings attributed to Paul.

46. Only here in the New Testament.

ἀλαλάζον ('a noisy gong or a clanging cymbal') in 13.1;[47] πίστις ὥστε ὄρη μεθιστάναι ('faith so as to remove mountains') in 13.2;[48] χρησ-τεύομαι ('to be kind') in 13.4;[49] περπερεύομαι ('to boast') in 13.4;[50] παροξύνομαι ('to be irritable') in 13.5;[51] βλέπω...δι' ἐσόπτρου ('to see...in a mirror') in 13.12;[52] αἴνιγμα ('indirect image') in 13.12;[53] and πρόσωπον πρὸς πρόσωπον ('face to face') in 13.12.[54] In addition, ψωμίζω ('to dole out') in 13.3 appears elsewhere only at Rom. 12.20, in a quotation from Prov. 25.21.[55]

In my judgment, the presence of so many *hapax legomena* in the span of only 14 verses[56] constitutes a rather strong argument Pauline authorship of 1 Corinthians 13.

c. *Content*

It is my judgment that a number of features of the content of 1 Corinthians 13 call into serious question both Pauline authorship of the passage and Pauline inclusion of the passage between chs. 12 and 14 of the Corinthian letter. Some of these have already been mentioned in the discussion of whether 1 Corinthians 13 really belongs between chs. 12 and 14, but there are others.

Absence of Christology. Titus and others have noted as 'un-Pauline' the complete absence of christology or indeed of any reference to

47. Smit ('The Genre of 1 Corinthians 13', p. 200) observes: 'In classical antiquity the comparison of a garrulous orator with a hollow-sounding instrument like a gong or a cymbal occurs regularly. The bipartite formula which is found here however is rare. It probably is an onomatopoiea or echoism.'

48. Smit, 'The Genre of 1 Corinthians 13', p. 200: 'The expression "to move mountains" is originally a grotesque metaphor. In Jewish as well as in Greek milieus it has lost much of its force and has become a proverbial expression.'

49. Only here in the New Testament, but also in *1 Clem.* 13.2; 14.3.

50. Only here in the New Testament.

51. Only at Acts 17.16 elsewhere in the New Testament.

52. Only here in the New Testament, but cf. Jas 1.23. Smit ('The Genre of 1 Corinthians 13', p. 201) observes: 'To "see in a mirror" is, in classical Greek as well as in Jewish-Hellenistic authors, a common metaphor for the indirect way by which man knows God'.

53. Only here in the New Testament.

54. Only here in the New Testament, but cf. Gen. 32.31; Judg. 6.22 LXX.

55. Only at these two places in the New Testament.

56. I am including 12.31b in this verse count.

Christ (or God) in 1 Corinthians 13.[57] Other scholars, however, do not see this as an argument against Pauline authorship. Conzelmann, for example, attributes it to 'Paul's Hellenistic Jewish schooling',[58] and Fee raises a warning against circular reasoning: 'lack of Christology suggests it is not by Paul; therefore, Paul is not its original author because it lacks Christology'.[59] My own judgment is that the total absence of christology in 1 Corinthians 13 is, to say the least, unusual for Paul, and that it may well, *in combination with other cogent considerations*, constitute a significant argument against Pauline authorship of the passage.

Faith. Titus also suggests that the juxtaposition of 'faith' and 'love' in 1 Corinthians 13—and, I would add, the apparent subordination of the former to the latter—arouses suspicions regarding Pauline origin.[60] Moreover, the implied definition of 'faith' in 1 Corinthians 13 (namely, that which enables one 'to remove mountains') appears to bear little resemblance to what Paul understands by 'faith' throughout his letters.

'In a mirror darkly'. Titus asks, 'Would Paul be willing to conclude that now *we see in a mirror darkly*?'[61] 'It is true', he continues, 'that [Paul] could say, "We walk by faith and not by sight" (II Cor. 5.7), but to "walk by faith" does not mean shadowy reflections; it means, rather, to walk by the light of the knowledge of the glory of God in the face of Jesus Christ (II Cor. 4.6)'.[62]

Eschatology. According to 1 Corinthians 13, prophecy, tongues and knowledge will pass away 'when the perfect comes', and we shall 'see face to face' and 'understand fully'. Titus asks, 'Does the writer here

57. Titus, 'Did Paul Write I Corinthians 13?', p. 300; see, e.g., Meeks, *The Writings of St. Paul*, p. 41 n.6.

58. Conzelmann, *1 Corinthians*, p. 220.

59. Fee, *The First Epistle to the Corinthians*, p. 626 n. 8. My own view is that what Fee terms 'circular reasoning' is in fact, at least as he phrases it, rather a 'tautology'. Moreover, I believe that Fee's own argument comes perilously close to circular reasoning: assuming that 1 Corinthians 13 (at least in its present form) is by Paul, Fee then concludes that, *because it is by Paul*, it no doubt presupposes 'the thoroughly theological, christological understanding of ἀγάπη that [Paul] demonstrates everywhere'. Fee apparently regards this conclusion, then, as some sort of confirmation of Pauline authorship.

60. Titus, 'Did Paul Write I Corinthians 13?', pp. 300-301.

61. Literally, 'For now we see through a mirror in a riddle (or "indirect image")'.

62. Titus, 'Did Paul Write I Corinthians 13?', p. 302.

equate the perfect with the end of the age?' and 'Is this Pauline eschatology?'[63]

Spiritual gifts. As already noted, the attitude toward *spiritual gifts* in 1 Corinthians 13 not only differs from that expressed in chs. 12 and 14 but even appears to be significantly non-Pauline: as Titus notes, 'Whatever may be said of spiritual gifts as an annoyance, it remains true that the import of chapter 14 [of 1 Corinthians] is to stress their importance. Indeed Paul outdoes all others in the gift of tongues. Yet in chapter 13 their importance is minimized'.[64]

Martyrdom. In 1 Cor. 13.3, there may be a reference to martyrdom. Here, we encounter what Fee terms 'one of the truly difficult' textual choices in the New Testament.[65] Although the manuscript evidence would appear to support the reading, 'if I deliver my body in order that I might boast', most scholars prefer the variant, 'if I deliver my body in order that I might be burned'.[66] If the latter is indeed the correct reading, it may, as Fee indirectly suggests, pose a problem so far as Pauline authorship of the passage is concerned: 'Even though martyrdom by fire was not unknown among the Jews, this had not yet become a Christian phenomenon; the fiery persecutions of Nero are still at least a decade away'.[67]

Faith, hope and love. It is often suggested that the triad faith, hope and love is something of a commonplace in Paul.[68] Thus, the presence of the triad in 1 Corinthians 13 is seen as a mark of Pauline authorship. Titus notes, however, that 'the triad appears [only] rarely in combination in Paul's letters' and that, where it does occur, the 'practical references have little resemblance to the abstract faith, hope and love'

63. Titus, 'Did Paul Write I Corinthians 13?', p. 302.

64. Titus, 'Did Paul Write I Corinthians 13?', p. 302.

65. Fee, *The First Epistle to the Corinthians*, p. 629 n. 18.

66. Fee, *The First Epistle to the Corinthians*, pp. 633-34; cf. however, p. 629 n. 18: 'Paul most likely wrote, "if I hand over my body that I might boast"'. For the same conclusion, see Smit, 'Two Puzzles', pp. 255-56.

67. Fee, *The First Epistle to the Corinthians*, p. 634. For Fee, this is an argument against taking 'in order that I might be burned' as the original reading.

68. See, e.g., 1 Thess. 1.3; 5.8; Gal. 5.5-6; Rom. 5.1-5; and perhaps 1 Thess. 3.6. Indeed, Meeks (*The Writings of St. Paul*, p. 42 n. 9) refers to it as 'a cliché for Paul, perhaps already in pre-Pauline Christianity and even in Hellenistic Judaism'. Although Titus ('Did Paul Write I Corinthians 13?', p. 301) rejects this notion, he does refer to the phrase as 'a familiar Pauline formula'.

of 1 Corinthians 13.[69] Titus also notes 'that the combination of the triad is not confined to Paul's writings'.[70] Thus, Fee believes 'that this was a familiar triad in early Christian preaching',[71] and A.M. Hunter has suggested that the words 'these three' (τὰ τρία ταῦτα) might be translated as 'you know, the well-known three'.[72] Although Fee and Hunter assume that the triad is *earlier* than Paul,[73] it should be noted that most of the examples are *later* than the Apostle.[74] All of this suggests, in my judgment, that if the triad (in whichever sequence) was indeed a commonplace, it was a commonplace not uniquely in Paul but rather in various strands of early Christianity, particularly post-Pauline Christianity.[75] Thus, I do not see the presence of the triad in 1 Corinthians 13 as an argument for Pauline authorship.

Knowledge. More than half a century ago, Robert Martyr Hawkins noted as a possible argument against Pauline authorship of 1 Corinthians 13 'the place that is given to knowledge, especially the idea that knowledge will ultimately come to fulness and completion'.[76] Most scholars assume that Paul is here thinking in eschatological terms.[77] If

69. Titus, 'Did Paul Write I Corinthians 13?', p. 301. The sequence of the three elements in both 1 Thess. 1.3 and 5.8 is faith, love, hope, not the faith, hope, love of 1 Cor. 13.13. The sequence faith, hope, love in Rom. 5.1-5 is to be expected, because in Rom. 4 Paul deals with justification by faith and in Rom. 5.6-11 he picks up on the idea of God's love. Gal. 5.5-6 also has the sequence faith, hope, love.

70. Titus, 'Did Paul Write I Corinthians 13?', p. 301; see, e.g., Col. 1.4-5; Eph. 4.2-5; 1 Pet. 3.8; Heb. 6.10-12; 10.22-24; *Barn*. 1.4; 11.8; and Polycarp, *Phil*. 3.2-3. Titus notes ('Did Paul Write I Corinthians?', p. 301) 'that in I Peter the ideas are not barely stated as in I Thessalonians 1:3 and I Corinthians 13:13, but appear in formal discussion', suggesting that this 'was [also] true of the text which formed the original triad of which I Corinthians 13 was the concluding member'.

71. Fee, *The First Epistle to the Corinthians*, p. 650; cf. A.M. Hunter, *Paul and his Predecessors* (Philadelphia: Westminster Press, rev. edn, 1961), pp. 33-35.

72. Hunter, *Paul and his Predecessors*, p. 34.

73. See also, e.g., Conzelmann, *1 Corinthians*, p. 229: 'Paul may have found the formula already in the Hellenistic community'.

74. These are the examples in Colossians, Ephesians, 1 Peter, Hebrews, Barnabas and Polycarp.

75. For a discussion of the triad that assumes Pauline authorship of 1 Cor. 13, see, e.g., Conzelmann, *1 Corinthians*, pp. 229-31.

76. Hawkins, *The Recovery of the Historical Paul*, p. 195. Hawkins himself, however, regarded the interpolation hypothesis regarding 1 Cor. 13 as 'unlikely'.

77. E.g. Conzelmann, *1 Corinthians*, p. 228.

the materials regarding knowledge are read in mystical terms, however, the resulting interpretation appears strikingly non-Pauline.[78]

d. *Conclusion*

Overall, I regard the content of 1 Corinthians 13 as constituting a strong argument not only against the original placement of the passage between chs. 12 and 14 but also against Pauline authorship.

5. *Text-Critical Considerations*

Although this is not mentioned by Titus, I believe that text-critical considerations should play a significant role in the identification of interpolations. The strongest positive evidence for interpolation, of course, would be *direct* text-critical evidence (the absence of a passage from one or more of the manuscripts, particularly early manuscripts, and/or the location of the passage at different places in the various manuscripts).[79] Indeed, some scholars insist that this is virtually a prerequisite for identifying any passage as an interpolation.[80] In the case of 1 Corinthians 13, I am aware of no such direct text-critical evidence.

It is important, however, that the absence of text-critical evidence be seen as precisely what it is: the *absence* of evidence. The extant manuscript evidence goes back no further than the late second-century, and it is clear that even the earliest extant manuscript, P^{46}, represents an *edited* collection of the letters, including, as it does, parts of both pseudo-Pauline and non-Pauline writings.[81] It is precisely during the period *prior* to the late-second century, however, that interpolations would most likely have appeared, and these *early* interpolations are precisely the ones that would have left no textual traces. In short, the absence of direct text-critical evidence for interpolation is of little

78. In the thought of those rejecting the mystical interpretation there may be some circular reasoning: 1 Cor. 13 is Pauline; Paul thinks in eschatological rather than mystical terms; therefore, 1 Cor. 13 is to be interpreted in eschatological rather than mystical terms; therefore, a mystical interpretation of 1 Cor. 13 may not be used as an argument against Pauline authorship.

79. See, e.g., Jn 7.53–8.11, which almost all scholars regard as a non-Johannine interpolation. In the Pauline letters, see Rom. 16.25-27 and 1 Cor. 14.34-35.

80. See, e.g., Ellis, 'The Silenced Wives of Corinth (I Cor. 14:34-5)', p. 220; and 'Traditions in 1 Corinthians', p. 488 and p. 498 n. 58.

81. Pseudo-Pauline are Colossians and Ephesians; non-Pauline is Hebrews.

negative value in refuting an otherwise cogent argument for interpolation.

There are, however, at least two types of *indirect* text-critical evidence that might support an argument for interpolation. One of these—admittedly requiring an argument from silence—is the failure of one or more early Christian writers to refer to a passage at a place where the subject matter, point of view and/or use of other related passages would appear to call for such a reference. This might indicate that the author was unaware of the passage (presumably because it was absent from the manuscript[s] at hand). Indirect text-critical evidence of this type does appear to exist in the case of 1 Corinthians 13. A number of references to other passages in 1 Corinthians can be found in *1 Clement* and the letters of Ignatius (probably also in Polycarp's *Letter to the Philippians* and in the *Didache*).[82] With one possible exception, however, I can find no reference to 1 Corinthians 13 prior to the latter part of the second century (that is, not until Irenaeus, Clement of Alexandria and Tertullian).[83]

The one possible exception is *1 Clem.* 49.2–50.2. Here, not long after admonishing the readers to 'take up the epistle of the blessed Paul the Apostle' (47.1), making clear reference to 1 Cor. 1.11-12 (*1 Clem.* 47.3), and apparently alluding to 1 Cor. 12.8-9 (*1 Clem.* 48.5), the author provides a moving panegyric or encomium on love.[84] Some scholars find reflections of 1 Corinthians 13 in this passage.[85] In my own judgment, however, this is unlikely. A close comparison of

82. See the Reference Index in Kirsopp Lake, *The Apostolic Fathers* (LCL; 2 vols.; Cambridge, MA: Harvard University Press, 1912–13), II, p. 395; and J. Allenbach *et al.*, *Biblia Patristica: Index des citations et allusions bibliques dans la littérature patristique* (4 vols.; Paris: Éditions du Centre National de la Recherche Scientifique, 1975–87), I, pp. 444-74.

83. Allenbach *et al.*, *Biblia Patristica*, I, pp. 465-67.

84. It is my own judgment that this ends at 50.2, but others believe that it continues further.

85. E.g. Lake, *The Apostolic Fathers*, I, p. 92 and II, p. 395; and Allenbach *et al.*, *Biblia Patristica*, I, p. 466. For a careful comparison of 1 Cor. 13 and *1 Clem.* 49.1-6 that assumes *1 Clement*'s use of 1 Cor. 13, see, e.g., Barbara E. Bowe, 'The Rhetoric of Love in Corinth: From Paul to Clement of Rome', in Julian V. Hills with Richard B. Gardner *et al.* (eds.), *Common Life in the Early Church: Essays Honoring Graydon F. Snyder* (Harrisburg, PA: Trinity Press International, 1998), pp. 244-57; see also, e.g., Donald A. Hagner, *The Use of the Old and New Testaments in Clement of Rome* (NovTSup, 34; Leiden: E.J. Brill, 1973), pp. 185-213.

1 Clem. 49.5 and 1 Cor. 13.4-7 discloses that, apart from the repeated reference to 'love' (ἀγάπη), there are virtually no verbal parallels between the two passages. To be sure, both assert that love is 'patient' (μακροθυμεῖ), but the wording of the assertion is different.[86] Similarly, both assert that love 'bears all things', but the Greek words for 'bears' are different.[87] Finally, both passages deny that love is 'arrogant' or 'haughty', but again the wording is different.[88] Indeed, as Barbara E. Bowe notes, the passage in *1 Clement* shares exactly with 1 Corinthians 13 'only the verb "endure" (μακροθυμεῖ) and the repetition of ἀγάπη, πάντα, and οὐδέν'.[89] In my judgment, these similarities are not sufficient to indicate that the author of either passage was familiar with the other. Indeed, the two passages appear to represent either essentially independent treatments of the virtue of love or perhaps independent and partial renditions of some earlier encomium on love.[90]

The primary purpose of *1 Clement* is to resolve a controversy in Corinth over leadership in the church. As one way of accomplishing this, the author appeals both directly and indirectly to the authority of Paul. Indeed, according to Andreas Lindemann, he 'seems…to take it as self-evident that he should make use of Paul's letter in support of his own argumentation'. Thus, he 'refers to Paul just where he seems to require the support of apostolic authority in relation to the strife in Corinth', and 'he declares that the apostle, in his own letter to the Corinthians, had already provided the solution to the very problem they now faced'.[91] In *1 Clement*, the second explicit appeal to Paul (and, in fact, an appeal specifically to 1 Corinthians!) comes at 47.1-3. This is only 40 lines before the passage (*1 Clem*. 49.2–50.2) regarded by many as a reflection of 1 Corinthians 13. Moreover, an apparent allusion to

86. 1 Cor. 13.4 reads ἡ ἀγάπη μακροθυμεῖ ('love is patient') while *1 Clem*. 49.5 has πάντα μακροθυμεῖ ('it is patient in all things').

87. 1 Cor. 13.7 has στέγει, while *1 Clem*. 49.5 reads ἀνέχεται.

88. 1 Cor. 13.4 reads οὐ φυσιοῦται ('it is not arrogant') while *1 Clem*. 49.5 has οὐδὲν ὑπερήφανον ('[there is] nothing haughty' [in love]').

89. Bowe, 'The Rhetoric of Love', pp. 255-56.

90. See, e.g., the encomia on *Erōs* in Plato, *Symp*. 197C-E, and Maximus of Tyre, *Diss*. 20.2.

91. Andreas Lindemann, 'Paul in the Writings of the Apostolic Fathers', in William S. Babcock (ed.), *Paul and the Legacies of Paul* (Dallas: Southern Methodist University Press, 1990), pp. 25-45 (32, 31).

1 Cor. 12.8-9 in *1 Clem.* 48.5 appears only eight lines before the passage in question (49.2–50.2.)[92]

In light of the author's purpose in writing *1 Clement*, his clear desire for Pauline authority to support his admonitions to the Corinthians, and the fact that he was obviously familiar with much of what we know as 1 Corinthians (including material in ch. 12), I find it almost impossible to imagine that this author knew 1 Corinthians 13 but failed to cite it at this point and even used a different passage with similar content. Substantively, 1 Corinthians 13 would have suited his purposes at least as well as the passage he used, and it would have had the added advantage of possessing apostolic (that is, Pauline) authority. In short, my own judgment is that the author of *1 Clement* almost certainly did not know 1 Corinthians 13. Because the author obviously was familiar with other parts of 1 Corinthians, this appears to support the view that this author's copy (or copies) of 1 Corinthians did not include ch. 13. Thus, the chapter may well be a later addition to the text of Paul's Corinthian letter.

A final possible argument for viewing 1 Cor. 12.31b–14.1a as a non-Pauline interpolation has already been noted: the presence of an apparently insignificant textual variant in 12.31a. Here, the better attested reading is 'but be zealous for the greater (μείζονα) gifts'; some manuscripts, however, read, 'but be zealous for the better (κρείττονα or κρείσσονα) gifts'. It is possible that 'better' (κρείττονα or κρείσσονα) was the original reading but that it was changed to 'greater'—either by an interpolator or by a later editor—to provide a clearer link with 13.13, which states that love is 'greater' (μείζων) than faith and hope.

6. *Conclusion*

It is my judgment that 1 Cor. 12.31b–14.1a forms an independent, self-contained unit, that it was not originally located between chs. 12 and 14, that it was not composed by Paul, and that it was inserted in the Corinthian letter by someone other than Paul. Titus suggests that the interpolation may have been made by someone who 'disagreed with Paul's exaltation of prophecy and "corrected" it in terms of his [*sic*] own evaluation of love as the supreme way'.[93] Titus also suggests that the interpolation 'has served its purpose well', because, 'after reading

92. The lines are counted as they appear in Lake, *Apostolic Fathers*.
93. Titus, 'Did Paul Write I Corinthians 13?', p. 300.

the inspiring panegyric on love, the force of chapter 14 with its stress on prophecy is lost to the average reader, so that he [*sic*] scarcely knows that it is there at all'.[94] Another possibility, of course, is that 1 Corinthians 13 was inserted into the Corinthian letter by someone who, for whatever reason, assumed it to be Pauline in origin and, again for whatever reason, decided to place it between what we now know as chs. 12 and 14.

94. Titus, 'Did Paul Write I Corinthians 13?', p. 302.

Chapter 8

ROMANS 1.18–2.29*

1. *Introduction*

More than two decades ago, J.C. O'Neill argued that Rom. 1.18–2.29 is a non-Pauline interpolation.[1] Because he finds numerous glosses and interpolations in both Romans and Galatians,[2] however, his views have not been well received by most scholars. Indeed, as I noted in my Introduction, Victor Paul Furnish asserts that O'Neill's conclusions reflect 'highly subjective judgments about content and tone...intermixed with often-questionable generalizations about the apostle's style and vocabulary', resulting in 'a Paul created in the interpreter's own image'.[3] More peremptorily, Joseph A. Fitzmyer declares that 'short shrift...has to be given to the proposals of O'Neill'.[4] One reviewer of

* This chapter represents a slightly revised version of my article 'Romans 1.18–2.29: A Non-Pauline Interpolation?'. It is included here, with permission of the original publisher.

1. O'Neill, *Paul's Letter to the Romans*, pp. 40-56. 'Non-Pauline interpolation' means that the material was both composed and inserted into the Roman letter by someone other than Paul (the author and the interpolator, however, may or may not have been the same person). Other scholars who have regarded Rom. 1.18–2.29, either in whole or in part, as a non-Pauline interpolation include: Loisy (*The Origins of the New Testament*, p. 250; and *idem*, *The Birth of the Christian Religion* [trans. L.P. Jacks; New Hyde Park, NY: University Books, 1962 (French original, 1933)], p. 363 n. 21); Hawkins (*The Recovery of the Historical Paul*, pp. 79-86; Harrison (*Paulines and Pastorals*, p. 81); and, more recently, Munro (*Authority in Paul and Peter*, pp. 112-13, 155-60).

2. On Galatians, see O'Neill, *The Recovery of Paul's Letter to the Galatians*; see also Loisy, *Remarques sur la littérature épistolaire*, *passim*; Couchoud, 'Reconstitution et classement des Lettres'; and 'La première édition de Saint Paul'; and Hawkins, *The Recovery of the Historical Paul*, pp. 14-20, 291-92, *et passim*.

3. Furnish, 'Pauline Studies', p. 325.

4. Fitzmyer, *Romans*, p. 65; cf. p. 270: 'The passage is scarcely an interpolation into Paul's text'.

O'Neill's book on Romans observes, however: 'Scholars will find this a challenging and stimulating treatment of Romans, and may even decide that some of its arguments for Pauline and non-Pauline sections must be treated very seriously'.[5] It is my intention not only to treat very seriously O'Neill's views regarding Rom. 1.18–2.29 but also to support and strengthen his argument that the passage is a non-Pauline interpolation.

2. *Text-Critical Evidence for Interpolation*

There is no direct text-critical evidence for regarding 1.18–2.29, or any part of it, as a non-Pauline interpolation. So far as I can ascertain, it appears—indeed, at the same location—in all of the early manuscripts and versions. There is, however, some indirect text-critical evidence suggesting the absence of 1.19–2.1 from one or more early manuscripts.

According to Theodor Zahn and Adolf von Harnack, Rom. 1.19–2.1 did not appear in Marcion's 'authentic' text of Romans.[6] Most scholars (including Harnack) assume that Marcion eliminated these verses because he objected to something in their content.[7] A number of years ago, however, P.-L. Couchoud argued that it was Marcion who preserved the original text of the Pauline letters and that the now-extant

5. Anonymous, 'Talking Points from Books', *ExpTim* 86 (1975), pp. 257-59 (258).

6. Theodor Zahn, *Geschichte des neutestamentlichen Kanons* (2 vols.; Erlangen: Deichert, 1888–92), II, p. 516; Adolf von Harnack, *Marcion: The Gospel of the Alien God* (trans. John E. Steely and Lyle D. Bierman; Durham, NC: Labyrinth, 1990 [German original, 1924]), p. 34. For a summary of the evidence, see Harrison, *Paulines and Pastorals*, p. 79. On the difficulties involved in reconstructing Marcion's text of the Pauline letters, see John Knox, *Marcion and the New Testament: An Essay in the Early History of the Canon* (Chicago: University of Chicago Press, 1942), pp. 46-53. For an argument that 'Marcion's role was not the creation of a new text but the adaptation of an already existing Pauline Corpus', see John J. Clabeaux, *A Lost Edition of the Letters of Paul: A Reassessment of the Text of the Pauline Corpus Attested by Marcion* (CBQMS, 21; Washington: Catholic Biblical Association, 1989), quotation from p. 4.

7. See, e.g., Harnack, *Marcion*, p. 34: 'he eliminated 1:19–2:1 completely because this bit of natural religion had to go counter to his opinions, just as did the idea that men [*sic*] are given up by God to the most dreadful vices as punishment'.

manuscripts include numerous interpolations.[8] Although this view has generally been rejected, P.N. Harrison suggested some years ago that 'in this particular instance [namely, Rom. 1.19–2.1] Couchoud came nearer to the truth than he himself realized'.[9]

Harrison noted that Marcion's text omits not only 1.19-32, which Marcion no doubt would have found objectionable, but also 2.1, to which he would have had no plausible objection.[10] For Harrison, the most likely explanation for the omission of 2.1 was that the entire passage, 1.19–2.1, 'had no place in the text of Romans used by Marcion, being an interpolation added by some scribe'.[11] Harrison then cited various aspects of the linguistic evidence to be discussed below to support his view that Rom. 1.19–2.1 is a non-Pauline interpolation.[12]

Along with the considerations of language, context and ideational content, this bit of textual history may support the view that at least Rom. 1.19–2.1 is an interpolation.[13]

8. Couchoud, 'La première édition de Saint Paul' and 'Reconstitution et classement des Lettres'.

9. Harrison, *Paulines and Pastorals*, p. 80.

10. Harrison, *Paulines and Pastorals*, p. 81: 'on Harnack's own showing… Marcion included in his Gospel the words "judge not that ye be not judged, condemn not that ye be not condemned" [Luke 6:37]… So there is nothing in this verse to which Marcion could or did object. Yet it was as certainly missing in the Apostolicon as the fourteen verses preceding it.'

11. Harrison, *Paulines and Pastorals*, p. 81.

12. Harrison, *Paulines and Pastorals*, pp. 82-85. According to Munro (*Authority in Paul and Peter*, pp. 112-13), Rom. 1.19–2.1 'is to be dissociated from its context in Romans' and 'associated with the Pastorals'; in addition, the passage 'bears a close relation to [what Munro terms] the later [Pastoral] stratum in the ten-letter corpus' (quotations from p. 113).

13. Following Harrison, Munro (*Authority in Peter and Paul*, pp. 112-13, 155-60) regards Rom. 1.19–2.1 (but not 1.18 or 2.2-29) as non-Pauline. She sees both ὦ ἄνθρωπε πᾶς ὁ κρίνων in 2.1 (cf. ὦ ἄνθρωπε ὁ κρίνων in 2.3) and οἱ τὰ τοιαῦτα πράσσοντες in 1.32 (cf. τοὺς τὰ τοιαῦτα πράσσοντας in both 2.2 and 2.3) as parts 'of the seam connecting later to earlier material' (p. 155). In her view (p. 155), 'Rom. 1:19ff, concerning the revelation of God through the creation, follows awkwardly after Rom. 1:18, which speaks of the revelation of God's wrath from heaven. If, however, Rom. 2:2ff is joined to Rom. 1:18, a smooth sequence results. The theme of the judgement of God in Rom. 2:2 follows naturally after that of the wrath of God in Rom. 1:18, and the thought of God's judgement "according to truth" in Rom. 2:2 forms an effective contrast to "the ungodliness and unrighteousness of men who possess the truth in unrighteousness" (Rom. 1:18)'. Although

3. *Linguistic Evidence for Interpolation*

Much of the language of Rom. 1.18-32 and, to lesser extent, that of Romans 2 appears to be distinctively non-Pauline. Because of significant differences, however, between 1.18-32 and ch. 2 so far as language is concerned, the two sections will be examined separately.

a. *The Language of Romans 1.18-32*

Regarding Rom. 1.18-32, O'Neill asserts that 'the language in which the argument is expressed is unlike Paul's usual language in both vocabulary and style'.[14] The basic data regarding vocabulary are the following:[15] the passage contains 109 different nouns, adjectives and verbs;[16] of these 109, 15 (13.76 per cent) are found nowhere else in the New Testament,[17] 10 (8.26 per cent) appear elsewhere in the New Testament but not in the Pauline corpus,[18] four (3.67 per cent) are shared only with pseudo-Pauline[19] and other non-Pauline New Testament writings,[20] and five (4.59 per cent) are shared only with pseudo-Pauline

Munro's observations are clearly plausible, it is my own judgment that they are outweighed by arguments against the authenticity of Rom. 2.

14. O'Neill, *Paul's Letter to the Romans*, p. 41.

15. Many of these data are set forth by Harrison (*Paulines and Pastorals*, pp. 82-83). At some points, however, my numbers differ from his because, unlike him, I regard Ephesians, Colossians and 2 Thessalonians as pseudo-Pauline.

16. Not included are articles, conjunctions, prepositions, demonstratives, personal pronouns, relative pronouns, reflexive pronouns, or the negative particle.

17. Καθοράω, θειότης, ματαιόομαι, ἀλάσσω (×2), σεβάζομαι, χρῆσις (×2), ἐκκαίομαι, ὄρεξις, κακοήθεια, ψιθυριστής, κατάλαλος, θεοστυγής, ἐφευρετής, ἀσύνθετος and ἀνελεήμων. In addition, ἀναπολόγητος appears elsewhere in the New Testament only at Rom. 2.1, which, as part of the larger passage under consideration, may well be non-Pauline.

18. Γνωστός, αΐδιος, φάσκω, πετεινός, τετράπους, ἑρπετόν, φυσικός (×2), ἀσχημοσύνη, καθήκω and φόνος. In addition, ἀτιμάζω occurs elsewhere in the Pauline corpus only at Rom. 2.23, which, as part of the larger passage under consideration, may well be non-Pauline. Καθήκω appears at Acts 22.22; otherwise, however, it appears in early Christian literature only in *1 Clement*, 'where it has quite explicit connections with a hierarchical ordering of human relationships' (Munro, *Authority in Paul and Peter*, p. 159).

19. I regard the Pastorals, Ephesians, Colossians and 2 Thessalonians as pseudo-Pauline.

20. Ψεῦδος, ὑπερήφανος, ἀπειθής and ἀόρατος (the last occurs in Colossians, which Harrison regards as authentically Pauline).

writings.[21] In short, almost a third of the nouns, adjectives and verbs in Rom. 1.18-32—a total of 34 words or 31.19 per cent—appear nowhere else in the authentic Pauline letters[22] (particularly noteworthy is the vocabulary beginning with the last two words of v. 29 and continuing through to v. 31: here, 12 of the 15 words are not otherwise attested in the authentic letters of Paul). In addition, Rom. 1.18-32 contains 16 words that appear elsewhere in the authentic Pauline writings only once. Of the 16, four occur only in quotations from the Old Testament,[23] two appear only in Gal. 3.28 (often regarded as a pre-Pauline baptismal formula),[24] and two are found only in Romans 2 which, as part of the larger passage under consideration, may well be non-Pauline;[25] this leaves only eight that are likely to have originated with Paul himself.[26] Thus, at least 50 (45.87 per cent) of the 109 nouns, adjectives and verbs in Rom. 1.18-32 appear not to represent typically Pauline vocabulary.[27] Finally, it should be noted that ὀργὴ Θεοῦ (1.18) occurs elsewhere in the New Testament only in the pseudo-Pauline Ephesians (5.6) and

21. Νοέω, ὑβριστής, ἀλαζών, ἄστοργος and ποίημα.

22. Harrison counts 30 such words, and O'Neill (*Paul's Letter to the Romans*, p. 41), 'at least twenty-nine' (apparently O'Neill, like Harrison, assumes that Ephesians and Colossians are Pauline). Noting that the remainder of Romans contains only 231 words that appear nowhere else in the authentic Pauline writings, Harrison (*Paulines and Pastorals*, pp. 82-83, where exact statistics are given) concludes that Rom. 1.18-32 (one page in the Westcott-Hort text) contains 'more than three times as many words which do not occur elsewhere in the Paulines as the remaining twenty-five pages of Romans have on the average' (note: if Harrison also regarded Ephesians and Colossians as pseudo-Pauline, the number 231 would be somewhat higher).

23. Ἀσέβεια (Rom. 11.26; cf. Isa. 11.26), σκοτίζομαι (Rom. 11.10; cf. Ps. 68.24), ἀσύνετος (Rom. 10.19; cf. Deut. 32.21) and μωραίνω (1 Cor. 1.20; cf. Isa. 19.11).

24. θῆλυς and ἄρσην.

25. Ἀναπολόγητος (Rom. 2.1) and ἀτιμάζω (Rom. 2.23).

26. Κτίζω (1 Cor. 11.9), πάθος (1 Thess. 4.5), ἀντιμισθία (2 Cor. 6.13), πλάνη (1 Thess. 2.3), ἀπολαμβάνω (Gal. 4.5), πονηρία (1 Cor. 5.8), μεστός (Rom. 15.14), and γονεῖς (2 Cor. 12.14).

27. In addition, Rom. 1.18-32 contains eight words that appear elsewhere in the undoubtedly authentic Pauline letters only twice: ἄφθαρτος (1 Cor. 9.25; 15.52), λατρεύω (Rom. 1.9; Phil. 3.3), πλεονεξία (2 Cor. 9.5; 1 Thess. 2.5), κακία (1 Cor. 5.8; 14.20), φθόνος (Gal. 5.21; Phil. 1.15), δόλος (2 Cor. 12.16; 1 Thess. 2.3), ἄξιος (Rom. 8.18; 1 Cor. 16.4) and συνευδοκέω (1 Cor. 7.12, 13). These, too, might well be regarded as not typically Pauline.

Colossians (3.6) and in Revelation (19.15), and that γονεῦσιν ἀπειθεῖς (1.30) appears elsewhere only in the pseudo-Pauline 2 Timothy (3.2).

Winsome Munro, who regards Rom. 1.19–2.1 (but not 1.18 or 2.2-29) as a non-Pauline interpolation, emphasizes the affinities between the vocabulary of this passage and that of other proposed interpolations and the pseudo-Pauline writings.[28] For example, she notes that πάθος (1.26) appears elsewhere in the New Testament only at the pseudo-Pauline Col. 3.5 and at 1 Thess. 4.5, which she regards as part of an interpolation. Similarly, both Rom. 1.19–2.1 and 1 Cor. 11.3-16 (which both Munro and I regard as a non-Pauline interpolation[29]) 'use the relatively unusual New Testament words' εἰκών,[30] φύσις,[31] κτίζειν[32] and ἀτιμία,[33] 'and do so in very similar ways'. Finally, the phrase γονεῦσιν ἀπειθεῖς ('disobedient to parents') in 1.30 appears elsewhere in the New Testament only in the pseudo-Pauline 2 Tim. 3.2.[34]

28. Munro, *Authority in Paul and Peter*, pp. 155-60.

29. See Chapter 5.

30. Rom. 1.23; 1 Cor. 11.7. According to Munro (*Authority in Paul and Peter*, p. 156), only in Rom. 1.23 and 1 Cor. 11.7 is there a direct connection between εἰκών and the account of the creation of man [*sic*] in Gen. 1.26 LXX. Elsewhere in the Pauline corpus, εἰκών always refers 'to the image of God as applied to man [*sic*]' but in such a way as to indicate a contrast between the present and future (intended) status of humankind.

31. Rom. 1.26; 1 Cor. 11.14. In both passages, according to Munro, 'to err is to behave in such a way as to oppose or change nature, and right conduct is behavior that accords with nature'; indeed, these two passages 'are alone in the New Testament in representing nature, clearly identifiable with the created order, as the right norm for behaviour' (p. 157).

32. Rom. 1.25; 1 Cor. 11.9. According to Munro (*Authority in Paul and Peter*, pp. 156-57), only in these two passages and in the pseudo-Pauline 1 Tim. 4.3 does the verb refer to 'creation as the norm for moral judgment': 'In all three contexts evil consists in rejecting or opposing the world as God has created and ordered it'.

33. Rom. 1.26; 1 Cor. 11.14. In these two passages and in the pseudo-Pauline 2 Tim. 2.20, according to Munro, 'the term refers to dishonour in the sense of 'blameworthy disgrace' which is the result of culpable error'; elsewhere in the Pauline corpus, however, 'the word is used to refer simply to lack of prominence and external importance, without necessarily implying any blame' (*Authority in Paul and Peter*, pp. 157, 158).

34. Note also in the pseudo-Pauline Col. 3.20 and Eph. 6.1 that children are to 'be obedient' (ὑπακούειν) to parents.

In my judgment, these data regarding vocabulary suggest that Pauline authorship of Rom. 1.18-32 is highly unlikely. One might argue, of course, that the distinctive vocabulary of Rom. 1.18-32 results from its distinctive subject matter. This argument founders, however, on the fact that the *vocabulary* of the passage is *most* distinctive at precisely the point where the *subject matter* is *least* distinctive: the 'vice' list in 1.29-31. The authentic Pauline letters contain five other such lists,[35] and a comparison of the vocabulary in these lists with that in Rom. 1.29-31 indicates relatively little overlap. Romans 1.29-31 lists a total of 21 vices; of the 21, however, only six (28.57 per cent) appear in one or more of the other lists.[36] Alternatively, the other five lists enumerate a total of 28 vices; of the 28, however, only six (21.43 per cent) appear in Rom. 1.29-31. At the same time, however, there is significantly more overlap *among* the other five lists: all of the six vices in 1 Cor. 5.10-11 (100 per cent) appear in one or more of the other lists,[37] as do five of the six (83.33 per cent) in Rom. 13.13,[38] nine of the 11 (81.82 per cent) in 2 Cor. 12.20-21,[39] 11 of the 15 (73.33 per cent) in Gal. 5.19-21,[40] and seven of the 11 (63.64 per cent) in 1 Cor. 6.9-10.[41] In short, although the vocabularies of the other vice lists in the authentic Pauline letters exhibit a significant degree of overlap, the vocabulary of Rom. 1.29-31 is distinctively different.

It should also be noted that, of the 21 vices in Rom. 1.29-31, eight (38.10 per cent) also appear in the Pastoral Letters,[42] seven of them

35. Rom. 13.13; 1 Cor. 5.10-11; 6.9-10; 2 Cor. 12.20-21; Gal. 5.19-21; in the pseudo-Pauline writings, Eph. 5.3-5; Col. 3.5-8; 1 Tim. 1.9-10; 6.4-5; 2 Tim. 3.2-4; Tit. 1.7; 3.3 (cf. also 1 Pet. 2.1; 4.3; 4.15).

36. Two appear in three lists: ἔρις (Rom. 13.13; 2 Cor. 12.20; Gal. 5.20) and πλεονεξία (πλεονεξία in Rom. 1.29 but the cognate πλεονέκτης in 1 Cor. 5.10; 6.10); and four (ἀδικία, ψιθυρίστης, κατάλαλος and φθόνος) appear in only one list (ἀδικία in Rom. 1.29 but the cognate ἄδικός in 1 Cor. 6.9; ψιθυριστής in Rom. 1.29 but the cognate ψιθυρισμός in 2 Cor. 12.20; κατάλαλος in Rom. 1.30 but the cognate καταλαλία in 2 Cor. 12.20; φθόνος in both Rom. 1.29 and Gal. 5.21).

37. Three in one other list, one in two other lists, and two in three other lists.

38. Two in one other list and three in two other lists.

39. Five in one other list, two in two other lists, and two in three other lists.

40. Five in one other list, three in two other lists, and three in three other lists.

41. Three in one other list, two in two other lists, and two in three other lists.

42. Κακία (Tit. 3.3), φθόνος (1 Tim. 6.4; Tit. 3.3), ἔρις (1 Tim. 6.4; Tit. 3.9), ὑβριστής (1 Tim. 1.13), ὑπερήφανος (2 Tim. 3.2), ἀλαζών (2 Tim. 3.2), γονεῦσιν ἀπειθής (2 Tim. 3.2), and ἄστοργος (2 Tim. 3.3).

(33.33 per cent) in vice lists[43] and four of these (19.05 per cent) in the same passage.[44] Thus, the vocabulary of Rom. 1.29-31 is closer to that of the Pastoral vice lists than to that of the authentically Pauline lists.[45]

Significant, too, is the fact that some of the items included in the other lists but not in Rom. 1.29-31 are vices that Paul elsewhere singles out for vigorous attack. For example, Rom. 1.29-31 does not include πορνεία/πορνεύειν/πόρνος. Elsewhere, however, Paul has a great deal to say about πορνεία/πορνεύειν/πόρνη/πόρνος,[46] associating the terms with conduct that is prevalent among Gentiles but not to be tolerated among the people of God (a concern closely related to that of Rom. 1.18-32). Similarly, Rom. 1.29-31 omits εἰδωλολατρία/εἰδωλολάτρης, about which Paul speaks elsewhere.[47] Because πορνεία/πορνεύειν/πόρνος appears in four of the five other vice lists and εἰδωλολατρία/εἰδωλολάτρης in three of the five and both are the object of serious concern elsewhere in Paul's writings, it is difficult to understand why Paul would have omitted them from such a lengthy list as that in Rom. 1.29-31!

In short, not only is the vocabulary of Rom. 1.18-32 distinctively non-Pauline, it is also most *non-Pauline* (and, indeed, apparently *pseudo-Pauline*) precisely at the point where one would expect it to be most *Pauline*: in the vice list in 1.29-31.

In addition, Rom. 1.18-32 contains a number of stylistic features that appear not to be typically Pauline. As P.N. Harrison notes, the passage exhibits 'a fondness for words beginning with α-privative': by his count, Romans in its entirety contains only 48 α-privative words, of which 17 (35.42 per cent) are in this one passage.[48] In addition, Calvin L. Porter has called attention to certain repetitive features suggesting that the passage is 'a speech constructed for the ears, for hearing'.

43. All except ὑβριστής.

44. 2 Tim. 3.2-3: ὑπερήφανος, ἀλαζών, γονεῦσιν ἀπειθής and ἄστοργος.

45. Noting that the vice list in Rom. 1.29-31 is similar to that in *1 Clem.* 35.5, Munro (*Authority in Paul and Peter*, p. 159) suggests the possibility that the former may be dependent upon the latter rather than *vice versa* (as is usually assumed).

46. E.g. 1 Cor. 5.1-13; 6.12-20; 7.2; 10.8; 1 Thess. 4.3-8.

47. 1 Cor. 10.7, 14-22; note the juxtaposition of εἰδωλολατρία and πορνεία in 1 Cor. 10.7-8. To be sure, Rom. 1.23, 25, earlier in the same passage, appears to have εἰδωλολατρία in mind; nevertheless, it is surprising to find it missing from the vice list in 1.29-31.

48. Harrison, *Paulines and Pastorals*, p. 83; cf. Hawkins, *The Recovery of the Historical Paul*, p. 80.

These include the following items in 1.22-31: (1) παρέδωκεν αὐτοὺς ὁ Θεός appears three times (1.24, 26, 28); (2) a form of the verb ἀλλάσσω appears three times (1.23, 25, 26); (3) the dative-case ending –ιᾳ appears four times in the same verse (1.29); and (4) there is an alliterative sequence of four words beginning with the negative α and ending with –ους in the same verse (1.31). Further, Porter notes that 'the discourse as a whole is dominated by the repeated use of third person plural verbs' ending in –σαν, –ξαν or –σιν;[49] observing that 'no other section of Romans contains such a concentration', Porter suggests that 'in an oral presentation the endings of these Greek verbs would have been as striking as is the "they" in an English translation'. Finally, Porter notes that the passage contains 'thirteen occurrences of plural forms of the pronoun αὐτός...and one instance of the plural reflexive ἑαυτοῖς'.[50] All of this, in Porter's view, contributes to a 'strong and dominant "they/them" sense of the speech'.[51] Such features are not prominent, however, elsewhere in the Pauline writings.

These linguistic data indicate that the language of Rom. 1.18-32 is distinctively non-Pauline in character and, in my judgment, suggest that Paul was not the author of the passage. Such data are not sufficient, of course, to demonstrate that someone other than Paul added 1.18-32 to the Roman letter, for it is possible that Paul incorporated an originally non-Pauline passage into his own letter, perhaps even adapting and revising it to suit his purposes. To show that 1.18-32 not only was composed by someone other than Paul but also was added to the Roman letter by someone other than Paul, it will be necessary to consider both the context and the ideational content of the passage.

b. *The Language of Romans 2*

The language of Romans 2 is somewhat less striking than that of 1.18-32, but it too appears not to be typically Pauline. Chapter 2 contains seven words that occur nowhere else in the New Testament,[52] nine that

49. Three in v. 21, one in v. 22, one in v. 23, three in v. 25, one in v. 26, one in v. 27, one in v. 28, and two in v. 32.

50. Some manuscripts have a second instance at 1.24.

51. Calvin L. Porter, 'Romans 1.18-32: Its Role in the Developing Argument', *NTS* 40 (1994), pp. 210-28 (218-19).

52. Σκληρότης, ἀμετανόητος, δικαιοκρισία, ἀνόμως (×2), γραπτός, ἐπονομάζομαι and ἱεροσυλέω.

appear elsewhere in the New Testament but not in the Pauline corpus,[53] one that is shared only with pseudo-Pauline and other non-Pauline New Testament writings,[54] one that is shared only with pseudo-Pauline writings,[55] and two that appear elsewhere in the New Testament only in Rom. 1.18-32 which, as part of the larger passage under consideration, may well be non-Pauline.[56] This comes to a total of at least 18 or perhaps 20 words in Romans 2 that are non-Pauline. In addition, the chapter contains two words that appear elsewhere in the authentic writings of Paul only in quotations from the Old Testament[57] and eight other words that appear only once elsewhere in the authentic writings of Paul.[58] To be sure, this represents a significantly lower proportion of non-Pauline words than is the case with 1.18-32. Nevertheless, ch. 2 contains a somewhat higher concentration of *hapax legomena* than is typical of the Pauline writings.[59] This, in my judgment, suggests that the vocabulary of the chapter should be regarded as at least marginally non-Pauline. Because the linguistic evidence here is less striking than in 1.18-32, however, the context and ideational content become particularly important for determining whether ch. 2 is Pauline.

c. *The Language of Romans 1.18–2.29 as a Whole*

As regards the entire passage, Rom. 1.18–2.29, O'Neill finds 'at least forty-nine words' that do not occur elsewhere in the writings of Paul. He suggests that this be compared 'with a total of nineteen words not found elsewhere in Paul which occur in an equal stretch of *Romans* around this chapter and a half (excluding the explicit Old Testament quotations)'.[60] My own judgment is that the language of Rom. 1.18–2.32 is such as to indicate that 1.18-32 almost certainly was composed

53. Ἀκροατής, ποιητής, κατηγορέω, ἐπαναπαύομαι, ὁδηγός, τυφλός, παιδευτής and βδελύσσομαι.

54. Προσωπολημψία.

55. Μόρφωσις.

56. Ἀναπολόγητος (2.1; cf. 1.20) and ἀτιμάζω (2.23; cf. 1.24).

57. Κλέπτω (×2) and μοιχεύω (×2), both in Rom. 13.9.

58. Ἀνοχή, καταφρονέω, χρηστός, μετάνοια, θυμός, λογισμός, ἀπολογέομαι and παραβάτης.

59. By Harrison's count, each page of the Pauline letters as a whole contains an average of only 9.24 words that do not occur elsewhere in the authentically Pauline writings; for Rom. 2, however, the number is roughly 13.33.

60. O'Neill, *Paul's Letter to the Romans*, p. 41.

by someone other than Paul and that the same may well be true regarding ch. 2.

4. *Contextual Evidence for Interpolation*

According to C.K. Barrett, 'The first and most difficult problem to be solved' regarding Rom. 1.18–2.29 'is the question of its place in the argument of the epistle'. Some regard it as part of 'a long digression' between Paul's brief summary of the Christian gospel in 1.16-17 and his development of 'the theme of the saving righteousness of God' that begins in 3.21. Thus, 'the digression deals...with the state of mankind [*sic*] apart from the Gospel; it is therefore by no means irrelevant to a presentation of the Gospel, but it is not directly connected with 1.17'.[61] Most scholars see a closer connection between 1.18–2.29 and its immediate context, however, arguing that it 'is intended to demonstrate (or illustrate) the universal sinfulness of all (3.9, 20), so as to lay the ground for Paul's solution: righteousness by faith in Christ'.[62]

Such interpretations of Rom. 1.18–2.29, however, are problematic. In 1.16-17, Paul introduces the theme of the gospel—'the righteousness of God...revealed through faith for faith'—and declares that the gospel is 'the power of God for salvation to every one who has faith'. At 1.18, however, there is an abrupt shift both of subject matter and of tone. Suddenly and without explanation, the subject is no longer *the gospel as the revelation of God's saving righteousness*; now, it is *the wrath of God* that is revealed against wicked people who, despite the evidence of creation, have lapsed into idolatry and, as a result, have fallen into all manner of immoral conduct (1.18-32).[63] This is followed by a stern warning to those who judge others that their own evil conduct may well lead to the same condemnation (2.1-11) and the assertion that God

61. C.K. Barrett, *A Commentary on the Epistle to the Romans* (HNTC; New York: Harper & Row, 1957), p. 33. Barrett insists, however, that the passage is directly connected with 1.16-17.

62. E.P. Sanders, *Paul, the Law, and the Jewish People* (Philadelphia: Fortress Press, 1983), p. 123; cf., e.g., Porter, 'Romans 1.18-32', p. 210.

63. See, e.g., Porter, 'Romans 1.18-32', pp. 212-13: 'The transition from δικαιοσύνη Θεοῦ revealed in the gospel (1.16-17) to ὀργὴ Θεοῦ revealed from heaven (1.18) raises a major theological conundrum, the relationship of God's righteousness to God's wrath. The solution to that puzzle is not evident in the text.' There is no explicit reference to Gentiles in Rom. 1.18-32, but they likely were in the mind of the author.

judges all people, both Jews and Gentiles, on the basis of their 'works' (2.12-29).

Any direct ideational link between 1.16-17 and 1.18–2.29 would appear to require that δικαιοσύνη in 1.17 be translated as 'justice' (that is, 'righteous judgment' or even 'just punishment'),[64] not as '[saving] righteousness'. With such a translation, ἀποκαλύπτεται γὰρ ὀργὴ Θεοῦ ('for God's wrath is revealed') in v. 18 would be virtually synonymous with δικαιοσύνη γὰρ Θεοῦ...ἀποκαλύπτεται ('for God's righteousness is revealed') in v. 17, and 1.18-32 would represent an elaboration of the causes for and nature of this 'wrath'. It is surely clear, however, that δικαιοσύνη in v. 17 does not mean 'justice' in this sense. As Fitzmyer has cogently argued, Paul here (and elsewhere) uses δικαιοσύνη Θεοῦ to denote 'the quality whereby God actively acquits his sinful people, manifesting toward them his power and gracious activity in a just judgment'.[65] The phrase refers, in other words, to God's (saving) righteousness. Thus, the possible ideational link between 1.17 and 1.18-32 disappears.

Moreover, the very notion of 'God's wrath' (ὀργή) is totally unexpected—and, many would say, even inappropriate—at this point in the letter.[66] It is in no way anticipated in what precedes. Indeed, everything in the letter up to this point has been decidedly 'upbeat'. Paul is thankful for the faith of the Roman Christians (v. 8), he has long wished to visit them (vv. 9-10, 13a), he anticipates that he and they will 'be mutually encouraged by each other's faith' (vv. 11-12), and he looks forward with optimism to preaching the gospel in Rome (vv. 13b-15)—the gospel that is 'the power of God for salvation to every one who has faith' (v. 16). Despite the fact that Paul has never visited Rome, his tone is warm and intimate. Then, at v. 18, abruptly and without warning, both the subject matter and the tone become shockingly different: what in 1.1-17 has been a personal communication to 'you' becomes in vv. 18-32 a stinging castigation of human wickedness focusing upon a 'they' that is never explicitly identified, followed in

64. Cf. Rom. 2.5, where 'day of wrath' (ἡμέρα ὀργῆς) and 'day of revelation of God's righteous judgment' (ἡμέρα ἀποκαλύψεως δικαιοκρισίας τοῦ Θεοῦ) appear to be synonymous.

65. Fitzmyer, *Romans*, p. 257; cf. pp. 257-63.

66. Romans does elsewhere speak of 'wrath' (ὀργή), even indicating that it is God who 'inflicts' the wrath (3.5; cf. 5.9; 9.22). As already noted, however, the phrase ὀργὴ Θεοῦ does not appear elsewhere in the authentic Pauline writings.

ch. 2 by a similarly scathing critique of a 'you' that is hypocritically guilty of judging 'them'. This has nothing whatever to do with Rom. 1.1-17 and, indeed, appearing at this point in the letter, would almost certainly have surprised and shocked its Roman readers.

It is also important to note the abrupt shifts both in audience and in 'person' in the first three chapters of Romans. In 1.1-17, Paul speaks in the *second* person to a *Gentile* audience.[67] Almost certainly, however, 1.18–2.29 is addressed to a *Jewish* audience—1.18-32 speaking in the *third* person about Gentiles and ch. 2 speaking in the *second* person primarily to Jews themselves. Beginning at 3.1, however, Paul is apparently addressing a *Gentile* audience as in 1.1-17, this time, however, speaking in the *third* person about Jews.[68] These shifts in audience and 'person' are most readily explained, in my judgment, not as some rhetorical device adopted by a single author (Paul)[69] but rather as evidence of disruption in the text.

In short, there appears to be nothing in 1.18–2.29 that would suggest any link with 1.1-17. Romans 3.1, however, picks up on the notion in 1.16-17 that salvation is for 'every one who has faith', both Jew and Greek, and raises the question, 'If salvation is for *every* one who has faith, does the Jew have any advantage over the Gentile?'[70] Following a provisional 'Yes' (3.2), Paul's considered answer is a resounding 'No!' (3.9-10). As O'Neill so cogently observes, it is by no means clear how the intervening material, Rom. 1.18–2.29, 'would fit into the train of thought so strikingly begun' in 1.16-17 and continued in 3.1, for 'there seems to be no point to the argument in this context'.[71] Indeed, if 1.18–2.29 were missing, the transition from Rom. 1.16-17 to Rom. 3.1 would appear both intelligible and smooth, and Paul's basic argument would in no way be affected.

67. See Rom. 1.5-6, 13, 14-15.

68. Paul shifts to the *first* person in Rom. 3.5, but this appears to be merely a rhetorical shift (see the rhetorical questions in 3.5, 7-8). In 3.9, the implied subject of the first person plural verb προεχόμεθα is almost certainly 'Jews'; if so, here for the first time in Romans Paul explicitly identifies himself as a Jew.

69. Or even as evidence that Paul is addressing a 'mixed' audience (both Gentiles and Jews).

70. If the words 'to the Jew first and also to the Greek' are original in 1.16, the question would follow almost inevitably. It may be, however, that these words were added by an interpolator precisely for the purpose of linking 1.18-32 with 1.16-17 (see 'the Jew first and also the Greek' in 2.9, 10).

71. O'Neill, *Paul's Letter to the Romans*, p. 41.

There are only two significant verbal links between Rom. 1.18–2.29 and 1.1-17. The first is the verb ἀποκαλύπτεται (1.17 and 1.18). As already noted, however, the *subject* of revelation is different in the two verses: in v. 17, it is the saving righteousness of God; in v. 18, it is the wrath of God. O'Neill suggests further that, while the verb is a true *present* tense in v. 17 ('the righteousness of God *is being revealed*'), it probably refers in v. 18 to the *future* ('the wrath of God *will be revealed*').[72] At one point O'Neill assumes that all of 1.18-2.29 'was written by some later commentator on Paul' and that this commentator 'used a verbal similarity [namely, ἀποκαλύπτεται], in writing v. 18, to make a bridge between Paul's argument and his own' (that is, that he 'deliberately designed the connection').[73] Elsewhere, however, O'Neill suggests that 1.18–2.29 was not 'composed especially for insertion into *Romans* at all' but rather represents 'a traditional tract which belongs essentially to the missionary literature of Hellenistic Judaism'; in this case, it may well have been the 'striking similarity' (that is, the use of the verb ἀποκαλύπτεται) that 'first suggested the happy juxtaposition of the two venerable documents'.[74] My own judgment is that this latter suggestion is most likely accurate.

The second significant verbal link between Rom. 1.18–2.29 and 1.1-17 is the phrase, 'the Jew first and also the Greek' (1.16 and 2.9, 10). As in the case of ἀποκαλύπτεται, of course, it is possible that the author of 1.18–2.29 'used a verbal similarity...to make a bridge between Paul's argument and his own'.[75] It is at least equally possible, however, that an interpolator added the phrase 'both to Jew first and to

72. O'Neill, *Paul's Letter to the Romans*, p. 42; cf. Hans-Joachim Eckstein, '"Denn Gottes Zorn wird vom Himmel her offenbar werden": Exegetische Erwägungen zu Röm 1.18', *ZNW* 78 (1987), pp. 74-89 (74-79). This, however, is debatable. In 1.24, 26, 28, the writer three times declares that 'God gave [aorist tense] them up', with the possible intimation that 'impurity' and 'dishonoring of their bodies' (v. 24), 'dishonorable passions' (v. 26), and 'a base mind' and 'improper conduct' (v. 28) constitute the (present, not future) revelation of God's wrath. Note, too, 2.2: 'the judgment of God rightly falls [present tense] upon those who do such things'. Clearly, however, the judgment is regarded as *future* in 2.5-10, 16. Porter ('Romans 1.18-32', p. 213) separates Rom. 1.18-32 from ch. 2 and maintains 'that God's judgment is portrayed in 1.18 (ἀποκαλύπτεται) as a present reality'.

73. O'Neill, *Paul's Letter to the Romans*, pp. 43, 54.

74. O'Neill, *Paul's Letter to the Romans*, pp. 53-54.

75. O'Neill, *Paul's Letter to the Romans*, p. 43.

Greek' to v. 16 for the specific purpose of providing a link with 1.18–2.29. The phrase is not needed in 1.16-17 and, indeed, is somewhat surprising in light of the fact that only Gentiles, not Jews, have been mentioned thus far in the letter (Rom. 1.5, 13, 14). The only distinction made prior to 1.16 is not between 'Jews' and 'Greeks' but rather between 'Greeks' and 'barbarians' (1.14).

Whatever may be said regarding these two *verbal* links, it has already been noted that there is no apparent relation between 1.18–2.29 and 1.1-17 so far as *content* is concerned. The situation is somewhat less clear, however, regarding the relation of Rom. 1.18–2.29 to the material that *follows*. One might argue that the question of possible Jewish 'advantage' over Gentiles provides continuity between ch. 2 and 3.1-20: ch. 2 indicates that they have no advantage, 3.1-4 provisionally suggests that they do, but 3.9-20 asserts categorically that they do not, thus agreeing with the position of ch. 2. It is at least possible, however, that just as the appearance of ἀποκαλύπτεται in 1.17 may have suggested the appropriateness of adding 1.18–2.29 immediately thereafter, so too the apparent similarity of theme between ch. 2 and 3.1-20 may have reinforced an interpolator's inclination to insert 1.18–2.29 precisely at this point in Paul's Roman letter.

A possible argument against viewing 1.18–2.29 as an interpolation is the usual translation of Paul's statement in 3.9: 'We have previously charged (προατιτάομαι) that all people, both Jews and Greeks, are under the power of sin'.[76] Most interpreters find this 'previous charge' in 1.18–2.29,[77] thus establishing a clear link between 1.18–2.29 and ch. 3. In fact, however, no such charge is made in 1.18–2.29. Regarding 1.18-32, O'Neill notes: 'the writer is not arguing that all Gentiles are sinners'; 'the argument is that idolaters are prone to immorality, not that all Gentiles are immoral'.[78] To be sure, 1.18-32 is followed immediately by a warning to those who judge others that their own evil conduct will lead to the same condemnation (2.1-11) and the assertion that God judges Jews and Gentiles on the same basis (2.12-29). It is clear that 2.12-29 refers to both Jews and Gentiles, and if, as most

76. Cf. Rom. 3.23: 'all have sinned and fall short of the glory of God'.

77. E.g. William Sanday and Arthur C. Headlam, *A Critical and Exegetical Commentary on the Epistle to the Romans* (ICC; Edinburgh: T. & T. Clark, 5th edn, 1902), p. 77.

78. O'Neill, *Paul's Letter to the Romans*, p. 41.

interpreters assume, 1.18-32 refers to Gentiles and 2.1-11 to Jews,[79] then Rom. 1.18–2.29 does in fact suggest that *some* Jews and *some* Gentiles are sinners. In ch. 2, however, there is also reference to people, both Jews and Gentiles, who will gain eternal life through their good deeds (Rom. 2.6-7, 9-10) and, indeed, the declaration that 'justification' is possible through obedience to the law.[80] E.P. Sanders asserts that 'Paul's case for universal sinfulness, as it is stated in Rom. 1.18–2.29, is not convincing'.[81] I would go further: there *is* no charge in Rom. 1.18–2.29 'that *all* people, both Jews and Greeks, are under the power of sin' (Rom. 3.9). Indeed, there is no such charge *anywhere* in the Roman letter prior to 3.9. Thus, it is quite possible, in my judgment, that an interpolator added 1.18–2.29 before ch. 3 precisely because it at least *comes close* to suggesting that both Jews and Greeks are sinners and, in its absence, there is nothing remotely akin to such an accusation in Romans prior to 3.9.

It may well be the case, however, that προῃτιασάμεθα in Rom. 3.9 is not to be translated as 'we *have previously* charged' at all. The preposition πρό can mean 'before' in terms of either time or place; thus, as a verbal prefix, it can quite properly be translated as 'before' or 'beforehand' in a temporal sense, but it can also have other meanings such as 'publicly'. Thus, προαιτιάομαι may mean simply 'to charge publicly' or 'openly', with no reference at all to temporality.[82] Moreover, the *aorist* tense of the verb may well be an 'epistolary' aorist,[83] in which case it has a *present*, not a past, reference. In short, προῃτιασάμεθα in Rom. 3.9 may mean nothing more than 'we [now] charge publicly' or 'we [now] charge openly'. If so, Paul is here making the charge *for the first time* (at least so far as his Roman letter is concerned). Thus, it is by no means clear that Rom. 3.9 requires a *previous* charge 'that all people, both Jews and Greeks, are under the power of sin'. Indeed, Paul's basis for this charge appears to be the scriptural proof-texts that follow

79. There is debate regarding whether 2.1-11 refers only to Jews; see, e.g., Dieter Zeller, *Juden und Heiden in der Mission bei Paulus: Studien zum Römerbrief* (Stuttgart: Katholisches Bibelwerk, 2nd edn, 1976), p. 149 and n. 36.

80. Rom. 2.13: 'For it is not the hearers of the law who are righteous before God, but the doers of the law who will be justified'; cf. 2.12-29 in its entirety.

81. Sanders, *Paul, the Law, and the Jewish People*, p. 125.

82. Because neither BAGD nor LSJ cites any appearance of the verb other than at Rom. 3.9, its meaning here remains unclear.

83. See BDF, §334.

in vv. 10-18, not some empirical description of human behavior, actual or imagined.[84] Some later interpreter of Paul, however, might well have translated προαιτιᾶσθαι as 'to charge previously' (as have modern translators), regarded the aorist as a historical aorist (as have modern translators), and thus seen the need for something that would substantiate or at least illustrate the charge. As already indicated, this may account for the addition of 1.18–2.29 prior to ch. 3.

In summary, it is difficult to relate Rom. 1.18–2.29 in any convincing way to the preceding material in Paul's letter to the Romans, and its relation to the material that follows is at best strained. Thus, the passage may well be an interpolation, added between 1.17 and ch. 3 because of (1) the verbal link ἀποκαλύπτεται at the beginning of the passage,[85] (2) the possibility of projecting the question of Jewish 'advantage' from ch. 3 back into ch. 2, and (3) the apparent need for a charge of universal sinfulness prior to 3.9.

5. *Ideational Evidence for Interpolation*

Much of the ideational content of Romans 2, and to a somewhat lesser extent that of Rom. 1.18-32, is non-Pauline and even anti-Pauline. As in the case of language, however, there are significant differences between 1.18-32 and ch. 2 so far as content is concerned; for this reason, the two sections will again be considered separately.

a. *The Ideational Content of Romans 1.18-32*

In my judgment, the content of Rom. 1.18-32 not only supports the view that the passage was not composed by Paul but also strongly suggests that it was someone other than Paul who inserted it into the Roman letter. Indeed, I believe that this case has inadvertently been made rather convincingly by Porter.

Commentators have long recognized striking similarities between Rom. 1.18-32 and certain Hellenistic Jewish writings of the period,

84. If so, Rom. 3.9 is to be viewed not as a *conclusion* based on alleged empirical evidence, as most have assumed, but rather as a *theologoumenon* based on Scripture.

85. If 'to the Jew first and also to the Greek' is original to 1.16, this would provide another verbal link; as already suggested, however, an interpolator may well have added this phrase to 1.16.

including particularly the Wisdom of Solomon.[86] Many have concluded, therefore, that 'Romans 1.18-32...is a denunciation of the Gentiles formulated [by Paul] in accord with traditional Jewish reasoning'.[87] William Sanday and Arthur C. Headlam go further, however, asserting that 'there are clear indications of the use by the Apostle of the Book of Wisdom'.[88] Porter carries the argument further still: arguing that Rom. 1.18-32 'is a self-contained discourse similar to that used in Hellenistic Judaism in order to establish, maintain and strengthen a well-defined boundary and distance between the Jewish community and the Gentiles', he maintains that Paul first quotes the discourse (without identifying it as the position of his opponents) and then, beginning in 2.1, 'challenges, argues against, and refutes both the content of the discourse and the practice of using such discourses'. In short, according to Porter, 'the ideas in Rom. 1.18-32 are not Paul's' but rather 'are ideas which obstruct Paul's Gentile mission theology and practice' and against which Paul argues throughout his letter to the Romans.[89]

Porter cites a number of points at which Rom. 1.18-32 is in conflict with Paul's views as stated elsewhere in Romans:[90] (1) in 1.18-32 the divine 'wrath' is exercised by 'handing over' sinful humans 'to the power and authority of another',[91] while Paul elsewhere 'asserts that God holds back and delays wrath rather than 'handing over' and 'turning loose';[92] (2) 'God's judgment is portrayed in 1.18...as a present reality while in 2.5...and 2.6...it remains in the future';[93] (3) 'throughout Romans Paul unequivocally and forcefully states that judgment belongs to God',[94] while 1.18-32 'judges and calls upon the hearers to

86. For a summary of similarities between the Wisdom of Solomon and Rom. 1.18-32, see Brendan Byrne (*Romans* [SP, 6; Collegeville, MN: Liturgical, 1996], pp. 64-65.

87. Victor Paul Furnish, *The Moral Teaching of Paul: Selected Issues* (Nashville: Abingdon Press, 2nd edn, 1985), p. 74; cf. pp. 74-77; cf. Byrne, *Romans*, pp. 64-65.

88. Sanday and Headlam, *A Critical and Exegetical Commentary*, p. 51; for a chart showing the similarities, see pp. 51-52.

89. Porter, 'Romans 1.18-32', quotations from p. 215.

90. Porter, 'Romans 1.18-32', pp. 213-15.

91. Rom. 1.24, 26, 28: παρέδωκεν αὐτοὺς ὁ Θεός.

92. Rom. 2.4; 3.26; cf. 3.25.

93. This assumes that Rom. 1.18-29 and Rom. 2 have different authors. On the 'time' question, see n. 72 above.

94. Rom. 2.2, 3, 16; 3.19; 14.10, 12.

judge as well'; (4) Romans 4 'establishes God's provision for the Gentiles even before the time of Jesus Christ' and asserts 'that God "gives life to the dead and calls into existence the things that do not exist"', while 1.18-32 declares that God 'hand[s] persons over to the power of death'; and (5) elsewhere in Romans 'the necessity for the gospel lies not in the human condition of "wickedness" and "ungodliness", as some have claimed, but in God'.

According to Porter, the real intent of 1.18-32 is 'to drive a wedge' between Jews and Gentiles.[95] This, however, would be in sharp opposition to Paul's emphatic desire to bring Jews and Gentiles together in the Christian community. Further, the notion that God has 'handed [the Gentiles] over to' immoral conduct leading to death would appear to contradict the very point of Paul's mission to the Gentiles. Moreover, and this is not mentioned by Porter, the apparent appeal to 'natural revelation' in 1.19-21 (cf. also v. 32) is without parallel elsewhere in the Pauline writings and appears to be in conflict with 1 Cor. 1.21 ('in the wisdom of God, the world did not know God through wisdom').[96] It should also be noted that, while 'the responsibility for human sin...is laid clearly at the feet of human beings' in Rom. 1.18-32, elsewhere in Romans 'sin' is characterized as 'an oppressive power that ensnares and dominates the lives and actions of people'.[97] Finally, there is nothing specifically 'Christian' in Rom. 1.18-32. A devout non-Christian Jew and, indeed, many non-Christian Gentiles could, without any difficulty, subscribe to everything in the passage.

In short, it appears that the content of Rom. 1.18-32 is not only non-Pauline but even anti-Pauline at significant points.

Porter, while emphasizing the conflict between Rom. 1.18-32 and the views of Paul, nevertheless argues that Paul included the passage in the

95. Porter, 'Romans 1.18-32', p. 219.

96. Käsemann (*Commentary on Romans*, p. 41) raises the possibility of a conflict with Paul's 'eschatology and christology' but then concludes (pp. 41-44) that no such conflict is evident. Similarly, Fitzmyer (*Romans*, pp. 273-74) argues that such conflict 'is far from clear'. Note Paul's Areopagus speech in Acts 17.22-31, which does include such an appeal. For the relation between Rom. 1.19-21 and Acts 17.22-31, see, e.g., Philipp Vielhauer, 'On the "Paulinism" of Acts' (trans. Wm. C. Robinson, Jr, and Victor Paul Furnish), in Leander E. Keck and J. Louis Martyn (eds.), *Studies in Luke-Acts: Essays Presented in Honor of Paul Schubert* (Nashville: Abingdon Press, 1966), pp. 33-50 (34-37).

97. Charles B. Cousar, *The Letters of Paul* (IBT; Nashville: Abingdon Press, 1996), pp. 119-20.

Roman letter precisely for the purpose of refuting it. According to Porter, 'That Paul sometimes includes in his letters a statement or a saying of his readers or opponents without identifying it as such has been widely acknowledged by interpreters and translators'.[98] This is surely true, but none of the examples previously noted is anywhere near the length of Rom. 1.18-32.[99] In my own judgment, it is most unlikely that Paul would include such a lengthy non-Pauline (anti-Pauline) passage, without identifying it as such, simply for the purpose of refuting it. Indeed, if the subtlety of his alleged rhetorical strategy has escaped all interpreters until the present, it is doubtful that it would have been recognized by his original readers (or hearers). As Harrison so aptly phrased it, 'with all due respect, I cannot see St. Paul lifting a passage like this from anywhere'.[100] In short, I regard Porter's analysis of Rom. 1.18-32 as a strong argument not only against Pauline authorship of the passage but also against Pauline insertion of the passage into the Roman letter.

b. *The Ideational Content of Romans 2*

If Porter has inadvertently made a strong case that Rom. 1.18-32 is a non-Pauline interpolation, I believe that E.P. Sanders has made an even stronger case with regard to Romans 2.[101] Sanders notes that 'what is said about the law in Romans 2 cannot be fitted into a category otherwise known from Paul's letters', and, for this reason, he consigns his own treatment of the chapter to an appendix.[102] Specific points at which Romans 2 appears to 'conflict with positions which Paul elsewhere adopts' include the following: (1) 'the...statement that those who do the law will be righteoused (2.13)';[103] (2) 'Paul's statement about

98. Porter, 'Romans 1.18-32', p. 222.

99. Porter cites Hurd (*The Origin of I Corinthians*) to support his claim. All of the examples noted by Hurd, however, are *very* brief: 1 Cor. 6.12, 13; 7.1; 8.1, 4, 5-6, 8; 11.2. To my knowledge, the longest proposed example is 1 Cor. 11.3-7b (Alan Padgett, 'Paul on Women in the Church: The Contradictions of Coiffure in 1 Corinthians 11.2-16', *JSNT* 20 [1984], pp. 69-86).

100. Harrison, *Paulines and Pastorals*, p. 84.

101. O'Neill (*Paul's Letter to the Romans*, pp. 45-56) makes many of the same points as Sanders, but I focus on Sanders' discussion because he, unlike O'Neill, is unwilling to regard it as an interpolation.

102. Sanders, *Paul, the Law, and the Jewish People*, pp. 123-35.

103. Sanders prefers 'to righteous' as the translation of δικαιοῦν.

repentance (2.4)'; (3) 'the "hearing and doing" theme (2.13)', which 'has numerous parallels in Jewish literature, but none in Paul's letters'; (4) 'the phrase δίκαιος παρὰ τῷ Θεῷ' (2.13), which 'is also without a Pauline parallel and appears to rest on a Semitic Jewish formulation'; (5) 'the statement...that Gentiles who keep the law will judge Jews who do not' (2.17), which 'is at variance with Paul's view that Christians ("the saints") will judge the world (1 Cor. 6.1)'; and (6) 'the emphasis on actually doing the law' and thereby gaining justification.[104]

Of particular significance is the emphasis upon justification by 'works' (ἔργα) of the law and judgment based upon obedience to the law.[105] As Sanders notes, the point of ch. 2 'is not that no one *can* keep the law' because 'several verses mention those who do keep it'; moreover, 'the condemnation of the Jews is that they do not keep the law, or do not keep it well enough, not that they keep it in the wrong spirit'; and finally, 'those who keep the law *will condemn* those who do not (2.18)'.[106]

Sanders suggests 'that the best way to read all of Rom. 1.18-2.29 is as a synagogue sermon', the point of which 'is to have its hearers become better Jews on strictly non-Christian Jewish terms, not to lead them to becoming true descendants of Abraham by faith in Christ':[107] 'what is at stake is whether or not one is a good Jew, a good Jew as judged not on the basis of sharing Abraham's faith, but of obedience to the law'.[108] Sanders' conclusion is: 'I find, in short, no distinctively Pauline imprint in 1.18-2.29, apart from the tag in 2.16'.[109]

Not surprisingly, Sanders asks, 'Why is the chapter in Romans at all?' His only answers are: (1) the chapter 'puts Jew and Gentile on the same footing; not...as Paul does in Romans 3 and 4 (all have equal opportunity to be righteoused by faith in Christ), but nevertheless on equal footing'; thus, 'different parts of it, though not in a consistent or objective way, lead up to 3.9'; and (2) in the special circumstance of

104. Sanders, *Paul, the Law, and the Jewish People*, p. 125.

105. Cf. O'Neill, *Paul's Letter to the Romans*, p. 47.

106. Sanders, *Paul, the Law, and the Jewish People*, p. 126 (his emphasis).

107. Sanders, *Paul, the Law, and the Jewish People*, p. 129.

108. Sanders, *Paul, the Law, and the Jewish People*, p. 13; cf. O'Neill, *Paul's Letter to the Romans*, p. 53.

109. 'on that day when, according to my gospel, God judges the secrets of people by Christ Jesus' (Rom. 2.16).

'writing to a church which he did not know, Paul may have used traditional material to an unusual degree'.[110]

Sanders specifically rejects the idea that Rom. 1.18–2.29 is an interpolation, citing, rather, the frequent observation that even if Paul did not himself compose some of the material in his letters, 'he did incorporate it, and he could not have done so if it went completely against the grain'.[111] Such a response, however, obviously begs the question of whether Paul did in fact incorporate this passage into the Roman letter. Moreover, it comes perilously close to circular argumentation: Paul incorporated the passage into the letter; he would not have done so if it 'went completely against the grain'; thus, the passage does not go 'completely against the grain'; *ergo*, it could well have been inserted into the letter by Paul. My own judgment is that the material *does* go 'completely against the grain' and was incorporated into the Roman letter by someone other than Paul.

Although he declines to treat Romans 2 as an interpolation, Sanders does note that 'there is a difference' between Romans 2 and other passages often viewed as Pauline inclusions of non-Pauline material: Phil. 2.6-11 and Rom. 1.3-4, for example, are christological in their content, but Romans 2 'at no points reflects specifically Christian thinking'. To be sure, 'Paul's virtue and vice lists [also] do not reflect a particularly Christian point of view', but Romans 2 'stands out because it deals directly with salvation and makes salvation dependent on obedience to the law'. It is because of 'what is said about the law in Romans 2' that the passage 'cannot be fitted into a category otherwise known from Paul's letters'.[112] My own judgment, therefore, is that, despite his disclaimer, Sanders has made a convincing case for viewing Romans 2 as a non-Pauline interpolation.

6. *Comparative Evidence for Interpolation*

Under 'Linguistic Evidence for Interpolation' (pp. 169-76), it was noted that much of the vocabulary of Rom. 1.18–2.29 appears to be not only non-Pauline but also typically pseudo-Pauline. Of particular note in this regard is the 'vice' list in Rom. 1.29-31. Here, the vocabulary is much closer to that of the pseudo-Pauline vice lists than to that of the

110. Sanders, *Paul, the Law, and the Jewish People*, p. 131.
111. Sanders, *Paul, the Law, and the Jewish People*, p. 131.
112. Sanders, *Paul, the Law, and the Jewish People*, pp. 131-32.

other vice lists in the authentically Pauline letters. This suggests that Rom. 1.18–2.29 may well have originated not with Paul himself (or with someone earlier than Paul) but rather within the same circles of post-Pauline Christianity that produced the pseudo-Pauline writings.

7. *Situational, Motivational and Locational Evidence for Interpolation*

It would be difficult if not impossible to determine whether the particular situation leading to the composition of Rom. 1.18–2.29 might have been pre-Pauline, contemporary with Paul or post-Pauline. Romans 1.18-32 appears to reflect an anti-Gentile bias. It could have been written by a Jewish Christian, but, as already noted, none of its content is specifically Christian; thus, in my own judgment, it most likely originated within Jewish, not Christian, circles. Its rather sweeping and general condemnation of what apparently were regarded as typically Gentile vices, however, suggests the absence of any *specific* situation calling for its composition.

Chapter 2, by way of contrast, is much more even-handed in its treatment of both Jews and Gentiles, indicating that both will be judged in terms of their obedience to the law. It may well be the case that 1.18-32 and ch. 2 were written by different authors; indeed, ch. 2 may originally have been intended as a response to 1.18-32.[113] Except for the words διὰ Χριστοῦ ᾿Ιησοῦ (‘through Christ Jesus’) in v. 16, however, ch. 2 is as devoid of any specifically Christian content as is 1.18-32. Thus, it too could have been written either by a Jew or by a Jewish Christian. Here again, however, my own judgment is that the author was most likely not a Christian. The most that can be said regarding why ch. 2 was written is that the author was concerned by the hypocrisy of Jews who were judging non-Jews for not following the Jewish law.

In short, it simply is impossible to determine the exact situation(s) that led to the composition of Rom. 1.18–2.29. As to why the passage was inserted into Paul’s Roman letter—and precisely at its present location—my best guess has already been indicated. Romans 3.9 may have been interpreted as requiring a ‘previous’ charge that *all* Jews and

113. This is Porter’s view (‘Romans 1.18-32’), but, as noted above, he believes that it was Paul who both included 1.18-32 in his letter and then composed ch. 2 as a partial response.

Greeks are under the power of sin, and 1.18–2.29 may have been inserted to provide something *approximating* such an accusation. This, however, is necessarily speculative. Thus, the principal arguments for viewing the passage as a non-Pauline interpolation are based upon the contextual, linguistic, ideational and, to a lesser extent, the comparative evidence.

8. *Conclusion*

My own examination of the language, context and ideational content of Rom. 1.18–2.29 leads me inescapably to the conclusion that O'Neill was right: the entire passage is a non-Pauline interpolation.

Chapter 9

OTHER LIKELY INTERPOLATIONS (1)

As I noted in my Introduction, the list of proposed interpolations in the Pauline letters has become rather lengthy. It has by no means been my intention, however, to examine all of these proposed interpolations. In Chapter 4, by way of illustrating the various types of evidence that might point to interpolation, I devoted considerable attention to 1 Cor. 14.34-35, a passage that is now viewed as an interpolation by many scholars. Then, in Chapters 5, 6, 7 and 8, I argued that four additional passages—1 Cor. 11.3-16; 2.6-16; 12.31b–14.1a; Rom. 1.18–2.29—are also non-Pauline interpolations. In this and the next chapter, in rather cursory fashion, I propose to look at another five passages: Rom. 16.25-27, 2 Cor. 6.14–7.1, 1 Thess. 2.13-16, Rom. 13.1-7 and 1 Cor. 10.1-22. The first four of these are regarded as non-Pauline interpolations by a significant number of scholars, and, in my own judgment, a strong case has been made that the fifth is also an interpolation.

In my discussion of these five passages, I will not offer a critical evaluation of the arguments for interpolation, nor will I respond to scholars who have attempted to refute these arguments. Rather, in each case, I will simply summarize the case for interpolation.

The overall thrust of the entire book, then, will have been the identification of what I myself regard as 10 probable interpolations in the Pauline letters. As has already been suggested, however, the identification of these 10 implies the almost certain presence of others, perhaps many others, only some of which are likely thus far to have been recognized.

1. *Romans 16.25-27*

The authenticity of the doxology normally labeled Rom. 16.25-27 has long been questioned,[1] and it is now widely regarded as a non-Pauline

1. See, e.g., J.B. Lightfoot, 'M. Renan's Theory of the Epistle to the Romans',

interpolation.[2] Walter Schmithals has argued that the doxology was originally intended as the ending not just of Romans but of an early collection of Paul's letters,[3] but cogent arguments against this view have been presented by Harry Gamble, Jr.[4] Other scholars have maintained that the doxology originated as the conclusion of a 14-chapter version of Romans, perhaps in Marcionite circles.[5] While rejecting a Marcionite origin,[6] Gamble agrees that the doxology first stood at the end of a shortened, 14-chapter version of the letter and was subsequently moved variously to the end of ch. 15 and the end of ch. 16.[7] Larry W. Hurtado, however, has examined Gamble's arguments and concluded that they are 'very weak and inconclusive'. In Hurtado's view, the doxology may well have originated to conclude Romans 16 and subsequently been adopted as the ending for a shortened, 14-chapter version of Romans.[8]

JP 2 (1869), pp. 264-95; reprinted as 'The Structure and Destination of the Epistle to the Romans. A', in J.B. Lightfoot, *Biblical Essays* (London: Macmillan, 1893], pp. 287-320); F.J.A. Hort, 'On the End of the Epistle to the Romans', *JP* 3 (1871), pp. 51-80; reprinted as 'The Structure and Destination of the Epistle to the Romans. B', in Lightfoot, *Biblical Essays*, pp. 321-51; and J.B. Lightfoot, 'The Epistle to the Romans', *JP* 3 (1871), pp. 193-214; reprinted as 'The Structure and Destination of the Epistle to the Romans. C', in Lightfoot, *Biblical Essays*, pp. 352-74.

2. Werner Georg Kümmel (*Introduction to the New Testament* [trans. Howard Clark Kee; Nashville: Abingdon Press, rev. edn, 1975], p. 316 n. 39) lists a number of scholars who, 'more recently', have viewed Rom. 16.25-27 as 'a non-Pauline supplement'. For a summary of discussion in the 1970s, see, e.g., Larry W. Hurtado, 'The Doxology at the End of Romans', in Epp and Fee (eds.), *New Testament Textual Criticism*, pp. 185-99 (185-87). The most comprehensive treatment, which concludes that the passage is a non-Pauline interpolation, is Kamlah, 'Traditionsgeschichtliche Untersuchungen zur Schlussdoxologie des Römerbriefes'.

3. Schmithals, *Paul and the Gnostics*, pp. 258-59; and *Der Römerbrief als historisches Problem*, pp. 108-24.

4. Gamble, *The Textual History*, pp. 121-23.

5. E.g. Matthew Black, *Romans* (NCB; London: Oliphants, 1973), pp. 26-29, 184-85; C.E.B. Cranfield, *A Critical and Exegetical Commentary on the Epistle to the Romans* (ICC; 2 vols.; Edinburgh: T. & T. Clark, 1975–79), I, p. 8; II, pp. 808-809; cf., e.g., Karl Paul Donfried, 'A Short Note on Romans 16', *JBL* 89 (1970), pp. 441-49 (447-48); and Kümmel, *Introduction to the New Testament*, p. 317.

6. Gamble, *The Textual History*, pp. 107-11.

7. Gamble, *The Textual History*, pp. 123-24, 130-32.

8. Hurtado, 'The Doxology', pp. 192-99.

Gamble cites three arguments for regarding the doxology as a non-Pauline interpolation: (1) 'in terms of style, the conclusion of a letter with a doxology stands in clear contrast to Paul's habit of concluding with the grace-benediction'; (2) 'the terminological and conceptual affinities of the doxology lie mainly with the deutero-Pauline letters (Ephesians, the Pastorals)'; and (3) 'textual observations demonstrate that the doxology was originally appended to the fourteen-chapter text of Romans', which cannot have originated with Paul.[9] Thus, in his view, the evidence for interpolation is primarily text-critical, contextual, linguistic, ideational and comparative in nature.

a. *Text-Critical Evidence for Interpolation*

Brendan Byrne notes that the 'textual credentials' of the material commonly labeled Rom. 16.25-27 are 'uncertain;'[10] somewhat more categorically, J.K. Elliott asserts that 'the conclusion to the epistle to the Romans is a major problem in textual criticism'.[11] First, it is to be noted that the verses are missing altogether in some witnesses. According to Origen, they did not appear in the text used by Marcion (second century), and a text without the doxology is implied by Priscillian (fourth century)[12] and attested by Jerome (fourth/fifth centuries); in addition, the verses are missing in the ninth-century bilingual uncial manuscripts F (Codex Augiensis)[13] and G (Codex Boernerianus),[14] the fourteenth-

9. Gamble, *The Textual History*, p. 123. Note, however, Hurtado's argument that the doxology may have originated to conclude ch. 16.

10. Byrne, *Romans*, p. 461.

11. J.K. Elliott, 'The Language and Style of the Concluding Doxology to the Epistle to the Romans', *ZNW* 72 (1981), pp. 124-30 (124). For summaries and discussions of the evidence, see, e.g., Kurt Aland, 'Der Schluss und die ursprüngliche Gestalt des Römerbriefes', in *idem*, *Neutestamentliche Entwürfe* (TBü, 63; Munich: Chr. Kaiser Verlag, 1979), pp. 284-301; and Gamble, *The Textual History*, pp. 22-29.

12. Implied both by Priscillian's failure to include the doxology in 'a concordance of the Pauline letters under ninety canons or headings' and by his 'failure to mention it under the two headings which would seem to demand reference to it' (Gamble, *The Textual History*, p. 25).

13. The doxology appears after 16.24 in the Latin text but is missing in the parallel Greek column.

14. Six blank lines appear between 14.23 and 15.1, suggesting 'that the scribe of G had reason to think that after 14.23 was the place where the doxology should

century minuscule 629, and the ninth-century Latin Manuscript g.[15] Further, the doxology appears not to have been present in the exemplar from which the sixth-century uncial D (Codex Claromontanus) was copied,[16] and Gamble argues cogently that it was originally absent from the Old Latin text as a whole.[17] The text-critical principle of 'transcriptional probability'—what a scribe is most likely to have done—suggests that, on the face of it, the addition of such a doxology would be more likely than its deletion. Thus, the absence of these verses from some of the witnesses suggests that they may be a later addition to the text of Paul's Roman letter.

Second, although the doxology does appear in the vast majority of the witnesses, it is variously located, appearing after ch. 15 in the oldest surviving manuscript (the late-second or early-third century P^{46}), after ch. 16 in most of the 'best' witnesses,[18] after ch. 14 in a large number of witnesses, after both ch. 14 and ch. 16 in a few witnesses including the fifth-century Codex Alexandrinus (A), and after both ch. 14 and ch. 15 in one fourteenth-century manuscript (1506). Such variation indicates great uncertainty in the early Church regarding the appropriate location of the passage.[19] Together with the omission of the verses by some witnesses, this further strengthens the case for viewing the passage as a later addition. Moreover, if the doxology originated as the conclusion for a shortened, 14-chapter version of Romans, as Gamble and others believe, it is unlikely to be Pauline.

Finally, two interesting textual variants in the doxology suggest that it may, in its original form, have been regarded by some as an inappropriate conclusion to Paul's Roman letter and therefore modified. The first of these variants is the addition in v. 26 of καὶ τῆς ἐπιφανείας τοῦ κυρίου ἡμῶν ᾿Ιησοῦ Χριστοῦ ('and the appearance of our Lord

occur, but that it was lacking in the manuscript from which he was copying' (Metzger, *A Textual Commentary*, p. 535).

15. The Latin parellel to the Greek Codex Boernerianus (G).

16. For evidence, see, e.g., Metzger, *A Textual Commentary*, p. 535.

17. Gamble, *The Textual History*, pp. 24-29.

18. Including the fourth-century ℵ (Codex Sinaiticus) and B (Codex Vaticanus), the fifth-century C (Codex Ephraemi Syri Rescriptus), and the sixth-century D (Codex Claromontanus).

19. The matter is complicated by the fact that there is strong evidence for the existence of three different versions of the Roman letter, one consisting of 14 chapters, one of 15 chapters, and one of 16 chapters; see, e.g., Gamble, *The Textual History*, especially pp. 15-35, 96-126.

Jesus Christ') after διά τε γραφῶν προγητικῶν ('through prophetic writings')[20]—an apparent attempt further to 'Christianize' the doxology by specifying that the μυστήριον ('mystery') had been 'manifested' (φανερωθέντος) not only through 'prophetic writings' but pre-eminently through 'the appearance of our Lord Jesus Christ'. The second textual variant is either the omission of ᾧ[21] or the substitution of αὐτῷ[22] in v. 27. As William Sanday and Arthur C. Headlam note, 'both [of] these look very much like corrections',[23] perhaps intended to make clear that the ascription of praise was directed toward 'the only wise God', not toward 'Jesus Christ'.[24]

All of this—the omission of the doxology in some witnesses, its placement at various locations in others and the textual variants within it—suggest that the verses may well be a later addition to Paul's Roman letter.

b. *Contextual Evidence for Interpolation*

As already indicated, the doxology normally labeled Rom. 16.25-27 is variously located in the early witnesses: at the end of ch. 14, at the end of ch. 15, at the end of ch. 16, at the end of both ch. 14 and ch. 16 and at the end of both ch. 15 and ch. 16. In view of evidence for the early existence of a 14-chapter version, a 15-chapter version, and a 16-chapter version of Romans, it appears that the doxology, in whichever location, was originally intended as the conclusion of Paul's letter to the Romans. Ending a letter with a doxology, however, is not otherwise a feature of the Pauline corpus. To be sure, doxologies do appear elsewhere in the authentically Pauline letters,[25] as they do in other early Christian writings,[26] but they never come at the end of a Pauline letter. Indeed, every other letter in the Pauline corpus (including Hebrews)

20. Origen and manuscripts known to Jerome.

21. The fourth-century Codex Vaticanus (B) and a few other witnesses.

22. The ninth-century Codex Porphyrianus (P) and a few other witnesses.

23. Sanday and Headlam, *A Critical and Exegetical Commentary*, p. 435.

24. As ᾧ would properly indicate; see Sanday and Headlam, *A Critical and Exegetical Commentary*, pp. 435-36.

25. Rom. 11.36b; Gal. 1.5; Phil. 4.20.

26. Pseudo-Pauline writings: Eph. 3.20-21; 1 Tim. 1.17; 2 Tim. 4.18b; other early Christian writings: Heb. 13.21; Jude 24–25; *1 Clem.* 64.1; 65.2b; *Mart. Pol.* 20.2.

concludes not with a doxology but rather with a benediction.[27] It is perhaps for this reason that a few ancient witnesses add a benediction—ἡ χάρις τοῦ κυρίου ἡμῶν 'Ιησοῦ Χριστοῦ μετὰ πάντων ὑμῶν. ἀμήν ('the grace of our Lord Jesus Christ [be] with all of you. Amen')—after v. 27. Doxologies do appear, however, at the conclusion of some post-Pauline Christian letters.[28] Thus, the location of the doxology at the end of Paul's letter to the Romans constitutes an argument for interpolation.[29]

It is also significant that, while the other doxologies in the authentically Pauline letters appear to grow out of and reflect the immediately preceding material in the letter,[30] Rom. 16.25-27 represents a 'self-contained' body of material that bears little relation to its immediate context; in this respect, it is more closely akin to post-Pauline and particularly pseudo-Pauline doxologies.[31] Thus, both the location of Rom. 16.25-27 at the very end of the letter and its apparent independence from the immediately preceding material raise questions regarding its authenticity.

c. *Linguistic Evidence for Interpolation*

Linguistic evidence for viewing Rom. 16.25-27 as a non-Pauline interpolation involves matters of both style and vocabulary. As regards *style*, none of the other three doxologies in the authentically Pauline

27. Authentically Pauline letters: 1 Cor. 16.23 (followed only by 'My love be with you all in Christ Jesus. Amen'); 2 Cor. 13.14; Gal. 6.18; Phil. 4.23; 1 Thess. 5.28; Phlm. 25; pseudo-Pauline writings: 2 Thess. 3.18; Col. 4.18c; Eph. 6.24; 1 Tim. 6.21b; 2 Tim. 4.22b; Tit. 3.15c. As Hurtado ('The Doxology at the End of Romans', p. 190) notes, 'I Cor. 16:24 (a concluding love wish) is technically an exception'; Gamble (*The Textual History*, p. 82), however, regards this as 'not a formal element, but only an *ad hoc* addition which is best regarded as a postscript'.

28. E.g. Jude 24–25; 2 Pet. 3.18a; *1 Clem.* 65.2b; *Mart. Pol.* 22.3; *2 Clem.* 20.5.

29. For an attempt to refute—or at least diminish the force of—this argument, see, e.g., Hurtado, 'The Doxology', pp. 189-90.

30. See, e.g., Benjamin W. Bacon, 'The Doxology at the End of Romans', *JBL* 18 (1899), pp. 167-76 (173): 'Doxologies are frequent in Paul, but do not occur without adequate occasion in the immediate context. In general it appears to be the mention of "the good and acceptable and perfect will of God", when his goodness, wisdom, and power stand revealed in their inexpressible greatness, that calls for these ejaculations.'

31. Elliott, 'The Language and Style', p. 130.

letters even approaches the length or syntactical complexity of Rom. 16.25-27. Two of the others are virtually identical: Rom. 11.36b (αὐτῷ ἡ δόξα εἰς τοὺς αἰῶνας, ἀμήν) and Gal. 1.5 (ᾧ ἡ δόξα εἰς τοὺς αἰῶνας τῶν αἰώνων, ἀμήν), and the third, Phil. 4.20 (τῷ δὲ Θεῷ καὶ πατρὶ ἡμῶν ἡ δόξα εἰς τοὺς αἰῶνας τῶν αἰώνων, ἀμήν), is only slightly longer. While Rom. 16.25-27 contains 53 words, Rom. 11.36b has only seven words, Gal. 1.5 only nine, and Phil. 4.20 only 14. In the pseudo-Pauline writings, however, the doxologies are longer, in one case coming rather close to the length of Rom. 16.25-27.[32] Moreover, as J.K. Elliott notes, the syntax of Rom. 16.25-27 is much more complicated than that of the three undoubtedly Pauline doxologies: 'Three prepositional phrases depend on the infinitive στηρίξαι; three participles in apposition qualify μυστηρίου; two prepositional phrases illuminate φανερωθέντος'; moreover, there are 'three indirect objects including one relative' and 'one dative of time', 'διά appears twice, κατά three times and εἰς three times'; finally, 'no finite verb is expressed'. According to Elliott, 'this suggests a well-rehearsed and liturgically inspired composition'.[33] Thus, quite apart from its content, the literary style of Rom. 16.25-27 calls attention to itself as not typically Pauline.

In addition, although some of the vocabulary of the doxology is typically Pauline, much of it is not. Following a detailed word-by-word analysis of the language of the passage, Elliott summarizes his findings as follows:

> Three phrases in particular brand the doxology as non-Pauline. These are χρόνοις αἰωνίοις, γραφῶν προφητικῶν and κατ' ἐπιταγὴν τοῦ αἰωνίου Θεοῦ. Τὸ κήρυγμα Ἰησοῦ Χριστοῦ and σοφῷ Θεῷ are unique expressions in the New Testament. Κήρυγμα and ἐπιταγή seem to bear a more general meaning than is found elsewhere in the New Testament and this possibly indicates a later date when these terms had become less specific. Τῷ δυναμένῳ and στηρίξαι belong to the language of doxologies although the parallels to Paul's writings are not precise. Κατὰ ἀποκάλυψιν μυστηρίου is an expression with differences from the authentic Pauline letters. Σεσιγμένου has a different usage from the rest of Paul's epistles.[34]

32. Although 1 Tim. 1.17 contains only 18 words, Eph. 3.20-21 has 37. Cf. also Jude 24-25 (42 words).

33. Elliott, 'The Language and Style', p. 129.

34. Elliott, 'The Language and Style', p. 129. For details, see the entire discussion (pp. 125-29).

Elliott concludes that, 'although some of the vocabulary closely parallels Paul's own writings,[35] the doxology is unlikely to be from his pen'. In his view, there is simply 'too high a percentage of unusual or unique expressions' in the scope of 'the fifty odd words of the doxology'.[36]

d. *Ideational Evidence for Interpolation*

The most significant ideational argument for viewing Rom. 16.25-27 as a non-Pauline interpolation is its reference to the 'revelation of [the] mystery that had been kept silent for eternal ages but was now made manifest' (ἀποκάλυψιν μυστηρίου χρόνοις αἰωνίοις σεσιγημένου φανερωθέντος δὲ νῦν). To be sure, there are references elsewhere in the authentically Pauline letters to 'mystery' (μυστήριον),[37] either in the singular or in the plural, and Paul's message, the 'gospel', is perhaps labeled a 'mystery'.[38] Elsewhere in the authentically Pauline letters, however, it is only in 1 Cor. 2.6-16 that such a 'hidden but now revealed' schema appears,[39] and I have argued in Chapter 6 that this passage is a non-Pauline interpolation. Otherwise, this 'revelation schema' appears only in pseudo-Pauline[40] or other post-Pauline texts.[41]

35. See, e.g., Sanday and Headlam, *A Critical and Exegetical Commentary*, pp. 433-36.

36. Elliott, 'The Language and Style', p. 129.

37. Rom. 11.25; 1 Cor. 2.1, 7; 4.1; 13.2; 14.2; 15.51. Note, however, the significant textual evidence for μαρτύριον ('testimony') rather than μυστήριον ('mystery') at 1 Cor. 2.1. Further, I have argued in Chapters 6 and 7 that 1 Cor. 2.6-16 and 1 Cor. 12.31b–14.1a are non-Pauline interpolations. This leaves only Rom. 11.15; 1 Cor. 2.1; 4.1; 14.2; 15.51, as undoubtedly Pauline uses of 'mystery' (μυστήριον). In the pseudo-Pauline writings, the term is much more frequent: 2 Thess. 2.7; Col. 1.26, 27; 2.2; 4.3; Eph. 1.9; 3.3, 4, 9; 5.32; 6.19; 1 Tim. 3.9. Indeed, according to Byrne (*Romans*, p. 354), the word is 'virtually a technical term' in Colossians and Ephesians, used 'to express what God has accomplished in Jesus Christ'.

38. 1 Cor. 2.1 (if μυστήριον is the correct reading) and perhaps 1 Cor. 4.1.

39. To be sure, 2 Cor. 4.3-4 speaks of the gospel being 'veiled' (κεκαλυμμένον), but it is 'veiled' only to 'the unbelievers' (οἱ ἄπιστοι), and it is 'the god of this age' (ὁ θεὸς τοῦ αἰῶνος τούτου), not God, who has 'blinded' them. Moreover, the temporal scheme—'once hidden but now revealed'—is missing in 2 Cor. 4.3-4.

40. Col. 1.26; Eph. 3.4-6, 8-11; 2 Tim. 1.9-11; Tit. 1.2-3.

41. 1 Pet. 1.20; Ignatius, *Magn.* 6.1; *Herm. Sim.* 9.12.2-3.

e. *Comparative Evidence for Interpolation*

It has already been noted that, apart from Romans, the authentically Pauline letters never end with a doxology but post-Pauline letters sometimes do. Further, as has been noted, post-Pauline doxologies, like that at the end of Romans, tend to be longer and more complex in their syntactical structure than the authentically Pauline doxologies. In addition, some of the vocabulary of Rom. 16.25-27 is more typical of post-Pauline doxologies than of the authentically Pauline ones. Included here are the phrase τῷ δὲ δυναμένῳ ('to the one being able'),[42] στηρίξαι ('to strengthen')[43] and μόνος ('only') as a quality of God.[44] Finally, as noted above, the 'hidden-but-now-revealed mystery' notion is characteristic of the post-Pauline and particularly pseudo-Pauline writings but not of the authentically Pauline letters. All of this suggests that the Rom. 16.25-27 was both composed and added to Paul's Roman letter by someone other (and later) than Paul.

f. *Situational, Motivational and Locational Evidence for Interpolation*

Any discussion of situational, motivational and locational evidence for interpolation in the case of Rom. 16.25-27 is, of course, complicated by the fact that these verses appear at various locations in Paul's letter to the Romans. Whether the doxology originated as the conclusion of a 14-chapter, a 15-chapter or a 16-chapter version of Romans, however, the situation, motivation and location would appear obvious. Without the doxology, a 14-chapter version would end quite abruptly and uncharacteristically with Paul's discussion of eating (ch. 14); in short, some sort of ending would be required. Similarly, without the doxology, a 16-chapter version would end somewhat abruptly and uncharacteristically with greetings but nothing else.[45] The situation is somewhat different for a 15-chapter version, because ch. 15 does end with a short benediction, 'The God of peace be with you all. Amen'. Even this, however, is not a typical ending for a Pauline letter, all of which,

42. Eph. 3.20; Jude 24; *Mart. Pol.* 20.2.

43. Used as an attribute of God in the context of a doxology at 1 Pet. 5.10.

44. 1 Tim. 1.17; Jude 25; *2 Clem.* 20.5; cf. 1 Tim. 6.15; Rev. 4.

45. To be sure, some witnesses add the benediction, 'The grace of our Lord Jesus Christ be with you all, amen', after 16.23, but, like the addition of the doxology, this addition was almost certainly a secondary attempt to 'complete' what otherwise appeared to be an incomplete document.

except that in Galatians, include not only a benediction but also some type of greeting. Thus, like the 14-chapter and 16-chapter versions, a 15-chapter version of Romans would appear to require something more at the end.

g. *Conclusion*
On the basis primarily of text-critical, contextual, linguistic, ideational and comparative evidence, most scholars have concluded—correctly, in my judgment—that the doxology normally labeled Rom. 16.25-27 is a non-Pauline interpolation.[46]

2. *2 Corinthians 6.14–7.1*

Victor Paul Furnish notes that 'whether [2 Cor. 6.14–7.1] actually belongs where it is located in our canonical 2 Cor has been discussed since early in the nineteenth century, and whether it can be attributed to Paul himself has been discussed almost as long'.[47] These verses have variously been viewed as: (1) composed by Paul specifically for inclusion at their present location in 2 Corinthians; (2) composed by Paul for some other occasion[48] but subsequently included at their present location either by Paul or by someone else; (3) composed by someone other than Paul but included at their present location by Paul; or (4) both composed by someone other than Paul and included at their present location by someone other than Paul (not necessarily the same person).[49] It is evidence for this fourth view—that 2 Cor. 6.14–7.1 is a non-Pauline interpolation in both senses of 'non-Pauline'—that is to be presented in what follows.[50]

46. Hurtado ('The Doxology', p. 185) insists that 'the question of the origin of the doxology remains open'; indeed, in his view (p. 199), 'It is still possible that the doxology was Paul's conclusion to Romans 16'.

47. Furnish, *II Corinthians*, p. 371.

48. Perhaps as part of the earlier letter mentioned in 1 Cor. 5.9-11.

49. For a good summary of scholarship since the Reformation, see William J. Webb, *Returning Home: New Covenant and Second Exodus as the Context for 2 Corinthians 6.14–7.1* (JSNTSup, 85; Sheffield: JSOT Press, 1993), pp. 16-30; see also e.g., Furnish, *II Corinthians*, pp. 375-83.

50. This view has been accepted by a number of scholars including Rudolf Bultmann (*Exegetische Probleme des zweiten Korintherbriefes* [SEÅSup, 9; Uppsala: Wretman, 1947], p. 307 n. 17; *idem*, *Theology of the New Testament* [trans.

a. *Text-Critical Evidence for Interpolation*

All of the early witnesses include 2 Cor. 6.14–7.1 at its present location. Thus, there is no direct text-critical evidence for viewing the verses as a later addition. There are within the passage, however, some apparently insignificant textual variants that might indicate an uneasiness on the part of some early copyists regarding the passage and perhaps even an desire to make it accord more closely with other Pauline materials. In v. 15, several witnesses including the sixth-century Codex Claromantanus (D) read Χριστῷ rather than Χριστοῦ, and Βελιάν rather than Βελιάρ.[51] Also in v. 15, the fourth-century Codex Vaticanus (B) and a few other witnesses have πιστοῦ rather than πιστῷ; similarly, in v. 16 Codex Claromantus and a few other witnesses read μοι rather than μου. In 7.1, the oldest extant manuscript, P^{46}, reads πνεύματι rather than πνεύματος. More significantly so far as the possibility of interpolation is concerned, a number of witnesses, including P^{46}, read 'for *you* are God's temple' (ὑμεῖς γὰρ ναὸς Θεοῦ ἐστε) in v. 16 rather than 'for *we* are God's temple' (ἡμεῖς γὰρ ναὸς Θεοῦ ἐσμεν).[52] This may reflect an attempt to bring 2 Cor. 6.16 more closely in line with 1 Cor. 3.16 (ναὸς Θεοῦ ἐστε).[53] Similarly, in 7.1, P^{46} has 'love of God' (ἀγάπῃ Θεοῦ) rather than 'fear of God' (φόβῳ Θεοῦ); this, too, may reflect an attempt to make the passage more 'Pauline' in tone.[54] Only in conjunction with other compelling arguments, however, could these textual variants be seen as possible indications of interpolation.

Kendrick Grobel; 2 vols.; New York: Charles Scribner's Sons, 1955], p. 205); Bornkamm (*Die Vorgeschichte des sogenannten Zweiten Korintherbriefes*, p. 187; and 'The History of the Origin'); and Helmut Koester ('*GNOMAI DIAPHOROI*: The Origin and Nature of Diversification in the History of Early Christianity', *HTR* 58 [1965], pp. 279-317; reprinted in James M. Robinson and Helmut Koester, *Trajectories through Early Christianity* [Philadelphia: Fortress Press, 1971], pp. 114-57 [154]). The most important recent contributions have been made by Grossouw ('Over de echtheid van 2 Cor. 6,14–7,1'), Fitzmyer ('Qumrân and the Interpolated Paragraph'); Gnilka ('2 Cor 6:14–7:1 in the Light of the Qumran Texts'), and Betz ('2 Cor 6:14–7:1').

51. A few have Βελιάβ or Βελιάλ.

52. A few witnesses including the fifth-century Codex Alexandrinus (A) have 'for we are God's *temples*' (ἡμεῖς γὰρ ναοὶ Θεοῦ ἐσμεν).

53. See also 1 Cor. 3.17 (ὁ γὰρ ναὸς Θεοῦ ἅγιός ἐστιν, οἵτινές ἐστε ὑμεῖς) and 6.19 (τὸ σῶμα ὑμῶν ναὸς τοῦ ἐν ὑμῖν ἁγίου πνεύματός ἐστιν).

54. Elsewhere, Paul speaks of 'fear of God' only in Rom. 3.18, which is a quotation from Ps. 36.2 (LXX 35.2).

b. *Contextual Evidence for Interpolation*
Much more persuasive than any possible text-critical evidence for interpolation is the contextual evidence. As James Moffatt observed many years ago, 'In its present situation [2 Cor. 6.14–7.1] looks like an erratic boulder'.[55] More expansively, Alfred Plummer wrote, 'This strongly worded admonition to make no compromise with heathenism comes in so abruptly here that a number of critics suppose that it is a fragment of another letter and some maintain that the fragment is not by St. Paul'.[56] As these comments suggest, it is by no means apparent that 6.14–7.1 is related in any meaningful way to its immediate context. The passage appears to interrupt what would otherwise be a syntactically smooth and logically clear transition from the immediately preceding passage (6.11-13) to that which immediately follows (7.2-3). As Fitzmyer notes, 'In the preceding context (6.1-13) Paul is making an eloquent plea for his reconciliation with the Corinthian community, appealing to his own past experience and his efforts expended on their behalf'.[57] Verses 11-13 begin with Paul's assurance, 'Our mouth is open to you, Corinthians, our heart is wide' (τὸ στόμα ἡμῶν ἀνέῳγεν πρὸς ὑμᾶς, Κορίνθιοι, ἡ καρδία ἡμῶν πεπλάτυνται); they continue with his assertion, 'You are not restricted by us, but you are restricted in your own affections' (οὐ στενοχωρεῖσθε ἐν ἡμῖν, στενοχωρεῖσθε δὲ ἐν τοῖς σπλάγχνοις ὑμῶν); and they end with his appeal, 'And in return—I speak as to children—widen your hearts also' (τὴν δὲ αὐτὴν ἀντιμισθίαν, ὡς τέκνοις λέγω, πλατύνθητε καὶ ὑμεῖς). 'Then', as Fitzmyer puts it, 'comes the puzzling paragraph about avoiding relations with unbelievers (6,14–7,1)'.[58] Following this paragraph, 7.2-3 begins with essentially the same appeal as 6.13, 'Make room for us' (χωρήσατε ἡμᾶς); it continues with an assertion similar to that in 6.12, 'We have wronged no one, we have corrupted no one, we have taken advantage of no one' (οὐδένα ἠδικήσαμεν, οὐδένα ἐφθείραμεν, οὐδένα ἐπλεονεκτήσαμεν); and it ends with an assurance similar to that in 6.11, 'I do not say this to condemn you, for I said before that you are in our

55. James Moffatt, *An Introduction to the Literature of the New Testament* (ITL; Edinburgh: T. & T. Clark, 3rd edn, 1918), p. 125.

56. Alfred Plummer, *A Critical and Exegetical Commentary on the Second Epistle of St. Paul to the Corinthians* (ICC; New York: Charles Scribner's Sons, 1915), p. 204.

57. Fitzmyer, 'Qumrân and the Interpolated Paragraph', p. 271.

58. Fitzmyer, 'Qumrân and the Interpolated Paragraph', p. 271.

hearts, to die together and to live together' (πρὸς κατάκρισιν οὐ λέγω· προείρηκα γὰρ ὅτι ἐν ταῖς καρδίαις ἡμῶν ἐστε εἰς τὸ συναποθανεῖν καὶ συζῆν). In short, as Joachim Gnilka points out, 2 Cor. 6.14–7.1 'disturbs the continuity of the Epistle just where Paul is trying to win the love of the church at Corinth, by introducing the new concept of the Christian's relationship to the heathen'.[59]

Moreover, and to my knowledge this has not previously been noted, with the removal of 6.14–7.1, the now (re-)unified passage, 6.11-13 and 7.2-3, forms a perfect chiasmus:

- A^1 *Assurance of Affection* (6.11): 'Our mouth is open to you, Corinthians, our heart is wide'.
  - B^1 *Disclaimer of Responsibility for Alienation* (6.12): 'You are not restricted by us, but you are restricted in your own affections'.
    - C^1 *Appeal for Affection* (6.13): 'And in return—I speak as to children—widen your hearts also'.
    - C^2 *Appeal for Affection* (7.2a): 'Make room for us'.
  - B^2 *Disclaimer of Responsibility for Alienation* (7.2b-3a): 'We wronged no one, we corrupted no one, we took advantage of no one'.
- A^2 *Assurance of Affection* (7.3b): 'I do not say this to condemn you, for I said before that you are in our hearts, to die together and to live together'.

Surely, the appearance of this chiasmus following the removal of 2 Cor. 6.14–7.1 lends support to the interpolation hypothesis.

Finally, as Fitzmyer points out, 6.14–7.1 'has a self-contained, independent character, forming a unit intelligible in itself, like a short homily'.[60] The verses could easily stand alone, addressing, in radically exclusionary terms, the question of the relation between believers and unbelievers—a topic not raised in this fashion elsewhere in 2 Corinthians and certainly not addressed in the immediate context of 6.14–7.1. Indeed, the passage 'is devoid of any concrete details which would suggest that it was dealing with a specifically Corinthian problem'.[61]

In short, 2 Cor 6.14–7.1 would appear at best to be an inexplicable digression at its present location; at worst, a foreign intrusion.

59. Gnilka, '2 Cor 6:14–7:1 in the Light of the Qumran Texts', p. 48.

60. Fitzmyer, 'Qumrân and the Interpolated Paragraph', p. 217. Similarly, Betz ('2 Cor 6:14–7:1', p. 89) refers to the passage as a 'very carefully constructed' parenesis, 'a literary unity which appears to be complete in itself'.

61. Fitzmyer, 'Qumrân and the Interpolated Paragraph', pp. 271-72.

c. *Linguistic Evidence for Interpolation*

The linguistic evidence for viewing 2 Cor. 6.14–7.1 as non-Pauline is impressive. First, the 'artistically linked' chain of scriptural quotations (vv. 16c-18) is not characteristically Pauline. Elsewhere when 'Paul forms similar scriptural combinations (Rom. 3.10-18)', he often 'takes care to distinguish the individual quotations from one another and to identify the author (Rom. 9.25-29; 10.18-20; 15.9-12)'.[62] In addition, as Furnish notes, 'Paul nowhere else cites or even alludes to any of the scriptural passages reflected in 6.16c-18.[63] Finally, the introductory and closing citation formulas (καθὼς εἶπεν ὁ Θεὸς in v. 16 and λέγει Κύριος Παντωκράτωρ in v. 18) are not found elsewhere in the Pauline letters.[64]

Second, Paul does not elsewhere employ the kind of 'poetic parallelism' or series of contrasts exhibited in vv. 14-16a.[65]

Third, the three and a half verses preceding and following the catena of scriptural citations (6.16c-18) contain eight words not otherwise found in the authentically Pauline letters: ἑτεροζυγεῖν ('unevenly yoke') and μετοχή ('sharing') in 6.14; συμφώνησις ('harmony'), Βελιάρ ('Beliar') and μερίς ('share') in 6.15; συγκατά-θεσις ('agreement') in 6.16a; and καθαρίζω ('cleanse') and μολυσμός ('defilement') in 7.1. Of these eight words, six are found nowhere else in the New Testament, and the other two are relatively rare.[66] In addition, ἀνομία ('iniquity', 6.14) appears elsewhere in the authentically Pauline letters only at Rom. 4.7, which is a quotation of Ps. 32.1 (LXX 31.1) and at Rom. 6.19; and ἁγιωσύνη ('holiness'; 7.1) appears only at Rom. 1.4, which is

62. Gnilka, '2 Cor 6:14–7:1 in the Light of the Qumran Texts', p. 59.

63. Furnish, *II Corinthians*, p. 376.

64. A somewhat similar introductory formula appears at 2 Cor. 4.6 (ὁ Θεὸς ὁ εἰπών), but it is not followed by a literal scriptural quotation. The closing formula, λέγει Κύριος Παντοκράτωρ appears at 2 Kgs 7.8, only a few verses before the apparent source of the final citation in 2 Cor. 6.18 (2 Kgs 7.14), and this may account for its presence at 6.18.

65. Gnilka ('2 Cor 6:14–7:1 in the Light of the Qumran Texts', p. 54) says that 'Paul does not otherwise use this poetic style or a series of comparisons'.

66. Nowhere else in the New Testament: ἑτεροζυγεῖν, μετοχή, συμφώνησις, Βελιάρ, συγκατάθεσις and μολυσμός. Μερίς appears only at Lk. 10.42, Acts 8.21, 16.12 and the pseudo-Pauline Col. 1.12. Καθαρίζειν is fairly frequent in the Synoptic Gospels, Acts and Hebrews but appears elsewhere in the New Testament only at the pseudo-Pauline Eph. 5.26 and Tit. 2.14 and at Jas 4.8 and 1 Jn 1.7, 9.

generally regarded as part of a pre-Pauline formulation, and at 1 Thess. 3.13, which is part of benediction.[67]

Fourth, several of the words that appear elsewhere in the authentically Pauline letters are used differently in 2 Cor. 6.14–7.1. These include 'righteousness' (δικαιοσύνη)[68] and 'fellowship' (κοινω-νία)[69] in 6.14; 'believer' (πιστός)[70] in 6.15; 'promises' (ἐπαγ-γελίαι)[71] and

67. Within the catena and its closing formula, ἐμπεριπατεῖν (v. 16, part of the quotation from Lev. 26.12) occurs nowhere else in the New Testament, and παντοκράτωρ (v. 18, perhaps suggested by the same word at 2 Kgs 7.8), although frequent in the LXX appears elsewhere in the New Testament only at Rev. 1.8; 4.8; 11.17; 15.3; 16.7, 14; 19.6, 15; 21.22.

68. See, e.g., Gnilka, '2 Cor 6:14–7:1 in the Light of the Qumran Texts', p. 57: '*dikaiosunē* does not have the meaning here of grace and justice given by God to man [*sic*], which is the sense in which Paul [normally] uses this term, but connotes, as an antithesis to *anomia*, a practical manner of living in accordance with the commendments and will of God'.

69. Elsewhere in the authentically Pauline letters, κοινωνία means 'fellowship', 'communion', or 'sharing' with reference to personal relationships (Rom. 15.26; 1 Cor. 1.9; 10.16; 2 Cor. 8.4; 9.13; 13.13; Gal. 2.9; Phil. 1.5; 2.1; 3.10; Phlm. 6). Here, however, it refers in a much more impersonal way to the relation between 'light' and 'darkness'.

70. Although Paul elsewhere uses ἄπιστος to refer to 'unbelievers' (1 Cor. 6.6; 7.12-15; 10.27; 14.22-24; 2 Cor. 4.4), with one possible exception (Gal. 3.9), πιστός means 'worthy of belief', 'worthy of trust', 'reliable', 'faithful' and is applied to God or Christ (1 Cor. 1.9; 10.13; 2 Cor. 1.18; 1 Thess. 5.24) or to humans (1 Cor. 4.2, 17; 7.25). Here, however, πιστός is contrasted with ἄπιστος (v. 15), and the context strongly suggests that the two terms should be translated respectively as 'believer' (Christian) and 'unbeliever' (non-Christian). According to Gnilka ('2 Cor 6:14–7:1 in the Light of the Qumran Texts', p. 57), 'The later connotation [πιστός as "believer"] appears first in the preface to Eph. (1.1 *pistois en Christō Iēsou*) and is clearly defined in the Pastoral letters. Here the *pistoi* (without any further qualification) are the believers in Christ (1 Tim 4:10-12; 5:16).'

71. Only at Rom. 9.4, 15.8, 2 Cor. 1.20, Gal. 3.16 and Gal. 3.21 does Paul use the plural, ἐπαγγελίαι; elsewhere (Rom. 4.13, 14, 16, 20; 9.8, 9; Gal. 3.14, 17, 18 [×2], 22, 29; 4.23, 28), it is always the singular, ἐπαγγελία. In every case except two (Rom. 9.4; 2 Cor. 1.20), it is either specified or made clear from the context that it is God's promise to *Abraham* that is intended (even in 2 Cor. 1.20, Paul states that 'all the promises of God find their "Yes" in [Christ]', thus apparently alluding to the more specific notion of the promise to Abraham). Only in Rom. 9.4, therefore, is there a generalized reference to 'promises', and even here 'promises' is followed immediately by 'patriarchs' (v. 5), thus suggesting an apparent link between promise and Abraham). In 2 Cor. 7.1, where the plural (ἐπαγγελίαι) appears, the reference is specifically to 'these promises' (ταύτας...τὰς ἐπαγγελίας), which are

'make perfect' (ἐπιτελεῖν)[72] in 7.1. Also to be noted is what Gnilka terms 'The absolutely untheological use of "flesh" and "spirit" in the concluding admonition of 2 Cor 7.1'.[73]

In short, the linguistic features of 2 Cor. 6.14–7.1—both stylistic and terminological—would appear to constitute significant evidence against Pauline authorship of the passage, though not necessarily against Pauline inclusion of the verses at their present location in his letter to the Corinthians.

d. *Ideational Evidence for Interpolation*

Some of the central ideas in 2 Cor. 6.14–7.1 appear not to be Pauline. First, as Gnilka notes, 'The call in 2 Cor. 6.14–7.1 for a radical separation from a heathen environment does not seem to harmonize with the Pauline concept of the relationship heathen/Christian'.[74] Indeed, in 1 Corinthians, Paul favors the preservation of marriages between Christians and non-Christians (1 Cor. 7.12-16), he allows Christians to eat with non-Christians (1 Cor. 10.25-27), he regards speaking in tongues as a sign for unbelievers (1 Cor. 14.22), and he acknowledges that the elimination of any association with non-Christians would require that Christians 'go out of the world' (1 Cor. 5.9-10). This is a far cry from the attitude of 2 Cor. 6.14–7.1!

Second, as Furnish points out, 'nowhere else does the apostle suggest that the fulfillment of God's promises is contingent upon one's obedience to God's commands (6.17-18)'.[75] Elsewhere, Paul insists that 'the promises were made to Abraham and to his offspring' (Gal. 3.16) and that 'the promise to Abraham and his descendants...did not

spelled out in 6.16c-18 and which have no apparent relation either to Abraham or even specifically to Christ. Thus, the use of ἐπαγγελία in 2 Cor. 7.1 appears to be non-Pauline.

72. Elsewhere in the authentically Pauline letters (Rom. 15.28; 2 Cor. 8.6, 11 [×2]; Gal. 3.3; Phil. 1.6), ἐπιτελεῖν means 'to complete', 'to fulfill', or 'to end up'. Here, however, it means 'to make perfect'.

73. See Gnilka, '2 Cor 6:14–7:1 in the Light of the Qumran Texts', p. 58: 'it is "not impossible" that [Paul] should here conform to the popular idea that man [*sic*] is formed from "flesh" and "spirit", and that the two together mean simply man [*sic*]. This idea appears, for example, in 1 Cor. 5.3 and 7.34. However, nowhere does he speak of the "defilement of flesh and spirit", or of the need for purification from such defilement.'

74. Gnilka, '2 Cor 6:14–7:1 in the Light of the Qumran Texts', p. 63.

75. Furnish, *II Corinthians*, p. 376.

come through the law but through the righteousness of faith' (Rom. 4.13). Thus, it is not 'the adherents of the law' who inherit the promise but rather 'those who share the faith of Abraham' (Rom. 4.14-16).

Finally, the notion of 'defilement of flesh and spirit', together with the assumption that Christians have the ability to 'cleanse' themselves from such defilement 'and make holiness perfect in the fear of God' (7.1) appears not to be Pauline. Elsewhere, Paul speaks not of 'defilement' but rather of enslavement to sin,[76] and he views the remedy not as self-cleansing but rather the gift of 'God's righteousness (δικαιοσύνη)'.

In addition, as has already been intimated, at least some of these ideas appear to be not only un-Pauline but even anti-Pauline. Thus, John J. Gunther suggests that the following features of the passage 'are in no way incompatible with the views of Paul's opponents': 'the implicit loyalty to the law, the tendencies toward perfectionism and asceticism, the underlying dualism, and the conception of God's people as God's temple'.[77] More explicitly, Hans Dieter Betz maintains 'that the *theology* of 2 Cor. 6.14–7.1 is not only non-Pauline, but anti-Pauline'.[78] Indeed, the thrust of the verses is to urge Jewish Christians, who keep the Law, not to associate with Gentile Christians, who do not. In short, the passage 'represents a theological position very similar to, if not identical with, the one which Paul tries to disprove in Galatians'.[79] In support of this view, Betz notes that, while Paul's notion of divine promise 'is based entirely upon the tradition of God's promise to Abraham',[80] the promises referred to in 2 Cor. 7.1 'are grounded in the "covenant formula"' (Lev. 26.12). Further, 'By starting with the promise to Abraham, Paul is able radically to separate what in 2 Cor. 6.14–7.1 are equally radically identified: promise and observance of the Torah'.[81] All of this means, in the judgment of Betz and others, that Paul can neither have written 2 Cor. 6.14–7.1 nor been responsible for its inclusion at its present location.

76. E.g. Rom. 6.16-23.

77. John J. Gunther, *St. Paul's Opponents and Their Background: A Study of Apocalyptic and Jewish Sectarian Teachings* (NovTSup, 35; Leiden: E.J. Brill, 1973), pp. 308-13 (quotation from Furnish, *II Corinthians*, p. 376).

78. Betz, '2 Cor 6:14–7:1', p. 108.

79. Betz, '2 Cor 6:14–7:1', p. 88.

80. Gal. 3.6-29 and elsewhere.

81. Betz, '2 Cor 6:14–7:1', p. 103; see the entire discussion, pp. 103-107.

e. *Comparative Evidence for Interpolation*

Joseph A. Fitzmyer and Joachim Gnilka have pointed out numerous significant affinities between 2 Cor. 6.14–7.1 and the Qumran materials.[82] Such affinities by no means resolve the question of whether the passage is a non-Pauline interpolation, however, because Paul himself might have included Qumran-like materials in one of his own letters or, indeed, have been influenced by such materials.

At a few points, 2 Cor. 6.14–7.1 appears to be more closely akin to the post-Pauline than to the Pauline writings. First, the use of πιστός to refer to a 'believer' (that is, a Christian), though uncharacteristic of the authentically Pauline letters, is found in the pseudo-Pauline writings.[83] Second, as Furnish points out, while the address 'beloved' (ἀγαπητοί) in 7.1 does occur elsewhere in the authentically Pauline letters,[84] 'it is not a special characteristic of Pauline style'; rather, 'it is a feature of homiletical-hortatory style in general, and in fact occurs more often in the later New Testament letters than in Paul's'.[85] Third, as has already been noted, the noun μερίς (6.15) occurs nowhere else in the authentically Pauline letters, but it appears in the pseudo-Pauline Col. 1.12;[86] similarly, the verb καθαρίζειν (7.1) occurs in the pseudo-Pauline Eph. 5.26 and Tit. 2.14 but not elsewhere in the authentically Pauline letters.[87]

More specifically, Gnilka calls attention to similarities between the theme of 2 Cor. 6.14–7.1 and certain ideas that appear in the pseudo-Pauline Ephesians. These include not only the 'stress on keeping oneself spiritually aloof from the heathen, and on the dignity of the spiritual temple', but also 'the opposition to *akathartos*, and the sharply defined light-darkness dualism'.[88]

In conjunction with other compelling arguments, such evidence lends some support to the interpolation hypothesis regarding 2 Cor. 6.14–7.1.

82. Fitzmyer, 'Qumrân and the Interpolated Paragraph'; and Gnilka, '2 Cor 6:14–7:1 in the Light of the Qumran Texts'.

83. 1 Tim. 4.3, 10, 12; 5.16; 6.2.

84. Rom. 12.19; 1 Cor. 10.14; 15.58; 2 Cor. 12.19; Phil. 2.12; 4.1.

85. Furnish, *II Corinthians*, p. 365. See Heb. 6.9; Jas 1.16, 19; 2.5; 1 Pet. 2.11; 4.12; 2 Pet. 3.1, 8, 14, 17; 1 Jn 2.7; 3.2, 21; 4.1, 7, 11; Jude 3, 17, 20.

86. Also at the post-Pauline Lk. 10.42; Acts 8.21; 16.12.

87. Also at the post-Pauline Jas 4.8 and 1 Jn 1.7, 9.

88. Gnilka, '2 Cor 6:14–7:1 in the Light of the Qumran Texts', p. 69.

f. *Situational Evidence for Interpolation*

On the basis of its content, Betz maintains that the addressees of 2 Cor. 6.14–7.1 were Jewish Christians. He also suggests that, while this is impossible to prove, Paul's Antioch encounter with Jewish Christians including Cephas (Gal. 2.11-14) 'would fit perfectly as a *Sitz im Leben*'. In any case, he concludes that 'incidents like that at Antioch must have been the cause of 2 Cor. 6.14–7.1'. The question remains open, however, as to whether the passage is 'intentionally anti-Pauline'. In the final analysis, it can only be assumed 'that the redactor of the Pauline corpus, for reasons unknown to us, has transmitted a document among Paul's letters which in fact goes back to the movement to which Paul's opponents in Galatia belonged'.[89]

That 2 Cor. 6.14–7.1 was addressed to Jews, not Gentiles, would appear to be a reasonable conclusion. Whether Betz is further correct, however, in ascribing the passage 'to the movement to which Paul's opponents in Galatia belonged' is less certain. In any case, the verses appear to reflect a situation in which the 'mismating' of believers and unbelievers was regarded as problematic. This situation may well have existed during Paul's lifetime as well as later, but there is nothing elsewhere in the authentically Pauline letters to suggest that Paul regarded it as problematic in the same sense as did the author of 2 Cor. 6.14–7.1 or, if he did, that he would have addressed it in the same way.

g. *Motivational and Locational Evidence for Interpolation*

With specific reference to 2 Cor. 6.14–7.1, William J. Webb insists that 'proponents of interpolation theories must explain why and how a redactor would have placed a non-Pauline or anti-Pauline fragment into a letter under Paul's name and at a most unlikely point between 6.13 and 7.2'.[90] As Furnish notes, however, 'proponents of these theories have generally despaired of finding an explanation, and respond only with such comments as "difficult to answer"…"not clear"…"remains unsolved"…and "for reasons unknown"'.[91]

Gnilka proposes a partial explanation. Assuming that '2 Cor is in fact a collection of letters', he suggests that 6.14–7.1 'won a place in the collection because the editor believed it to be a fragment of a Pauline letter'. Gnilka must confess, however, that 'it is not clear what caused

89. Betz, '2 Cor 6:14–7:1', pp. 99-103, 108 (quotations from pp. 108 and 100).

90. Webb, *Returning Home*, p. 162.

91. Furnish, *II Corinthians*, p. 380.

[the editor] to place the fragment in its present context, because the majority of exegetes who support the collection-theory consider 2.14–7.1 (excluding 6.14–7.1) to be one epistle'.[92] It is, of course, possible that an isolated fragment might, either inadvertently or intentionally, have been included within an otherwise unified document.

Robert Jewett offers a more comprehensive explanation. He suggests that, 'in the context of competing Christian groups castigating each other as heretical' (that is, at the time when Paul's letters were edited), the verb πλατύνειν in 6.13 might well have been understood in the sense, 'be broad minded', and thus seen as 'a call to tolerance, a suitable guideline from the apostle himself to reject the trend toward separatism and institutional rigidity'. Such a call might, however, be interpreted as including 'a broad-minded attitude toward paganism'. Thus, the insertion of 2 Cor. 6.14–7.1 'would have been highly meaningful', for 'it sharply delimits the scope of Christian tolerance, forbidding close associations with "unbelievers"'.[93] Jewett's proposal provides both a possible motive for the interpolation and a reason for its insertion at precisely its present location.

h. *Conclusion*

On the basis primarily of contextual, linguistic and ideational evidence, many scholars have concluded that 2 Cor. 6.14–7.1 is a non-Pauline interpolation. In my own judgment, this is not an unreasonable conclusion.

92. Gnilka, '2 Cor 6:14–7:1 in the Light of the Qumran Texts', p. 67.
93. Jewett, 'The Redaction of I Corinthians', p. 395.

Chapter 10

OTHER LIKELY INTERPOLATIONS (2)

1. *1 Thessalonians 2.13-16*

In the nineteenth century, primarily because of 1 Thess. 2.13-16, Ferdinand Christian Baur and a few others denied Pauline authorship of 1 Thessalonians.[1] Today, however, most scholars regard the letter as authentic. Both in the nineteenth century and in the twentieth, however, various scholars have suggested that part or all of 1 Thess. 2.13-16 should be viewed as a non-Pauline interpolation.[2] In 1961, Karl Gottfried Eckart argued, primarily on the basis of its similarity to 1.2-10, that 2.13-16 was post-Pauline in origin.[3] As Robert Jewett notes, however, 'The hypothesis of an interpolation in 1 Thess. 2.13-16 has its most persuasive development in the work of Birger A. Pearson',[4]

1. Ferdinand Christian Baur, *Paul the Apostle of Jesus Christ, His Life and Work, His Epistles and His Doctrine: A Contribution to the Critical History of Christianity* (ed. and trans. Eduard Zeller and Allan Menzies; 2 vols.; London: Williams & Norgate, 2nd edn, 1875–76), II, pp. 84-97. For discussion, see, e.g., Moffatt, *An Introduction to the Literature of the New Testament*, pp. 69-73.

2. For survey's of the relevant literature, see, e.g., Pearson, '1 Thessalonians 2:13-16', p. 80; G.E. Okeke, 'I Thessalonians 2.13-16: The Fate of the Unbelieving Jews', *NTS* 27 (1980), pp. 127-36 (128); and Robert Jewett, *The Thessalonian Correspondence: Pauline Rhetoric and Millenarian Piety* (FF; Philadelphia: Fortress Press, 1986), pp. 36-37.

3. Eckart, 'Der zweite echte Brief des Apostels Paulus an die Thessalonicher'. Eckart also identifies 4.1-8, 10b-12 and 5.12-22 as non-Pauline interpolations, with 3.5 and 5.17 as 'linking material'. In addition, he finds evidence of two different authentically Pauline letters in 1 Thessalonians.

4. Jewett, *The Thessalonian Correspondence*, p. 37; cf. John C. Hurd, 'Paul Ahead of his Time: 1 Thess. 2:13-16', in Peter Richardson and David Granskou (eds.), *Anti-Judaism in Early Christianity* (SCJ, 2; Waterloo, Ontario: Wilfrid Laurier University Press, 1986), pp. 21-36 (26): 'Pearson's case is probably the best that can be built in favor of the theory of interpolation'.

who, in 1971, examined the content of the passage and concluded that it could only have been written in the post-70 CE period.[5] Finally, in 1983, a linguistic analysis of the verses led Daryl Schmidt to the view that they represent a later addition to Paul's Thessalonian letter.[6] The arguments for interpolation have been accepted by a number of scholars[7] but, after critical scrutiny, rejected by others.[8]

In the following summary of evidence for interpolation, I shall be heavily dependent upon the work of Pearson with some attention also to the contributions of Schmidt and others.

a. *Text-Critical Evidence for Interpolation*

There is no apparent text-critical evidence for viewing 1 Thess. 2.13-16 (or any portion of it) as a non-Pauline interpolation. The verses appear at the same location in all of the witnesses, and it would be difficult to

5. Pearson, 'I Thessalonians 2:13-16'.

6. Schmidt, '1 Thess 2.13-16'; see also his 'Identifying Seams in Authentic Pauline Letters'.

7. E.g. Hendrikus Boers, 'The Form Critical Study of Paul's Letters: I Thessalonians as a Case Study', *NTS* 22 (1976), pp. 140-58 (151-52); Helmut Koester, '1 Thessalonians—Experiment in Christian Writing', in F. Forrester Church and Timothy George (eds.), *Continuity and Discontinuity in Church History: Essays Presented to George Huntston Williams on the Occasion of His 65th Birthday* (SHCT, 19; Leiden: E.J. Brill, 1979), pp. 33-44; *idem*, *Introduction to the New Testament*, II, p. 113; and Norman A. Beck, *Mature Christianity in the 21st Century: The Recognition and Repudiation of the Anti-Jewish Polemic of the New Testament* (Shared Ground among Jews and Christians, 5; Philadelphia: American Interfaith Institute/World Alliance; New York: Crossroad, rev. edn, 1994), pp. 76-84.

8. E.g. Ernest Best, *A Commentary on the First and Second Epistles to the Thessalonians* (HNTC; New York: Harper & Row, 1972), pp. 29-30, responding only to Eckart's work; Joseph Coppens, 'Miscellanées bibliques. LXXX. Une diatribe antijuive dans I Thess., II, 13-16', *ETL* 51 (1975), pp. 90-95; Raymond F. Collins, 'A propos the Integrity of I Thes.', *ETL* 55 (1979), pp. 67-106; Okeke, 'I Thessalonians 2.13-16'; Ingo Broer, '"Antisemitismus" und Judenpolemik im Neuen Testament: Ein Beitrag zum besseren Verständnis von 1 Thess 2:14-16', *BN* 29 (1983), pp. 59-91; Broer, '"Der Ganze Zorn Ist Schon Über Sie Gekommen"'; Karl Paul Donfried, 'Paul and Judaism: I Thessalonians 2:13-16 as a Test Case', *Int* 38 (1984), pp. 242-53 (244-45); Jewett, *The Thessalonian Correspondence*, pp. 36-42; Hurd, 'Paul Ahead of his Time'; Jon A. Weatherly, 'The Authenticity of 1 Thessalonians 2.13-16: Additional Evidence', *JSNT* 42 (1991), pp. 79-98; and Carol J. Schlueter, *Filling Up the Measure: Polemical Hyperbole in 1 Thessalonians 2.14-16* (JSNTSup, 98; Sheffield: JSOT Press, 1994).

argue that the seemingly insignificant textual variants in vv. 13, 15 and 16 are indications of interpolation.

b. *Contextual Evidence for Interpolation*

Pearson and others have treated much of the contextual evidence for interpolation under the heading of 'form criticism'. A normal Pauline thanksgiving formula appears in 1 Thess. 1.2-10 (εὐχαριστοῦμεν τῷ Θεῷ πάντοτε περὶ πάντων ὑμῶν...), but a similar formula also appears at 3.13 (καὶ διὰ τοῦτο καὶ ἡμεῖς εὐχαριστοῦμεν τῷ Θεῷ ἀδιαλείπτως...).[9] This repetition of the thanksgiving formula, which is not otherwise found in the authentically Pauline letters, has been variously explained. According to Paul Schubert, 1 Thess. 1.2–3.13 forms a single 'thanksgiving' section, even though it is 'highly complex' and of 'excessive length', there is no 'formal transition' between 2.16 and 2.17, and 2.14-16 includes 'some extraneous matter'.[10] Jack T. Sanders, however, argues cogently that the thanksgiving which begins at 1.2 ends at 1.10 and that 2.13 marks the beginning of a second thanksgiving, which, in turn, continues to 4.1.[11] Going further, Walter Schmithals maintains that 2.13 (the beginning of the second thanksgiving) is the point at which two originally different (Pauline) letters were joined together by an editor.[12]

Hendrikus Boers attempts to resolve the problem by examining the first part of v. 13 (καὶ διὰ τοῦτο καὶ ἡμεῖς εὐχαριστοῦμεν τῷ Θεῷ ἀδιαλείπτως ὅτι παραλαβόντες...).[13] In his view, the first καί 'functions [simply] as a copulative particle' (that is, a link between v. 13 and the preceding material in vv. 1-12), διὰ τοῦτο points not back to what precedes but 'forward to the clause which begins with ὅτι',[14] and the

9. See also 3.9 (τίνα γὰρ εὐχαριστίαν δυνάμεθα τῷ Θεῷ ἀνταποδοῦναι περὶ ὑμῶν...) for what some have regarded as yet a third thanksgiving formula.

10. Paul Schubert, *Form and Function of the Pauline Thanksgiving* (BZNW, 20; Berlin: Alfred Töpelmann, 1939), pp. 21-26.

11. Jack T. Sanders, 'The Transition from Opening Epistolary Thanksgiving to Body in the Letters of the Pauline Corpus', *JBL* 81 (1962), pp. 348-62 (356).

12. Walter Schmithals, 'Die Thessalonicherbriefe als Briefkomposition', in Erich Dinkler (ed.), *Zeit und Geschichte: Dankesgabe an Rudolf Bultmann zum 80. Geburtstag* (Tübingen: J.C.B. Mohr [Paul Siebeck], 1964), pp. 295-315; and his *Paul and the Gnostics*, pp. 179-80.

13. Boers, 'The Form Critical Study of Paul's Letters', pp. 151-52.

14. See, however, Weatherly, 'The Authenticity of 1 Thessalonians 2.13-16',

second καί 'should not be taken with ἡμεῖς, but with the verb that follows' (εὐχαριστοῦμεν). Thus, the appropriate translation would be, 'And for the following (reason) we also give thanks to God unceasingly, namely, that having received...' This means, according to Boers, that v. 13 is not a continuation of the earlier thanksgiving but rather the introduction of a new one, intended to parallel that in 1.2-10. In short, the phrase καὶ διὰ τοῦτο καὶ ἡμεῖς 'would give exact expression to the intention of an interpolator who wanted to incorporate the anti-Jewish polemic of verses 14-16 as a parallel to the thanksgiving of i.2-10'. This, in his judgment, lends support to other arguments for viewing 1 Thess. 2.13-16 as a secondary interpolation.

Further, the transitions from 2.12 to 2.13 and particularly from 2.16 to 2.17 are abrupt and appear somewhat contrived. The first 12 verses of ch. 2 speak of Paul's visit to Thessalonica, and the last four report the sequel to this visit; in both sections, the focus is upon the Thessalonians and Paul himself. The anti-Jewish polemic of vv. 13-16, however, interrupts this narrative. The removal of these verses would result in a transition between vv. 12 and 17 that is both smooth and logical.

Thus, according to Boers, 'The problem of the structure of I Thess. finds a simple resolution when ii.13-16 is recognized as an interpolation'.[15] He summarizes the matter as follows:

> Gone is the unusually long thanksgiving section with its two sub-themes. The removal of ii.13-16 makes evident that, although iii.9f. has all the *formal* characteristics of a thanksgiving formula, it does not function as such, i.e., to introduce a thanksgiving period. The apostolic apology [2.1-12] and *parousia* [2.17–3.13] sections, which have already been recognized as intimately related, are reconnected. The shift of focus from the Thessalonians in ii.12 back to Paul himself in vv. 17ff. is clearly indicated by the ἡμεῖς δέ. With that the first three chapters of 1 Thessalonians regain a more 'normal' structure: on the thanksgiving (i.2-10) follows the central section (ii.1-12) and then the apostolic *parousia* (ii.17–iii.11) which is concluded with the benediction of iii.12. In iii.10 Paul is evidently still concerned with his '*parousia*'. On the benediction follows the exhortation section of iv.1ff.[16]

p. 82: 'if 1 Thess. 2.13-16 is an interpolation, διὰ τοῦτο is the interpolator's device to integrate the material into the context, not an indication that the verses are self-contained'.

15. Boers, 'The Form Critical Study of Paul's Letters', p. 158.
16. Boers, 'The Form Critical Study of Paul's Letters', p. 152.

In short, 'The letter [now] has a completely normal form: prescript i.1; thanksgiving i.2-10; apostolic apology ii.1-12; apostolic *parousia* ii.17–iii.13; exhortation iv.1–v.22; and conclusion v.23-8'.[17]

As Pearson summarizes the matter, form-critical considerations suggest that 'vv. 13-16 do not belong to Paul's original letter at all, but represent a later interpolation into the text'.[18] According to Norman A. Beck, a form-critical analysis leads to the conclusion that 1 Thess. 2.13-16 'is extraneous' and must therefore be seen as either a Pauline excursus or a non-Pauline interpolation; in his judgment, however, a theological analysis of the verses clearly tips the scales in favor of non-Pauline interpolation.[19]

c. *Linguistic Evidence for Interpolation*

The linguistic evidence for viewing 1 Thess. 2.13-16 as a non-Pauline interpolation has been discussed most fully by Schmidt.[20] At the outset, Schmidt eschews both the usual reliance upon 'lists of words and phrases' and more recent 'computer-aided "stylistic analysis"' that focuses upon such items as 'sentence-length and common-word frequency'—the former because of its 'lack of appropriate linguistic criteria' and the latter because 'such statistics...are of very limited usefulness in the analysis of a short passage such as 1 Thess. 2.13-16'.[21] Rather, Schmidt provides a detailed examination of the 'syntactical pattern' of 1 Thess. 2.13-16, particularly as this pattern relates to that of the material immediately preceding and following (1 Thess. 1.2–2.12 and 2.17–3.10). Here, 'syntactical pattern' refers to 'three levels of syntactical relationships: (1) the formation of noun and verb phrases, including those traditionally called "clauses", (2) the sequence of phrases in a sentence, and (3) the connection between sentences'.

According to Schmidt's analysis, 1 Thess. 1.2–2.12 and 2.17–3.10 exhibit essentially 'the same basic pattern' so far as syntax is concerned.[22] This pattern includes frequency and complexity of 'embeds' (dependent clauses), the way in which 'embeds' are introduced, conjunctions connecting 'matrix sentences' (main clauses), and noun and

17. Boers, 'The Form Critical Study of Paul's Letters', p. 158.
18. Pearson, 'I Thessalonians 2:13-16', p. 91.
19. Beck, *Mature Christianity in the 21st Century*, p. 78.
20. Schmidt, '1 Thess 2.13-16'.
21. Schmidt, '1 Thess 2.13-16', p. 271.
22. Schmidt, '1 Thess 2.13-16', pp. 271-73.

prepositional phrases. The disputed passage, 1 Thess. 2.13-16, however, is significantly different.[23] Verse 13 is distinctive in its use of the conjunction καί,[24] the construction καὶ διὰ τοῦτο,[25] the introduction of the initial 'embed' with ὅτι rather than a participle,[26] and the 'troublesome' use of 'the noun phrase' λόγον ἀκοῆς παρ' ἡμῶν τοὺς Θεοῦ following the participle παραλαβόντες.[27] Verses 14-16a are even more out of harmony with the pattern of the larger section', with 'more embeds than any other sentence in the whole section', 'significantly more levels of embedding', a different structure in the 'embeds', the 'unusual feature' (v. 15) of 'the separation of the nouns κύριον and Ἰησοῦν by the participle',[28] the unusual noun phrase in v. 15: τῶν ἐκκλησιῶν τοῦ Θεοῦ τῶν οὐσῶν ἐν τῇ Ἰουδαίᾳ ἐν Χριστῷ Ἰησοῦ,[29] and the position of ἀδελφοί between μιμηταὶ ἐγενήθητε and τῶν ἐκκλησιῶν in v. 14.[30] In short, vv. 14-16a 'are not "completely incorporated" into the syntactical pattern of the rest of this larger section'; rather, 'the

23. Schmidt, '1 Thess 2.13-16', pp. 273-76.

24. 'Nowhere else in 1 Thessalonians is καί used to connect two matrix sentences' (Schmidt, '1 Thess 2.13-16', p. 273).

25. Schmidt, '1 Thess 2.13-16', p. 273: 'no other undisputed letter of Paul uses the construction καὶ διὰ τοῦτο (though it is imitated in 2 Thess 2:11)'.

26. 'The thanksgiving formula used here is an abbreviation of the opening one in 1:2-5, but more importantly, it is also the second of the two types that Paul developed, having a content ὅτι-embed instead of participles, similar to Rom. 1:8 and 1 Cor. 1:4, and the type imitated in 2 Thess 1:3 and 2:13' (Schmidt, '1 Thess 2.13-16', p. 273).

27. 'The relationship of the three components to the head noun is not clear' (Schmidt, '1 Thess 2.13-16', p. 275). The entire phrase 'can be analyzed as an amalgamation of several different "Pauline" constructions, each one found somewhere in the Pauline corpus, but the final combination itself is not typical of Pauline syntax' (p. 276).

28. 'Elsewhere in Paul they always appear together' (Schmidt, '1 Thess 2.13-16', p. 273).

29. 'The noun ἐκκλησία is followed by (1) a genitive [noun phrase], (2) the adnominal equative participle with a locative [prepositional phrase], and (3) the "in Christ" [prepositional phrase]. Each of the three constructions is Pauline, but the combination of all three is not' (Schmidt, '1 Thess 2.13-16', p. 274).

30. 'In the more than 50 times Paul uses the vocative ἀδελφοί, it always comes at a natural syntactical break in the sentence, such as between complete noun phrases, not between parts of the same noun phrase' (Schmidt, '1 Thess 2.13-16', p. 275).

syntax of these lines deviates as much from the surrounding pattern as does the content'.[31]

Schmidt's conclusion is that: (1) 'the content of 2.13-16 does not fit well into 1 Thessalonians, nor into Pauline thought in general'; (2) 'formally this section intrudes into the overall structure of the whole letter'; (3) 'the linguistic evidence suggests that it did not come from the same editor as the rest of the letter, but is rather built around a conflation of Pauline expressions'.[32] In his judgment, 'the interpolation hypothesis seems to be the best explanation for all three of these matters, especially since Birger Pearson has already offered a very plausible setting for such an interpolation'.

d. *Ideational Evidence for Interpolation*

As Jon A. Weatherly observes, 'For most exegetes, the decisive factor in judging 1 Thess. 2.13-16 an interpolation is its apparent theological contradiction of Romans 11, especially vv. 25-32'.[33] This view is articulated in some detail by Pearson.[34] Focusing initially on v. 16c, Pearson argues that 'wrath' (ὀργή) 'is to be taken in an eschatological sense', and, however it is to be translated, εἰς τέλος indicates 'the finality of the wrath that has come upon the Jews';[35] thus, 'the passage excludes categorically any possibility for the Jews except the naked wrath of God'.[36] Given Paul's pride in 'his achievements in Judaism prior to his "conversion"' (Gal. 1.14; Phil. 3.5-6) and his continuing 'refer[ences] to himself as a Jew' (Gal. 2.15; Rom. 11.1), it is 'virtually impossible to ascribe to Paul the *ad hominem* fragment of Gentile anti-Judaism in v. 15 [πᾶσιν ἀνθρώποις ἔαντίων]'; further, 'the thought that God's wrath has come upon the Jewish people with utter finality (v. 16) is manifestly foreign to Paul's theology which, unique in the New Testament, expresses the thought that God has *not* abandoned his ancient covenant people (Rom. 9.1), and indeed "all Israel will be

31. Schmidt, '1 Thess 2.13-16', p. 273.

32. Schmidt, '1 Thess 2.13-16', p. 276.

33. Weatherly, 'The Authenticity of 1 Thess. 2.13-16', pp. 82-83.

34. Pearson, '1 Thessalonians 2:13-16'. For a somewhat different summary of the evidence that reaches the same conclusion, see Beck, *Mature Christianity in the 21st Century*, pp. 79-81.

35. Pearson, '1 Thessalonians 2:13-16', p. 81.

36. Pearson, '1 Thessalonians 2:13-16', p. 82.

saved" (Rom. 11.26)'.[37] Indeed, it strains credulity to believe that the author of 1 Thess. 2.13-16 could also have written Rom. 9.1-5a:

> I am speaking the truth in Christ, I am not lying; my conscience bears me witness in the Holy Spirit that I have great sorrow and unceasing anguish in my heart. For I could wish that I myself were accursed and cut off from Christ for the sake of my brethren, my kinsmen by race. They are Israelites, and to them belong the sonship, the glory, the covenants, the giving of the law, the worship, and the promises; to them belong the patriarchs, and of their race, according to the flesh, is the Christ.

John C. Hurd also notes that Paul by no means had 'an attitude of revulsion toward his preconversion days'; indeed, 'when Paul made the magnificent comparison between his former life within Judaism and his new life as a Christian in Phil. 3.4-7 he did not contrast bad and good, but rather a very considerable good and an infinitely better good'. Further, according to Hurd, when Paul refers to his own persecution of Christians in Gal. 1.13-17, he speaks of it not as 'part of the sin of Israel' but rather as 'evidence of his [own] zeal, albeit misguided'.[38] In addition, 'it is hardly possible that Paul himself would have written in [such a] detached way about the churches in Judea suffering at the hands of the Jews, since according to Gal. 1.13-14 Paul himself had formerly persecuted the church and tried to destroy it'.[39] Finally, Paul 'never attributes the death of Jesus to the Jews'.[40] Thus Hurd concludes 'that in the other Pauline letters Paul's attitude toward Judaism both theologically and autobiographically stands in sharp contrast to the sentiments expressed in the Thessalonian passage'.[41]

Along somewhat different lines, the reference to the readers as 'imitators' (μιμηταί) of 'the churches of God in Judea' is uncharacteristic of Paul, who elsewhere, even in 1 Thessalonians, speaks of his readers as 'imitators' (μιμηταί) only of himself[42] and indirectly of Christ.[43] Moreover, the statement in 2.16c that 'the wrath *has* come (ἔφθασεν)

37. Pearson, '1 Thessalonians 2:13-16', pp. 85-86.
38. Hurd, 'Paul Ahead of his Time', p. 22.
39. Beck, *Mature Christianity in the 21st Century*, p. 79.
40. 1 Cor. 2.8 blames the crucifixion on 'the rulers of this age' (οἵ ἄρχοντες τοῦ αἰῶνος τούτου). In Chapter 6, however, I argued that 1 Cor. 2.6-16 is a non-Pauline interpolation.
41. Hurd, 'Paul Ahead of his Time', p. 22.
42. 1 Cor. 4.16; 11.1; Phil. 3.17; 1 Thess. 1.6; cf. 2 Thess. 2.7-9.
43. E.g. 1 Cor. 11.1; 1 Thess. 1.6.

upon them' appears to be at odds with the reference in 1.10 to 'the wrath that is coming' (ἐρχομένης).

In short, as Pearson notes, 'there are some basic incompatibilities between I Thessalonians 2.15f. and Paul's thought as expressed elsewhere in his epistles'.[44] Such considerations lead Beck to the conclusion: 'it seems almost certain that a redactor, from a theological and political position similar to that expressed in Acts of the Apostles, inserted what we call 2.13-16 into 1 Thessalonians'.[45]

e. *Comparative Evidence for Interpolation*

Affinities between 1 Thess. 2.13-16 and certain materials in the Synoptic Gospels have often been noted. In a general sense, as Pearson points out, both this passage and the Gospel of Matthew reflect a situation in which 'the final break between church and synagogue [has] occurred' and 'the relations between Jews and Christians are now acutely polemical'.[46] More specific are the striking similarities between these verses and Lk. 11.47-52 and its parallel in Mt. 23.29-36. Particularly noteworthy in this regard are the words of Mt. 23.31-32:

> Thus you witness against yourselves, that you are the sons of those who murdered the prophets (ὑιοί ἐστε τῶν φονευσάντων τοὺς προφήτας; cf. τῶν...ἀποκτεινάντων...τοὺς προφήτας in 1 Thess. 2.15). Fill up, then, the measure of your fathers (καὶ ὑμεῖς τὸ μέτρον τῶν πατε̂ρων ὑμῶν, cf. εἰς τὸ ἀναπληρῶσαι ἀὐτῶν τὰς ἁμαρτίας πάντοτε in 1 Thess. 2.16b).

Some scholars, noting such similarities, have suggested that Paul was using pre-Synoptic tradition at 1 Thess. 2.13-16.[47] In light of the fact that the Synoptic materials also appear to presuppose a post-70 situation, however, a more likely explanation is that the author of 1 Thess. 2.13-16 knew one or more of the Synoptic Gospels. In any case, such similarities between a suspected interpolation in a Pauline letter and documents that are clearly post-Pauline in date cannot be ignored. Indeed, they suggest a similar situation for both sets of materials.

44. Pearson, '1 Thessalonians 2:13-16', pp. 85-86.

45. Beck, *Mature Christianity in the 21st Century*, p. 81.

46. Pearson, '1 Thessalonians 2:13-16', p. 93.

47. E.g. J.B. Orchard, 'Thessalonians and the Synoptic Gospels', *Bib* 19 (1938), pp. 19-42 (23-25); R. Schippers, 'The Pre-Synoptic Tradition in I Thessalonians II 13-16', *NovT* 8 (1966), pp. 223-34; and Donfried, 'Paul and Judaism: I Thessalonians 2:13-16 as a Test Case', *Int* 38 (1984), pp. 242-53 (248-49).

f. *Situational Evidence for Interpolation*

Despite suggestions to the contrary, Pearson insists that 'the aorist ἔφθασεν [v. 16c] must be taken as referring to an event that is now past, and the phrase εἰς τέλος underscores the finality of the "wrath" that has occurred'.[48] Thus, 'I Thessalonians 2.16c refers to the destruction of Jerusalem in 70 A.D.', because only this event in the first century would 'lend itself to such apocalyptic theologizing'.[49] It is insufficient, however, 'merely to excise this one sentence as a post-70 gloss', for 'it constitutes the conclusion to the material represented in the participial clauses of vv. 15 and 16 modifying τῶν Ἰουδαίων in v. 14'.[50] Thus, if v. 16c is post-Pauline, so too are vv. 15 and 16a-b.

Further, according to Pearson, other than in 1 Thess. 2.14, the New Testament nowhere 'indicate[s] that the churches in Judaea suffered persecution at the hands of the Jews between 44 AD and the outbreak of the war against Rome';[51] indeed, it appears that 'there was no significant persecution of Christians in Judaea before the war'.[52] In addition, it is doubtful 'that the Thessalonian Christians were actually suffering systematic persecution in the apostolic period', as 1 Thess. 2.14 suggests.[53] In short, v. 14 'stands out as...historically incongruous',[54] because 'it is only in the period post-70 that an editor working with the text of Paul's letter to the Thessalonians, in a situation of local (presumably Gentile) persecution against the church in Thessalonica, could hold up as a shining example "the churches of God which are in Judaea"'.[55]

Thus, as Hurd observes, 'the Thessalonian passage is anomalous and seems out of place if taken as an utterance of Paul, but it fits well with

48. Pearson, '1 Thessalonians 2:13-16', pp. 82-83.

49. Pearson, '1 Thessalonians 2:13-16', p. 83.

50. Pearson, '1 Thessalonians 2:13-16', p. 83.

51. Pearson, '1 Thessalonians 2:13-16', p. 86.

52. Pearson, '1 Thessalonians 2:13-16', p. 87. To be sure, Acts 8.1b-3 reports Jewish persecution of the church in Judea in the 30s and even links Paul himself with this persecution (see also Gal. 1.13, 23; 1 Cor. 15.9; Phil. 3.6). This, however, is clearly earlier than the period specified by Pearson (44–56 CE). Moreover, Paul's own letters indicate nothing regarding the location of his 'persecuting' activities (Gal. 1.23 perhaps implies that it was in Judea), and the historicity of Acts has long been a matter of dispute.

53. Pearson, '1 Thessalonians 2:13-16', p. 87.

54. Pearson, '1 Thessalonians 2:13-16', p. 88.

55. Pearson, '1 Thessalonians 2:13-16', p. 94.

the post-70 C.E. attitude of the church'.[56] Pearson concludes that like the author of the pseudo-Pauline 2 Thessalonians, the interpolator has 'use[d] Pauline words and phrases from a genuine letter [that is, 1 Thessalonians] in order to provide a putative "Pauline" framework for a new message'.[57]

g. *Motivational Evidence for Interpolation*

According to Pearson, the purpose of 1 Thess. 2.13-16 is, 'in circumstances of persecution, to encourage the readers with reference to the embattled Christians in Palestine and to underscore now in a post-70 situation the "united front" of all Christians against the Jews who have at last suffered in the destruction of their city and temple the ultimate rejection and judgment from God'.[58]

h. *Locational Evidence for Interpolation*

So far as I can ascertain, neither Pearson nor others have directly addressed the question of why the interpolation would have been inserted at precisely its present location in Paul's letter to the Thessalonians. If it was to be added to the letter at all, however, this would appear to be the only logical place. Verses 1-12 speak of Paul's activity in Thessalonica, and v. 12 even summarizes something of the content of his message (referred to in v. 9 as 'the gospel of God'). Then, the interpolation begins (v. 13) by making reference to the readers' reception of the message (termed 'the word of God which you heard from us').[59] Nowhere else in 1 Thessalonians would such a reference appear to fit.

i. *Conclusion*

On the basis primarily of contextual (including form-critical), linguistic, and ideational considerations, a strong case has been made for viewing 1 Thess. 2.13-16 as a non-Pauline interpolation. Moreover, the case has been buttressed by comparative, situational and motivational considerations.

56. Hurd, 'Paul Ahead of his Time', p. 23.

57. Pearson, '1 Thessalonians 2:13-16', p. 91.

58. Pearson, '1 Thessalonians 2:13-16', p. 91.

59. As noted above, the Greek here is problematic (λόγον ἀκοῆς παῤ ἡμῶν τοῦ Θεοῦ).

2. *Romans 13.1-7*

Even scholars who regard Rom. 13.1-7 as authentically Pauline and/or appropriately located in Paul's Roman letter acknowledge that the passage presents problems for the exegete. Otto Michel, for example, refers to it as 'an independent insertion' that Paul included in his letter to the Romans;[60] similarly, Ernst Käsemann speaks of 'an independent block' that 'in many respects...is unique to Paul' and acknowledges that 'it can be pointedly called an alien body in Paul's exhortation'.[61] More concisely, Brendan Byrne observes that 'at this point the reader is confronted by perhaps the strangest and most controversial passage in the entire [Roman] letter'.[62] Thus, it is not surprising that some scholars regard Rom. 13.1-7 as a non-Pauline interpolation.[63] Their arguments are based upon a confluence of different types of evidence.[64]

a. *Text-Critical Evidence for Interpolation*

J.I.H. McDonald observes that 'textual criticism establishes a strong presumption in favour of the authenticity of Rom. 13.1-7'.[65] What he means, of course, is that the passage appears—and, indeed, appears at the same location—in all of the early manuscripts. Thus, there is no direct text-critical evidence for interpolation.

A number of years ago, however, Ernst Barnikol argued that the author of *1 Clement*[66] could not have known Rom. 13.1-7, that it was

60. Otto Michel, *Der Brief an die Römer übetsetzt und erklärt* (KEK; Göttingen: Vandenhoeck & Ruprecht, 4th edn, 1966), p. 312.

61. Käsemann, *Commentary on Romans*, pp. 350, 352.

62. Byrne, *Romans*, p. 385.

63. See especially, Barnikol, 'Römer 13'; Kallas, 'Romans xiii.1-7'; Schmithals, *Der Römerbrief als historisches Problem*, pp. 185-97; O'Neill, *Paul's Letter to the Romans*, pp. 15, 207-209; Munro, *Authority in Paul and Peter*, pp. 16-19, 56-57; and *idem*, 'Romans 13:1-7'.

64. In my own summary of the evidence for interpolation, I rely most heavily upon the work of Barnikol ('Römer 13') and Kallas ('Romans xiii.1-7'). It should also be noted, however, that Michel (*Der Brief an die Römer*), while accepting Pauline inclusion of Rom. 13.1-7 in his letter to the Romans, noted a number of arguments against Pauline authorship of the passage; thus, I shall also refer to his work at appropriate places.

65. J.I.H. McDonald, 'Romans 13.1-7: A Test Case for New Testament Interpretation', *NTS* 35 (1989), pp. 540-49 (540).

66. Usually dated c. 95–96 CE. According to Laurence L. Welborn ('Clement,

missing from Marcion's text of Romans (c. 130 CE), that the earliest evidence for the passage is a fragment quoted by Origen from Heracleon (c. 145–180 CE), and that the first ecclesiastical writer to cite the passage was Irenaeus (late-second century). Such evidence suggests that the verses may have been missing from early copies of Paul's Roman letter[67] and thus constitutes indirect text-critical evidence for viewing Rom. 13.1-7 as a possible interpolation.

b. *Contextual Evidence for Interpolation*

Three types of contextual evidence suggest that Rom. 13.1-7 may be a secondary addition to the text of Paul's Roman letter. First, as James Kallas notes, 'there is unmistakable evidence that the latter part of [Romans] has been subjected to some kind of alteration'. This is indicated by the problematic nature of the relation of ch. 16 to the remainder of Romans, the evidence for second-century texts of Romans ending with ch. 14, and the presence of four closing benedictions in chs. 15 and 16.[68] Although such evidence by no means constitutes a positive argument for interpolation, it does, according to Kallas, lend some credence to the conjecture that Rom. 13.1-7 might be a secondary addition.[69]

Second, 'this little section of seven verses has always been recognized by theologians as a self-contained envelope completely independent of its context'.[70] Thus, Käsemann refers to the passage as 'an independent block',[71] and McDonald observes that 'the inner logic of the passage is completely self-contained'.[72] That the passage can stand alone, without reference to its context, is indicated by 'the fact that many monographs have been written on just this one section, treating the passage and extracting its essence without any reference being necessarily made to the sections preceding or following'.[73] In addition, there is nothing elsewhere in Paul's letter to the Romans that would

First Epistle of', *ABD*, I, p. 1060), however, 'one may place the composition of *1 Clement* between A.D. 80 and 140'.

67. Barnikol, 'Römer 13', pp. 81-82, 113-18.
68. Rom. 15.13, 33; 16.24 (in some manuscripts), 25-27.
69. Kallas, 'Romans xiii.1-7', p. 365.
70. Kallas, 'Romans xiii.1-7', pp. 365-66.
71. Käsemann, *Commentary on Romans*, p. 352.
72. McDonald, 'Romans 13.1-7', p. 542.
73. Kallas, 'Romans xiii.1-7', p. 366.

16:25-27
+
13:1-7

suggest a reason for inclusion of a passage dealing with relation between Christians and 'governing authorities'.

Third, 'not only is this section independent of its context, but i actually interrupts the context'.[74] Indeed, according to Käsemann, Rom. 13.1-7 can be seen as 'an alien body in Paul's exhortation'.[75] Barnikol observes that Rom. 12.18-21 'with its admonition to peace and to renunciation of vengeance and with the instruction of active love of the enemy finds its continuation not in the pericope that affirms the Imperium [13.1-7] but rather in 13.8-10, in the command of love as the true fulfillment of the Law'.[76] Similarly, Kallas notes that Romans 12 and 13.8-10 appear to represent a deliberate and smoothly-flowing 'development by Paul of synoptic-type teaching'. Then, 'into this homogeneous material' are 'thrust' the apparently unrelated verses regarding Christians and the governing authorities. 'If that envelope were not there the two chapters would move forward much more normally than is now the case'.[77] As Byrne summarizes the argument, 'the removal of 13.1-7 from the text of Romans leaves a smooth flow across 12.9-21–13.8-10, governed by the overall theme of love, with the "eschatological" ending (13.11-14) reinforcing the ethical appeal'.[78] In short, Rom. 13.1-7 'is a self-contained treatment of a special theme not immediately related to what precedes or follows, and...this new theme is abruptly introduced with no organic literary connexion to its surroundings'.[79] Of particular interest in this regard is the fact that 13.1-7 makes no reference whatsoever to 'love' (ἀγάπη), which clearly is the overriding theme both in 12.9-21 (immediately prior to 13.1-7) and in 13.8-10 (immediately following).

Also significant in this regard is the fact that, although Rom. 13.8–15.13 is closely related to ch. 12, it makes no reference to submission to the governing authorities, which is the theme introduced in 13.1-7. Indeed, its opening admonition (13.8) to 'owe no one anything except to love one another' (μηδενὶ μηδὲν ὀφείλετε εἰ μὴ τὸ ἀλλήλους ἀγαπᾶν) is somewhat surprising, coming, as it does, immediately after the closing command in 13.7: 'Pay to all what is owed…' (ἀπόδοτε πᾶσιν τὰς

74. Kallas, 'Romans xiii.1-7', p. 366.
75. Käsemann, *Commentary on Romans*, p. 352.
76. Barnikol, 'Romans 13', p. 74.
77. Kallas, 'Romans xiii.1-7', p. 366.
78. Byrne, *Romans*, pp. 385-86.
79. Kallas, 'Romans xiii.1-7', p. 366.

ὀφειλὰς...).[80] It could well be the case, however, that the near juxtaposition of ὀφείλετε (v. 8) and ὀφειλάς (v. 7) represents the presence of 'link words connecting originally separated units'.[81]

Finally, a close verbal parallel between 13.8 (immediately following the disputed passage) and 12.17 (shortly before the passage) calls for attention. In 12.17a Paul admonishes his readers to 'repay no one evil for evil' (μηδενὶ κακὸν ἀντὶ κακοῦ ἀποδιδόντες), and the remainder of the chapter (vv. 17b-21) simply spells out the meaning of this admonition. Then, immediately following 13.1-7, there is the command in v. 8a to 'owe no one anything except to love one another' (μηδενὶ μηδὲν ὀφείλετε εἰ μὴ τὸ ἀλλήλους ἀγαπᾶν), which is amplified in the next few verses (vv. 8b-10). According to Michel, the μηδενί both in 12.17a and in 13.8a serves to introduce a paraphrase of the commandment to love one's neighbor.[82] As was noted in Chapter 4, such verbal repetition is sometimes an indication of interpolation, where the second appearance of the word or phrase in question represents an attempt to resume the line of thought prior to the interpolation.

c. *Linguistic Evidence for Interpolation*

Some of the vocabulary of Rom. 13.1-7 appears not to be typically Pauline. Three words appear only here in the authentically Pauline letters: ἀντιτάσσεσθαι ('to resist')[83] and διαταγή ('ordinance')[84] in v. 2 and φόρος[85] ('tax' or 'tribute') in vv. 6 and 7. In addition, four words appear only once elsewhere in the authentic letters: τάσσειν ('to set in place') in v. 1,[86] φορεῖν ('to bear') in v. 4,[87] ἔκδικος ('avenging') in v. 4,[88] and προσκαρτερεῖν ('to attend to') in v. 6.[89] Finally, several

80. Barnikol, 'Romans 13', p. 74.

81. Munro, *Authority in Paul and Peter*, p. 57. According to Munro, ὀφειλάς (v. 7) might be 'an adaptation' to ὀφείλετε (v. 8), ὀφείλετε (v. 8) might be 'intended to provide a connecting link' for ὀφειλάς (v. 7), or both words might have 'been included with the purpose of making contact with each other'.

82. Michel, *Der Brief an die Römer*, p. 312.

83. Elsewhere in the New Testament at Acts 18.6; Jas 4.6; 5.6; 1 Pet. 5.5.

84. Elsewhere in the New Testament at Acts 7.53.

85. Elsewhere in the New Testament at Lk. 20.22; 23.2.

86. 1 Cor. 16:15; elsewhere in the New Testament at Mt. 28.16; Lk. 7.8; Acts 13.48; 15.2; 22.10; 28.23.

87. 1 Cor. 15.49; elsewhere in the New Testament at Mt. 11.8; Jn 19.5; Jas 2.3.

88. 1 Thess. 4.6; nowhere else in the New Testament.

words that also appear elsewhere in the Pauline letters carry a different meaning in Rom. 13.1-7. These include ἐξουσία (Rom. 13.1, 2, 3),[90] ὑπερέχειν (Rom. 13.1),[91] ἔπαινος (Rom. 13.3),[92] τελεῖν (Rom. 13.6)[93] and ὀργη (13.4, 5).[94]

Regarding the style of Rom. 13.1-7, Barnikol states that it is 'a decree-style'. The verses are 'apodictic propositions of an imposed system' reflecting 'the new style of the monarchical power of the bishop', not 'the cautious style of the missionary of the first century, who seeks to persuade and who must even reckon with factionalism'. In short, the style of Rom. 13.1-7 would be more appropriate to the second century than to the first.[95] In this respect, it stands in marked contrast to the style of the ethical admonitions immediately preceding and following (12.1-21; 13.8-14), which begin in 12.1 not with a command but rather with an appeal (παρακαλῶ) based on 'the mercies of

89. Rom. 12.12; elsewhere in the New Testament at Mk 3.9; Acts 1.14; 2.42, 46; 6.4; 8.13; 10.7; Col. 4.2 (pseudo-Pauline).

90. Elsewhere at Rom. 9.21; 1 Cor. 7.37; 8.9; 9.4, 5, 6, 12, 18; 11.10 (in my judgment, part of a non-Pauline interpolation; see Chapter 5); 15.24; 2 Cor. 10.8; 13.10; never, however, with reference to *political* power.

91. Elsewhere only at Phil. 2.3, 3.8 and 4.7 in the sense not of exercising political power but rather of surpassing or excelling; in 1 Pet. 2.13, however, the meaning is the same as in Rom. 13.1.

92. Elsewhere only at Rom. 2.29 (in my judgment, part of a non-Pauline interpolation; see Chapter 8); 1 Cor. 4.5; 2 Cor. 8.18; Phil. 1.11; 4.8. In Rom. 2.29 and 1 Cor. 4.5, the reference is to approval from God; in Phil. 1.11, praise of God. In Phil. 4.8, ἔπαινος means 'a thing worthy of praise'. Apart from Rom. 13.3, only at 2 Cor. 8.18 is the reference apparently to approval of humans by humans, and even here the wording is somewhat ambiguous: τὸν ἀδελφὸν οὗ ἔπαινος ἐν τῷ εὐαγγελίῳ διὰ πασῶν τῶν ἐκκλησίων. According to Barnikol ('Romans 13', p. 75), '"Επαινος is used of God in Eph. 1.6, 12, 14 and Phil. 1.11, as also in 1 Cor. 4.5 (with ἀπό), Rom. 2.29 (with ἐκ) of God and humans, otherwise only in 2 Cor. 8.18 of humans...(without ἐκ), besides Rom. 13.1 with ἐκ.'

93. Elsewhere only at Rom. 2.27 (in my judgment, part of a non-Pauline interpolation; see Chapter 8), 2 Cor. 12.9 and Gal. 5.16; but not with the meaning 'pay' as in Rom. 13.6.

94. Barnikol ('Romans 13', p. 75) states that ὀργή refers to 'wrath' or 'anger' elsewhere in the Pauline letters (Rom. 1.18; 2.5, 8; 3.5; 4.15; 5.9; 9.22; 12.19; 1 Thess. 1.10; 2.16; 5.9), generally specified as *God*'s wrath, while in Rom. 13.4-5 it has to do with 'punishment' inflicted by human agencies.

95. Barnikol, 'Romans 13', p. 75.

God' (διὰ τῶν οἰκτιρμῶν τοῦ Θεοῦ) and end in 13.11-14 with an eschatological rationale. Indeed, the 'apodictic' style of Rom. 13.1-7 is noticeably different from that of the entire section, Rom. 12.1-21; 13.8–15.13. Along the same lines, Michel suggests that the style and type of argumentation in Rom. 13.1-7 are reminiscent of 'a Jewish-Hellenistic wisdom-teaching'.[96]

d. *Ideational Evidence for Interpolation*

Three features of the content of Rom. 13.1-7 suggest that it may have been written and/or included in Paul's Roman letter by someone other than Paul. The first and most general of these features is the fact that there is no reference to Christ in these verses; indeed, there is nothing specifically 'Christian' or even 'Jewish' about the passage. Thus, J.C. O'Neill observes that 'both Christian and Jewish tradition commanded respect for earthly rulers, but never the absolute obedience laid down in this section'; his conclusion, therefore, is that 'Romans 13.1-7 is neither Christian nor Jewish in origin'. In O'Neill's judgment, the 'eight injunctions' that comprise the passage were 'collected together by a Stoic teacher and given Stoic philosophical grounding in the first saying (v. 1)'.[97]

The second ideational feature calling for attention is the fact that this is the only passage in the authentically Pauline letters that addresses the issue of the relation of the Christian to the State *per se*. As Barnikol phrases it, 'The pericope Romans 13,1-7 is a unit *sui generis*'.[98]

The third and most important ideational feature is the fact that Rom. 13.1-7 appears to contradict a number of basic ideas expressed by Paul in other contexts. Romans 13.1-7 expresses a quite positive view regarding the nature and function of governmental authority. Such authority has been instituted by God for the maintenance of good and the punishment of evil, and those who resist this authority oppose the will of God. Indeed, the civil ruler is 'God's servant' (διάκονος). Elsewhere, however, Paul expresses a rather negative attitude toward the State, civil authorities and institutions, and the present world order in general. In 1 Cor. 6.1-8, for example, he insists that Christians not resort to the civil courts to settle their disputes, for these courts are administered by 'the unrighteous' (οἵ ἄδικοι) who are 'disdained'

96. Michel, *Der Brief an die Römer*, p. 289; cf. pp. 313-14.

97. O'Neill, *Paul's Letter to the Romans*, p. 208.

98. Barnikol, 'Romans 13', p. 74.

(ἐξουθενημένοι) in the Church. In Phil. 3.19-20, he asserts that the Christian's citizenship (πολίτευμα) is in heaven and not among those who 'set their minds on earthly things' (οἱ τὰ ἐπίγεια φρονοῦντες). In 1 Cor. 7.29-31, he advocates maintaining the *status quo* in human relationships and conditions because 'the form of this world is passing away' (παράγει γὰρ τὸ σχῆμα τοῦ κόσμου τούτου). In 1 Thess. 4.13–5.11, he expresses the apocalyptic hope and expectation of imminent liberation from this world (ἁρπαγησόμεθα ἐν νεφέλαις εἰς ἀπάντησιν τοῦ κυρίου εἰς ἀέρα καὶ οὕτως πάντοτε σὺν κυρίῳ ἐσόμεθα). Indeed, it is Paul's view that the present age can be characterized as 'the present evil age' (ὁ αἰὼν ὁ ἐνεστὼς πονηρός [Gal. 1.4]) precisely because it is under the control of 'the god of this age' (ὁ θεὸς τοῦ αἰῶνος τούτου [2 Cor. 4.4]). It is destined, however, to pass away and be replaced by a liberated cosmos (Rom. 8.21-22). Indeed, like others who held 'the eschatological-demonological world view of the apocalyptists', Paul would have seen 'Rome not as a benefactor but as a tyrant, an instrument not of God but of Satan'.[99] Thus, as Winsome Munro notes, 'What has caused perplexity [regarding Rom. 13.1-7] is how to reconcile subjection to the ἐξουσίαι (authorities) and ἄρχοντες (powers or rulers) with a world view that assumed the existence of hostile angelic powers standing behind earthly rulers and nations'.[100]

Even in the chapter immediately preceding Rom. 13.1-7, Paul appeals to his readers not to be 'conformed to this age' but rather to be 'transformed' in such a way that they will be able to determine for themselves (δοκιμάζειν) what is 'the good and pleasing and perfect will of God' (12.1-3). In the same chapter (vv. 9-21), he calls for an ethic that presupposes the pervasive presence and power of 'evil' (vv. 9, 17, and 21); the reality of 'tribulation' (v. 12), persecution (v. 14) and generally tenuous relations between Christians and non-Christians (v. 18); and the temptation to vengeance (vv. 19-20). All of this, in Barnikol's view, 'unanimously and clearly and completely rules out the absolute affirmation of government' found in Rom. 13.1-7.[101]

Moreover, as Barnikol observes, 'Romans 13,1-7 is un-eschatological, indeed anti-eschatological'.[102] According to Kallas, 'one of the

99. Kallas, 'Romans xiii.1-7', p. 369.
100. Munro, *Authority in Paul and Peter*, p. 16.
101. Barnikol, 'Romans 13', p. 76; cf. pp. 83-84.
102. Barnikol, 'Romans 13', p. 85.

constants of Pauline thought', even in his letter to the Romans,[103] 'is the expectation of a near end of the world'. In Rom. 13.1-7, however, 'the whole basic assumption of the author...is that the world will continue for an indefinitely long time'. This is particularly surprising in light of the strong eschatological appeal just a few verses later (vv. 11-13).[104]

Further, as Kallas notes, 'in every other place where Paul speaks of "governing authorities" or "rulers of this age" he is speaking of cosmic rulers, supernatural figures'. In Rom. 13.1-7, however, 'the reference is unmistakably to human figures, rulers of this world in a political sense'. Further, 'elsewhere in Paul the authorities are not only spiritual-angelic powers but more accurately demonic powers',[105] but 'here they are depicted as loyal servants of God carrying out His will'.[106]

Finally, 'it is Paul's usual view that it is the innocent one who suffers most of all in this world, it is the Christian who is most abused in this evil age ruled by malignant celestial hosts opposed to God'.[107] Romans 13.1-7, however, 'flatly says that it is the evildoer who is punished here and now by God's servants, and the good have nothing to fear'.[108] In summary, in Rom. 13.1-7 'both the eschatological hope has all but disappeared—the church is settling down, making peace with the world—and the demonological view has disappeared—the world is seen as under the full control of God'.[109]

e. *Comparative Evidence for Interpolation*

Kallas suggests that the disappearance of 'the demonological view' reflected in Rom. 13.1-7 can also be seen in later canonical literature. For example, while Paul viewed 'all cosmic entities [as] evil and opposed to God', Hebrews regards angels and cosmic beings 'as loyal servants of God' (Heb. 1.14).

It is also significant that 1 Peter contains a passage remarkably

103. Rom. 8.18-25; 13.11-13; 16.20.

104. Kallas, 'Romans xiii.1-7', p. 367.

105. E.g. 1 Cor. 2.6-8; Gal. 4.3-5; Col. 2.15; Eph. 6.12; and even Rom. 8.38-39. Note, however, that Colossians and Ephesians are likely pseudonymous; further, I have argued in Chapter 6 that 1 Cor. 2.6-16 is a non-Pauline interpolation.

106. Kallas, 'Romans xiii.1-7', p. 368.

107. Kallas, 'Romans xiii.1-7', p. 371. See, e.g., 2 Cor. 11.23-29; 12.7-10.

108. Kallas, 'Romans xiii.1-7', p. 374.

109. Kallas, 'Romans xiii.1-7', p. 374.

similar in content, tone and even vocabulary to Rom. 13.1-7.[110] This passage (1 Pet. 2.13-17) is part of a *Haustafel* or 'household code' (2.11–3.12), which, in addition to addressing the issue of submission to human rulers, also commands that slaves be submissive to their masters and wives to their husbands.[111] It is generally agreed that, while the *Haustafel* is not a feature of the authentically Pauline letters, it does appear in the pseudo-Pauline writings.[112] It is also noteworthy that the writings that contain *Haustafeln* sometimes include a command of submission to governing authorities.[113] Moreover, one of the characteristic features of the *Haustafel* is its use of the passive-voice verb 'be subject' (ὑποτάσσεσθαι).[114] Thus, the command to 'be subject' (ὑποτάσσεσθαι) to the governing authorities in Rom. 13.1-7 is much more closely akin to material found in the post-Pauline and particularly pseudo-Pauline writings than to that in the authentically Pauline letters.

Further, Barnikol argues that the 'absolute' affirmation of the authority and goodness of the government found in Rom. 13.1-7 goes even beyond the 'qualified' affirmation that appears in the 'trito-Pauline' Pastoral Letters and in *1 Clement*.[115] 1 Timothy calls for prayers on behalf of the authorities, 'that we may lead a quiet and peaceable life' (1 Tim. 2.1-2) but makes no mention of 'submissiveness'. Titus commands that Christians 'be submissive' and 'obedient' to rulers and authorities as a part of a more general admonition 'to speak evil of no one, to avoid quarreling, to be gentle and to show perfect courtesy to all people' (Tit. 3.1-2). The principal concern, in other words, is that Christians live in harmony with non-Christians. Similarly, *1 Clement* (60.4–61.2) calls for obedience and even submissiveness to rulers and governors in the context of a prayer for concord and peace and that God will 'direct their counsels according to that which is "good and pleasing" before [God], that they may administer with piety in peace and gentleness the power given to them by [God]'. Thus, both the

110. Note the same terminology in the two passages: ὑποτάσσεσθαι, ὑπερέχειν, ἐκδίκησις/ἔδικος, κακοποιεῖν/τὸ κακὸν ποιεῖν, ἔπαινος, and ἀγαθοποιεῖν/τὸ ἀγαθὸν ποιεῖν.

111. For a recent and succinct treatment of the *Haustafel*, see, e.g., David L. Balch, 'Household Codes', *ABD*, III, pp. 318-20.

112. Col. 3.18–4.1; Eph. 5.21–6.9; 1 Tim. 2.8-15; 5.1-2; 6.1-2; Tit. 2.1-10; 3.1.

113. Tit. 3.1; cf. 1 Tim. 2.2 and, of course, 1 Pet. 2.13-17.

114. Col. 3.18; Eph. 5.22, 24; Tit. 2.5, 9; 3.1; 1 Pet. 2.13, 18; 3.1, 5.

115. Barnikol, 'Römer 13', pp. 78-80, 81, 92-93.

Pastorals and *1 Clement* fall short of requiring the absolute affirmation of government commanded in Rom. 13.1-7. This suggests that the latter passage may have been written sometime in the second century, when the interests of an 'episcopal' church and an imperial state began to coincide more closely so far as peace, harmony and order were concerned.

f. *Situational, Motivational and Locational Evidence for Interpolation*
According to Kallas, 'The whole emphasis and approach [of Rom. 13.1-7] indicates a later date than Paul's life; a time when the eschatological fires had been banked, a time when the church later [*sic*] under suspicion in the Neronian persecutions must make clear its non-subversive nature by making a clear statement of loyalty to the ruling authorities'.[116] Similarly, according to O'Neill, 'the ultimate reason for the incorporation of this section is that the later Church would feel the need for some guidance in relations with the State in an apostolic letter to the Romans'.[117] Stated differently, the passage must have been 'written later than Paul at a time when the church was obliged, by the failure of the end to come, to re-evaluate the nature of the world' and to conclude 'that perhaps the world order—since it had not ceased—was not as demonic as had earlier been supposed and was therefore to be obeyed'.[118]

As to how Rom. 13.1-7, which he believes to have been Stoic in origin, 'gained a foothold in the Christian setting', O'Neill suggests 'two circumstances, one material and the other almost accidental'. The first, which relates to the more general question of how the material came to be included in a Christian writing, 'is the agreement of the teaching in the insertion with one strand of the Jewish-Christian tradition, the strand which acknowledges the divine source of earthly rulers' power, their authority to collect taxes, and their right to expect obedience and respect and prayers for their well-being'. The second circumstance, which addresses the question of the precise location of the insertion in Paul's Roman letter, 'is the purely verbal agreement between Romans 13.8 and the last sentence of the Stoic collection, Romans 13.7 [μηδενὶ μηδὲν ὀφείλετε εἰ μὴ τὸ ἀλλήλους ἀγαπᾶν and ἀπόδοτε πᾶσιν τὰς ὀφειλάς]'. According to O'Neill, 'The verbal similarity, with the

116. Kallas, 'Romans xiii.1-7', p. 368.
117. O'Neill, *Paul's Letter to the Romans*, p. 209.
118. Kallas, 'Romans xiii.1-7', pp. 370-71.

complete difference in concepts, is just what would appeal to a compiler of aphorisms or a glossator of aphorisms, for whom word-play is everything'.[119] In addition, the presence of at least four verbal links between Rom. 13.1-7 and the material immediately preceding should be noted: ὀργή ('wrath') in 13.4, 5 (see 12.19), ἔκδικος ('avenging') in 13.4 (see ἐκδικεῖν in 12.19), προσκαρτερεῖν ('to attend to') in 13.6 (see 12.12), and ἀποδιδόναι ('to repay') in 13.7 (see 12.17). Further, as Byrne notes, 'a theme of "good" (*agathon*) "bad" (*kakon*) runs through the entire context (12.2, 9, 17, 21; 13.3a, 3c, 4a, 4b, 4d; 13.10)', and it may be that 'a skillful interpolator...contrived this conformity to the language of the wider context'.[120]

It is also possible that the content of Rom. 13.1-7 accounts, at least in part, for its insertion at precisely its present location in Paul's Roman letter. Byrne notes 'the overall tendency of the parenesis from 12.3 onwards to "work outwards" from responsibilities and the demands of love within the Christian community (12.3-16), to those affecting relations with outsiders (12.17-21)'. In his view, 13.1-7 would represent a logical next step in this sequence; indeed, 'it naturally extends and specifies the command to "live peaceably with all" (12.18)'.[121] This may well be the case, but it should also be noted that 13.8-10 returns to the focus of 12.17-21 by restricting the scope of the parenesis to relations among individuals. Perhaps even more significant than the considerations cited by Byrne is the fact that 12.14-21 speaks of persecution and 'enemies'; indeed, it concludes with a command against taking vengeance. Such references might easily call to mind the most obvious potential agents of persecution, namely the governing authorities, and suggest an opening for a passage regarding these authorities.

It is true, of course, that any reasons an interpolator might have had for inserting Rom. 13.1-7 at precisely its present location in Paul's Roman letter can just as easily serve as arguments for Pauline authorship and/or inclusion of the passage. Thus, such considerations as have just been advanced have cogency only if there are other compelling grounds for viewing the material as an interpolation. As has already been noted, however, there appear to be such compelling grounds—at least in the minds of some scholars.

119. O'Neill, *Paul's Letter to the Romans*, pp. 208-209.

120. Byrne, *Romans*, p. 386. It should be noted, however, that Byrne himself rejects the interpolation hypothesis.

121. Byrne, *Romans*, p. 386.

3. *1 Corinthians 10.1-22*

In an article published in 1990, Lamar Cope noted 'that Paul's advice about "idol meat" in 1 Corinthians 8 and 10 is problematic'.[122] On the one hand, ch. 8 and 10.23–11.1 indicate 'that...idol meat is in itself neutral and one's only compunction about eating it is a concern for the other person' (p. 115); indeed, even eating in an idol's temple is challenged (8.10) '*only* on the grounds that it might harm "a weak brother"' (p. 116). Finally, there is here 'no hint of any feeling that idols are dangerous "demons"' (p. 116). On the other hand, 10.1-22 insists that 'the eating of meat in an idol's temple is forbidden outright' (p. 115) precisely 'because it involves fellowship with demons' (p. 116), which is to say, idolatry.

Rejecting the notion that the problem is to be solved by assigning the materials to two originally separate letters,[123] Cope suggested 'that the likelihood is strong that 10.1-22 is an interpolation by a later editor intended to bring Paul into line with the widely held views of subsequent Christianity' (p. 115).[124] His arguments were based primarily on considerations of 'vocabulary, style, and content' (p. 119).

According to Cope, the evidence that 1 Corinthians 8 and 10.23–11.1 are authentically Pauline 'seems to be overwhelming' (p. 119). There are a number of verbal 'connectors back and forward between these

122. Cope, 'First Corinthians 8–10' (quotation from pp. 114-15). Page numbers for subsequent quotations from Cope's article will be indicated in parentheses in the body of the text.

123. Cope quotes John Coolridge Hurd, Jr (*The Origin of 1 Corinthians* [New York: Seabury; London: SPCK; Macon, GA: Mercer University Press, 2nd edn, 1983], p. 132), as follows: 'scholars who subdivide I Cor. consider the discrepancies between [8; 10.23–11.1] and [10.1-22] great enough to show that [the latter] was not written at the same time as [the former] but small enough to allow [the latter] to have been written by the same author, to the same group, and on the same topic as [the former]. These scholars allow Paul to be inconsistent with himself concerning the Corinthians' use of idol meat from one letter to the next, but they do not allow the inconsistency in a single letter. This distinction is, therefore, possible but somewhat subtle.'

124. Cope's suggestion has attracted little attention. For example, Fee (*The First Epistle to the Corinthians*) fails even to mention it, and Collins (*First Corinthians*, p. 307), after briefly summarizing the argument, concludes: 'Cope's radical view finds no support in the manuscript tradition. It would, moreover, require of Paul a kind of epistolary consistency that is not his style.'

sections and the rest of the letter', and, 'even more strikingly, the fundamental argument of these sections is echoed in abbreviated form in Romans 14–15' (p. 119). In short, '1 Corinthians 8 and 10.23–11.1 show every sign of being a coherent part of the main body of this letter' (p. 122). 'As soon as the question is raised, however, concerning 10.1-22, one notices a vast difference': 'the vocabulary has shifted radically, the style of argument has become midrashic, and the advice is in sharp contrast' to ch. 8 and 10.23–11.1 (p. 119). Moreover, 'there is no hint of any parallel to 1 Corinthians 10.1-22 in Romans' (p. 117), or, indeed, anywhere else in the authentically Pauline letters.

As regards style, Cope notes that 'Paul's other midrashim are limited and precise',[125] while that in 1 Cor. 10.1-22 'is elaborate and strained'.[126] While the latter 'could be from Paul', it would mean that 'he has wandered far more technically into the arena of midrashic exegesis than at any other point in the letters' (p. 119).

In addition, much of the vocabulary of 1 Cor. 10.1-22 appears not to be typically Pauline. Included here are the 'sacramental' sense of κοινωνία ('participation', 'communion' or 'fellowship') in vv. 16-21,[127] the word δαιμόνια ('demons') in vv. 20 and 21,[128] the use of οἱ πατέρες ('the fathers') in v. 1 to refer to the Wilderness generation,[129] ἐπιθυμητής ('desirer') in v. 6,[130] ἐκπειράζειν ('to test') in v. 9,[131] τυπικῶς ('typologically' or 'figuratively') in v. 11,[132] τὰ τέλη τῶν αἰώνων ('the

125. Gal. 3.15-18; 4.21-31; 2 Cor. 3.7-10; Rom. 4.1-15. According to Cope ('First Corinthians 8–10', p. 119), 'only once, in the seed/seeds reading of Galatians 3:15, is the reader stretched beyond the range of simple application of the biblical text'.

126. Cope cites ('First Corinthians 8–10', p. 119) the imprecise 'reference to the people of Israel being "baptized" into Moses', the identification of *pneumatikos food* and *pneumatikos drink* with manna and water from the Rock, 'the rather esoteric tradition of the Rock following the Exodus community', and the identification of the Rock with Christ.

127. Elsewhere (1 Cor. 1.9; 2 Cor. 8.4; Gal. 2.9; Phil. 1.5; 2.1; 3.10), the term refers simply to 'community fellowship' (Cope, 'First Corinthians 8–10', p. 120).

128. Elsewhere in the Pauline corpus only at the pseudo-Pauline 1 Tim. 4.1.

129. Elsewhere (Rom. 9.15; 11.28; 15.8), οἱ πατέρες refers to 'the forefathers' or 'the patriarchs' (cf. also the singular, πατήρ, in Rom. 4.11, 12, 16, 17, 18; 9.10).

130. Nowhere else in the entire New Testament, although Paul uses the cognate noun ἐπιθυμία numerous times.

131. Only here in the Pauline corpus.

132. Nowhere else in the New Testament or the LXX.

ends of the ages') in v. 11,[133] and ἔκβασις ('way of escape') in v. 13.[134] In short, according to Cope, 'In just these 22 verses, there are at least 10 cases of words found only here in material attributed to Paul, several of them *hapax legomena* in the New Testament'. Further, 'there are two compound phrases found only here also, and there are at least five cases where terms are used with a special meaning occurring only here, although the terms are used by Paul elsewhere with a regular, but different meaning' (p. 120 n. 18).

Cope acknowledges that, 'because the topic of 10.1-22 and its midrashic character are somewhat unique, the striking oddities of phrasing and vocabulary alone might not render 10.1-22 suspect as being non-Pauline'. He goes on to note, however, that 'taken together with the problems of content and context, they greatly increase the difficulties for holding the passage to be genuine'. Nevertheless, for Cope, 'the crux of the issue is substantive' (p. 120).

It is sometimes suggested that 1 Corinthians 8 and 10.23–11.1 speak simply of the private consumption of meat that has been offered to idols and then sold in the marketplace while 1 Cor. 10.1-22 refers to sacrificial meals in an idol's temple. Thus, there is no real conflict between the two: the former is to be decided on the basis of Christian conscience and consideration for one's brothers and sisters in the faith; the latter is prohibited. It should be noted, however, that 10.1-22 includes in v. 10 a reference to 'you, the one having knowledge, reclining at table in an idol's temple (ἐν εἰδωλείῳ κατακείμενον)'. Further, appealing to the work of Wendell L. Willis,[135] Cope argues 'that there was little or no difference in the Hellenistic mind in the meaning of meal fellowship in different locations and settings', whether temples, private homes, or even cemeteries (p. 121). Thus, in his view, 1 Corinthians 8 and 10.23–11.1 are concerned not just with private consumption of meat but rather 'with private dining, with cultic dining, and with being an invited guest', all of which are 'governed by the principle that meat and location are neutral so one may eat *unless* it offends a weaker brother's conscience' (p. 122). In 1 Cor. 10.1-22, however, Christians are forbidden to eat and drink 'in an idol's temple' (p. 122) because to do so involves them in the worship of demons.

133. Only here in Paul's letters.

134. Elsewhere in the New Testament only at Heb. 13.7.

135. Wendell L. Willis, *Idol Meat in Corinth: The Pauline Argument in 1 Corinthians 8 and 10* (SBLDS, 68; Chico, CA: Scholars Press, 1985).

This leads to what Cope terms 'the heart of the issue of the authenticity of this passage': 'the equation of idols and *demons*' (p. 121). Citing the work of Richard A. Horsley,[136] Cope observes that 'within Judaism itself there were two distinctive traditions of polemic against idols or false gods'. The first (found particularly in Deutero-Isaiah) 'derided the heathen gods as nothing and their worship as foolishness' (p. 121 n. 19). According to Cope, this attitude is reflected not only in 1 Corinthians 8 and 10.23–11.1 but also in such passages as Rom. 1.19-23,[137] Gal. 4.8a and 1 Thess. 1.9. Further, 'in these places and several others, where Paul had ample opportunity to condemn idol worship as trucking with demons, he did not do so' (p. 121). Thus, in Cope's view, Paul's attitude is clear: heathen deities are nothing.

The second attitude toward idols or false gods,[138] however, viewed them as 'subordinate cosmic powers' to whom non-Jews were subjected but who should be avoided by Jews (p. 121 n. 19). This is the attitude reflected in 1 Cor. 10.1-22. Elsewhere in the authentically Pauline letters, however, idol worship is never condemned 'as trucking with demons' (p. 121)—in other words, idols are never equated with demons.[139] Further, the Christian sacrament is not elsewhere associated so closely both with Jewish experience and worship (10.18; cf. vv. 1-4) and with pagan ritual (10.14-22). Thus, 'it is very difficult to show that Paul held the position' expressed in 1 Cor. 10.1-22.

Cope's summary of the evidence for viewing 1 Cor. 10.1-22 as a non-Pauline interpolation is the following:

> 1 Corinthians 8 and 10.23-11.1 show every sign of being a coherent part of the main body of [1 Corinthians]. But 10.1-22 is deeply suspect. The passage exhibits non-Pauline terminology and, more strikingly, Pauline terminology used in an uncharacteristic way. It presents an ornate and flawed midrashic support unique in the Pauline corpus. It argues a position on eating in an idol's temple that is not supported anywhere else in the genuine letters. The position is contrary to one expressed earlier in

136. Richard A. Horsley, 'Gnosis in Corinth: I Corinthians 8.1-6', *NTS* 27 (1980), pp. 32-51.

137. See Chapter 8, however, for the argument that Rom. 1.18–2.32 is a non-Pauline interpolation.

138. Found in such passages as Deut. 4.19; 29.25; Jer. 16.19; Mal. 1.11.

139. Cope argues that 'the weak and beggarly elemental spirits' (τὰ ἀσθενῆ καὶ πτωχὰ στοιχεῖα) in Gal. 4.9 and the 'principalities' (ἀρχαί) and 'powers' (δυνάμεις) in Rom. 8.38 are not really parallels to δαιμόνια ('demons') in 1 Cor. 10.20, 21.

> Galatians and later in Romans. The passage interrupts the flow of thought from 8.1-11 to 10.23 whatever one does with chapter 9. For all of these reasons, the critic ought to consider seriously the likelihood that 10.1-22 is a later non-Pauline interpretation [*sic*] (p. 122).

As to why 1 Cor. 10.1-22 was inserted into Paul's Corinthian letter, Cope accepts John C. Brunt's demonstration 'that the Pauline position [that is, the position articulated in 1 Cor. 8 and 10.23–11.1] on the treatment of idolatry was largely ignored in the church at the turn of the century' (p. 122); rather, the eating of meat offered to idols was strictly prohibited.[140] Thus, 'the editor/redactor(s) of the Pauline letters [likely] wanted to bring Paul into line with the dominant anti-temple worship position of the church a generation later'. In short, Cope asks, 'How better to diffuse a libertarian or Gnostic use of Paul's advice on meat offered to idols than to insert a section condemning the practice in the middle of that advice?' (p. 123).

4. *Conclusion*

In Chapters 9 and 10, I have attempted to present the arguments of other scholars for viewing Rom. 16.25-27, 2 Cor. 6.14–7.1, 1 Thess. 2.13-16, Rom. 13.1-7 and 1 Cor. 10.1-22 as non-Pauline interpolations. As indicated at the beginning of Chapter 9, I have neither offered critical evaluation of these arguments nor responded to attempts to refute them. In conclusion, however, I should note that I myself find the arguments persuasive. I should also reiterate my own conviction that, in addition to these five passages and the five I discussed in Chapters 4 to 8 (1 Cor. 14.34-35; 1 Cor. 11.3-16; 1 Cor. 2.6-16; 1 Cor. 12.31b–14.1a; Rom. 1.18–2.29), there are likely to be more—perhaps many more—non-Pauline interpolations in the letters generally regarded as authentically Pauline.

140. John C. Brunt, 'Rejected, Ignored, or Misunderstood? The Fate of Paul's Approach to the Problem of Food Offered to Idols in Early Christianity', *NTS* 31 (1985), pp. 113-24. See, e.g., Acts 15; Rev. 2.12-17, 18-29; *Did.* 6.3; Justin, *Dial.* 35.

Epilogue

INTERPOLATIONS AND THE CANONICAL AUTHORITY OF SCRIPTURE

In a recent conversation with a well-educated and rather sophisticated friend who is not an academic but is a committed Christian, I was attempting to explain the nature of my work on 'interpolations' in the Pauline letters. When I had finished, he asked me, 'Just which passages are you throwing out?' Similarly, another friend wanted to know which parts of the letters I was 'debunking'. I suspect that these responses would not be atypical. Indeed, even among scholars and church leaders, there may be some apprehension that the kind of work I am doing amounts to 'tampering' with the Scriptures. It is for this reason that I have decided to append a brief epilogue on 'Interpolations and the Canonical Authority of Scripture'. I should note at the outset, however, that I myself am not a theologian—either by training or by inclination. Thus, I do not propose to deal in any detail with the questions of 'Canon' or the 'authority' of Scripture. Rather, I shall offer two simple observations regarding the relation of my work to these questions.

The first observation is that the identification of a passage as a non-Pauline interpolation is not to be viewed as a judgment regarding the importance, validity, truth, relevance or authority of the passage. Such an identification represents simply the literary-historical conclusion that the passage in question was both written by someone other than Paul and included at its present location in one of the Pauline letters by someone other than Paul. This conclusion, however, says nothing at all about the importance, validity, truth, relevance or authority of the passage. Such matters should, in my judgment, be decided on grounds quite different than literary-historical ones. Indeed, to make the validity of a document, or any portion thereof, dependent upon the identity of the person who wrote it and/or made use of it would appear to constitute an egregious example of *argumentum ad hominem*. Thus, although I do not believe that Paul wrote 1 Corinthians 13 (indeed, I have no idea who the author might have been), nor do I believe that he included it in his letter to the Corinthian Christians, I nevertheless regard the passage as an important, relevant and even authoritative piece of literature.

The second observation is that the identification of a passage as a non-Pauline interpolation is not to be viewed as a call for its removal from the New Testament Canon. Indeed, if any of the possible reasons for removal of such a passage were to be judged valid, logical consistency would require the removal of most of what now constitutes the New Testament. More specifically, I note the following points.

The first possible reason for the removal of non-Pauline interpolations from the New Testament Canon is that such interpolations represent secondary, indeed foreign insertions into the texts of the letters in which they now appear. As was noted in Chapter 1, however, it is widely agreed that other writings in the New Testament are composed of various layers or strata of material. This is certainly true of the Synoptic Gospels; indeed, according to the most popular source theory, Matthew and Luke are simply rewritten and expanded versions of Mark. It is probably also true of the Fourth Gospel and Acts of the Apostles. Nevertheless, so far as I am aware, there has been no attempt for this reason to remove these writings from the Canon of the New Testament or even to identify and retain only the earliest recoverable version of each document. Thus, it is clear that secondary and even foreign strata of material are not necessarily barred from inclusion in the Canon of the New Testament.

A second possible reason for the removal of non-Pauline interpolations from the New Testament Canon is that such interpolations were not written by Paul. This, however, is true of most of the writings that constitute the New Testament. Nevertheless, so far as I am aware, there has been no attempt for this reason to remove these writings from the Canon. Indeed, it has apparently been only Marcion and his followers[1] who have insisted that Christian Scripture be limited to the Pauline writings (and even Marcion also included the Gospel according to Luke). Thus, it is clear that non-Pauline authorship is no necessary bar to inclusion in the Canon of the New Testament.

A third possible reason for the removal of non-Pauline interpolations from the New Testament Canon is that the authorship of such interpolations is not only non-Pauline but indeed unknown. This too, however,

1. Second century and later.

is also true of most of the writings that constitute the New Testament. Indeed, the authorship of only seven books—Romans, 1 and 2 Corinthians, Galatians, Philippians, 1 Thessalonians and Philemon—is relatively certain. Of the other 20, nine are anonymous (author unknown),[2] and perhaps as many as 11 are pseudonymous (written by people other than those whose names they bear).[3] Nevertheless, so far as I am aware, there has been no attempt for this reason to remove these writings from the New Testament Canon. Thus, it is clear that unknown authorship is no necessary bar to inclusion in the Canon of the New Testament.

A fourth possible reason for the removal of non-Pauline interpolations from the New Testament Canon is that such interpolations are, at least by implication, falsely attributed to someone other than their actual authors.[4] This too, however, is also true of a number of the writings that constitute the New Testament. As already indicated, perhaps as many as 11 of these writings are pseudonymous, including perhaps

2. All four of the Gospels, Acts of the Apostles, Hebrews and the three 'Johannine' letters. The names 'Matthew', 'Mark', 'Luke' and 'John' appear only in the superscriptions or titles of the gospels, but these superscriptions were added later, probably in the second century. Most scholars agree that Acts was written by the author of Luke's Gospel, but, as already indicated, the identity of this author is uncertain. To be sure, there are relatively early traditions that attribute the Gospels and Acts to the people whose names appear in the superscriptions, but we have no way of verifying these traditions. They may simply reflect attempts to legitimate writings that, for other reasons, were deemed important and worthy of inclusion in the Canon. There was considerable debate in the early church regarding both the authorship of Hebrews and its inclusion in the Canon. The final decision was that it was Pauline in origin and should be in the New Testament. I know of no modern scholar, however, who believes Hebrews to have been written by Paul. Two of the Johannine letters (2 and 3 John) are attributed to 'the elder', but the identity of this 'elder' is unknown. Many scholars believe that one or more of the letters were written by the author of John's Gospel, but, as already indicated, the identity of this author is uncertain.

3. This is almost certainly the case with some of the letters ascribed to Paul: the Pastoral Letters (1 and 2 Timothy and Titus), probably Ephesians and Colossians, and perhaps 2 Thessalonians. Beyond the Pauline Corpus, 2 Peter is almost certainly pseudonymous, and the same is probably true of James, Jude and 1 Peter. In addition, many believe Revelation, like most apocalyptic writings, to be pseudonymous (even if it was written by John, whose name it bears, however, it is by no means certain just who this 'John' was).

4. By inserting an interpolation into one of the Pauline letters, the interpolator implies that Paul either wrote the passage or himself included it in his letter.

seven that are attributed to Paul. Nevertheless, so far as I am aware, there has been no attempt for this reason to remove these writings from the New Testament Canon. Thus, it is clear that false attribution—even explicit false attribution—is no necessary bar to inclusion in the Canon of the New Testament.

A fifth and final possible reason for the removal of non-Pauline interpolations from the New Testament Canon is that such interpolations exhibit ideational features that are non-Pauline and at times even anti-Pauline. This too, however, is also true, to a greater or lesser extent, of other writings that constitute the New Testament. It can be argued that most of these writings are more or less *non*-Pauline in outlook and, indeed, that a few are deliberately *anti*-Pauline. As regards the latter, I note only Mt. 5.17-20 with its strident defense of 'the law and the prophets',[5] Jas 2.14-26 with its insistence upon the necessity of both 'faith' and 'works',[6] and perhaps 2 Pet. 3.15b-17 with its warning against 'lawless people' who 'twist to their own destruction' the things in Paul's letters that are 'hard to understand'. Nevertheless, so far as I am aware, there has been no attempt for this reason to remove these writings from the Canon.[7] Thus, it is clear that non-Pauline and even anti-Pauline ideational features are no necessary bar to inclusion in the Canon of the New Testament.

In short, most of the writings comprising the New Testament exhibit non-Pauline ideational features and some even anti-Pauline features, some of these writings are attributed to people other than their actual authors, most are of non-Pauline and indeed unknown origin, and some contain multiple strata of material. Moreover, all of this is well known,

5. Note Matthew's repeated use of δικαιοσύηνη ('righteousness')—the same word (translated 'justification') used frequently by Paul. Indeed, Matthew could be seen, at least in part, as a debate with Paul regarding the proper meaning and basis of δικαιοσύνη.

6. Note that both James and Paul cite Gen. 15.6 in support of their position (Jas 2.23; Rom. 4.3; Gal. 3.6). Note, too, that both agree regarding the necessity to keep the *entire* law (Jas 2.10-11; Gal. 3.10).

7. To be sure, Martin Luther characterized the Letter of James as 'an epistle of straw' because 'it has nothing of the nature of the gospel about it', denied its apostolic authorship, and consigned it, along with Hebrews, Jude and Revelation to the end of his translation of the New Testament; see, e.g., Sophie Laws, *A Commentary on the Epistle of James* (HNTC; San Francisco: Harper & Row, 1980), p. 1. So far as I know, however, Luther made no formal proposal to eliminate James from the Canon. Furthermore, all versions of the New Testament continue to include it.

not only by New Testament scholars but also by the graduates of reputable theological seminaries. So far as I am aware, however, no responsible scholar or ecclesiastical leader has, for this reason, called for the removal of any of these writings from the New Testament Canon. Indeed, the Church has long since decided, *de facto* if not *de jure*, that neither the presence of multiple strata of material, non-Pauline and indeed unknown and even 'false' authorship, nor non-Pauline and even anti-Pauline ideas constitutes a necessary bar to inclusion of a document within the Canon. If this is the case regarding entire documents, why should it not also apply to specific passages within documents? In principle, the recognition that 1 Cor. 14.34-35, for example, is a non-Pauline interpolation is not so different from the acknowledgment that the Gospel according to Luke is composed of various strata of material, that the Gospel according to John is of unknown authorship, that the Letter to the Ephesians is pseudonymous, and that the Letter of James is non-Pauline and even anti-Pauline in flavor.[8] If these documents are to be retained in the New Testament Canon, what possible basis could there be for the removal of 1 Cor. 11.34-35 or other non-Pauline interpolations?

It should also be noted that when the early Church eventually arrived at a consensus regarding the limits of the Canon, the various documents were included in their final, 'canonical' form, not in some putative earlier or 'original' form and not with the proviso that any parts later judged to be secondary were to be removed. Thus, any non-Pauline interpolations that might then have appeared in the Pauline letters became a part of the Canon of Christian Scripture. To this day, they remain a part of this Canon and must be dealt with as such. The precise meaning of 'Canon of Christian Scripture' and the status implied by inclusion in this Canon are, of course, historically, culturally and individually conditioned and subject to continual revision and varied interpretation. Whatever the meaning and status may be, however, the passages that I and other scholars regard as non-Pauline interpolations are included in this Canon. The decision that they are non-Pauline in no way removes them from this category, nor, in my judgment, should it.

It is, of course, conceivable that some might wish to eliminate the non-Pauline interpolations from the Canon of Christian Scripture

8. In the case of James, we are faced with non-Pauline, unknown and probably pseudonymous authorship as well as non-Pauline and even anti-Pauline ideational features.

simply because they are non-Pauline interpolations. Any decision to do so, however, would face virtually insuperable difficulties. Quite apart from the problem of agreement regarding exactly which passages are in fact non-Pauline interpolations and the question of who would have the authority to carry out such excisions, there would be other complications. For example, many contemporary Christians might be inclined to remove 1 Cor. 14.34-35 and 1 Cor. 11.3-16 because of their misogynistic sentiments, 1 Thess. 2.13-16 because of its vitriolic anti-semitism, or Rom. 13.1-7 because of its unconditional acceptance of civil authority. But what about the magnificent doxology in Rom. 16.25-27, the sublime panegyric on love in 1 Corinthians 13, or the remarkably even-handed treatment of Jews and Gentiles in Romans 2? Surely, their elimination would impoverish the store of Christian Scripture! In short, my own judgment is that if there were to be any move to delete individual passages from the New Testament, the decision should be made on grounds other than the literary history of the passages in question. I seriously doubt, however, both the wisdom and the practicality of any such move.

Much more realistic, in my own view, is acceptance of the simple fact that, as has often been noted, churches and individual Christians almost inevitably rely upon 'a canon within the Canon'. On the basis of this 'canon within the Canon', they assess other parts of the Bible, emphasizing that which is compatible and, for the remainder, either reinterpreting it in light of the more compact canon, disregarding it as having been superceded by further illumination, or simply ignoring it. Such, of course, is not a legitimate path for literary-historical scholarship, but it may be the only recourse for those who wish to use the biblical writings as a basis for Christian faith and practice.

In summary, then, the identification of a passage as a non-Pauline interpolation represents neither a judgment regarding its importance, validity, truth, relevance or authority nor a call for its removal from the Canon of Christian Scripture. It is simply a scholarly conclusion regarding the literary history of the passage in question and of the document in which it now appears. What is to be done with this conclusion, if anything, is out of the hands of the scholar *qua* scholar.

BIBLIOGRAPHY

Aland, Kurt, 'Der Schluss und die ursprüngliche Gestalt des Römerbriefes', in *idem*, *Neutestamentliche Entwürfe* (TBü, 63; Munich: Chr. Kaiser Verlag, 1979), pp. 284-301.

—'Glosse, Interpolation, Redaktion und Komposition in der Sicht der neutestamentlichen Textkritik', in Walther Eltester (ed.), *Apophoreta: Festschrift für Ernst Haenchen* (BZNW, 30; Berlin: W. de Gruyter, 1964), pp. 7-31; reprinted in his *Studien zur Überlieferung des Neuen Testaments und seines Textes* (ANTT, 2; Berlin: W. de Gruyter, 1967), pp. 35-57.

Aland, Kurt, and Barbara Aland, *The Text of the New Testament: An Introduction to the Critical Editions and to the Theory and Practice of Modern Textual Criticism* (trans. Erroll F. Rhodes; Grand Rapids: Eerdmans; Leiden: E.J. Brill, 2nd edn, 1989).

Allenbach, J. *et al.*, *Biblia Patristica: Index des citations et allusions bibliques dans la littérature patristique* (4 vols.; Paris: Editions du Centre National de la Recherche Scientifique, 1975–87).

Amador, J.D.H., 'Revisiting 2 Corinthians: Rhetoric and the Case for Unity', *NTS* 46 (2000), pp. 92-111.

Anonymous, 'Covering of the Head', *EJR*, p. 101.

Anonymous, *Federal Rules of Evidence: 1998–99 Edition including Amendments Effective December 1, 1998* (St Paul, MN: West Group, 1998).

Anonymous, 'Head, Covering of', *UJEnc*, V, pp. 262-63.

Anonymous, 'Talking Points from Books', *ExpTim* 86 (1975), pp. 257-59.

Bacon, Benjamin W., 'The Doxology at the End of Romans', *JBL* 18 (1899), pp. 167-76.

Baird, William, '"One against the other": Intra-Church Conflict in 1 Corinthians', in Robert T. Fortna and Beverly R. Gaventa (eds.), *The Conversation Continues: Studies in Paul and John in Honor of J. Louis Martyn* (Nashville: Abingdon Press, 1990), pp. 116-36.

Balch, David L., 'Household Codes', *ABD*, III, pp. 318-20.

Barnikol, Ernst, 'The Non-Pauline Origin of the Parallelism of the Apostles Peter and Paul: Galatians 2:7-8' (trans. Darrell J. Doughty with B. Keith Brewer), *JHC* 5 (1998), pp. 285-300 (German original published in Ernst Barnikol [ed.], *Forschungen zur Entstehung des Urchristentums des Neuen Testaments und der Kirche* [Kiel: Walter G. Mühlau, 1931]).

—*Prolegomena zur neutestamentlichen* Dogmengeschichte. II. *Philipper 2. Der marcionitische Ursprung des Mythos-Satzes Phil. 2,6-7* (FEUNTK, 7; Kiel: Mühlau, 1932).

—'Römer 13: Der nichtpaulinische Ursprung der absoluten Obrigkeitsbejahrung von Römer 13,1-7', *Studien zum Neuen Testament und zur Patristik: Erich Klostermann zum 90. Geburtstag dargebracht* (ed. Der Kommission für spätantike Religionsgeschichte, Deutsche Akademie der Wissenschaften zu Berlin; TU, 77; Berlin: Akademie Verlag, 1961), pp. 65-133.

Barrett, C.K., *A Commentary on the Epistle to the Romans* (HNTC; New York: Harper & Row, 1957).

—*A Commentary on the First Epistle to the Corinthians* (HNTC; New York: Harper & Row, 1968).

—*The Gospel According to St. John: An Introduction with Commentary and Notes on the Greek Text* (Philadelphia: Westminster Press, 2nd edn, 1978).

Barton, Stephen C., 'Paul's Sense of Place: An Anthropological Approach to Community Formation in Corinth', *NTS* 32 (1986), pp. 225-46.

Bauer, Walter, *Orthodoxy and Heresy in Earliest Christianity* (trans. Team from Philadelphia Seminar on Christian Origins; ed. Robert A. Kraft and Gerhard Krodel; Philadelphia: Fortress Press, 1971).

Baur, Ferdinand Christian, *Paul the Apostle of Jesus Christ, His Life and Work, His Epistles and His Doctrine: A Contribution to the Critical History of Christianity* (ed. and trans. Eduard Zeller and Allan Menzies; 2 vols.; London: Williams & Norgate, 2nd edn, 1875–76).

Beare, F.W., *A Commentary on the Epistle to the Philippians* (HNTC; San Francisco: Harper & Row, 1959).

—'Canon of the New Testament', *IDB*, I, pp. 520-32.

Beck, Norman A., *Mature Christianity in the 21st Century: The Recognition and Repudiation of the Anti-Jewish Polemic of the New Testament* (Shared Ground among Jews and Christians, 5; Philadelphia: American Interfaith Institute/World Alliance; New York: Crossroad, rev. edn, 1994).

Bedale, Stephen, 'The Meaning of κεφαλή in the Pauline Epistles', *JTS* 5 (1954), pp. 211-15.

Best, Ernest, *A Commentary on the First and Second Epistles to the Thessalonians* (HNTC; New York: Harper & Row, 1972).

Betz, Hans Dieter, '2 Cor 6:14–7:1: An Anti-Pauline Fragment?', *JBL* 92 (1973), pp. 88-108.

Black, Matthew, *Romans* (NCB; London: Oliphants, 1973).

Boers, Hendrikus, 'The Form Critical Study of Paul's Letters: I Thessalonians as a Case Study', *NTS* 22 (1976), pp. 140-58.

Bolling, George Melville, *The External Evidence for Interpolation in Homer* (Oxford: Clarendon Press, 1925).

Bornemann, W., *Die Thessalonicherbriefe* (KEK, 10; Göttingen: Vandenhoeck & Ruprecht, 5th and 6th edn, 1894).

Bornkamm, Günther, *Die Vorgeschichte des sogenannten Zweiten Korintherbriefes* (SHAW, 2; Heidelberg: Winter, 1961); reprinted with Addendum in his *Gesammelte Aufsätze*. IV. *Geschichte und Glaube* (BEvT, 53; Munich: Chr. Kaiser Verlag, 1971), pp. 162-94.

—'The History of the Origin of the So-Called Second Letter to the Corinthians', *NTS* 8 (1961–62), pp. 258-64.

—*Paul* (trans. D.M.G. Stalker; New York: Harper & Row, 1971).

Boucher, Madeleine, 'Some Unexplored Parallels to 1 Cor 11,11-12 and Gal 3,28: The New Testament on the Role of Women', *CBQ* 31 (1969), pp. 50-58.

Bowe, Barbara E., 'The Rhetoric of Love in Corinth: From Paul to Clement of Rome', in Julian V. Hills with Richard B. Gardner *et al.* (eds.), *Common Life in the Early Church: Essays Honoring Graydon F. Snyder* (Harrisburg, PA: Trinity Press International, 1998), pp. 244-57.

Broer, Ingo, '"Antisemitismus" und Judenpolemik im Neuen Testament: Ein Beitrag zum besseren Verständnis von 1 Thess 2:14-16', *BN* 29 (1983), pp. 59-91.

—'"Der Ganze Zorn Ist Schon Über Sie Gekommen": Bemerkungen zur Interpolationshypothese und zur Interpretation von 1 Thess 2,14-16', in Raymond F. Collins (ed.), *The Thessalonian Correspondence* (BETL, 87; Leuven: Leuven University Press/ Peeters, 1990), pp. 137-59.

Brown, Raymond E., *The Gospel According to John (xiii–xxi): Introduction, Translation, and Notes* (AB, 29A; Garden City, NY: Doubleday, 1970).

Brunt, John C., 'Rejected, Ignored, or Misunderstood?: The Fate of Paul's Approach to the Problem of Food Offered to Idols in Early Christianity', *NTS* 31 (1985), pp. 113-24.

Bultmann, Rudolf, *Exegetische Probleme des zweiten Korintherbriefes* (SEÅSup, 9; Uppsala: Wretman, 1947); reprinted in his *Exegetica: Aufsätze zur Erforschung des Neuen Testaments* (ed. Erich Dinkler; Tübingen: J.C.B. Mohr [Paul Siebeck], 1967), pp. 298-322.

—'Glossen im Römerbrief', *TLZ* 72 (1947), pp. 197-202.

—*The Second Letter to the Corinthians* (trans. Roy A. Harrisville; Minneapolis: Augsburg, 1985).

—*Theology of the New Testament* (trans. Kendrick Grobel; 2 vols.; New York: Charles Scribner's Sons, 1951–55).

Byrne, Brendan, *Romans* (SP, 6; Collegeville, MN: Liturgical Press, 1996).

Carrez, M., 'Le "nous" en 2 Corinthiens', *NTS* 26 (1980), pp. 474-86.

Charlesworth, James H., 'Christian and Jewish Self-Definition in Light of the Christian Additions to the Apocryphal Writings', in E.P. Sanders with A.I. Baumgarten and Alan Mendelson (eds.), *Jewish and Christian Self-Definition*. II. *Aspects of Judaism in the Greco-Roman Period* (Philadelphia: Fortress Press, 1981), pp. 27-55.

—'Reflections on the SNTS Pseudepigrapha Seminar at Duke on the Testaments of the Twelve Patriarchs', *NTS* 23 (1977), pp. 296-304.

Clabeaux, John J., *A Lost Edition of the Letters of Paul: A Reassessment of the Text of the Pauline Corpus Attested by Marcion* (CBQMS, 21; Washington: Catholic Biblical Association, 1989).

Clark, Kenneth W., 'The Theological Relevance of Textual Variation in Current Criticism of the Greek New Testament', *JBL* 85 (1966), pp. 1-16.

Clemen, Carl, *Die Einheitlichkeit der paulinischen Briefe an der Hand der bisher mit bezug auf die aufgestellten Interpolations- und Compilationshypothesen* (Göttingen: Vandenhoeck & Ruprecht, 1894).

Collins, John J., 'Sibylline Oracles', *ABD*, VI, pp. 2-6.

Collins, Raymond F., 'A propos the Integrity of I Thes.', *ETL* 55 (1979), pp. 67-106.

—*First Corinthians* (SP, 7; Collegeville, MN: Liturgical Press, 1999).

—*Letters That Paul Did Not Write: The Epistle to the Hebrews and the Pauline Pseudepigrapha* (GNS, 28; Wilmington, DE: Michael Glazier, 1988).

Comfort, Philip W., and David P. Barrett (eds.), *The Complete Text of the Earliest New Testament Manuscripts* (Grand Rapids: Baker Book House, 1999).

Conzelmann, Hans, *1 Corinthians: A Commentary on the First Epistle to the Corinthians* (trans. James W. Leitch; Her; Philadelphia: Fortress Press, 1975).

Cope, Lamar, '1 Cor 11.2-16: One Step Further', *JBL* 97 (1978), pp. 435-36.

—*First Corinthians 8–10: Continuity or Contradiction?* (ATRSup, 11; Evenston, IL: Anglican Theological Review, 1990).

Coppens, Joseph, 'Miscellanées bibliques. LXXX. Une diatribe antijuive dans I Thess., II, 13-16', *ETL* 51 (1975), pp. 90-95.

Couchoud, P.-L., 'La première édition de Saint Paul', *RHR* 94 (1926), pp. 242-63.

—'Reconstitution et classement des Lettres de Saint Paul', *RHPR* 87 (1923), pp. 8-31.

Cousar, Charles B., *The Letters of Paul* (IBT; Nashville: Abingdon Press, 1996).

Cranfield, C.E.B., *A Critical and Exegetical Commentary on the Epistle to the Romans* (ICC; 2 vols.; Edinburgh: T. & T. Clark, 1975–79).

Dautzenberg, Gerhard, 'Botschaft und Bedeutung der urchristlichen Prophetie nach dem ersten Korintherbrief (2.6-16, 12-14)', in J. Panagopoulos (ed.), *Prophetic Vocation in the New Testament and Today* (NovTSup, 45; Leiden: E.J. Brill, 1977), pp. 131-61.

Delobel, Joël, '1 Cor 11:2-16: Towards a Coherent Explanation', in A. Vanhoye (ed.), *L'apôtre Paul: Personalité, style et conception du ministère* (BETL, 73; Leuven: Leuven University Press/Peeters, 1986), pp. 369-89.

Dentan, Robert C., 'Hair', *IDB*, II, p. 512.

Detering, Hermann, 'The Dutch Radical Approach to the Pauline Epistles', *JHC* 3 (1996), pp. 163-93.

Deutsch, Gotthard, and Kaufmann Kohler, 'Bareheadedness', *JE*, II, pp. 530-33.

Donfried, Karl Paul, 'A Short Note on Romans 16', *JBL* 89 (1970), pp. 441-49.

—'Paul and Judaism: I Thessalonians 2:13-16 as a Test Case', *Int* 38 (1984), pp. 242-53.

Doty, William G., *Letters in Primitive Christianity* (GBS; Philadelphia: Fortress Press, 1973).

Doughty, Darrell J., 'Pauline Paradigms and Pauline Authenticity', *JHC* 1 (1994), pp. 95-128.

Eckart, Karl Gottfried, 'Der zweite echte Brief des Apostels Paulus an die Thessalonicher', *ZTK* 58 (1961), pp. 30-44.

Eckstein, Hans-Joachim, '"Denn Gottes Zorn wird vom Himmel her offenbar werden": Exegetische Erwägungen zu Röm 1 18', *ZNW* 78 (1987), pp. 74-89.

Ehrman, Bart D., *The Orthodox Corruption of Scripture: The Effect of Early Christological Controversies on the Text of the New Testament* (Oxford: Oxford University Press, 1993).

Elliott, J.K., 'The Language and Style of the Concluding Doxology to the Epistle to the Romans', *ZNW* 72 (1981), pp. 124-30.

Ellis, E. Earle, '"Spiritual" Gifts in the Pauline Community', *NTS* 20 (1974), pp. 128-44.

—'The Silenced Wives of Corinth (I Cor. 14:34-5)', in Epp and Fee (eds.), *New Testament Textual Criticism*, pp. 213-20.

—'Traditions in 1 Corinthians', *NTS* 32 (1986), pp. 481-502.

Enslin, Morton Scott, *The Ethics of Paul* (Apex edn; New York: Abingdon Press, 1957).

Epp, Eldon Jay, 'Textual Criticism: New Testament', *ABD*, VI, pp. 412-35.

—'Western Text', *ABD*, VI, pp. 909-12.

Epp, Eldon Jay, and Gordon D. Fee (eds.), *New Testament Criticism: Its Significance for Exegesis; Essays in Honour of Bruce M. Metzger* (Oxford: Clarendon Press; New York: Oxford University Press, 1980).

Epp, Eldon Jay, and George W. MacRae (eds.), *The New Testament and Its Modern Interpreters* (BMI, 3; Philadelphia: Fortress Press; Atlanta: Scholars Press, 1989).

Eshbaugh, Howard, 'Textual Variants and Theology: A Study of the Galatians Text of Papyrus 46', *JSNT* 3 (1979), pp. 60-72.

—'Theological Variants in the Western Text of the Pauline Corpus' (unpublished doctoral dissertation, Case Western Reserve University, 1975).

Farmer, William R., *The Last Twelve Verses of Mark* (SNTSMS, 25; Cambridge: Cambridge University Press, 1974).

Fee, Gordon D., *The First Epistle to the Corinthians* (NICNT; Grand Rapids: Eerdmans, 1987).

Feldman, Louis H., 'Josephus', *ABD*, III, pp. 981-98.

Fitzer, Gerhard, *Das Weib schweige in der Gemeinde: Über den unpaulinischen Charakter der mulier-taceat Verse in 1. Korinther 14* (TEH NS, 110; Munich: Chr. Kaiser Verlag, 1963).

Fitzmyer, Joseph A., 'A Feature of Qumrân Angelology and the Angels of I Cor. xi.10', *NTS* 4 (1957–58), pp. 48-58; reprinted with a 'Postscript' in Murphy-O'Connor (ed.), *Paul and Qumran*, pp. 31-47, and in Joseph A. Fitzmyer, *Essays on the Semitic Background of the New Testament* (London: Geoffrey Chapman, 1971; paperback edn; Missoula, MT: Scholars Press, 1974), pp. 187-204.

—'Qumrân and the Interpolated Paragraph in 2 Cor 6,14–7,1', *CBQ* 23 (1961), pp. 271-80.

—*Romans: A New Translation with Introduction and Commentary* (AB, 33; New York: Doubleday, 1993).

Fortna, Robert Tomson, *The Gospel of Signs: A Reconstruction of the Narrative Source Underlying the Fourth Gospel* (SNTSMS, 11; Cambridge: Cambridge University Press, 1970).

Frend, W.H.C., *Martyrdom and Persecution in the Early Church: A Study of a Conflict from the Maccabees to Donatus* (Garden City, NY: Doubleday, 1967).

Fridrichsen, Anton, Prescript to E. Hoffmann, 'Zu 1 Cor. 13 und Col. 3,14', in Anton Fridrichsen (ed.), *Otto Lagercrantz Mnemosynon* (ConNT, 3; Leipzig: Lorentz, 1938), p. 28.

Friedrich, Gerhard, '1. Thessalonicher 5,1-11, der apologetische Einschub eines Späteren', *ZTK* 70 (1973), pp. 288-315.

Furnish, Victor Paul, *II Corinthians: Translated with Introduction, Notes, and Commentary* (AB, 32A; Garden City, NY: Doubleday, 1984).

—*The Moral Teaching of Paul: Selected Issues* (Nashville: Abingdon Press, 2nd edn, 1985).

—'Pauline Studies', in Epp and MacRae (eds.), *The New Testament and Its Modern Interpreters*, pp. 321-50.

Gamble, Harry Y., *Books and Readers in the Early Church: A History of Early Christian Texts* (New Haven: Yale University Press, 1995).

—'Canon: New Testament', *ABD*, I, pp. 852-61.

—'The Canon of the New Testament', in Epp and MacRae (eds.), *The New Testament and Its Modern Interpreters*, pp. 201-43.

—*The New Testament Canon: Its Making and Meaning* (GBS; Philadelphia: Fortress Press, 1985).

—'The Redaction of the Pauline Letters and the Formation of the Pauline Corpus', *JBL* 94 (1975), pp. 403-18.

—*The Textual History of the Letter to the Romans: A Study in Textual and Literary Criticism* (SD, 42; Grand Rapids: Eerdmans, 1977).

Gaston, Lloyd, 'Angels and Gentiles in Early Judaism and in Paul', *SR* 11 (1982), pp. 65-75.

Gillespie, Thomas W., 'Interpreting the Kerygma: Early Christian Prophecy According to 1 Corinthians 2:6-16', in James E. Goehring *et al.* (eds.), *Gospel Origins and Christian Beginnings: In Honor of James M. Robinson* (FFasc, 1; Sonomo, CA: Polebridge Press, 1990), pp. 151-66.

Gnilka, Joachim, '2 Cor 6.14–7.1 in the Light of the Qumran Texts and the Testaments of the Twelve Patriarchs', in Murphy-O'Connor (ed.), *Paul and Qumran*, pp. 48-68.

Grant, Robert M., 'Hellenistic Elements in 1 Corinthians', in Allen Wikgren (ed.), *Early Christian Origins: Studies in Honor of Harold R. Willoughby* (Chicago: Quadrangle, 1961), pp. 60-66.

—*Heresy and Criticism: The Search for Authenticity in Early Christian Literature* (Louisville, KY: Westminster/John Knox Press, 1993).

—*The Letter and the Spirit* (New York: Macmillan; London: SPCK, 1957).

—'Marcion and the Critical Method', in Peter Richardson and John C. Hurd (eds.), *From Jesus to Paul: Studies in Honour of Francis Wright Beare* (Waterloo, Ontario: Wilfrid Laurier University Press, 1984), pp. 207-15.

Grossouw, Willem K.M., 'Over de echtheid van 2 Cor 6,14–7,1', *StC* 26 (1951), pp. 203-206.

Gunther, John J., *St. Paul's Opponents and Their Background: A Study of Apocalyptic and Jewish Sectarian Teachings* (NovTSup, 35; Leiden: E.J. Brill, 1973).

Hagen, Wayne H., 'Two Deutero-Pauline Glosses in Romans 6', *ExpTim* 92 (1981), pp. 364-67.

Hagner, Donald A., *The Use of the Old and New Testaments in Clement of Rome* (NovTSup, 34; Leiden: E.J. Brill, 1973).

Harnack, Adolf von, *Marcion: The Gospel of the Alien God* (trans. John E. Steely and Lyle D. Bierma; Durham, NC: Labyrinth, 1990 [German original, 1924]).

Harrison, P.N., *Paulines and Pastorals* (London: Villiers, 1964).

Hawkins, Robert Martyr, *The Recovery of the Historical Paul* (Nashville: Vanderbilt University Press, 1943).

—'Romans: A Reinterpretation', *JBL* 60 (1941), pp. 129-40.

Héring, Jean, *The First Epistle of Saint Paul to the Corinthians* (trans. A.W. Heathcote and P.J. Allcock; London: Epworth Press, 1962).

Hirsch, Emanuel, 'Stilkritik und Literaranalyse im vierten Evangelium', *ZNW* 43 (1950–51), pp. 129-43.

Hooker, M.D., 'Authority on her Head: An Examination of I Cor.xi.10', *NTS* 10 (1964), pp. 410-16.

—'Christology and Methodology', *NTS* 17 (1971), pp. 480-87.

Horn, Friedrich Wilhelm, '1 Korinther 15,56—ein exegetischer Stachel', *ZNW* 82 (1991), pp. 88-105.

Horsley, Richard A., *1 Corinthians* (ANTC; Nashville: Abingdon Press, 1998).

—'Gnosis in Corinth: I Corinthians 8.1-6', *NTS* 27 (1980), pp. 32-51.

Hort, F.J.A., 'On the End of the Epistle to the Romans', *JP* 3 (1871), pp. 51-80; reprinted as 'The Structure and Destination of the Epistle to the Romans. B', in Lightfoot (ed.), *Biblical Essays*, pp. 321-51.

Hunter, A.M., *Paul and his Predecessors* (Philadelphia: Westminster Press, rev. edn, 1961).

Hurd, John C., 'Paul Ahead of his Time: 1 Thess. 2:13-16', in Peter Richardson with David Granskou (eds.), *Anti-Judaism in Early Christianity* (SCJ, 2; Waterloo, Ontario: Wilfrid Laurier University Press, 1986), pp. 21-36.

Hurd, John Coolidge, Jr, *The Origin of I Corinthians* (New York: Seabury; London: SPCK, 1965; Macon, GA: Mercer University Press, 2nd edn, 1983).

Hurley, J.B., 'Did Paul Require Veils or the Silence of Women? A Consideration of I Cor 11:2-16 and I Cor 14:33b-36', *WTJ* 35 (1973), pp. 190-220.

Hurtado, Larry W., 'The Doxology at the End of Romans', in Epp and Fee (eds.), *New Testament Textual Criticism*, pp. 185-99.

Jewett, Robert, *The Redaction of 1 Corinthians and the Trajectory of the Pauline School* (JAARSup, 44; Missoula, MT: American Academy of Religion, 1978).

—*The Thessalonian Correspondence: Pauline Rhetoric and Millenarian Piety* (FF; Philadelphia: Fortress Press, 1986).

Johansson, Nils, 'I Cor. XIII and I Cor. XIV', *NTS* 10 (1964), pp. 383-92.

Kähler, Else, *Die Frau in den paulinischen Briefen unter besonderer Berücksichtigung des Begriffes der Unterordnung* (Zürich: Gotthelf, 1960).

Kallas, James, 'Romans xiii.1-7: An Interpolation', *NTS* 11 (1965), pp. 365-74.

Kamlah, Ehrhard, 'Traditionsgeschichtliche Untersuchungen zur Schlussdoxologie des Römerbriefes' (unpublished doctoral dissertation, University of Tübingen, 1955).

Käsemann, Ernst, *Commentary on Romans* (trans. Geoffrey W. Bromiley; Grand Rapids: Eerdmans, 1980).

Keck, Leander E., *Paul and His Letters* (PC; Philadelphia: Fortress Press, 2nd edn, 1988).

—'Romans 15:4: An Interpolation?', in John T. Carroll, Charles H. Cosgrove and E. Elizabeth Johnson (eds.), *Faith and History: Essays in Honor of Paul W. Meyer* (SPHS; Atlanta: Scholars Press, 1990), pp. 125-36.

—'The Post-Pauline Interpretation of Jesus' Death in Rom 5,6-7', in Carl Andresen and Günter Klein (eds.), *Theologia Crucis—Signum Crucis: Festschrift für Erich Dinkler zum 70. Geburtstag* (Tübingen: J.C.B. Mohr [Paul Siebeck], 1979), pp. 237-48.

Keck, Leander E., and Victor Paul Furnish, *The Pauline Letters* (IBT; Nashville: Abingdon Press, 1984).

Kittel, Gerhard, and Gerhard von Rad, 'δοκέω, δόξα, δοξάζω, συνδοξάζω, ἔνδοξος ἐνδοξάζω, παράδοξος', *TDNT*, II, pp. 233-53.

Knox, John, *Chapters in a Life of Paul* (ed. Douglas R.A. Hare; Macon, GA: Mercer University Press; Leuven: Peeters, rev. edn, 1987).

—'The Epistle to the Romans: Introduction and Exegesis', *IB*, IX, pp. 355-668.

—*Marcion and the New Testament: An Essay in the Early History of the Canon* (Chicago: University of Chicago Press, 1942).

Koester, Helmut, '1 Thessalonians—Experiment in Christian Writing', in F. Forrester Church and Timothy George (eds.), *Continuity and Discontinuity in Church History: Essays Presented to George Huntston Williams on the Occasion of his 65th Birthday* (SHCT, 19; Leiden: E.J. Brill, 1979), pp. 33-44.

—'*GNOMAI DIAPHORI*: The Origin and Nature of Diversification in the History of Early Christianity', *HTR* 58 (1965), pp. 279-317; reprinted in James M. Robinson and Helmut Koester, *Trajectories through Early Christianity* (Philadelphia: Fortress Press, 1971), pp. 114-57.

—*Introduction to the New Testament*. II. *History and Literature of Early Christianity* (Berlin: W. de Gruyter, 2nd edn, 2000).

—'The Text of I Thessalonians', in Dennis E. Groh and Robert Jewett (eds.), *The Living Text: Essays in Honor of Ernest W. Saunders* (Lanham, MD: University Press of America, 1985), pp. 220-32.

—'The Text of the Synoptic Gospels in the Second Century', in Petersen (ed.), *Gospel Traditions in the Second Century*, pp. 19-37.

—'φύσις, φυσικός, φυσικῶς', *TDNT*, IX, pp. 251-77.

Krentz, Edgar M., 'Thessalonians, First and Second Epistles to the', *ABD*, VI, pp. 515-23.

Kümmel, Werner Georg, *Introduction to the New Testament* (trans. Howard Clark Kee; Nashville: Abingdon Press, rev. edn, 1975).

Lake, Kirsopp, *The Apostolic Fathers* (LCL; 2 vols.; Cambridge, MA: Harvard University Press, 1912–13).

Laws, Sophie, *A Commentary on the Epistle of James* (HNTC; San Francisco: Harper & Row, 1980).

Lehmann, Eduard, and Anton Fridrichsen, 'I Kor. 13: Eine christlich-stoische Diatribe', *TSK* 94 (1922), pp. 55-95.

Lightfoot, J.B., 'M. Renan's Theory of the Epistle to the Romans', *JP* 2 (1869), pp. 264-95; reprinted as 'The Structure and Destination of the Epistle to the Romans. A', in Lightfoot, *Biblical Essays*, pp. 287-320.

—'The Epistle to the Romans', *JP* 3 (1871), pp. 193-214; reprinted as 'The Structure and Destination of the Epistle to the Romans. C', in Lightfoot (ed.), *Biblical Essays*, pp. 352-74.

Lightfoot, J.B. (ed.), *Biblical Essays* (London: Macmillan, 1893).

Lindemann, Andreas, 'Paul in the Writings of the Apostolic Fathers', in William S. Babcock (ed.), *Paul and the Legacies of Paul* (Dallas: Southern Methodist University Press, 1990), pp. 25-45.

Loisy, Alfred Firmin, *The Birth of the Christian Religion* (trans. L.P. Jacks; New Hyde Park, NY: University Books, 1962 [French original, 1933]).

—*The Origins of the New Testament* (trans. J.P. Jacks; New Hyde Park, NY: University Books, 1962 [French original, 1936]).

—*Remarques sur la littérature épistolaire du Nouveau Testament* (Paris: Nourry, 1935).

Lovering, Eugene Harrison, Jr, 'The Collection, Redaction, and Early Circulation of the Corpus Paulinum' (unpublished doctoral dissertation, Southern Methodist University, 1988).

MacDonald, Dennis Ronald, 'A Conjectural Emendation of 1 Cor 15:31-32: Or the Case of the Misplaced Lion Fight', *HTR* 73 (1980), pp. 265-76.

—*The Legend and the Apostle: The Battle for Paul in Story and Canon* (Philadelphia: Westminster Press, 1983).

—*There is No Male and Female: The Fate of a Dominical Saying in Paul and Gnosticism* (HDR, 20; Philadelphia: Fortress Press, 1987).

Magne, Jean, 'A Summary History of the Eucharist' (unpublished paper, 1999).

—*From Christianity to Gnosis and From Gnosis to Christianity: An Itinerary through the Texts To and From the Tree of Paradise* (trans. A.F.W. Armstrong; rev. Jean Magne; BJS, 286; Atlanta: Scholars Press, 1993).

—'Les paroles sur la coupe', in Joël Delobel (ed.), *Logia: Les paroles de Jésus—The Sayings of Jesus: Mémorial Joseph Coppens* (BETL, 59; Leuven: Peeters/Leuven University Press, 1982), pp. 485-90.

Mann, C.S., *Mark: A New Translation with Introduction and Commentary* (AB, 27; Garden City, NY: Doubleday, 1986).

Marxsen, Willi, *The Beginnings of Christology: A Study in Its Problems* (trans. Paul J. Achtemeier; FFBS, 22; Philadelphia: Fortress Press, 1969).

Maurer, Karl, *Interpolation in Thucydides* (MBCBSup, 150; Leiden: E.J. Brill, 1995).

McDonald, J.I.H., 'Romans 13.1-7: A Test Case for New Testament Interpretation', *NTS* 35 (1989), pp. 540-49.

McKenzie, John L., *Dictionary of the Bible* (Milwaukee: Bruce, 1965).

Meeks, Wayne A. (ed.), *The Writings of St. Paul: Annotated Text, Criticism* (NCE; New York: W.W. Norton, 1972).

Meier, John P., *A Marginal Jew: Rethinking the Historical Jesus*. I. *The Roots of the Problem and the Person* (ABRL; New York: Doubleday, 1991).

—'On the Veiling of Hermeneutics (1 Cor 11:2-16)', *CBQ* 40 (1978), pp. 212-26.

Merklein, Helmut, 'Die Einheitlichkeit des ersten Korintherbriefes', *ZNW* 75 (1984), pp. 153-83.

Metzger, Bruce M., *A Textual Commentary on the Greek New Testament: A Companion Volume to the United Bible Societies' Greek New Testament (Third Edition)* (London: United Bible Societies, 1971).

—*The Text of the New Testament: Its Transmission, Corruption, and Restoration* (Oxford: Oxford University Press, 3rd edn, 1992).

Meyer, Ben F., *The Aims of Jesus* (London: SCM Press, 1979).

Michel, Otto, *Der Brief an die Römer übersetzt und erklärt* (KEK; Göttingen: Vandenhoeck & Ruprecht, 4th edn, 1966).

Moffatt, James, *An Introduction to the Literature of the New Testament* (ITL; Edinburgh: T. & T. Clark, 3rd edn, 1918).

Mowry, Lucetta, 'The Early Circulation of Paul's Letters', *JBL* 63 (1944), pp. 73-86.

Munro, Winsome, 'A Paradigmatic Shift in Pauline Studies?' (unpublished paper presented at the 1983 Annual Meeting of the Society of Biblical Literature, Dallas, Texas).

—'Authority and Subjection in Early Christian "Paideia" with Particular Reference to the Pauline Corpus and 1 Peter' (unpublished doctoral dissertation, Columbia University, 1974).

—*Authority in Paul and Peter: The Identification of a Pastoral Stratum in the Pauline Corpus and 1 Peter* (SNTSMS, 45; Cambridge: Cambridge University Press, 1983).

—'Criteria for Determining the Authenticity of Pauline Letters: A Modest Proposal' (unpublished paper prepared for the Paul Seminar of the Westar Institute, Santa Rosa, California, 1994).

—'Interpolation in the Epistles: Weighing Probability', *NTS* 36 (1990), pp. 431-43.

—'Patriarchy and Charismatic Community in "Paul"', in Judith Plaskow and Joan Arnold Romero (eds.), *Women and Religion* (ASR, 1; Missoula, MT: American Academy of Religion/Scholars Press, rev. edn, 1974), pp. 189-98.

—'Post-Pauline Material in 1 Cor 10, 11, and 14 with Confirmation from 2 Cor 6.14–7.1' (unpublished paper, 1977).

—'Romans 13:1-7: Apartheid's Last Biblical Refuge', *BTB* 20 (1990), pp. 161-68.

—'Two Strata in 1 Cor. 10 and 11' (unpublished paper presented at the 1971 Annual Meeting of the Society of Biblical Literature, Atlanta, Georgia).

Murphy-O'Connor, Jerome, *I Corinthians* (NTM, 10; Wilmington, DE: Michael Glazier, 1979).

—'1 Corinthians 11:2-16 Once Again', *CBQ* 50 (1988), pp. 265-74.

—*Becoming Human Together: The Pastoral Anthropology of St. Paul* (GNS, 2; Wilmington, DE: Michael Glazier, 2nd edn, 1982).

—'Freedom or the Ghetto (1 Cor. VIII,1-13; X,23–XI,1)', *RB* 85 (1978), pp. 543-74.

—'Interpolations in 1 Corinthians', *CBQ* 48 (1986), pp. 81-94.

—'The Non-Pauline Character of 1 Corinthians 11:2-16?', *JBL* 95 (1976), pp. 615-21.

—*Paul the Letter-Writer: His World, His Options, His Skills* (GNS, 41; Collegeville, MN: Liturgical Press, 1995).

—'Sex and Logic in 1 Corinthians 11:2-16', *CBQ* 42 (1980), pp. 482-500.
Murphy-O'Connor, Jerome (ed.), *Paul and Qumran: Studies in New Testament Exegesis* (SNTE; Chicago: Priory, 1968).
Niccum, Curt, 'The Voice of the Manuscripts on the Silence of Women: The External Evidence for 1 Cor 14.34-5', *NTS* 43 (1997), pp. 242-55.
Okeke, G.E., 'I Thessalonians 2.13-16: The Fate of the Unbelieving Jews', *NTS* 27 (1980), pp. 127-36.
Olson, K.A., 'Eusebius and the *Testimonium Flavianum*', *CBQ* 61 (1999), pp. 305-22.
O'Neill, J.C., 'Glosses and Interpolations in the Letters of St Paul', in Elizabeth A. Livingstone (ed.), *Papers presented to the Fifth International Congress on Biblical Studies held at Oxford, 1973* (TU, 126; *SE*, 7; Berlin: Akademie Verlag, 1983), pp. 379-86.
—*Paul's Letter to the Romans* (Baltimore: Penguin Books, 1975).
—*The Recovery of Paul's Letter to the Galatians* (London: SPCK, 1972).
Orchard, J.B., 'Thessalonians and the Synoptic Gospels', *Bib* 19 (1938), pp. 19-42.
Orr, William F., and James Arthur Walther, *I Corinthians: A New Translation: Introduction with a Study of the Life of Paul, Notes, and Commentary* (AB, 32; Garden City, NY: Doubleday, 1976).
Padgett, Alan, 'Paul on Women in the Church: The Contradictions of Coiffure in 1 Corinthians 11.2-16', *JSNT* 20 (1984), pp. 69-86.
Pagels, Elaine, *The Gnostic Gospels* (New York: Random House, 1979).
Palmer, Humphrey, *The Logic of Gospel Criticism: An Account of the Methods and Arguments Used by Textual, Documentary, Source, and Form Critics of the New Testament* (London: Macmillan; New York: St Martin's, 1968).
Payne, Philip B., 'Fuldensis, Sigla for Variants in Vaticanus, and 1 Cor 14.34-5', *NTS* 41 (1995), pp. 240-62.
—'MS. 88 as Evidence for a Text without 1 Cor 14.34-5', *NTS* 44 (1998), pp. 152-58.
Payne, Philip B., and Paul Canart, 'The Originality of Text-Critical Symbols in Codex Vaticanus', *NovT* 42 (2000), pp. 105-13.
Pearson, Birger A., '1 Thessalonians 2:13-16: A Deutero-Pauline Interpolation', *HTR* 64 (1971), pp. 79-94.
Pervo, Richard I., 'Social and Religious Aspects of the "Western" Text', in Dennis E. Groh and Robert Jewett (eds.), *The Living Text: Essays in Honor of Ernest W. Saunders* (Lanham, MD: University Press of America, 1985), pp. 229-41.
Peters, Melvin K.H., 'Septuagint', *ABD*, V, pp. 1093-1104.
Petersen, William L. (ed.), *Gospel Traditions in the Second Century: Origins, Recensions, Text, and Transmission* (CJA, 3; Notre Dame: University of Notre Dame Press, 1989).
Pfeiffer, Rudolf, *History of Classical Scholarship from the Beginnings to the End of the Hellenistic Age* (Oxford: Clarendon Press, 1968).
Plummer, Alfred, *A Critical and Exegetical Commentary on the Second Epistle of St. Paul to the Corinthians* (ICC; New York: Charles Scribner's Sons, 1915).
Porter, Calvin L., 'Romans 1.18-32: Its Role in the Developing Argument', *NTS* 40 (1994), pp. 210-28.
Price, Robert M., 'Apocryphal Apparitions: 1 Corinthians 15:3-11 as a Post-Pauline Interpolation', *JHC* 2 (1995), pp. 69-99.
—'The Evolution of the Pauline Canon' (unpublished paper prepared for the Paul Seminar of the Westar Institute, Santa Rosa, California, 1995).

Puskas, Charles B., Jr, *The Letters of Paul: An Introduction* (GNS; Collegeville, MN: Liturgical Press, 1993).

Ramsay, William M., *The Cities of St. Paul: Their Influence on His Life and Thought* (London: Hodder & Stoughton, 1907).

Refoulé, François, 'Unité de l'Epître aux Romains et histoire du salut', *RSPT* 71 (1987), pp. 219-42.

Richardson, Alan, *An Introduction to the Theology of the New Testament* (New York: Harper & Row, 1958).

Rylaarsdam, J. Coert, 'Nazarite', *IDB*, III, pp. 526-27.

Sanday, William, and Arthur C. Headlam, *A Critical and Exegetical Commentary on the Epistle to the Romans* (ICC; Edinburgh: T. & T. Clark, 5th edn, 1902).

Sanders, E.P., *Jesus and Judaism* (Philadelphia: Fortress Press, 1985).

—*Paul, the Law, and the Jewish People* (Philadelphia: Fortress Press, 1983).

Sanders, Jack T., 'First Corinthians 13: Its Interpretation Since the First World War', *Int* 20 (1966), pp. 159-87.

—'The Transition from Opening Epistolary Thanksgiving to Body in the Letters of the Pauline Corpus', *JBL* 81 (1962), pp. 348-62.

Sanford, Eva Matthews, 'Propaganda and Censorship in the Transmission of Josephus', *TPAPA* 66 (1935), pp. 127-45.

Schenk, Wolfgang, 'Der 1. Korintherbrief als Briefsammlung', *ZNW* 60 (1969), pp. 219-43.

—*Die Philipperbriefe des Paulus: Kommentar* (Stuttgart: W. Kohlhammer, 1984).

—'Korintherbriefe', *TRE*, XIX, pp. 620-40.

Schippers, R., 'The Pre-Synoptic Tradition in I Thessalonians II 13-16', *NovT* 8 (1966), pp. 223-34.

Schlier, Heinrich, 'κεφαλή, ἀνακεφαλαιόομαι', *TDNT*, III, pp. 673-82.

Schlueter, Carol J., *Filling Up the Measure: Polemical Hyperbole in 1 Thessalonians 2.14-16* (JSNTSup, 98; Sheffield: JSOT Press, 1994).

Schmidt, Daryl, '1 Thess 2.13-16: Linguistic Evidence for an Interpolation', *JBL* 102 (1983), pp. 269-79.

—'Identifying Seams in Authentic Pauline Letters: Evidence for Letter Fragments and Interpolations' (unpublished paper prepared for the Paul Seminar of the Westar Institute, Santa Rosa, California, 1998).

—'Response', in George D. Kilpatrick, *A Textus Receptus Redivivus? Protocol of the Thirty-Second Colloquy, 12 March 1978* (ed. Edward C. Hobbs; CHSHMCP, 32; Berkeley: The Center for Hermeneutical Studies in Hellenistic and Modern Culture, 1978), pp. 24-26.

Schmithals, Walter, *Der Römerbrief als historisches Problem* (SNT, 9; Gütersloh: Gerd Mohn, 1975).

—'Die Korintherbriefe als Briefsammlung', *ZNW* 64 (1973), pp. 263-88.

—'Die Thessalonicherbriefe als Briefkompositionen', in Erich Dinkler (ed.), *Zeit und Geschichte. Dankesgabe an Rudolf Bultmann zum 80. Geburtstag* (Tübingen: J.C.B. Mohr [Paul Siebeck], 1964), pp. 295-315.

—*Gnosticism in Corinth: An Investigation of the Letters to the Corinthians* (trans. John E. Steely; Nashville: Abingdon Press, 1971).

—*Paul and the Gnostics* (trans. John E. Steely; Nashville: Abingdon Press, 1972).

Schnelle, Udo, '1 Kor 6:14—Eine nachpaulinische Glosse', *NovT* 25 (1983), pp. 217-19.

Schubert, Paul, *Form and Function of the Pauline Thanksgiving* (BZNW, 20; Berlin: Alfred Töpelmann, 1939).
Schüssler Fiorenza, Elisabeth, *In Memory of Her: A Feminist Theological Reconstruction of Christian Origins* (New York: Crossroad, 1983).
—'The Study of Women in Early Christianity: Some Methodological Considerations', in Thomas J. Ryan (ed.), *Critical History and Biblical Faith: New Testament Perspectives* (APCTS; Villanova: College Theology Society/Horizons, 1979), pp. 30-58.
Scroggs, Robin, *The Last Adam: A Study in Pauline Anthropology* (Philadelphia: Fortress Press, 1966).
—'Paul and the Eschatological Woman', *JAAR* 40 (1972), pp. 283-303.
—'Paul: Chauvinist or Liberationist?', *CC* 89 (1972), pp. 307-309.
Smit, J.F.M., 'The Genre of 1 Corinthians 13 in the Light of Classical Rhetoric', *NovT* 33 (1991), pp. 193-216.
—'Two Puzzles: 1 Corinthians 12.31 and 13.3: A Rhetorical Solution', *NTS* 39 (1993), pp. 246-64.
Smith, Morton, *Jesus the Magician* (New York: Harper & Row, 1978).
Snodgrass, Klyne, ' "Western Non-Interpolations" ', *JBL* 91 (1972), pp. 369-79.
Spicq, C., *Agapè dans le Nouveau Testament: Analyse de Textes* (EBib; 3 vols.; Paris: J. Gabalda, 1958–59).
Stowers, Stanley K., 'Greek and Latin Letters', *ABD*, IV, pp. 290-93.
—*Letter Writing in Greco-Roman Antiquity* (LEC, 5; Philadelphia: Westminster Press, 1986).
Strecker, Georg, *History of New Testament Literature* (trans. Calvin Katter; Harrisburg, PA: Trinity Press International, 1997).
Strugnell, John, 'A Plea for Conjectural Emendation in the New Testament, with A Coda on 1 Cor 4:6', *CBQ* 36 (1974), pp. 543-58.
Swete, Henry Barclay, *An Introduction to the Old Testament in Greek* (rev. Richard Rusden Ottley; Cambridge: Cambridge University Press, 2nd edn, 1914).
Talbert, Charles H., 'A Non-Pauline Fragment at Romans 3 24-26?', *JBL* 85 (1966), pp. 287-96.
Theissen, Gerd, *Psychological Aspects of Pauline Theology* (trans. John P. Calvin; Philadelphia: Fortress Press, 1987).
Thiselton, Anthony C., 'Realized Eschatology at Corinth', *NTS* 24 (1978), pp. 510-26.
Titus, Eric L., 'Did Paul Write I Corinthians 13?', *JBR* 27 (1959), pp. 299-302.
Trobisch, David, *Die Entstehung der Paulusbriefsammlung: Studien zu den Anfängen christlicher Publizistik* (NTOA, 10; Freiburg: Universitätsverlag; Göttingen: Vandenhoeck & Ruprecht, 1989).
—*Paul's Letter Collection: Tracing the Origins* (Minneapolis: Fortress Press, 1994).
Trompf, G.W., 'On Attitudes toward Women in Paul and Paulinist Literature: 1 Corinthians 11:3-16 and Its Context', *CBQ* 42 (1980), pp. 196-215.
Vielhauer, Philipp, 'On the "Paulinism" of Acts' (trans. Wm. C. Robinson, Jr, and Victor Paul Furnish), in Leander E. Keck and J. Louis Martyn (eds.), *Studies in Luke-Acts: Essays Presented in Honor of Paul Schubert* (Nashville: Abingdon Press, 1966), pp. 33-50.
Vööbus, Arthur, 'Syriac Versions', *IDBSup*, pp. 848-54.
Walker, William O., Jr, '1 Corinthians 2.6-16: A Non-Pauline Interpolation?', *JSNT* 47 (1992), pp. 75-94.
—'1 Corinthians 11:2-16 and Paul's Views Regarding Women', *JBL* 94 (1975), pp. 94-110.

—'An Unexamined Presupposition in Studies of the Synoptic Problem', *RL* 48 (1979), pp. 41-52.

—'The Burden of Proof in Identifying Interpolations in the Pauline Letters', *NTS* 33 (1987), pp. 610-18.

—'Interpolations in the Pauline Letters', in Stanley E. Porter and Brook W.R. Pearson (eds.), *Pauline Studies*. I. *The Pauline Canon* (Leiden: E.J. Brill, forthcoming).

—'Is First Corinthians 13 a Non-Pauline Interpolation?', *CBQ* 60 (1998), pp. 484-99.

—'Romans 1.18–2.29: A Non-Pauline Interpolation?', *NTS* 45 (1999), pp. 533-52.

—'Text-Critical Evidence for Interpolations in the Letters of Paul', *CBQ* 50 (1988), pp. 622-31.

—'The "Theology of Woman's Place" and the "Paulinist" Tradition', *Sem* 28 (1983), pp. 101-12.

—'The Vocabulary of 1 Corinthians 11.3-16: Pauline or Non-Pauline?', *JSNT* 35 (1989), pp. 75-88.

Wallace-Hadrill, D.S., 'Eusebius of Carsarea and the *Testimonium Flavianum* (Josephus, *Antiquities*, XVIII. 63f.)', *JEH* 25 (1974), pp. 353-62.

Weatherly, Jon A., 'The Authenticity of 1 Thessalonians 2.13-16: Additional Evidence', *JSNT* 42 (1991), pp. 79-98.

Webb, William J., *Returning Home: New Covenant and Second Exodus as the Context for 2 Corinthians 6.14–7.1* (JSNTSup, 85; Sheffield: JSOT Press, 1993).

Weiss, Johannes, *Der erste Korintherbrief* (KEK, 5; Göttingen: Vandenhoeck & Ruprecht, 9th edn, 1910).

Welborn, Laurence L., 'Clement, First Epistle of', *ABD*, I, pp. 1055-60.

White, John L., 'Letter', *HCBD*, p. 601.

—*Light from Ancient Letters* (FFNT; Philadelphia: Fortress Press, 1986).

Widmann, Martin, '1 Kor 2 6-16: Ein Einspruch gegen Paulus', *ZNW* 70 (1979), pp. 44-53.

—'Der Israelit Paulus und sein antijüdischer Redaktor: Eine literarkritische Studie zu Röm. 9–11', in Ernst Ludwig Ehrlich and Bertold Klappert with Ursula Ast (eds.), *'Wie gut sind deine Zelte, Jaakow...' Festschrift zum 60. Geburtstag von Reinhold Mayer* (Gerlingen: Bleicher, 1986), pp. 150-58.

Wiles, Maurice F., *The Divine Apostle: The Interpretation of St. Paul's Epistles in the Early Church* (Cambridge: Cambridge University Press, 1967).

Willis, Wendell Lee, *Idol Meat in Corinth: The Pauline Argument in 1 Corinthians 8 and 10* (SBLDS, 68; Chico, CA: Scholars Press, 1985).

Wisse, Frederik W., 'Textual Limits to Redactional Theory in the Pauline Corpus', in James E. Goehring *et al.* (eds.), *Gospel Origins and Christian Beginnings: In Honor of James M. Robinson* (FFasc, 1; Sonoma, CA: Polebridge Press, 1990), pp. 167-78.

—'The Nature and Purpose of Redactional Changes in Early Christian Texts: The Canonical Gospels', in Petersen (ed.), *Gospel Traditions in the Second Century*, pp. 39-53.

Ydit, Meir, 'Head, Covering of the', *EncJud*, VIII, pp. 2-6.

Zahn, Theodor, *Geschichte des neutestamentlichen Kanons* (2 vols.; Erlangen: Deichert, 1888–92).

Zeitlin, Solomon, 'The Christ Passage in Josephus', *JQR* 18 (1927–28), pp. 237-40.

—*Josephus on Jesus with Particular Reference to the Slavonic Josephus and the Hebrew Josippon* (Philadelphia: The Dropsie College for Hebrew and Cognate Learning, 1931).

—*The Rise and Fall of the Judaean State: A Political, Social and Religious History of the Second Commonwealth.* I. *37 B.C.E.–66 C.E.* (Philadelphia: Jewish Publication Society of America, 2nd edn, 1969).

Zeller, Dieter, *Juden und Heiden in der Mission bei Paulus: Studien zum Römerbrief* (Stuttgart: Katholisches Bibelwerk, 2nd edn, 1976).

Zuntz, Günther, *The Text of the Epistles: A Disquisition Upon the Corpus Paulinum* (Oxford: Oxford University Press, 1953).

INDEX

INDEX OF REFERENCES

BIBLE

OTHER ANCIENT REFERENCES

INDEX OF AUTHORS